James Bernard, Composer to Count Dracula

Also by David Huckvale
and from McFarland

Touchstones of Gothic Horror: A Film Genealogy of Eleven Motifs and Images (2010)

Hammer Film Scores and the Musical Avant-Garde (2008)

James Bernard, Composer to Count Dracula

A Critical Biography

DAVID HUCKVALE

Foreword by Ingrid Pitt

McFarland & Company, Inc., Publishers
Jefferson, North Carolina, and London

The present work is a reprint of the illustrated case bound edition of James Bernard, Composer to Count Dracula: A Critical Biography, *first published in 2006 by McFarland.*

LIBRARY OF CONGRESS CATALOGUING-IN-PUBLICATION DATA

Huckvale, David.
James Bernard, composer to Count Dracula : a critical biography; foreword by Ingrid Pitt / David Huckvale.
p. cm.
Includes filmography, bibliographical references, and index.

ISBN 978-0-7864-6613-9
softcover : 50# alkaline paper ∞

1. Bernard, James, 1925–2001. 2. Composers—England—Biography. 3. Motion picture music—Analysis, appreciation. I. Title.
ML410.B5557H83 2012
781.5'42092—dc22 2005026329

British Library cataloguing data are available

Manufactured in the United States of America

McFarland & Company, Inc., Publishers
Box 611, Jefferson, North Carolina 28640
www.mcfarlandpub.com

Acknowledgments

James Bernard died before this book was published, but he did live long enough to read and approve of my draft manuscript, and my principal thanks are to him. He gave so much of his time to this project, to say nothing of entrusting me with his precious manuscript scores. James also very generously arranged for us both to visit the British Film Institute to examine the handful of his films that were not commercially available on video at the time, and whenever I visited him at his home he was always the most hospitable and charming of hosts. My afternoons spent in his company are very special memories indeed.

Particular thanks go to James' brother-in-law and sister, Sir David and Lady Mary Lees, for their very generous financial support, and to their son, Jeremy Lees, who, along with Christopher Hughes, kindly arranged copyright permission for me to use material owned by the Bernard Estate. Many thanks also to Dr. Jenny Doctor and the Britten-Pears Foundation for allowing me to reproduce the letters from Benjamin Britten in full. I was the first researcher to whom James revealed these valuable letters, and it has been a great privilege to reproduce them in their entirety in this book. I am also grateful to Geoffrey Wansell for putting me in touch with the late Peter Carter-Ruck and the Terence Rattigan Estate, which granted permission to include the Terence Rattigan material; Rosamund Strode and the Holst Foundation for permission to include the letters from Imogen Holst; Charmian Lyons at Music Sales Ltd., Kate Bullock at IMP, David Stoner at Silva Screen Records and Louise Thompson at Bridge Films Ltd. for arranging music copyright permissions.

Thanks also to Max Charles Davies and Phillip Neil Martin at Twelfth Night Music (www.maxcharlesdavies.com), who so professionally transformed my original musical examples into such elegant printed examples; Marcus Hearn, for his help with the illustrations; Ingrid Pitt, who so kindly volunteered to write a foreword for this book; Christopher Lee, Geoffrey Toone, Anthony Hinds, Aida Young, Graham Skeggs and Eric Tomlinson, for sharing their reminiscences with me on the telephone; Leonard Salzedo and Philip Martell who both, back in the 1980s, set me on the road that ultimately led to this book; Dr. Methuen Clarke, who kindly gave up a Saturday morning when I appeared quite unannounced at his home in Northampton, and who told me all about Walter Hussey and St. Matthew's Church; the staff at the Puckrup Hall Hotel and Wellington College; the fount of all wisdom, Dr. Gail-Nina Anderson, who prevented me from giving up hope; fellow author and close friend of James, Gary Smith, for his always encouraging support; Tony Sellors, for many things— not least his enthusiastic willingness to feature James' music on BBC Radio 3, and Lionel Cummings for the excellent photograph of James, resplendent at the piano in his yellow cardigan and surrounded by his much-loved lilies.

Finally, I would like to dedicate this book, not only to the memory of James Bernard and all his loyal fans but also to Andrew McMillan and my wonderful parents, Iris and John, without whom, of course, none of this would have been possible.

Scars of Dracula
Music by James Bernard
© 1970 EMI Film and Theatre Music Ltd, London WC2H 0QY
Reproduced by permission of International Music Publishers Ltd.
All Rights Reserved.

The Plague of the Zombies
Music by James Bernard
© 1966 Twentieth Century Music Corp, USA
Worldwide print rights controlled by Warner Bros. Publications Inc./IMP Ltd.
Reproduced by permission of International Music Publications Ltd.
All Rights Reserved.

Frankenstein Created Woman
Music by James Bernard
© 1967 Twentieth Century Music Corp, USA
Worldwide print rights controlled by Warner Bros. Publications Inc./IMP Ltd.
Reproduced by permission of International Music Publication Ltd.
All Rights Reserved.

Frankenstein Must Be Destroyed
Music by James Bernard
© 1969 Warner–Tamerlane Publishing Corp., USA
Warner/Chappell Music Ltd., London W6 8BS
Reproduced by permission of International Music Publications Ltd.
All Rights Reserved.

The Legend of the Seven Golden Vampires
Music by James Bernard
© 1969 WB Music Corp., USA
Warner/Chappell Music Ltd., London W6 8BS
Reproduced by permission of International Music Publications Ltd.
All Rights Reserved.

Dracula (Horror of Dracula) (Bernard)
Universal Music Publishing Ltd.

The Stranglers of Bombay (Bernard)
Hammer Films Ltd./Universal
The Terror of the Tongs (Bernard)
Hammer Films Ltd./Universal

The Hound of the Baskervilles (Bernard)
Hammer Films Ltd./Universal

The Damned (Bernard)
Hammer Films Ltd./Universal

The Kiss of the Vampire (Bernard)
Hammer Films Ltd./Universal

The Secret of Blood Island (Bernard)
Hammer Films Ltd./Universal

The Gorgon (Bernard)
Hammer Films Ltd./Universal

Dracula — Prince of Darkness (Bernard)
Universal Music Publishing Ltd.

Frankenstein and the Monster from Hell (Bernard)
Famous Music Publishing Ltd.

Nosferatu
Music by James Bernard
Reproduced by permission of Silva Screen Music (publishers)

The Quatermass Experiment
Music by James Bernard
Reproduced by permission of Hammer Film Music Ltd.

X — The Unknown
Music by James Bernard
Reproduced by permission of Hammer Film Music Ltd.

Quatermass 2
Music by James Bernard
Reproduced by permission of Hammer Film Music Ltd.

The Curse of Frankenstein
Music by James Bernard
Reproduced by permission of the Trustees of the J. M. Bernard Will Trust.

Table of Contents

Foreword

by Ingrid Pitt

I always think that chewing over past mistakes and irrational decisions is an exercise in futility. As Edward Fitzgerald would have it, "nor all thy Piety nor wit Shall lure it back to cancel half a Line." Occasionally I do something, or, in this case, not do something, that I regret deeply. I keep telling myself it's too late but I can't stop thinking about it. Jimmy Bernard, Hammer composer *extraordinaire,* wrote music for numerous Hammer films. His product is instantly recognizable and on many occasions rescues a mediocre script and turns it into a memorable film. Where would *Dracula*, the movie, be without the haunting "Dra-Cu-La" throbbing away as a palpable underpinning to the action on screen? When I met Jimmy Bernard back in the 1970s, I was always teasing him about the way he diligently avoided having to work with me. Being a perfect gentleman, he always said it was a great sorrow to him as well and he would make sure that in the future an opportunity would arise for us to collaborate. The years went by and no such opportunity arose.

Bernard was a gentle gentleman in the Peter Cushing mode. Endlessly polite and interested in what everyone was doing. Rarely talking about his own not inconsiderable contributions to the film industry, but happy to discuss any potty project which might be trailed before him and make helpful, professionally-based suggestions. I told Jimmy I was making a short horror film, *Green Fingers*, with Paul Cotgrove from the British Film Commission. Instantly, Jimmy asked who had done the music. When I told him that nobody was lined up for it, he said it was perfect. He would do the score. I protested that the budget was minuscule and we couldn't possibly afford his fee. He took my hand and kissed it lightly, saying, "This is my gift to you for being such a delightful friend."

It was about this time that Jimmy became ill. It was painful to see him waste away. But he never let his illness drain his good humor or make him less available to those who loved him. In fact, it seemed to draw us closer. Since doing a job for the BBC in Argentina, I had been having a lot of trouble with my lungs. Although by this time he found great difficulty in speaking and even the smallest effort left him gasping for air, he was still concerned that I was having the same sort of trouble, but on a minor scale. A week before he died, I went and had tea with him in his beautiful home in Chelsea. Jimmy was getting tired but he still made a gallant effort

Hammer Holiday: James Bernard with Martine Beswick, Ingrid Pitt and Ingrid's husband, Tony (photograph James Bernard).

to get me to stay when I said I was leaving. We both pledged a get-together when we were 100 percent and as I left he called after me, "The champagne's on me next time." I spoke to him on the telephone a couple of times after that and he assured me that he was improving daily. I told him I was scheduled for a hospital visit to have my lungs checked out and he wished me luck. A few days later, after the examination, Jimmy rang and left a message on my answering machine, checking up on my state of health. To my eternal discredit, I never returned his call. A couple of days later, a mutual friend telephoned to say Jimmy was dead.

"...Nor all thy Tears wash out a Word of it."

Preface

My fascination with the music of James Bernard began with the release of a *Dracula* LP record in 1974.[1] Narrated by Christopher Lee, this "horrifying tale of vampirism" was liberally supplied with blood-curdling sound effects and some of the most sonorous music that I, a boy of thirteen at the time, had ever heard. "Who was James Bernard?" I asked myself. But apart from the fact that he had written the scores for some of Hammer's most famous horror films, very few of which I had seen at that time, I could find no satisfying answer. I had a similarly profound experience when I discovered Wagner in the soundtrack of *Nosferatu, Phantom der Nacht (Nosferatu the Vampyre,* Gaumont/Werner Herzog Filmproduktion, dir. Werner Herzog, 1979). Now my question was "Who was Wagner?" Fortunately, there were rather more readily available answers to that one. While I was absorbing the world of mythological music-drama, I began to recognize certain similarities between Wagner's methods and the horror films I found equally fascinating. Then, one snowy evening in the bedroom of a rather Draculean hotel in the Lake District, where I was staying on holiday with my parents, I happened to catch a late-night TV screening of *The Kiss of the Vampire* (Rank/Hammer, dir. Don Sharp, 1964). The sight of actor Barry Warren sitting at a sumptuously rococo grand piano and "performing" Bernard's specially composed "Vampire Rhapsody" made a huge impression on me and, combined with my growing interest in the music of Liszt and Scriabin, it crystallized a desire to explore the nineteenth-century origins of film music.

It took quite a few more years before I finally met James Bernard in person whilst I was researching for my Ph.D. in 1987. Invited up to the comfortable Battersea flat in which he was staying during a visit from Jamaica, my first glimpse of him was of a fawn lisle sock and an elegant shoe peeping out from behind a half-open door. He greeted me as though we were lifelong friends, promptly offered me a glass of excellent red wine and chatted to me all morning and well into the afternoon about his film music, illustrating his fascinating reminiscences at the piano as we went along. The previous day, a film crew from the BBC had interviewed him for the documentary *Hammer— The Studio That Dripped Blood* (produced by Nick Jones and David Thompson) but he was quite happy to repeat everything he had told them especially for my benefit and afterwards insisted on paying my bus fare back home. It was a memorable occasion. Years passed, and I was fortunate enough to be able to interview him again, this time for a BBC radio series about film music.[2] Thanks to the enthusiasm of my producer, Tony Sellors, this project in turn led to my involvement with another radio program,[3] which brought together both James Bernard (talking about his score for F. W. Murnau's silent classic *Nosferatu* [Prana, 1921]) and Christopher Lee, who was promoting his just-released CD of operatic arias. Sad to say, it wasn't possible to interview them both together, but, as it happened, they only narrowly avoided meeting each other. Unbeknownst to me, Mr. Lee had just recorded an interview about the second edition of his autobiography in the studio that we were about to use, but having turned around to direct James to the toilets I had missed him walk past. Spinning around, who should I see but the tall figure so familiar from all those horror films, striding towards the same toilet, not clad in a billowing cape but at least wearing a suitably continental loden coat. When James reappeared, I asked if he had said hello to the man with whom so much of his music is associated. "Good heavens!" he exclaimed. "I saw someone tall standing next to me, but I had no idea I was taking a pee next to Count Dracula!"

It proved more difficult to entice Lee back to the BBC but at the eleventh hour I succeeded. He had fond memories of his collaboration with Hammer's most famous composer on a chant for *She* (Associated British–Pathé/Hammer, dir. Robert Day, 1965), which his character of Billali, the high priest, was to have sung at one of the impressive ritual ceremonies. This was never used in the finished film but Lee remembered it and even began to sing it to me. When, many years later, Lee and Peter Cushing were asked to record the commentary of another television documentary about Hammer films called *Flesh and Blood: The Hammer Heritage of Horror.* James, who was friendly with its director, Ted Newsom, arranged the transport and travelled with Lee and Newsom to meet Cushing, who was very ill with cancer. A small recording studio not far from Cushing's home in Whitstable had been selected for the recording session, and, amazingly, this was the very first time that Lee, Cushing and Bernard had ever been together in one room. Only a few weeks later, Cushing was dead.

All biographers look for skeletons in the cupboards of the people they are writing about, and this story certainly has some skeletons in it. But James enthusiastically brought them out of the cupboard for me, dusted them off and encouraged me to put them on display. It has been a fascinating experience to write about the man whose film scores made such an impact on me as a boy, and I am sure that after reading this book everyone will agree with Marianne in *The Kiss of the Vampire* that the music, to say nothing of the life of James Bernard, has been very exciting indeed.

Note

Elizabeth Lutyens composed the scores for several horror films during the 1960s, as well as the Hammer thrillers *Never Take Sweets from a Stranger* (Columbia/Hammer, dir. Cyril Frankel, 1960) and *Paranoiac* (Rank/Hammer, dir. Freddie Francis, 1963). In her autobiography she explained that "both film and radio music must be written not only quickly but with the presumption that it will only be heard once.

Its impact must be immediate. One does not grow gradually to love or understand a film score like a string quartet."[4]

In order to achieve this immediacy of impact, composers often use a well-established musical vocabulary rooted in the Western Romantic tradition. More modern idioms, such as **atonality**[5] and **serialism**, are usually employed from within an overall perspective of **tonality**. In mainstream film scores, dissonance is rarely liberated from its traditional signification.

This is not a formal semiological study, but my general approach has been in the spirit of that branch of linguistics, which argues that language is a system of signs. While music does not operate in the same way as a verbal language, both language and music are undeniably systems of communication. Within the context of the English language, the word "tree," for example, signifies, quite arbitrarily, the signified object known as a tree. Similarly, the musical **interval** of a **tritone**, within certain contexts, has come to signify the concept of "evil." Both "tree" and "tritone" are arbitrary "symbolic" signs whose meaning has been imposed upon them. Music, like onomatopoeia in language, can also convey what semiology designates as an "iconic" meaning by imitating certain acoustic phenomena such as bird song or thunderstorms. Examples of symbolic signs and iconic signs will be found in the pages which follow, though they will not be referred to as such.

All composers, whether they write for the screen or not, are influenced by their predecessors, and many different composers have often used similar melodic shapes and harmonic structures to convey certain shared extra-musical "meanings" or, if we are speaking semiologically, "significations."

It is certainly possible to argue that the reason why the film scores studied in this book are still resonant and durable is due to the reservoir of just such evocative musical signs upon which they draw. The same might be said in particular of Wagner, whose use of archetypal musical signs accounts for the powerful sense of mythic recognition one experiences when listening to his music-dramas; what Thomas Mann described as the "richness of meaning, evocative power and allusive magic" of the Wagnerian experience.[6]

Musical communication, especially in film, takes place on a largely subliminal level and no matter how unaware of musical tradition an audience may be, it is still responding to a shared legacy of musical signs, even if that legacy has been inherited exclusively through the experience of film music. The analytical sections of this book aim to reveal some of the more resonant origins of these musical signs in an attempt to explain their efficacy as well as to illuminate an historical continuum between twentieth-century film music and aspects of nineteenth-century music, which in many interesting ways anticipated it.[7]

"Something you've composed yourself? How exciting!"

—*Marianne (Jennifer Daniel) in* The Kiss of the Vampire

1

The Long Shadow of Castle Bernard

No human being could have passed a happier childhood than myself. My parents were possessed by the very spirit of kindness and indulgence.

—Victor Frankenstein in Mary Shelley's *Frankenstein*[1]

Appropriately, there are both barons and the English equivalent of counts in the ancestry of a composer associated with so many Frankenstein and Dracula films. James Bernard was indeed related to an aristocratic Irish family, which flourished in the market town of Bandon in County Cork, about twenty miles south of Cork itself. The founder of the dynasty was Francis Bernard, a landowner who rose to be a member of the Irish parliament, becoming Baron Bandon in 1755 and the first Earl in 1800. There is also an ancestral seat, known as Castle Bernard, which is now a romantic, ivy-covered ruin. Forced out into the grounds to watch her home being put to the torch by Sinn Fein on June 21, 1921, the Countess defiantly sang "God Save the King" many times over.[2] Unfortunately, the King did not save the castle. It was an event that was to be repeated cinematically in *Scars of Dracula* (EMI/Hammer, dir. Roy Ward Baker, 1970), Hammer's sixth Dracula film, in which the Count's residence suffered the same fate as Castle Bernard, though the arsonists in that case were revolting peasants of uncertain European nationality rather than members of the IRA.

With the death of the fifth Earl, the earldom became extinct, though Lady Jennifer Bernard, the Earl's daughter and James Bernard's second cousin, is now head of the clan. And it is with the grandmother of Lady Jennifer that the first definite connection between the Bernards of County Cork and James Bernard's own family can at last be made. There is a missing link that has so far eluded all attempts to establish a bloodline between the two Bernard families, but Lady Jennifer's mother, born Betty Edwards, was definitely the cousin of Col. Ronald Playfair St. Vincent Bernard, the composer's father.

Col. Bernard was born far away from Ireland, in Singapore. At that time (1888),

Singapore was very much a colonial city. The Raffles Hotel, which overlooks the sea with its parks, clubs and polo ground, was then at the height of its fame, reconciling European visitors to a tropical climate where it rains for over 180 days a year. Not much is known about Col. Bernard's own father, Frank, other than that he was what was then called a stock-jobber (or stockbroker), and quite a wealthy one at that. Ronald, however, was destined for a career as a professional soldier in the Indian Army, for at that time the sun had yet to set on the British Empire. He married twice. His first wife, Kathleen Cleland, came from a family of coal merchants. She followed her husband out to India but unfortunately died of scepticemia after giving birth to a child in 1922, only a year after her marriage. The child didn't survive either, and it was some time before young James was to learn about his father's first marriage. When he did, it came as rather a shock.

Col. Bernard's second wife was Katherine Wigan, who met him in India while on a grand tour. She was acquainted with the influential family of Sir Louis Dane, an Indian civil servant and secretary to the Punjab government, who later rose to become foreign secretary to the government of India. Thanks to the Dane family, young Katherine was introduced to all the eligible officers, one of whom eventually became her future husband. Her father was the Reverend Percival Wigan, a gentleman who had taken holy orders but, according to his musical grandson, "never did much about it." The family home, which is now a hotel and golf club, was Puckrup Hall, situated just outside the village of Twyning near Tewksbury. This imposing Georgian mansion is appropriately credited with a resident ghost: a phantom lady is still said to sit on one of the settees in the Drawing Room; some people have heard a coach and horses driving about the grounds during the hours of darkness. It also has rather musical views. From the front one can see Bredon Hill, made famous in the poem by A. E. Housman, which was later set to music as part of Ralph Vaughan Williams' song-cycle *On Wenlock Edge*. From the back, the Malvern Hills, with their evocative Elgarian associations, roll elegiacally across the horizon; and it was on the Broadwood in the day nursery of Puckrup Hall that young James Bernard first started to play the piano. He had another early musical experience there when he was about seven years old and asked for permission to stay up late to hear the great Italian tenor Giovanni Martinelli singing in Verdi's *Otello* on the radio. It marked the beginning of a life long love of that com-

Col. Ronald Playfair St. Vincent Bernard, MC, DSO—the composer's father (courtesy Bernard Estate).

poser's operas, which in due course exerted their influence over his own compositions.

These musical instincts were the inheritance of some notable ancestors on his mother's side of the family. *Her* mother, the wife of Reverend Percy Wigan, was Catherine Henslowe, and she was a descendant of Philip Henslowe, the well-known contemporary of Shakespeare who had managed the Rose Playhouse and Swan Theater in London's Bankside. Bernard's love of acting and his youthful desire to go on the stage can surely be traced back to that colorful personality. There is also a connection with Thomas Arne, the eighteenth-century composer of *Rule, Britannia!,* via Arne's wife, Cecilia Young. She had been one of the most noted singers of her day and much admired by Handel. Her niece, Polly (Mary), whom she educated, had married the French composer François-Hippolyte Barthélemon and the daughter of that marriage, Cecilia Maria, later married into the Henslowe family. Therefore, though the connection to Arne is only tenuous, Bernard could claim a direct (if rather complicated) bloodline descent from a once celebrated French composer. Indeed, he later inherited Bathélemon's violin as well as the portrait of him painted by Thomas Gainsborough.

Mrs. Katherine Bernard, the composer's mother (courtesy Bernard Estate).

Barthélemon was born in 1741 in Bordeaux, but had moved in 1764 to London where he became a leading figure in the city's musical life. He wrote only one serious opera, *Pelopida* (first performed in 1766), but composed quite a lot of incidental music for the theater. He was also a great friend of Haydn, whom he entertained when that composer came to London to give his celebrated series of concerts for the impresario Johann Peter Salomon. Barthélemon is often credited with having given Haydn the idea of composing *The Creation.* An unpublished memoir of Barthélemon, written by an anonymous member of the Henslowe family, which was inherited by the Bernard family, describes his character as:

> Of an unbounded generosity, open, irritable, and incautious; without guile or suspicion in himself, he became an easy dupe and prey to the designing craft of others. Even in his religion that amiable and self-destructive tendency bore sway; he admired too much the harmlessness of the dove, because he did so in exclusion of the serpent's wisdom. [...] In his personal stature Barthélemon might be almost called diminutive, a defect, which if it really were one, was more than fully redeemed by the perfection of his features, the muscular and shapeful elegance

"I am glad that it is old and big. I myself am of an old family and to live in a new house would kill me" (Dracula, in Bram Stoker's *Dracula*). Puckrup Hall, the home of the Bernard family — now a hotel and golf club.

Meet the Ancestor: James Bernard with Gainsborough's portrait of Barthélemon (courtesy Julieta Preston).

> of his make, the politeness of his address, the variety of his accomplishments, the extent of his attainments, the energy of his mind, and the goodness of his heart."[3]

Barthélemon's generosity of spirit was certainly handed down to James Bernard who, while not an "easy dupe," certainly became a victim of "the designing craft of others" during his time in Jamaica—with near-fatal results.

The memoir continues with a description of Barthélemon's facility for composing music at speed in collaboration with the actor, David Garrick:

> Barthélemon, looking over [Garrick's] shoulder, actually wrote an accompanied melody to the song as quickly as the other penned the poetry. "There, Sir, " at length exclaimed the manager, "is my song." "And there, Sir," returned Barthélemon, "is the music to it!" Astonished and delighted at this unlooked for musical impromptu, Garrick invited the composer to dine with him that day in company with Dr Johnson."

The ability to work at white hot speed is, of course, essential for a film composer as well. In fact, the gothic subject matter of Hammer's most famous products during the 1950s and 1960s had been foreshadowed by the succession of "Gothick" melodramas in vogue during Barthélemon's lifetime. Barthélemon's theater music, though not written for specifically "Gothick" plays, would certainly have conformed to the kind of music required by them; so Bernard's future musical career was really a continuation of family tradition.

Katherine Bernard was herself quite unmusical, but her husband, though he may not have enjoyed such an interesting musical pedigree, nonetheless had a pleasant singing voice and was very fond of performing Edwardian ballads. One song he particularly enjoyed was Alma Goetz's setting of a poem by Ethel Clifford called *Mélisande in the Wood.* The words ("Lean down to the water, Mélisande, / And look at your mirror'd face....") exploited the imagery of *Pelléas et Mélisande,* the then-fashionable symbolist drama by the Belgian playwright and Nobel prize winner, Maurice Maeterlinck. Appropriately, Maeterlinck's play was later set to music by Debussy, another of Bernard's favorite composers. Although Col. Bernard found Debussy and Ravel "a bit too modern," it was nonetheless through other kinds of music that father and son became very close.

Col. Bernard was also an excellent tennis player and had appeared at Wimbledon as well as being an Army boxing and fencing champion. Unfortunately, he also suffered from very high blood pressure and was eventually invalided out of the army, much to his dismay, in 1938. After looking around for a suitable job, he became bursar to St. Albans Boys School, but with the outbreak of the Second World War military expertise was of course in great demand again and he was asked back by the Army to become chief liaison officer to the Free Dutch, whose headquarters were based at Wolverhampton. This entailed another move to a large Victorian House called "Lawnwood" and it was there that Col. Bernard suffered two cerebral hemorrhages after going out on night exercises. The first one was a warning shot, because he recovered. Then, feeling much better again, he was tempted to go off on another exercise. The next morning, Mrs. Bernard told James the sad news that his father had died in the night. It was a very peaceful way for a soldier to pass away, and after a brief hesitation, Mrs. Bernard decided to take James' three-year old sister, Mary, to see the body. (Brother Bill was by that time serving in the Army and living away from home.) Together, widow, daughter and son stood by the bed in the sunlit room to say a last goodbye.

Dying from a brain hemorrhage in Wolverhampton is a far cry from the exciting and rather glamorous life of commanding a Gurkha regiment on the Northwest frontier, where Col. Bernard's youngest son, James Michael, was born on September 20, 1925, at what was then the little hill station of Nathia Gali in the foothills of the Himalayas. At that time Col. Bernard was ADC to Gen. Sir William Riddell Birdwood, the commander-in-chief of the Indian Army. "Birdie," as he was always known, had been a famous World War I hero and military secretary to Lord Kitchener in India. When the commander-in-chief was in Delhi, Col. Bernard and his family would follow him to live in the complex of buildings that had been designed by Sir Edwin Lutyens; but in the hot weather the family would to go up to the hill station at Simla. James Bernard remembered this vividly:

> It was just like *The Jewel in the Crown.* My childish memory is of looking out of the window from this little train chugging up the hillsides of the Himalayas and looking down into a vast valley which was filled with crimson rhododendrons. Even the thought of it now fills me with a thrill of the past.[4]

Ready for Battle: Bill Bernard (left) and James Bernard in Gurkha uniform, October 1930 (courtesy Bernard Estate).

James and his older brother Bill had an English nanny who was much loved by the whole family. On several occasions she rescued the boys from dangerous wildlife. Once, a cobra slithered into the bathroom and Nanny Rogerson came to the rescue. "He's just having a drink," she reassured the children. "He won't hurt us if we stay quite still." Bernard also remembered encountering a very poisonous little snake called a krait:

> It was the sort of snake that Cleopatra might have had in her bowl of figs or apricots. One day I saw one of these lying completely still in the dusty, dry arid sort of soil and I thought it was a stick. I was about to pick it up when Nanny snatched me away — so she probably saved my life.

Another time the boys had a little pet bear for a playmate; and, of course, they were very fond of their little sealyham dog, called Squiggy. When in Delhi they enjoyed going out on picnics, sometimes up at the Red Fort; but like so many of the famous sights of India, the Red Fort was overrun with hordes of monkeys who took a special delight in tormenting the poor creature. Squiggy, however, was a lucky dog. Not only did he manage to avoid being killed by the treacherous monkeys, he also survived an earthquake. Col. and Mrs. Bernard were fortunately away at the time of the terrible Quetta earthquake of 1935, as were their children, but when they returned they were dismayed to find their home reduced to a pile of rubble. Squiggy, however, ran out of the ruins completely unhurt, wagging his tail enthusiastically.

Col. Bernard eventually became the commander of a hill station at Malakand, in an area of the Northwest frontier, which was surrounded by hostile hill tribesmen, none too keen on the British Raj. As James Bernard explained:

> We could only get there on horseback and had to be escorted there under cover of armed guards. It was quite a glamorous environment, looking back. There we were, the only little children at a remote hill fort in India! We got made a great fuss of, Bill and myself, by the Gurkhas. They were wonderful, short, strong, wiry hill tribesmen who were incredibly brave — and bloodthirsty when it comes to it; but they used to make a tremendous fuss of us and my mother always loved the photo of us two little tiny boys dressed in Gurkha uniforms! So we had happy times.

Mrs. Bernard was an attractive, spirited woman. Born to be the wife and mother of a British colonial family, she devoted a great deal of her time to charitable good works. During the First World War she became a voluntary ambulance driver and nursed wounded soldiers at the front. When she later accompanied her younger son on his first visit to Wellington College as a school boy, she immediately recognized one of the porters who had only one leg. He was amazed when she told him how she remembered applying the tourniquet which saved his life.

But before going to Wellington, Bernard was sent to The Elms, a prep school in the Malvern Hills, run by the Singleton family. There he had singing and piano lessons with a certain Miss Gosden, and he soon became her star pupil. She was a large lady and he always felt rather sorry for her when, on hot days, big patches of sweat would stain her cotton frocks while she was trying to keep control of her class of less-than-sympathetic charges. It was also during his time at The Elms that Bernard became fascinated by the movies. He caused some consternation amongst the staff when he asked if he could subscribe to a magazine called *Film Weekly*. This was considered so unusual a request that permission had to be sought from his parents to make sure that they approved of this dubious influence on his young life. Fortunately, they did and with the help of this magazine he soon became an avid film fan. This interest coincided with his already clearly defined sexual orientation, for whenever he went to the cinema to see Johnny Weissmuller as Tarzan he always hoped that the actor's loincloth would fall off. He kept on hoping but, of course, it never did.

Bernard's love of things supernatural was also ingrained from an early age. At home he was brought up on the fairy tale books of Andrew Lang, which had wonderful illustrations of witches and flying carpets, beautiful princesses locked up in castles and even more beautiful princes who had been turned into frogs. Though his family weren't tremendous film fans, he was treated to a performance of *Snow White and the Seven Dwarfs* (David Hand, Walt Disney, 1937); before that, his father had taken him to see the romantic comedy *I Dream Too Much* (RKO, dir. John Cromwell, 1935) in which a French singer marries an American composer. It starred Lily Pons and Henry Fonda, with music by the doyen of Hollywood composers, Max Steiner. One scene in particular attracted his attention: Lily Pons finds herself without any pajamas and is lent a pair by Fonda. The borrowed pair is, of course, far too big for her, and causes embarrassment, which gives rise to some charming comedy: "It was so touching and sweet," Bernard remembered. As soon as he had sufficient pocket money, he rushed out to buy the record of the title song, "I Dream Too Much," sung by Pons herself. On the B-side he was introduced to the bell-song from Delibes' opera *Lakmé*. The record shop in Cheltenham where he bought it soon became his Mecca. His next disc was of the great Polish pianist Paderewsky playing Chopin's E flat Nocturne; and hand in hand with his love of Chopin came a fascination with the transcendental technique of Liszt. One of Liszt's studies had a title that fascinated him as much as the music: "*Feux Follets,*" or "Will-o-the-wisps." Combining the thrill of the supernatural with lashings of virtuoso showmanship, he couldn't resist buying a recording of it by Louis Kentner.[5]

Later, during his time at Wellington College, Bernard often took himself off to the movies and was fascinated by Lon Chaney, Jr., and Bela Lugosi in *Frankenstein Meets the Wolf Man* (Universal, dir. Roy William Neill, 1943). He also loved Romantic adventure. *The Call of the Wild* (Twentieth Century Fox, dir. William Wellman, 1935), starring Clark Gable, was a particular favorite. Little did he realize that he would later compose the music for another famous series of Frankenstein films, as well as one of Hammer's most successful Romantic adventures—a film based on H. Rider Haggard's 1887 novel, *She*. It was also during his time at Wellington that he would meet a very famous English composer who would play an important role in his future life and and career.

2

"Virtutis Fortuna Comes"*

Wellington College Chapel

Quietness falls on peoples' souls to-night,
When all the air is filled with murmuring
And leaves begin to talk outside these walls,
Within whose stern defence and welcome
People have prayed and thought,
And do again to-night in this intensity of prayer.
All that is God is here
Within these walls,
Bare as they are,
And in the air
A countless beat of hearts
And speaking silence,
A cup of blood from these dark centuries.
All that is God within the heads of these at prayer,
Crushed in tight-flexed fingers and tense arms,
Held in twisted hands and shadowed hair.
I am dead to all else but this eternity,
I am dissolved and nothing in reality,
I am scattered through this permanence of air,
Bodiless, a leaf in this still bowl.

James Bernard[1]

"*Virtutis Fortuna Comes,*" the motto of Wellington College, implies that good fortune doesn't just happen. Opportunities have to be sought out and taken advantage of; and that is exactly what Bernard had to do with regard to his musical career.

Situated at Crowthorne, near Wokingham in Berkshire, the College had been founded in 1857 by Prince Albert and built through public subscription as a school for the sons of British Army officers. By coincidence, Christopher Lee, whose father was also a military man, left the school in the very year that Bernard entered it, 1939. Not surprisingly, neither of them can remember the other as schoolboys. But for the future impersonator of Count Dracula, Wellington had few if any happy memories:

*"Good luck is the companion of courage"

> We didn't expect to be cosseted at a military school, even if it did have a Classical side. We played [rugby] on pitches frozen like lakes, and if we fell we bled, and were left to get on with it. The vivid smell of mud and blood together occur as a reprise through those years.[2]

Wellington was indeed run along military lines. An obituary in the December 1942 issue of the school magazine demonstrates the kind of spirit fostered by the school when describing the achievements of its head of catering, Major Ball. He had been in charge of the Army School of Cookery at Aldershot before joining the Wellington staff, and under his "command" the College kitchens were run like a well-planned military campaign, the preparation of food more like an all-out assault on enemy troops than the humble preparation of meat, vegetables and puddings:

> War always means waste. Men who can prevent waste and save precious stores are rare and valuable. [...Major Ball] gave us of his best. ... The kitchens began to bristle with machines, machines to slice bacon, to stuff sausages, peel and mash potatoes, to mix puddings and to freeze ice cream. ... Ball's whole heart was in his work. He was never tired of devising new methods of economy either of labour or of materials in the preparation of food. But these were only a means, not an end. It was a great thing if the Wellington boy was fed at the lowest cost of any public school, but only if at the same time he was better fed than any other boy. Ball's fame rapidly spread. Bursars, Headmasters, Chairmen of Governors came to visit him to ask his advice and solicit his help, which was always gladly given. He was a little surprised once on receiving a wire from a well-known school "Just found Cook dead in oven," but he was equal to the occasion and before 24 hours had passed had despatched [sic] the Wellington second cook to fill the unexpected gap.[3]

This was just the kind of military attitude that Lee found so hard to live with. For him it was a "terrible misuse [...] of the beautiful grounds set amongst silver beeches to hold parades and weapon training among them."[4] Bernard didn't like the military side of Wellington much either, but he made the best of it and ended up being quite good at it. Indeed, the training stood him in good stead during his later war service in the RAF. Like Lee, he was also a classical scholar; both of them were taught by Herbert H. Wright, the tutor in charge of the Combermere, Lee's schoolhouse. (Bernard's was the Hardinge.) Wright was known as Lofty because he stood six foot four and Lee recalls being beaten by him on numerous occasions. Bernard, however, got on very well with him.

The advantage of being in the classical sixth was that Bernard was excused cricket, which he hated. Being quite a good runner, he was allowed to get by on a little athletics before rushing back to the music school where he would practice the piano for the rest of the afternoon. In the Easter term they played hockey, which both Bernard and Lee hated, but the former made the best of playing rugby:

> I didn't mind the rugger because I thought, although I was supposed to be one of the artistic ones in the house, I would jolly well show that I could be quite butch. So I played with a great deal of vigor and I was a wing three-quarters. I was quite fast and I used to score tries. I even broke my wrist once and walked proudly about for the rest of the term with my wrist in plaster—and won my house colors.

There were, of course, many things to enjoy about contact sports at an all-male establishment if you were gay, which young Bernard certainly was in an active way that made him rather notorious. One incident, after he posted a proposition under the partition of a toilet cubicle, very nearly got him expelled: The recipient turned out to be the College's only unsympathetic prefect.

> I got a message that I was to go to the sixth form room and I thought, oh, good they're going to just beat me probably; but then that was changed and I was told to go and report to my tutor, who was a science master called Bertie Kemp who I suspect may also have been gay, though repressed. He later killed himself. Anyway, he brought out my little note and asked if I had written it. I said, "Oh, no, sir!," and then he said, "Are you telling the truth?" and I said, "Oh, no, sir!" I was about to be confirmed, and he said, "Now do you think in view of this that you ought to be confirmed?" What a curious reaction! I said, "Oh, please, sir, I must be confirmed because I've had all my confirmation presents from my great aunts!" So he did agree that the confirmation could go ahead. The term then came to an end and nothing had been said to anybody. When I came back I had a new housemaster who *was* gay—Robin Gordon Walker. He was so sympathetic and spoke in my favor when the acting headmaster, Boosie Gould, wanted to expel me. Robin said, "As your parents are so understanding, I feel you should write to them and tell them you're homosexual." I said, "Okay, if you want me to. I don't have any hangups, I don't feel guilty about it." I sat down and wrote to them and I got the most lovely letters back—sweet letters saying they didn't want me to think they loved me any the less. They both visited me but my father came in on his own, which I thought was very tactful, gave me a most affectionate hug, and reaffirmed that this news made no difference to his love for me but he wanted to talk to me about it, anxiously reminding me about what happened to Oscar Wilde. After our chat, Mother came in and she said nothing about it at all! Dad wasn't gay but he was all for male romantic friendships and I talked much more openly to him about gayness than I did to my mother.

In 1940, the war reached the heart of Wellington College itself when a German bomb killed the headmaster, Robert Longden. Both Lee and Bernard had fond memories of this much-loved man. Bernard remembered him as a man of great charm and personality, who used to invite senior boys to dinner and tea parties on Sunday afternoons. Quite the opposite of an old fogey, he was a young man, which made him particularly popular with the boys, all of whose names he learned by heart. Lee recalls that he "worked better for Bobby Longden that at any other time of my College life."[5] His death was a great blow to the school and Bernard vividly described the event in a letter he wrote to his parents:

> The Hardinge
> Wellington College
> 13/10/40
>
> Dear Mum and Dad
>
> [...]
>
> I expect you have already heard of the most sad death of the Master. Until he died, I never realised how much of a leader he was or how much he lit up college with his vitality. One misses him so much, one can hardly believe he's dead and that one will see him no more, walking round the quads or down to watch the games in the afternoon.

> [...]
> He was killed on Tuesday evening, as he was just going out after supper to look round college and see that all was well. A bomb landed almost on the porch of his house and he must have been killed instantly. Another bomb landed about 100 yards away but did no damage except for ruining part of a wall and a bike shed. The roof of the master's house was shattered, his car was blown into the bushes near by and the drive was ruined; many of the college windows were shattered, and the library was half-ruined what with shattered glass blowing in and the plaster showering of [sic] the ceiling.
> I shan't forget Wednesday morning for a long time; creeping out of our shelters where we'd slept all night, lots of us in our clothes owing to the earliness of the warning, going into a late breakfast in dressing-gowns and overcoats and standing about in little knots outside as the news flew from mouth to mouth that the Master was dead. At a quarter to ten prayers were held in the dining hall and Mr. Gould (now acting head) announced the sad news. The rest of the day we worked at clearing away debris or on the land while the junior forms continued work in the ordinary way.

Later in the same letter, he described his reaction to one of the concerts at Wellington, which had a very strong musical tradition:

> the Brahms [...] thrilled me from the depths of my heart. I don't know if you know that marvelous feeling which certain music can give you, if you listen with every inch of your attention and your eyes closed. I think it's the harmonies more than the actual melodies which have that power.

Wellington's director of music was Maurice Allen, a very temperamental man who was known to throw scores across the room when roused. He was nonetheless an important influence on Bernard's musical education. In fact, he took piano lessons from Allen, who also introduced him to the music of Benjamin Britten by playing him that composer's *Sonnets of Michelangelo*. Christopher Lee, who enjoyed singing in the school choir, also remembers performing Stanford's *The Revenge* under Allen's baton,[6] but Bernard took on rather more demanding musical roles. In the College Concert of July 1942, he performed one of the piano parts of Saint-Saëns' *Carnival of the Animals* alongside the brilliant Wellington piano teacher Ronald Timberley, whom Lee remembered as "splendid and rotund" in contrast to the "dark and sinister" Allen.[7] The school magazine, *The Wellingtonian*, recorded the event for posterity:

> The Orchestra played the minuet and trio from Haydn's "Bear Symphony," and accompanied J. M. Bernard and Mr. Timberley on two pianos in "Le Carnaval des Animaux." We hope it is not short memory to say that the Orchestra was better than usual; the brass has certainly improved; and in "Le Carnaval" the various soloists equalled the excellent standard of the pianists and the Orchestra.[8]

After *The Carnival of the Animals*, Timberley made way for John Goodall, a good friend of Bernard's, who was collaborating with him on a two-piano composition called *Phantasma*, which the school magazine modestly described as "pleasant."

However, Bernard was soon winning musical prizes and his platform appearances became increasingly frequent. The following year, *The Wellingtonian* obliquely reported that:

> J. M. Bernard's fine playing of the first movement of the Schumann Piano Concerto [...] was more than the usual schoolboy performance. By interpreting the music in his own way Bernard gave to the work a personality that, if lacking, would have left the audience wondering dimly about the secrets of the woodwind.[9]

Another concert displayed Bernard in a variety of different roles:

> Among the more remarkable performances were a brilliant effort, on the part of J. M. Bernard, in playing Rachmaninov's Prelude in G Minor, a work requiring of the pianist mature skill and meticulous technique. [...] The concert concluded with a Bourrée and March by Handel, played earnestly by the Music Society Orchestra, which was held together surprisingly well by its conductor, J.M. Bernard.
>
> Three imperfections were apparent — the Concert was, in some places, underrehearsed, the audience was too small and the short time passed too quickly.[10]

In July, Bernard gave "a decidedly mature and capable interpretation"[11] of César Franck's *Symphonic Variations*, and it's not surprising that he had by now developed ambitions to become a concert pianist. "But when you're at school and happen to have a certain facility of technique," he explained later, "you think it's all easy. It's only later when you go to the Royal College of Music you find out that you're hopeless." There were, however, several opportunities at Wellington to hear professional performances from visiting soloists such as the violinist Ida Haendel and pianist Harriet Cohen. The Boyd Neel Orchestra made an appearance in December 1942. But it was composition rather than piano-playing and conducting that brought Bernard to the attention of one of Wellington's most illustrious musical visitors. This was Benjamin Britten, who arrived in July 1943 just after having completed his opera *Peter Grimes.* He was visiting the school because he wanted to discuss the stage designs of the forthcoming premiere of that opera with Wellington's art master, Kenneth Green. As Britten's biographer Humphrey Carpenter has explained, Green had spent his childhood in Southwold, only a few miles to the north of Aldeburgh, but had become acquainted with Britten and Peter Pears through his son, who had got to know them as an evacuee.[12] Green, who painted both their portraits in 1943, was also a good stage designer, and Britten was convinced that he was the right man for the job.

Britten's visit coincided with one of the inter-house music competitions for which Bernard had composed a piece that had been written on the *Spur of the Moment* (its eventual title). It was scored for the unusual combination of trombone, piano and percussion in order to channel the enthusiasm of eight boys who wanted to take part as well as to demonstrate the technical progress of a boy called Cordeaux who was just beginning to learn the trombone. Bernard himself would preside at the piano. Britten was always interested in the musical activities of young people and he soon found out what was going on. Present at a rehearsal, he was fascinated by what he heard. The only problem was that there were seven eager percussionists and only six percussion instruments. Britten smiled, and immediately volunteered to help with the invention of an instrument to fill the gap.

They went on a spontaneous walk around the college grounds and experimented with what came to hand. First, Britten tried hitting two stones together but that didn't really make a very satisfactory noise. The stone emitted a spark and then broke.

After a while he saw a piece of drainpipe, picked it up and hit the stone against that instead. "It made a splendid 'clang,'" Bernard recalled, "so he said, 'That's our instrument. We'll call it the Pebble and Drainpipe.'" The problem solved, Bernard immediately set about writing a line for the new instrument and was rewarded with the singular honor of having his score inscribed, "Composed by James Bernard. Edited by Benjamin Britten."[13] The imaginative use of percussion in Bernard's film scores was anticipated in his detailed performance notes for this piece, which pointed out that "the surface of the tambourine must *not* be banged, but the wheels on the side of it made to revolve, and so jingle, with the flat surface of the hand."

When it came to the premiere, there was a lot of hard feeling because some of the masters' wives thought it unfair that Bernard had been helped by the great man. As a punishment, his piece was awarded only second prize. The masters' wives might also have been annoyed by the spectacle of Britten and Pears convulsed with giggles during another boy's recital of MacDowell's "To a Wild Rose" performed on the tuba. So audible was their amusement that they were asked to leave the room.

The masters' wives did, however, compliment Bernard on his subsequent performance of the role in Bernard Shaw's *Arms and the Man,* which had originally been played by Sibyl Thorndike. "I loved wearing drag," he confessed. "I had long earrings and I remember several of the masters' wives saying, 'You wear your earrings so well! You will have to give us lessons!'"

At that early stage, acting vied with music as a possible future career. Unlike Christopher Lee, who made few appearances in the school's theatrical productions, Bernard acted in school plays whenever he could. *The Wellingtonian* was, however, rather critical of Bernard's performance in the school production of *Twelfth Night* (a play for which he would later write music on the professional stage):

> He spoke and acted, as Malvolio, amazingly well; yet was his interpretation of the part *quite* all that it should be? Malvolio, we are told, was "sad and civil," a melancholy and punctilious civil servant with secret ambitions, not a mincing Osric in a golden chain. By burlesquing the part from the beginning Bernard lost half the effect of the box-hedge scene, where Malvolio's decorum and propriety crash in pathetic ruins, and he became instead a mere punchball for Sir Toby. Only in the last scene did he rise to the full heights of the pathos for which Shakespeare surely intended him.[14]

Bernard himself provided the details of a rather more impromptu performance in the letter to his parents that had also told of Robert Longden's death:

> [...] Since last Tuesday, we've been sleeping in the shelters every night; so last night we devised a variety show for entertainment in the shelter. Anyone could do a turn, and Goodall and I did a comic turn: we were two rather common old ladies in a tube station shelter in London. Goodall was Agatha Haggis and I was Bertha Lemon and we procured whigs [sic] and dresses and hats. I was old and fat and waddling, with a dead evening dress of white velvety stuff and orange shawls and grey hair. Goodall was younger, completely flat-breasted, and in a black dress with a black whig and old squashed red hat. We wrote our conversation before hand and composed several rather vulgar jokes and a stupid little song. I was a bit deaf and always mistook what Aggy said, and we both talked in awful haggy croaks and frequently burst into fits of howling cackles. [...] Some people thought

we had copied our jokes, but, actually, we composed them in about half-an-hour on Saturday afternoon.

Bernard also had several poems published in the school magazine, which demonstrated a similar precocity. "A Love Song," which appeared in the July 1943 edition, suggests an amorous adolescent encounter:

LOVE SONG

Hills have gone into the distance,
Day has fled into dusk
Evening loses all its silence
When the night throws off her mask.

Now the stillness is eternal
In this mid-point here in time;
We are lost in the eternal,
And our love is in the bloom.

You are mine, love, in the meadow;
Minutes do not pass us now;
Now it is that sun and shadow
Have not anything to show.[15]

"Words of the Trees" seems to reflect Bernard's indecision with regard to which artistic path he should follow on leaving school.

WORDS OF THE TREES

Those days have passed now,
When we wandered freely through the woods,
And talked,
And laughed,
And walked along a stairway to the stars;
And built our silly castles to the sun,
Which one by one
Have fallen since,
And now are gone;

The last one
Only this summer afternoon,
When I walked out alone,
And all the trees about me in the gloom
Spoke in quiet voices,
And told me I was late and old,
That I had made my choices,
That I had been too bold.
That I had chosen, wrongly,
Not my fate,
Or what the world might bring,
But rather, in my mind,
My own imagining.[16]

Meanwhile, however, a distraction arrived thanks to Britten and Pears:

45 A St Johns Wood High Street NW8
July 18th 1943

Dear Jim

This is only a note in great haste to thank you very much for sending me the copy of the Wellingtonians' Only (I much enjoyed it, especially your poem about Richelieu), and also to say that probably after all Peter Pears is not singing on the 4th — but he *is* singing Traviata on 31st July. If you would like our party on that date — let me know and I'll get tickets for as many as you say. Mind you round up quite a few and we'll make a good 'claque.' If you can't manage 31st — he's singing again on 7th I think, if that's better, but I expect you'll all be in camp then. Let me know soon — that's all.

How's the new song *and* my copy of the Spur of the Moment going ?

Love to all my friends including Lowe who made the faces and the boy with the drain-pipes— and of course Skinner — and to you.

Benjamin B.

A copy of *Spur of the Moment* was duly sent to Britten and is still lodged in the Britten-Pears Library at Aldeburgh. Britten also sent the required number of tickets for Pears' performance, and a group of operatically inclined Wellingtonians were subsequently crammed into a box at the New Theater in St. Martin's Lane where Pears was appearing with the Sadler's Wells Company. Britten had planned to take them all out to dinner at the Café Royal after the performance, but in the event he asked his friend, the Reverend Walter Hussey, to stand in for him, thereby sowing the seeds of another of Bernard's lifelong friendships, which was to have an impact on his musical education as well.

Hussey had first come into contact with Britten after he became the vicar of St. Matthew's Church in Northampton. Eager to revive the church's tradition of patronage to the arts, he had originally invited William Walton to compose a choral work for the Jubilee celebrations of the church. Walton, however, had declined, so Hussey turned to Britten, who accepted. The result was the cantata *Rejoice in the Lamb,* the first of several important artistic commissions from this enterprising cleric, which included a Madonna and Child sculpture by Henry Moore and a Crucifixion altar piece by Graham Sutherland. Later, when Hussey became Dean of Chichester Cathedral, he approached Leonard Bernstein to compose the *Chichester Psalms* and even commissioned a setting of the *Magnificat* and *Nunc Dimittis* by Bernard himself. Bernard always fondly remembered his first trip to the Café Royal with Hussey:

> They had this lovely great big downstairs room with marble topped tables. For the price of one lager or a coffee you could sit there all evening and chat. People like Auden and Isherwood used to go there. It was a great literary and artistic haunt. We went to the upstairs part where there was very good food — good for wartime days. I think in those days bread was a course: if you had bread that was one of the three courses. Anyway, we had a very jolly evening and Walter looked after us all. He must have taken my address because later on he wrote to me and said he'd love to see me again, so it was from that moment that our great friendship sprang up.

Hussey's letter arrived while Bernard was stationed at the top-secret codebreaking establishment at Bletchley Park in Buckinghamshire, fifty miles north of

London. Originally, Bernard had planned to go into the Air Force and become a fighter pilot, imagining that it would be "awfully glamourous." Unlike Britten and Kenneth Greene, he wasn't a conscientious objector and he wanted to do his bit for the war; but when one of his best friends at school, David Kingscote, got shot down and killed, Bernard thought twice about becoming a fighter pilot. Meanwhile, a squadron leader by the name of Bernard Shore came to Wellington to recruit suitable sixth-formers for Bletchley Park. In his musical capacity, Shore had been the leading viola player of the BBC Symphony Orchestra and had written several books about music, but on this visit to Wellington he was on the lookout for linguistic rather than musical talent because the job for which he was recruiting would involve learning Japanese. To Bernard, the classical scholar, it sounded far safer than being a fighter pilot but was just as glamourous, so he applied and was accepted.

Doing his bit: James Bernard in his Royal Air Force uniform. August 1944 (photograph Hay Wrightson).

> I left school at the end of the summer term 1943, signed up and was then sent on my two months hideous square bashing, marching up and down — but even then I found a chum called David Davenport who had been a ballet dancer and I remember him showing me the positions of ballet in the Naafi. One found chums in the most unlikely circumstances. Later on, when I was at Officers' Training Camp, we slept in Nissan huts and there were a lot of much older men all round me but I thought, well, at least I'm going to try to be as civilized as I can. I very much liked going to that famous shop, Floris, in Jermyn Street, because all Floris products are so nice — toiletries, talcum powders and aftershaves. I was armed with all these sorts of things and took them with me to the ablutions, as they were called. While I was there I showered myself with a great deal of Floris talcum powder (I think it was Roman Hyacinth), came back and got into bed. The other men said, "There's a tremendous pong round here. It smells like a whore house!" I kept very quiet and snuggled down into my bed; but in future I didn't use quite so much Floris talcum powder. Fortunately, my time in the Wellington Junior Training Corps stood me in good stead when it came to giving orders. I found I was rather good at it.

After his square bashing, he was sent to the School of African and Oriental Studies in London, which was part of London University. The course lasted for six months during the second blitz on London, and he was billeted in accommodation that was situated very near the BBC in Hallam Street. During the day he was force-fed Japanese; during the night he did his fair share of fire watching, picking his way through heaps of rubble the following morning on his way back to the University buildings. After successfully learning a thousand Japanese characters, he was sent to a code-breaking school at an Air Force interception site at Chicksands Priory in Bedfordshire, where he struggled somewhat but eventually passed the course. Then he was ready for the Top Secret code-breaking center at Bletchley Park in Buckinghamshire. It was code named Station X, and no one outside this establishment knew what its purpose was. Indeed, individuals within Station X weren't always sure about exactly what was going on. Originally a country mansion built for Sir Herbert Leon, a London stockbroker, the main building was a rather ungainly mixture of mock–Gothic and mock–Tudor surmounted by a green copper dome. If it had been built by the side of the Thames opposite Bray studios, Hammer would no doubt have called upon its services, along with those so often supplied by Oakley Court, the similarly eccentric mansion that featured in several of the company's most notable shockers. During the war, Bletchley Park's eccentric architecture housed some equally eccentric boffins, as one member of the Air Section recalled:

> There was a great degree of tolerance at Bletchley for eccentricities. There had to be because so many of the people were very, very eccentric indeed. At least half of the people there were absolutely mad. They were geniuses, no doubt many of them were extremely, extremely clever, but my goodness they were strange in ordinary life.
>
> So you did have this rather happy atmosphere of tolerance. Very eccentric behaviour was accepted fairly affectionately and I think people worked and lived there who couldn't possibly have worked and lived anywhere else. People who would obviously have been very ill at ease in a normal Air Force camp with its very strict modes of behaviour and discipline were very happy, very at ease in Bletchley.[17]

Bernard was immediately assigned to a code that was sent from Japanese merchant ships directly to headquarters in Berlin. If anything important was discovered, he had to rush to a secret room underground where he passed on the information to a man called Willy King, whose wife, Viva, he later got to know socially:

> She became a famous London hostess and she loved gays. Every Sunday she had an afternoon salon. The phrase gays used was, "Is he a friend of Mrs King?" Paul [Dehn, Bernard's future partner] and I used to use that. It's a very good phrase because you can use it in front of anyone. You can answer, "Well, I think he would like to know her but he hasn't met her yet."

There were plenty of gays at Bletchley Park during the war, mathematician Alan Turing and novelist Angus Wilson being two of the most famous. But Bernard was much too junior to have got to know them at that time. However, there were plenty of opportunities to socialize; even though there was a war on, the codebreakers of Bletchley Park had a great deal of fun after the hard work of the day was done. There were often musical evenings. "Brin Newton-John, an RAF officer in Hut 3 whose daughter Olivia became a well-known pop star, would sing German Lieder."[18] There were also dances, parties, fancy dress balls, RAF dance bands demonstrating the Jitterbug, Scottish country dancing and a drama group, which gave Sgt. Bernard, as he then was, the opportunity to act in several amateur theatrical productions.* In fact, he was still wondering about which direction to take after the war. Thinking ahead, he decided to write to the French star Yvonne Arnaud, who was not only an actress but also a very good concert pianist, well-known for her interpretation of Saint-Saëns' *Wedding Cake Caprice.* Madame Arnaud duly penned a charmingly Gallic reply in her generous and flowing hand. Her advice was that "the choice of a career must be decided by the individual alone[...]. One thing is certain — you do not achieve anything without a gift and *hard work*, both in Music and Theater."

So the indecision remained — but Britten had specifically asked his young friend to keep in touch. Indeed, just before joining the Air Force, Bernard had plucked up courage to make a spontaneous call on Britten at his London home in St. John's Wood High Street. It was there that the composer and Peter Pears were sharing an apartment with Erwin Stein, the senior editor at Boosey and Hawkes, and Stein's wife Sophie. It was Pears who opened the door and Bernard was given the warmest of welcomes. After tea and cakes, he realized to his delight that he had become "a chum":

> I had a very good friendship with Ben but it was never a sexual friendship at all. People tend to think, because of his reputation, that if one was an attractive young man and gay, one would have had an affair; but he was clearly not in that way attracted to me nor I to him, though I was absolutely attracted to him in every other way. He obviously thought I was a promising composer and liked my company and we became extremely close.[19]

During his time at Bletchley, Bernard occasionally travelled back to London in his Air Force uniform to turn pages for Britten's recitals at the Wigmore Hall, and during the next few years their friendship was to grow even closer. In the meantime, the war kept them apart; but he did meet Walter Hussey again, taking advantage of the London-to-Birmingham train line, which made travelling between Bletchley and Northampton so easy:

> He was the best kind of advertisement for Christianity in that he never thrust it down one's throat at all. If one went to stay with him for the weekend, as I did frequently, he would never say, "Now, I hope you'll be at communion in the morning!" He would say, "Sleep as long as you like — and Mrs. Cotton will do your breakfast."

Bernard remained at Bletchley Park for about two years, after which he received his commission and was moved to "a creepy old rectory in Old Wolverton." It was there that the future composer of the world's most famous Dracula theme first encountered Bram Stoker's equally famous novel. Bernard gave a graphic account of the experience in the notes he wrote for the Silva Screen CD reissue of the EMI *Dracula with Christopher Lee* LP he worked on with Philip Martell:

> The church and churchyard, with rectory close by, stood in a lonely cluster at the end of a long drive. The weather was freezing; the countryside lay under a pall of frozen snow. My bedroom was as cold as a grave, and from my window I looked out on gravestones and yew-trees, their white shrouds glimmering in the

**There was even an opportunity to hear Glenn Miller himself at a nearby U.S. Air Force base.*

> frosty moonlight. I was reading Bram Stoker's *Dracula*. Under my own heavy shroud of blankets I was still cold. I got up and fetched a tin hot-water bottle filled with almost boiling water. (Rubber bottles were scarce in those war-time days.) Clutching it to my chest, I climbed back into bed, and then, with the pervading warmth, drowsiness overcame me, and I fell into a marmoreal sleep, the book over my nose.
>
> In the morning I found my pyjama jacket pulled open, and the cold bottle pressed to my skin; beneath the bottle there had risen a large and angry blister. I have the scar to this day—the kiss of the vampire.[20]

But a far worse possible fate was looming on the horizon with the threat of being sent to India. He had no desire to return, during war time, to the country of his birth and he did all he could to persuade a friend to pull some strings to get him a job in the Air Ministry. That friend was Michael Meyer, later to become well-known as a leading translator of the plays of Ibsen and Strindberg. Situated conveniently behind the department store of Peter Jones was the Air Ministry building, where Bernard's congenial duties consisted of compiling a history of the Air Force. By that time he had encountered the even more congenial company of the poet, critic and future screenwriter, Paul Dehn, with whom he would live for the next thirty years. They were brought together while Bernard was stationed at Bletchley Park.

One of the people who had shared Bernard's wartime accommodation in London during his training was Anthony Easter-Bruce. Easter-Bruce had a friend called Geoffrey Wethered who had been a brilliant young barrister before the war but was now a colonel in Military Intelligence. He would often join Easter-Bruce and Bernard for dinner and trips to the theater; but Wethered was also friendly with Paul Dehn, and Bernard remembers first meeting his future partner for drinks at the family home of Easter-Bruce in Grosvenor Square. A short while later they met again, this time at Wethered's flat in Markham Square, just off Kings Road in Chelsea. Bernard had been invited to dinner there before embarking on his return train trip to Bletchley Park, on what was always referred to as the "midnight fornicator":

> I'd been feeling rather under the weather that afternoon. During dinner I began to feel extremely shivery and shaky and said to Jeffrey, "I really don't feel well." He took my temperature and I had 102 degrees, so he said, "You can't possibly go back to Bletchley tonight. You must stay here. I'll ring up in the morning." Of course he was a colonel so that was no problem.

Wethered telephoned Dehn, who was on leave that week, and asked him to come round to keep the invalid company.

> He was round in a flash: he'd fallen for me already!—and I found him so sympathetic. He came and sat by my bedside and I showed him my diary. Up to this stage we hadn't talked about gayness, so I left him the diary and he came back the next day and said some very constructive things about my poems. I was feeling much better and I was out of bed in my dressing gown, so we went into the drawing room where they had a good old 78 RPM record player. It sounds awfully corny but the record I wanted to listen to was Rachmaninoff's Second Piano Concerto; but this was better than a "Brief Encounter." It turned out to be a 30-year

encounter. We were sitting side by side on a small sofa and I was longing for him to put his arm around me. It was up to him to make the first move. He was very shy in that way—charmingly shy, modest—not thrusting in any way. I remember I got up to change the record and while I got up he put his arm out along the back of the sofa, so that if I sat down I would sit against his arm. I changed the record and came back to sit down and as I started to sit down I saw him starting to withdraw his arm, so I sat down very very quickly and trapped it! That started our 30-year love affair. It was wonderfully romantic!

Dehn, who was born on November 5, 1912, was later to become well-known for what his obituary in *The Times* described as "fastidiously expert film-scripts." These included *Goldfinger* (United Artists/Eon, dir. Guy Hamilton, 1964), *The Spy Who Came In from the Cold* (Salem/Paramount, dir. Martin Ritt, 1966) and *Murder on the Orient Express* (EMI, dir. Sidney Lumet, 1974). He also collaborated with Sir Lennox Berkeley and Sir William Walton on operatic projects.[21] A graduate of Shrewsbury School and Brasenose College, Oxford he became a critic and columnist before taking up an eighteen-year career as film critic for the *Sunday Chronicle, News Chronicle* and *Daily Herald*, as well as contributing to *Punch* and chairing the radio arts program called *The Critics.* He also became well-known and much admired in the 1940s and '50s as a lyric poet, much anthologized. He was just the man Bernard was looking for: "So," he explained, "I was suddenly whisked into this wonderful artistic, theater milieu. It was very thrilling for me."

However, Bernard was still in uniform and still uncertain about the direction his future career would take, so his role in this artistic world was very much that of a hanger-on. Desperate to be a civilian again, he wrote to Britten, hoping he would be able to arrange what was called a "class B" release for him. He received a friendly, though disappointing reply:

From Benjamin Britten

c/o Mrs Frank Bridge
Friston Field
Nr Eastbourne
Sussex
June 23rd 1946

My dear Jim

Thank you for your nice long letter. Sorry not to have answered it before but I have been and still am wildly busy with all-day rehearsals of Lucretia at Glyndebourne—this letter can only be a brief scrawl as a result.

I am afraid I can't at the moment raise your hopes about helping you to get a class B release—for the simple reason that my own movements are far too elaborate and unsettled to enable me to take on such a chap as you to help me with my work—useful as that would indubitably be for me.

For a year now, I shall not be in any one place for more than three weeks and I couldn't alas afford to take you around everywhere with me—at least not until the petrol restrictions are removed and I can tour in a grand (tho slightly uncertain) manner in the Rolls!! As soon as the position clarifies itself, we will discuss it—and if you are still in the R.A.F. we will see what we can do about pulling strings.

So, you've met Jimmy Smith.[22] What exalted circles you move in!
I hope your new flat with Paul materialises soon. How is he? We had a terrific time in Switzerland — enjoyed ourselves hugely. And am signed up to go back in the New Year which gives me courage to go on!! My — the food — and the clothes.

With love to you. Ben.

Meanwhile, Walter Hussey had managed to attract the attention of no less a star than the great Wagnerian soprano Kirsten Flagstad. Determined to acquire her services for St. Matthew's Church in Northampton, he had written to her completely out of the blue. To the amazement of all his friends (and perhaps, even Hussey himself), she accepted and agreed to give two recitals for him. Bernard was invited to meet her for the second of these, in which his brother, Bill, had also been involved, his duty having been to escort Miss Flagstad on her journey from Euston station in London up to Northampton. Hussey was determined to persuade Flagstad to perform the aria "*Ozean, du Ungeheuer*" ("Ocean, thou mighty monster") from Weber's opera *Oberon.* As Hussey recalled in his own memoirs,[23] she was, at first, equally determined to refuse. In the end, though, she was persuaded and was accompanied on the night of the performance by Harold Craxton, whose name is still familiar to pianists who play from his Associated Board edition of Beethoven piano sonatas. Flagstad was resplendent in "a special dress of deep plain cobalt blue"[24] which she had apparently ironed herself on Hussey's kitchen table while chatting to his housekeeper, Mrs. Cotton. After the concert, Hussey invited her and a group of friends, including Bernard, to dinner at the vicarage where Flagstad was persuaded to sing again. "It was all so charming," Bernard recalled, "and Flagstad was so fat and cozy."

The excitement of the Flagstad recital helped Bernard make up his mind about his future career. It would have to be musical, but how to set about it? First, he was lucky enough to indulge in a holiday trip to Italy. On his return, he turned for advice to Britten:

30 Markham Sq.
London SW3
Sept 4th 1947

My dear Ben

[...] I am last free of the bonds of the RAF! I was released a week or two ago[...]. Just before I was released Paul (who is very well) and I had three weeks holiday in Italy[...]; so I now feel entirely recovered from serving my country! I absolutely fell in love with Italy — its people and towns and food and everything.

I feel that I must now set about some really hard musical studying, as I am so far behind. [...] I really should love to see you again — *properly* not for a minute at the end of a concert — and I am very keen to talk to you about my future.

Could you possibly bear to have me for a night at Aldeburgh? [...]

Please be good, Ben, and answer this letter — I know what a bad letter writer you are! [...]

Britten replied:

Crag House
(undated)

Dear Jim

I am afraid it isn't any use you coming here at the moment—as it is my first bit of holiday for ages and I am up to my eyes in work (!) and besides, there are people staying here whom I have to see about business and things in the few spare moments I have.

But I'm in town in October for some weeks and we can possibly meet then. In the meantime—think of what exactly you want to do, and then I'll help you decide how to do it.

Actually, I should think that a government grant to either the R.C.M. [Royal College of Music] or R.A.M [Royal Academy of Music] (if there is one) would be the best thing. You could take piano and composition and get a good general musical education as well.

But will talk that over later.

Love, Ben

Eventually, Bernard settled on the Royal College. A musical future now lay before him but, as he was soon to find out, it wasn't going to be smooth sailing.

3

Amanuensis in Aldeburgh

"Your honor, I am at your disposal."

Claggart in Benjamin Britten's *Billy Budd*[1]

Soon after arriving at the Royal College, Bernard wrote to Britten again and received the following reply:

American Hotel
Amsterdam
February 23rd 1948

My Dear Jim

Thank you for your interesting letter. Sorry not to have replied before, but we are madly rushed out here, and have no time to sit down and think! Your experiences at the R.C.M. seem to be identical with mine. But all the same, dreary as most of it is, there are things to be got out of it. The thing which helped me was always to *insist* on dropping classes which were boring and a waste of time (it took some insisting, but worked in the end); and also to *insist* on changing professors who were useless, or who neglected one. Anson may be a nuisance and unsympathetic, but I should imagine could be worn down by determined tactics! The other thing which I should insist on is *more* time for composition. I don't know how this can be worked, but Howells might help. I hope he's sympathetic and will help you to get things performed.

I agree that the scruffy girls are a nightmare and a pest — it's maddening to have them around and in the way, but it's possible to ignore them. I shall be back in a week or two and could advise, if you want it, some more. So glad you got on well with David and Mama. He's a sweet child, but needs very gentle handling. I don't remember seeing the poems— they sound most romantic. Ah ... what an age it is!

I hope you and Paul are well. Peter picked up a bad cold in between Milan and Zürich and had to cancel 2 concerts. But he's well now and as usual Holland is at his feet. We spent a miraculous night in Venice. Were you ever there?

Love, please excuse short note

Ben

Britten's letter makes reference to several interesting characters. "David" was David Spencer, a child actor who had been vigorously promoted in the business by his mother. Born in Ceylon, he had started his career in radio after arriving in England in 1940. He came to Britten's attention after a broadcast of Honegger's *Joan of Arc* and was invited up to Glyndebourne to rehearse the role of Harry in Britten's 1947 opera *Albert Herring*. Spencer's only professional connection with Bernard was that he appeared in *The Stranglers of Bombay* (Columbia/Hammer, dir. Terence Fisher, 1960) in the role of Gopali. Privately, however, they became quite intimate for a while.

Pre–Hammer Glamour: James Bernard in a studio portrait from the 1940s (courtesy Bernard Estate).

Herbert Howells was Bernard's professor at the Royal College. Their relationship was very affable, but not, perhaps, quite as academically rigorous as it could have been, as Bernard himself explained:

> When I was studying with him, other composers were shining much more brightly than he was. He was a very gentle, unassuming man. Short with nice curly gray hair and a sweet, charming face. He was almost too kind and gentle. He was encouraging but I think I could have done with a teacher who was more challenging, who would say, "Go away and write an action scene for a film" or something. He didn't stretch me enough. He didn't teach me anything about orchestration. We just had charming weekly interludes. I was left to myself.

Howells did, however, take the trouble to write with advice on how to spend the holidays:

> 3 Beverley Close
> Barnes S.W. 13
> 10th August 1948
>
> My Dear Bernard
>
> Your letter chased me in and out of Wales, and now can be answered.
>
> Your queries remind me that Stanford's advice to us for the Long Vacation was two-fold:
>
> a) Don't do a stroke of work.
> b) Do whatever your mood and fancy dictate.
>
> His emphasis was always on a). Mine was always on b).

Throughout his time at the Royal College, more emphasis was placed on Bernard becoming a pianist than a composer:

> I was very keen on my piano playing. My piano professor was Kendall Taylor, but even those were very amiable lessons. I would learn something and he would listen to one playing and give a few suggestions but it was all very easy going. I did have a certain facility but not that tremendous facility you need as a concert pianist. I think I spent more time on practicing the piano which was barking up the wrong tree, really. I think if Herbert had realized he might have said, "Look, Jim, don't spend so much time on the piano. Concentrate more on composing—and why don't you orchestrate something?"

The other name Britten mentioned in his letter was Hugo Anson, the registrar of the R.C.M. When Bernard left the college, he was summoned to Anson's office and asked what he was going to do with his life. It was assumed that he would teach music, but Bernard had other ideas. "Oh no," he replied, defiantly, "I am going to be a composer and earn my living by composing." Anson laughed and told him not be so ridiculous. Only people like Vaughan Williams and Britten were able to do that! And on that parting shot, Bernard was sent out into a world that wasn't in the least interested in listening to his music. "One wasn't greatly encouraged," he remembered. He later caught sight of the director of the college, George Dyson, in the dinosaur hall of the Natural History Museum—exactly the right place, he thought, "for such a dry old stick."

Aside from these frustrations, though, student life was very pleasant. Bernard was living with Dehn in a comfortable furnished flat in Markham Square and he enjoyed his piano practice, even though it didn't lead anywhere. It was only after he left the College in 1949, with no letters after his name and no idea how he was to become a composer, that depression set in. He did, however, have a testimonial from Kendall Taylor, who, like Anson, rather assumed that Bernard's destiny was to be that of a piano teacher:

> 10 Lynton Road
> New Malden
> Surrey
> Malden 1731
> October 27. 49.
>
> Mr. James Bernard is a pianist of real musical intelligence and feeling and he has a high standard of technical attainment.
>
> During the time that he has studied with me at the Royal College of Music I have always found him keenly interested in every aspect of his work:—and he has got through a great deal of work.
>
> He has a thorough and sound knowledge of the technical principles of piano playing and I am confident that he will be able to hold the interest and to ensure the progress of his pupils.
>
> Kendall Taylor
> Professor: Royal College of Music, S.W. 7

If it hadn't been for the financial support of Paul Dehn, the life of a piano teacher might well have been unavoidable. This dependency, however, resulted in terrible moods, which usually boiled down to feeling guilty that he wasn't pulling his weight. Dehn would reply, "For goodness sake, Jimmy, this is my pleasure. We are chums

Markham Square, London S.W.3, Bernard and Dehn's first London home address.

and I want to do it. I have faith in you and I know that the time will come and I want to help you to that point. Then we'll share expenses."

One of the things they shared early on in their life together was an Academy Award for the original story of the film *Seven Days to Noon* (London Films, dir. John Boulting, 1950). This film later became associated with the Campaign for Nuclear Disarmament, reflecting, as it did, the then very real threat of an atomic war; but it wasn't conceived with any overt political program in mind. The idea for the story came to them when they had been on their way to spend the weekend with Bernard's mother. Faithful to the memory of her husband, Mrs. Bernard had never married again and now lived alone at Taylor's Farmhouse on the village green at Cranleigh in Surrey. Though the subject of gayness was never discussed, she was very fond of Dehn and was totally sympathetic, so their visits to Cranleigh were always very enjoyable:

> It was one of those wonderful summer evenings, without a cloud in the sky. We were going over Waterloo Bridge in the taxi and everything looked almost like a Canaletto. One of us said to the other, "Wouldn't it be terrible if all this was blown up by an atom bomb?" That was the beginning of it. Then we worked out the original story about a professor of atomic science, played by Barry Jones, who worked at an atomic establishment. Suddenly, he has a tremendous religious conversion and feels that the creation of atom bombs is wicked and must be stopped at all costs. He goes rather over the top and steals a small atomic device. I'm told that in those days there couldn't have been anything small enough to take out of a top secret establishment in a briefcase, though nowadays there would be; but

> that was a piece of poetic license. He then gives an ultimatum to the government and says, "Unless you agree to stop making all atom bombs and destroy your existing stockpile and announce this to the world, in seven days from tomorrow I shall blow up the whole of central London." So, the film is the story of how they find him.

Bernard and Dehn did not write the screenplay for the film; Dehn simply wrote a film treatment in three pages, which the Boultings bought outright for £3000. Their joint Oscar was in the category of Best Original Screen Story. In those days the Oscar ceremony was nowhere near as well publicized as it has subsequently become and the first thing either of them heard about it was from the *Evening Standard* newspaper. Bernard recalled:

> A few days later, a very affable man who represented the Academy of Motion Picture Arts and Sciences telephoned us and said, "I have your Oscars for you. Would you like me to bring them round?" We said, "Yes, would you come round tomorrow evening and have a drink with us?" So this affable man arrived in a taxi with a cardboard box and put it down on the carpet of our little sitting room in Chelsea and said, "They're in there." We gave him a gin and tonic, and then there was a lot of rustling of tissue paper and out came the Oscars. He said, "Well, congratulations!," and we all had another gin and tonic. Then he went away, and that was our Oscar ceremony!

The music for the film was composed by another old Wellingtonian, John Addison. There had, of course, been no suggestion that Bernard should write the score for his own story, and his dream of success as a composer still seemed a long way off. However, encouraged by their unexpected earnings from the film, they decided to move house. Their flat in Markham Square was barely large enough to accommodate them, let alone two Oscars as well, so this seemed the right time to look for somewhere with a little more room. They eventually went to view a property in Bramerton Street, just a few hundred yards further down Kings Road in Chelsea. After knocking at the door, they were received by a manservant who showed them into the living room and then vanished upstairs. While sitting on the sofa, Bernard happened to catch sight of a framed photograph and was amazed to find that it was of his cousin, Percy Ronald Gardner Bernard. He was the fifth and last Earl of Bandon, famous for having been the first to pilot a Vickers Victoria non-stop from Khartoum to Cairo. When the manservant returned, Bernard asked if the photo was indeed of "Paddy" Bandon, as he was known.

"Yes, indeed," the manservant replied, adding that he was the earl's bat-man. "Unfortunately," he continued, "Lady Bandon sends her apologies. She is unable to see you as she is taking a bath."

Bernard explained that he was a relative, and asked if he might be allowed to say hello through the bathroom door, which is exactly what he did. Lady Bandon, who was Lord Bandon's second wife, didn't know her unexpected caller, was as amazed at the coincidence as her visitors, but she still didn't emerge from her bath. Nor did she need to. "It seemed a very good omen," Bernard explained, so they took the house.

But new accommodation didn't solve Bernard's problem of how to get started as a composer. Fortunately, Britten came to the rescue later that same year with a modest proposal. Would Bernard care to visit him at Aldeburgh to help him with the preparation of his opera *Billy Budd*? It took no time at all for Bernard to accept the offer and begin one of the happiest years of his working life:

At home with Oscar: James Bernard with his Academy Award, 2000.

> All I did on *Billy Budd* was to copy out the vocal score. He was composing it as a vocal score. Ben was very understanding, because he knew I was living with Paul, so I'd go down and spend a week or ten days there and then he'd have a batch of stuff ready which I'd copied out and he'd say, "Go up to London and deliver it to Erwin Stein at Boosey and Hawkes, spend a few days with Paul and then come back." Once or twice he asked Paul down for the weekend. So it was all very charming and friendly. It was a most fascinating year. I became part of the household.[2] We'd start work in the morning. He liked to keep very disciplined hours, and be at the desk by nine. He'd sit at his big desk in the window never going near a piano, the music all coming from his head, and I'd sit at a big round table in the middle of the room and copy as he gave me the sheets.
>
> Then lunch would be announced. They had a wonderful housekeeper called Miss Hudson. He liked to have nursery food: boiled cod and parsley sauce followed by rice pudding and stewed plums. He might go to the piano on our way down to lunch just to try one chord. Peter Pears was the one who liked the good life and it was Peter who chose the wine. I remember once a time when they were delighted with a wine they had found in Germany called *Kröbernacktarsch*—which means "naked bottom." There was a picture of a cellarer who had caught a naughty little boy in the cellars stealing wine and had pulled down his trousers and was beating his bottom. They felt this was a great big giggle. It appealed to Ben, I think.
>
> So we'd have lunch. Ben would sometimes be rather silent and say, "Forgive me for being silent because the music's sort of brooding in me." Sometimes E.M. Forster was there and Eric Crozier. I suppose I was awfully brash. I used to tell them rude jokes which Peter enjoyed. Ben used to say he didn't understand the point and I had to explain them to him. And he'd shout, "Oh, Jim. How disgusting!" I used to get pleasure out of shocking them.
>
> After lunch he'd like to have a walk. Sometimes I'd go with him, and that was always fun because we could talk about anything. We used to walk across the marshes all round Aldeburgh on those high pathways above the marshes and by the river and through the streets of Aldeburgh and he'd tell me local legends like the story of the Black Shuck, because I'd already told him I was very into ghost stories. He told me that in that part of the world there's a legend about some-

thing called a Black Shuck, which is a huge black dog, which sometimes appears on the beach and follows people, but it's a ghost dog. I was fascinated by that. Other days he would say, "Jim, I'm going for a walk on my own because I need to compose while I'm walking." Other days he'd want to play squash. There was a prep school in Aldeburgh which had good squash courts and we were allowed to use those in the holidays. He was maddeningly good at everything. He used to beat me hollow at squash. I wasn't bad at tennis. I'd been taught well by my father but I'd never played squash before. Then he'd come back and have another session of work. After that he would knock off. He liked a dry martini cocktail made with gin. I'm sure it was shaken and not stirred. Ben loved about two of those before dinner. We'd then relax. Dinner would be slightly grander than lunch. After dinner, Ben and Peter would like to do songs or Ben would go to the piano and start playing. I remember one day Ben said, "Oh, I could never have been a concert pianist. Look at this Liszt Sonata. I could never have coped with that!" Then he played the first six pages absolutely brilliantly just reading it. He had this maddening facility! Sometimes I used to play two pianos with Ben but I used to get way behind because he was so good. I also remember playing arrangements of Balinese music by Colin McPhee. It was quite a little while before *The Prince of the Pagodas*.[3]

People felt they were taken up by Ben and then dropped, but I never felt that with him. Inevitably I became less close to him, but during that year I became very close to him, so close that I can remember occasions when — I suppose water was short, or something — when he'd have a bath and say, "Jim come and take the bath water after me." We'd be chatting like two boys in the bathroom. It was very close, very intimate, without any sexual connotation, although we used to talk about it. I used to try and get him to confess to me because I used to tell him about my naughtiness, but he always rather clammed up.

A steady flow of letters between the two men continued through 1952. On January 10, Britten wrote:

Jan 10th 1952

My Dear Jim

Apologies for silence — I've not forgotten you, nor the very nice, instructive, attractive book on rigging you and Paul sent us[4] – but life's been and still is, hectic.

I hope to be able to suggest a day or so for you to come down here before long — but at the moment the house is full and there'd be no peace for reflection. But we'll do it soon.

Thank you for being so gallant on my behalf with Neville Cardus[5] — really the critics have out-done themselves this time — but luckily it makes no difference to the public. Let this be a lesson to you, my dear — never take *any* notice of what the critics say, either good or bad. They are always 10 moves behind — and even when they by accident understand what a chap is trying to do, they wish he'd gone in the direction that they'd have liked. Remember also, it's easier to be funny (and therefore memorable) if you're being beastly — and it's dangerous to be enthusiastic, usually! Still, I mustn't start on King Charles' head....

Don't worry about the future — it isn't quite as dim as I'm sure you're feeling now.

Love and happy New Year to you both,
Ben

Bernard was indeed feeling despondent. He may have spent a year with Britten but he was still an unknown quantity in the musical world. At that stage, the dream of composing film music was obscured by his attempts to break into the concert world. He had already shown Britten the piano sonata he had composed in 1950 and Britten had been very encouraging. (Bernard subsequently consigned this piece to oblivion.) Thanks to his connection with the composer, he got to know the Australian pianist Noel Mewton-Wood, who had given the first performance of the revised version of Britten's Piano Concerto in 1946. He promised to perform Bernard's sonata at one of the concerts organized by the Society for the Promotion of New Music, the president of which was Sir Ralph Vaughan Williams. *Every*one who was *any*one in the musical world was either a vice-president or on the council of this august institution. Britten was a vice-president, along with Sir Arnold Bax, Sir Arthur Bliss, John Ireland and Sir William Walton. On the council was the prolific film composer William Alwyn along with two composers who were later to work for Hammer: Humphrey Searle, who scored *The Abominable Snowman* (Warner/Hammer/Clarion, dir. Val Guest, 1957), and Benjamin Frankel, who created the first serial score for a British film in his music for *The Curse of the Werewolf* (UniversalInternational/Hotspur/Hammer, dir. Terence Fisher, 1960). Intriguingly, when it received its premiere, Bernard's Sonata shared the program with a String Trio by Leonard Salzedo, who was later to score *The Revenge of Frankenstein* (Columbia/Hammer, dir. Terence Fisher, 1958). The concert took place on July 1, 1952, in the Great Drawing Room of the Arts Council of Great Britain in St. James' Square, followed by what Bernard called "one of those awful discussions afterwards" in which the merits and faults of the pieces just heard would be regurgitated.

Mewton-Wood was also gay, and when his partner, Bill Fredricks, died in 1953, he killed himself with prussic acid. Bernard got to know the pianist well who, like Britten, was very encouraging. "Noel was a brilliant pianist and a man of great intellect," Bernard recalled, " but he could throw off the intellectual thing and have giggles and fun!" However, the performance of the piano sonata very nearly didn't happen as the Society rejected it at first; Mewton-Wood insisted that the performance should go ahead. Lennox Berkeley, another member of the Society, also put in a good word for the composer (whom he knew socially), and after receiving a favorable reaction to a subsequent piece for two violins, Bernard set about the composition of an orchestral suite based on the subject of wild flowers. In the end, it came to nothing, and Bernard felt he ought to look for a more reliable source of income. He wrote to Britten and asked for a testimonial to use when the right opportunity arose. Britten was happy to oblige:

5th June 1952

My Dear Jimmy,

So sorry not to have answered you before — but I've been away and madly busy. I don't know *exactly* what you want as a testimonial, and so I've made the enclosed as un-precise as possible (hope it doesn't look too much like a good cook's character, though I'm sure that's appropriate too) — but if it's no good, bring it back and will have another shot.

[Enclosed Testimonial]

5th June 1952

To whom it may concern

I have a great admiration for the character and musical gifts of James Bernard. He has frequently worked for me in the past—work which needed skill, energy and determination, all of which he possessed in the highest degree. I can most warmly recommend him.

Benjamin Britten

In October, Bernard wrote again to Britten, hoping that he might be invited back to work as his assistant; but Britten realized that there would be no future for his protégé if he allowed him to follow that path. The letter he wrote marked a turning point for Bernard:

4 Crabbe St
Aldeburgh
Oct 18 '52

My Dear Jim

Please forgive the silence.

Actually, as you probably know ... there really wasn't anything else you could do to help me: this ruddy score—so I didn't bother you.

So now, my dear, your Budd labors have come to an end and this is only a scribble to thank you, more than I can say, for helping so invaluably. I have really been impressed with your ability and intelligence—and also your great concentration in sticking at a very dull job. I hope that the results of it aren't all negative and that you've learned a little about how to (and even how not to) write an opera. It has also been a very great pleasure in having you about the house. I can think of very, very few people I would have borne here during that wretched time of composition—you were the soul of tackt [sic] and good company to [sic]. (But it must have been hell for you!)

But now after all this interruption I hope you can get back 100% to your own work. When I am in London (as I shall be most of November) I hope to see you and see the 2 violin piece, and also the completed Piano Sonata. Keep in touch with me, anyhow, and let me know what's happening, if you want to come to some later Budd rehearsals I'm sure it'll be all right.

Aldeburgh goes on the same. The glorious Indian summer is over—when I played quite a bit of good tennis and enjoyed it hugely. I play a bit of squash—bad but joy with Nipper,[6] and good and exhausting with David Dow[7] (of Glemham—the Pan—do you remember?). Fidelity[8] and I went over the Borstall at Stimple Street—very touching and impressive. See Billy[9] a lot—and also his brother John who turns out to be sweet, but in a different way from Billy—complicated and neurotic. And so it all goes on ... nice, not exciting.

Love to you and also to Paul and thanks again for all you've done.

Ben

With this letter, Bernard realized that now he was on his own, as far as being a composer was concerned. He remained in friendly contact with Britten but knew, that, career-wise, he could not rely on that friendship.

Fortunately, there was soon to be an offer of work in London from the BBC. Through Dehn, Bernard had become acquainted with Lionel Gamlin, a very popular BBC Radio broadcaster who agreed to give Bernard four Wednesday lunchtime radio appearances over the Christmas holiday period as part of his magazine program *Hullo There!* The spots were called "They Shall Have Music," in which Bernard presented what the *Radio Times* described as "four musical rides off the beaten track." There were programs devoted to Water Music, Musical Birds (for which Dehn's interest in ornithology surely came in handy), Witches and Wizards.

Then, on April 18, 1953, Britten wrote with a "rather wild and urgent proposal": would Bernard care to go up to Aldeburgh for a Summer School, being organized by Imogen Holst and Peter Pears, at which some young performers might be persuaded to perform a few of Bernard's own works? "You could stay with us, and we'd eat communally," he suggested, adding, "You could also meet properly and talk to Imogen about the future (she's very keen to help you)."

Bernard declined the invitation in favor of a rather more exciting offer from the BBC. Again, it was thanks to Paul Dehn's wide circle of acquaintances that Bernard was introduced to the poet Patric Dickinson, who had been a regular contributor to the BBC third program in its early days. In 1953, he wrote a play called *The Death of Hector,* which was based on exactly that episode in Homer's *Iliad.* Dehn, a radio playwright himself, had always fought shy of suggesting Bernard as a composer for fear of being accused of nepotism. A play by Dickinson, however, was quite another matter and the poet courageously asked producer Val Gielgud, who was the head of BBC Radio drama as well as being the elder brother of Sir John (with whom Bernard also became friends later on), for permission to commission a score from this unknown newcomer. Permission was granted and it was agreed that the music would be scored for a small ensemble to perform alongside the actors. It was conducted in the studio by John Hollingsworth, who later became the musical supervisor of Hammer Films.

Born in London in 1916, Hollingsworth had been a student at the Guildhall School of Music and had joined the RAF in 1940. There he became associate conductor of the newly formed Royal Air Force Symphony Orchestra and went on tour with it both at home and abroad. During a concert engagement in Hollywood he had the opportunity to observe how film music was played and recorded. Then he came back to England with the RAF orchestra to conduct a score by Leighton Lucas[10] for the documentary film *Target for Tonight* (Crown Film Unit, dir. Harry Watt, 1941). A string of wartime documentary films followed before he flew out to Potsdam at the end of the war to give three concerts, again with the RAF orchestra, at the Three Powers Conference in the presence of Churchill, Stalin and Roosevelt. He was finally introduced to feature films by Muir Mathieson, head of music at Alexander Korda's London Films, where he worked on *Brief Encounter* (Eagle-Lion/Cineguild, dir. David Lean, 1945). But he also had ambitions outside the world of film music, becoming first assistant to Malcolm Sargent at the BBC Proms, and occasionally conducting Prom concerts himself. He was also, along with Robert Irving, one of the two chief conductors of the Royal Ballet at the Royal Opera House in London. Bernard recalled:

> He was a bit of a loner. John was quite a strange, very dear character. All the time I knew him he lived alone in a flat in a big, modernish, sort of '30s block in Ham-

mersmith called Latimer Court. His flat was very characterless with box-like rooms. It wasn't very roomy or cozy. He was a tall, good-looking man with a very pleasant face — tall and imposing. I think he was a bit insecure but when he realized he could trust Paul and me, we were allowed to become chums.

Hollingsworth was therefore the obvious choice of conductor for Bernard's first radio score, which they both agreed would require only a harp, flute and some percussion. It was first broadcast on September 1, 1953, with Leon Quartermaine in the leading role of Priam. The following week, after a repeat performance, Val Gielgud wrote to the composer, commenting on the "immense contribution your music made to whatever success the program may have had." From then on, Bernard began to get quite a lot of commissions for radio plays and worked for a number of radio producers, though he felt that he was still very much feeling his way:

> I remember being terrified because I'd only just stopped at the RCM and I was never taught orchestration at the RCM. I'm self-taught. I just hoped I was doing the right thing. I used to rush to Imogen Holst. After leaving work for Benjamin Britten, I said to him I would love to have someone with whom I could study or go to or take things to and he said, "Imo — Imogen Holst — is the person!" She was very helpful. I expect I went to her and said, "Is this okay? I haven't written something that's unplayable?"
>
> My model was Forsyth's[11] book on orchestration. I also used to use the book by Widor.[12] He wrote a wonderful book on orchestration. It has great lists of all the viable string chords in three parts, four parts — all that kind of thing. Terribly useful. I still have at hand Forsyth, Widor and Walter Piston[13] when I'm orchestrating now. Piston is excellent. I used to have a very good little one by Gordon Jacob.[14] In my early film scores, often the percussion was played by James Blades, the great percussionist. I used to consult him on matters of percussion and he was always very, very helpful. I could ring him up and ask him questions; but it was really just using those books and my imagination.
>
> In the early sessions, I was always amazed that they actually played what I'd written and didn't complain — and I'm still very conscious of that! When I'm writing for trombones, I always look at the diagram in Forsythe or Piston of trombone positions and make sure that I'm not changing at tremendous speed from the first position to the seventh position.

A string of commissions followed. On December 4, 1953, the BBC Radio Theater presented Julian Orde's *Dentist on the Dyke*, for which the pianist George Malcolm performed Bernard's music. A couple of weeks later, on December 18, Bernard provided the music for Jon Farrell's adaptation of Saint-Exupéry's *The Little Prince*, and he rounded off the year with music for a Revue at the Lyric Theater Hammersmith, which opened on December 23. Paul Dehn also contributed lyrics for three songs for this light-hearted entertainment starring Dora Bryan, Hermione Baddeley and Ian Carmichael: "Too Much Nostalgia," "Tailor Made" and "Riviera Goodbye." For the finale, Dehn collaborated with Bernard in a number entitled "Wrap Up Well," bringing the show, and the year, to a rousing conclusion. "Mr. James Bernard must have an honorable mention for his tuneful finale," wrote *The Stage* on New Year's Eve.

The following year, on March 21, Max Adrian starred in a BBC Radio production of Lope de Vega's *The Dog in the Manger ("El Perro del hortelano")*, and this time Bernard's score was conducted by Leighton Lucas; but his most important radio score was for *The Duchess of Malfi*, which followed on May 16. This had an all-star cast including Richard Burton as Antonio, Paul Scofield as Ferdinand and Peggy Ashcroft as the Duchess. In a March 31 letter to Britten, Bernard confessed that he found the work rather a strain "as the whole play is so unrelievedly grim." Conducted by Hollingsworth, the music was performed by the Boyd Neel Orchestra, the same that had visited Wellington College when Bernard had been a pupil there.[15] Alternating his original music with Renaissance string fantasias and virginal music by John Coporario, Orlando Gibbons, John Bull and Giles Farnaby, Bernard's score was eventually to lead to his first film for Hammer.

Seeking reassurance about his compositional technique, Bernard traveled up to Aldeburgh to discuss the radio project with Imogen Holst. He offered to pay for her time and trouble, but "Imo" wouldn't hear of it:

> 45 Crag Path
> Aldeburgh
> April 28th — 54
>
> Dear Jim
>
> Very many thanks for your letter, but you mustn't *dream* of paying for that Aldeburgh lesson when you had such an expensive journey! I shall keep the check against the next lesson, which must be an outsize one to balance that 29/10 train ticket!
>
> So glad the producer is pleased (so he *ought* to be!). And I'm glad it's the Boyd Neel. I'll be in London on May 4th and will ring you up.
>
> Ben's new opera[16] is *magnificent*: — the economy of material and the way it creates its own form is absolutely astounding. He seems much better in himself, though the arm still hurts a great deal.[17]
>
> Good luck to everything.
>
> Yours ever
> Imogen

Before that, however, in June, he had time to arrange Britten's *Variations on a Theme of Frank Bridge* for small orchestra to accompany the Ballet Rambert's new work by the South African choreographer John Cranko, called *Variations on a Theme.*[18] Bernard also managed to compose two more radio scores and complete a song cycle, which had been commissioned from him and Paul Dehn (who wrote the words) by Peter Pears. Pears had actually written to Bernard on the same day that the Rambert ballet project had closed, offering "10 guineas with no strings attached, except 1st performance right and perhaps a dedication of some sort. I might do them in November at the Wigmore."

The result was the song cycle *Shepherd's Warning*, setting poems by Dehn, which was indeed given its premiere at London's Wigmore Hall (November 12, 1954). "Thank you both so very much for the songs," Pears wrote on receiving them, enclosing with his letter a blank check. "I look forward enormously to working at them," he continued. "Like a fool I can't remember exactly what I offered you for them!! So sorry—can you fill it in as required and please thank Paul for the lovely words and yourself for the sweet songs." The performance brought together not only Peter Pears and James Bernard but also introduced the composer to the guitarist Julian Bream, who performed the accompaniment and was later to collaborate with Bernard on several of his film scores for the Rank Organization. Britten was in the audience "to cheer" as were most, though not all, of the critics. *The Times* (November 14, 1954) reported:

> The words of Paul Dehn had a neo-Caroline quality apt for musical setting. The shepherd wonders which is happier, his sheep or himself, and looks to bird, river, and vine for answer. When he asks the question again at the end the harmonies have changed to a more bitter tang. Meantime the images of the poems have provided the composer with suggestive figuration for the guitar. The work is original in conception, imaginative in execution, and telling in performance.

The *News Chronicle* (November 12, 1954) was equally enthusiastic:

> These new songs are settings of poems of acute observation of nature, and of the man curiously watching these things, by Paul Dehn.
>
> The composer, aware of the poet's vision, has provided a discreet commentary of the kind that illuminates the poems with a soft radiance and a clear light.

Desmond Shawe-Taylor in *The New Statesman* (November 27, 1954) was a little more ambivalent:

> Mr. Bernard writes clearly and sympathetically for both voice and guitar; his cycle began arrestingly, and contained one fresh and charming lyric ("The Bright Bird"). But it was noticeable that, if (as in "The Riverbed") the poet nodded, the composer too lost the air of spontaneity, which is his greatest asset.

The Daily Telegraph (November 13, 1954), however, was very uncomplimentary:

> Beyond an evident feeling for Paul Dehn's lyrics this had little to offer. The simplicity of the language was reminiscent of the Britten of the "Serenade." But the vast resource that must be behind such simplicity was lacking.

While it is true that the cycle does share a certain stylistic similarity to the sound world of Britten, Britten himself wrote a letter of encouragement, commiserating over the "beastly" review.

The "Prologue" is introduced by the guitar with a desolate descending **triplet** figure, which, with its **tied note**, is certainly an echo of the equally desolate first sea interlude from Britten's opera *Peter Grimes*:

James Bernard, *Shepherd's Warning*, "Prologue," bars 1–4

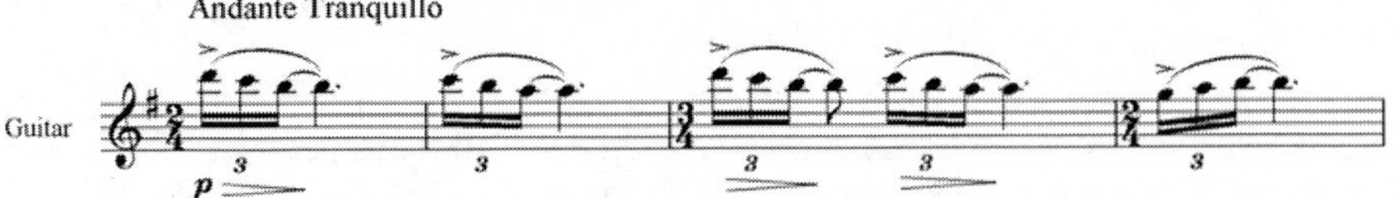

Example 1

The accompaniment of "The Bright Bird" is based on **fourths, intervals** that were to become very important in Bernard's future film scores:

James Bernard, *Shepherd's Warning*, "The Bright Bird," bars 1–2

Example 2

One can easily imagine Pears' mellow and flexible tenor voice performing the mellifluous **semiquavers** on the word "run" in the next song "The Riverbed":

James Bernard, *Shepherd's Warning*, "The Riverbed," bars 13–18

Example 3

And it is in this same song that Bernard introduces the clashing **major seconds**, which, along with even more discordant **minor seconds**, were to become so much a part of his Hammer trademark. The words these sounds accompany are also highly appropriate, given Bernard's later association with vampire films:

James Bernard, *Shepherd's Warning*, "The Riverbed," bars 45–49

"The Riverbed" is also notable for its consistent **polymetrical** scheme, which initially rather unnerved both Pears and Julian Bream during rehearsals.

Example 4

Bernard's friend, the pianist Ronald Kinloch-Anderson, wrote with his own congratulations, pinpointing the very characteristics that were later to make Bernard such a successful film composer:

> It seemed to me to be quite excellent in its simplicity and beauty and I was very struck by Jimmy's ability to suggest atmosphere and emotion by a very few notes, one or two—as they say—pregnant ideas which at once made a clear picture for the listener.

Of the other radio scores that followed hard on the heels of the song cycle, the first, which was broadcast on December 5, 1954, was for *The Mystery of Robert the Devil,* in which Anthony Jacobs and Valentine Dyall starred in a version of the supernatural legend that had inspired Giacomo Meyerbeer and Eugène Scribe's seminal 1831 French Grand Opera, *Robert le diable.* The play was produced by Frederick Bradnum, who took the trouble to write to Bernard after the broadcast, congratulating him on "a remarkably fine piece of music. I cannot tell you how much it helped."

Actor David Peel appeared as Cléante in the BBC's radio production of Molière's *The Miser* on May 23, 1955, and Hollingsworth was once again the conductor of Bernard's music for it. Hammer would later hire Peel to play Baron Meister in *The Brides of Dracula* (Universal-International/Hammer, dir. Terence Fisher, 1960); but back in 1955 the company was planning a modest feature film version of BBC Television's immensely popular science fiction series, *The Quatermass Experiment.* The stage was now set for Bernard's big break into the exciting world of the film business.

4

Trilogy of Terror

"They're ready to go into production and beat the world."

Broadhead (Tom Chatto) in *Quatermass 2* (Hammer, 1957)

Hammer had always been aware of the money to be made from big screen adaptations of popular BBC radio serials like *Life with the Lyons, The Man in Black* and *Dick Barton Special Agent.* Indeed, the company later resorted to the same tactic in the 1970s, converting small-screen sitcoms into big-screen comedies, with varying degrees of success. Back in the mid–1950s, with television in the ascendant, it was natural that Hammer should have looked to one of the most popular and startling television dramas yet to have appeared. Hammer selected their leading actor, Peter Cushing, from the BBC as well. He had come to Hammer's attention in the BBC's famous 1954 adaptation of George Orwell's *1984* (directed by Rudolph Cartier) and rapidly became known as "The Horror man of the BBC."[1]

From a musical point of view, Bernard also came to Hammer with a reputation for horror. As we shall see in the next chapter, he was to use part of his *The Duchess of Malfi* score for the first of Hammer's color films, *The Curse of Frankenstein* (Warner/Hammer, dir. Terence Fisher, 1957). Before that, however, a more contemporary brand of science fiction was to exercise his musical imagination.

Nigel Kneele's six-part television serial *The Quatermass Experiment* became Hammer's big-screen *The Quatermass Xperiment* (Exclusive/Hammer, dir. Val Guest, 1955). Prof. Bernard Quatermass (played by American character star Brian Donlevy) sends astronaut Victor Carroon (Richard Wordsworth) into space; on Carroon's return to Earth, it is discovered that an alien force has taken over his body and the astronaut gradually turns into a giant man-eating cactus. Quatermass and the police (represented by actor Jack Warner) follow its trail to Westminster Abbey where, with a splendid touch of irony, given the TV origins of this film, they interrupt a BBC outside-broadcast and promptly set about electrocuting the monster, courtesy of Battersea power station

The producer was Anthony Hinds, who had originally lined up the composer John Hotchkis[2] to write the music; but, as is so often the case with newcomers,

Bernard recalled that his first big break was the result of a last-minute change of plan:

> All I know is that Tony Hinds rang up John Hollingsworth and said, "John, we're in a bit of a fix because John Hotchkis is ill. He can't do the score for *The Quatermass Experiment* and we need someone pretty soon. Have you anybody tucked up your capacious sleeve?" And John said, "Well, yes, I think I might have someone who might suit." He rushed down to Bray Studios with the tape of my score for *The Duchess of Malfi*. Tony Hinds liked it and that's how it fell into my lap—and away I went.
>
> But at first, I simply didn't know how to start! In those days Hammer had a very good viewing theater in Soho in what is still called Hammer House. I used to go there and see the film reel by reel and take copious notes. I didn't dare say anything. I just did what I was told. They then sent me those terrible time sheets, and if there was something I didn't remember, the assistant director would fill me in with details.

A typical example of a time sheet (or cue sheet) is reproduced in Figure 1 (see page 47).

In the left hand column, the numbers of each cue are listed. Next to this, the action is broken down into a descriptive analysis, and the columns to the right of the page indicate the timings and film footage. Armed with this information, the composer is then left to get on with the job alone. Bernard always composed at the piano:

> I let the fingers do the talking! I also walk around a lot. What I like to do is have the whole thing fully sketched in short score on three or four staves before I do the orchestration. That's where the creative works comes in—inventing the material and having each section exactly timed. Then I can go to the orchestration and work at it fairly fast.

An example of Bernard's short score sketches for his later film *The Gorgon* (Columbia/Hammer, dir. Terence Fisher, 1964), can be seen in Figure 2 (see page 48).

Here, the main musical material (melody and supporting harmony) is condensed onto three staves, with an indication of the instrumentation penciled in above it.

Once the cue sheets are digested and the principal themes conceived, the next thing to work out is the tempo of each music section. Bernard had a specific way of working this out:

> I take a certain section and I first decide what tempo that sequence is going to need. If the beat underneath is going to be fast or slow, sixty beats a minute is very convenient. It works well for a lot of sections of music. But on the other hand, if you want the music to be fast, and double it to 120, it's not fast enough. It will work depending how many notes you get into each crotchet but often 120 is simply not enough. There are certain other tempi which I find it quite easy to work at. For instance, 144: Every twelve beats takes five seconds. I have the most elaborate way of doing it. Once I've got my initial material I often write out on a sheet of purely blank paper a series of just slashes with a pencil and through knowing the tempo I know how many of those slashes have got to happen to arrive at the next timing, and then I work out the tune against these slashes. If I'm in four beats in the bar and I'm going to arrive at the point of synchronization too soon, I may make a bar of five beats or six beats to give that extra time. Eighty beats to the minute

AMENDED SHEET 23-7-70

MUSIC CUES: 'SCARS OF DRACULA'

Reel/Sect.	Cue	Ftg.	Timing
4M2 cont. (AMENDED)			
119	C.U. TANIA, she licks her lips.	468½	5.12⅓
120	C.U. PAUL's bare neck.	472½	5.15
121	C.U. TANIA.	475½	5.17
122	She reveals her fangs	477	5.18
123	She goes down for a bite.	479	5.19⅓
124	Curtains thrown open by DRACULA	479½	5.19⅔
125	M.S. TANIA falls back away from PAUL as she hears DRACULA	480½	5.20⅓
126	M.S. DRACULA holding curtains open, looking very blood thirsty.	482½	5.21⅓
127	PAUL & TANIA in bed. TANIA horrified.	483½	5.22⅓
128	PAUL leaps to her rescue.	484	5.22⅔
129	C.S. DRACULA. PAUL tries to strangle DRACULA.	485½	5.23⅔
130	PAUL over DRACULA's shoulder. DRACULA thrusts PAUL away.	488½	5.25⅔
131	C.U. wash-stand. PAUL crashes into it.	490½	5.27
132	PAUL falls on the floor unconcious.	493	5.28⅔
133	M.S. DRACULA by TANIA in bed.	493½	5.29
134	DRACULA pulls back bedclothes and draws out knife.	495	5.30
135	C.S. DRACULA lunges forward with knife.	496½	5.31
136	C.U. TANIA receiving the blow.	498	5.32
137	TANIA's P.O.V. DRACULA lunging again.	499½	5.33
138	M.S. DRACULA stabbing TANIA.	500½	5.33⅔
139	TANIA's P.O.V. DRACULA withdraws enough to lunge again.	502½	5.35
140	C.U. TANIA being stabbed.	504½	5.36⅓
141	TANIA in pain after stab, rolling in pain.	505½	5.37
142	TANIA's P.O.V. DRACULA. He lunges again.	508	5.38⅔
143	TANIA over DRACULA's shoulder. DRACULA stabs yet again. The blood spurts on to her face.	509	5.39⅓
144	DRACULA stabs again.	512½	5.41⅔
145	M.S. DRACULA stands up, leaving knife in wound.	513	5.42
146	TANIA's P.O.V. he slowly bends down and drinks the blood.	517	5.44⅔

Figure 1

THE GORGON
1.M.1.
James Bernard
VLN
VLA
VC.
+ WW
BRASS + DB AND TIMPS.
VOICE ETC.
ORCH
VOICE AND NOVACHORD + HISS EFFECT
VIBRA.
BRASS OFF
+ BRASS (simile)

Figure 2

> is another very convenient one: four beats in three seconds. Seventy-two is another good one. So is ninety. Any number which will divide by twelve is good like 132 beats to the minute. The secret is timing. Some composers may be infinitely better composers than I am but they don't have the knack for synchronization.
>
> Philip Martell[3] used to tell me that Elizabeth Lutyens was hopeless at her maths. Once you've decided on the tempo of a particular section, you must know where your synch points are going to come. She was frightfully bad at doing this. Phil used to tell me, "Can you imagine! Liz —" as he called her "— Liz suddenly had a bar of 17/8 after a bar of 11/8!" She hadn't worked out how to make it happen quite simply. Normally you can make the synchronization happen in bars of three or four beats — or six. Sometimes in 5/4 or 7/4, though I prefer a slow tempo for that.
>
> I learned the importance of simplicity on the very first film I did: I did a fast section in 5/4 or 5/8 and I thought, "This will be very exciting!" When John Hollingsworth saw it, he did it, but he said, "You know, Jimmy, you'll find, when you get more experienced, that you really don't gain anything by that. You could just as well have worked it out and got just as much excitement, using a simpler time signature."

But before unveiling his score for *The Quatermass Experiment* to the Royal Opera House orchestra, who were to perform it, Bernard was keen to show it to Imogen Holst:

> She was very encouraging about it. At that stage she obviously wasn't going to try and make me change things — she was much too wise to do that. She saw I was up and away, but one wants somebody with experience to look things over. I was very keen to make sure that I hadn't written stuff that was impossible. That was a strong reason why I wanted her to look at it. And I wanted to be encouraged. She was a very sweet, warm lady, despite her eccentricities, and I played one or two bits through to her. I remember her saying, "Oh, gosh!" She sounded quite impressed — even a little dumbfounded by it, but dumbfounded in quite a good way! After that, I don't think I went on very long.

It was Hollingsworth's decision to limit Bernard's orchestral palette to strings and percussion, a decision that was dictated by expediency rather than any particular aesthetic considerations ("I don't think he trusted me with anything more than a small string orchestra!" Bernard recalled). However, the finished score perfectly complements the acerbic black-and-white images on screen, providing, as it does, a similarly "monochrome" sound world. Such an anti–Romantic approach to string writing is usually credited to Bernard Herrmann's score for *Psycho* (Shamley, dir. Alfred Hitchcock, 1960). Film music historian Roy M. Prendergast, for one, credits this development entirely to Herrmann's "revolutionary" approach:

> In utilizing a string orchestra Herrmann finally brought to the Hollywood film the idea that strings can have an extremely cold and piercing sound. For so many years Hollywood saw strings primarily as creating warmth and vibrancy. Herrmann reinforced his notion when he said in a 1971 interview, that he used only strings in his score to *Psycho* in order to "complement the black and white photography of the film with a black and white sound."[4]

History reveals, however, that it was actually James Bernard (admittedly in England rather than Hollywood) who first inverted the traditional function of strings in popular film.

The three-note theme that pervades *The Quatermass Experiment* couldn't be simpler, being merely a rising and falling **semitone**, proving that the simplest ideas are often the most effective when it comes to writing film music. Significantly, the theme's underlying harmony of **consecutive fourths** and **fifths** bears a striking resemblance to the *Czárdás Macabre*, a late piano work from 1881–82 by Franz Liszt, one of Bernard's favorite composers. Liszt had earlier piled fifths on top of each other in the opening bars of his *Mephisto Waltz No. 1* (composed in 1860) to suggest Mephistopheles tuning the open strings of his violin. Such harmonic daring broke all the rules in the middle of the nineteenth-century but by the time of *The Quatermass Experiment* **chromatic** consecutive fifths, in certain contexts, had usefully acquired an immediately recognizable signification of menace.

Franz Liszt, *Czárdás Macabre*, bars 1–4

Example 1a

James Bernard, *The Quatermass Experiment* 1M1, bars 6–11

Example 1b

Frequently, the rhythm of the "Quatermass" theme is played by the timpani alone, an orchestration that emphasizes the theme's predominantly metrical nature. In example two, the basses follow the timpani, while violins play **trills**, ***sul ponticello***, creating a characteristic Bernardian *frisson*.

James Bernard, *The Quatermass Experiment* 2M1, bars 6–7

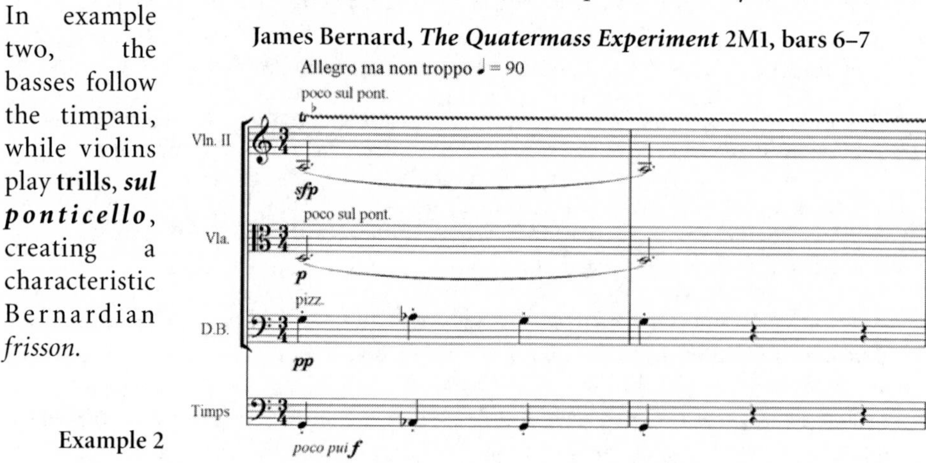

Example 2

Another of Bernard's characteristic fingerprints is the discordant interval of a **major second**, which he often sequences chromatically:

James Bernard, *The Quatermass Experiment* 3M3, bars 1–4

Example 3

Most astonishing of all, for an English film score of the mid–1950s, is Bernard's use of **tone-clusters.** It anticipated the musical style of Krzysztof Penderecki, whose principal works did not begin to appear until the 1960s. Bernard remained impressed by Hammer's adventurous approach to music in permitting such extreme musical idioms:

> I give full marks to Hammer and to Anthony Hinds, because he encouraged this. They never raised their eyebrows at the comparative weirdness of the sounds. I'd never even heard of Penderecki at that stage. In fact, I've always found atonal and twelve-tone music to be unappealing. I have a thing against it, but then I found myself doing the same kind of thing—it was the sort of sound I needed for the film—all from nobody's influence.[5]
>
> Val Guest, the director [of *The Quatermass Experiment*], was a charming man, but he never came to the sessions. He was like Terence Fisher. He left the music entirely to the music department—which is interesting because he did direct some musicals. In my memory, he never came near us when we were doing the music for *Quatermass*.

From a purely cinematic point of view, Bernard's approach again anticipates Herrmann's music for the *Psycho* shower scene. For that film, Herrmann exploited the clash of **false relations** and **minor seconds**. In *The Quatermass Experiment*, Bernard created an even more advanced tone cluster out of superimposed **sevenths** on tremolo strings, which occurs when Carroon reaches out for a vase of flowers while he is lying in a hospital bed in reel four (see example 4).

For the death of the monster at the end of the film, the strings again play piled-up fifths, but Bernard gives them an unusual timbre by asking the string players to execute the notes on the **wrong side of the bridge**. His marking, ***grottesco***, sums up the effect of this sound, which he was to use again and again for the immolation of a host of monsters in subsequent movies.

During the *Quatermass Experiment* recording session, Bernard was introduced to an up-and-coming composer who was later to make a name for himself in Hammer films:

> John [Hollingsworth] took me down to the recording because I didn't have a car in those days. He used to pick me up in his little red MG and drive very fast to the Anvil Studios and he said to me, "Oh, Jimmy, I hope you don't mind, I've asked a bright young composer to come to the recording because I think he's going to be very good in films. He's still at the Royal Academy. He's extremely bright and his name is Richard [Rodney] Bennett. And there was this lanky young man who was extremely nice and I was extremely impressed because without looking at the score he analyzed what I was doing.

James Bernard, *The Quatermass Experiment* 1M1, bar 8

Example 4

Hammer paid Bernard £100 for the score:

> I suppose in those long-ago days £100 was worth a bit more than it is now but it still seemed pretty small. My first three films for Hammer were all £100. It might have gone up to £400—that was the sort of range of fees one got. *She* was positively extravagant because I do know that Michael Carreras was a lavish sort of person. I think I got paid £650 for *She,* when I really hit the big time! I suppose Hammer knew perfectly well that the reason why composers were so keen to write film music was because of royalties. By then, everyone realized that if you write film music for a Hammer film, it was on the cards that you would do well from the point of view of royalties because most of them were so successful and worldwide. I'd have done the score for them for nothing—just for the royalties!
>
> It's not sour grapes, because I've not written concert music, but I truly do feel more pleased to have done those scores which have been heard by millions of people all over the world than to have written something for a Prom which might have had two performances and then vanished.

Far from vanishing, Hammer films soared in popularity after the success of the *Quatermass* films, a success that was in no small measure due to Bernard's innovative music. His scores introduced harmonies and orchestral effects that would have been quite new to the average late–1950s cinema-goer. A column in *The Star* newspaper (August 22, 1955) kept its readers up-to-date with Bernard's latest project:

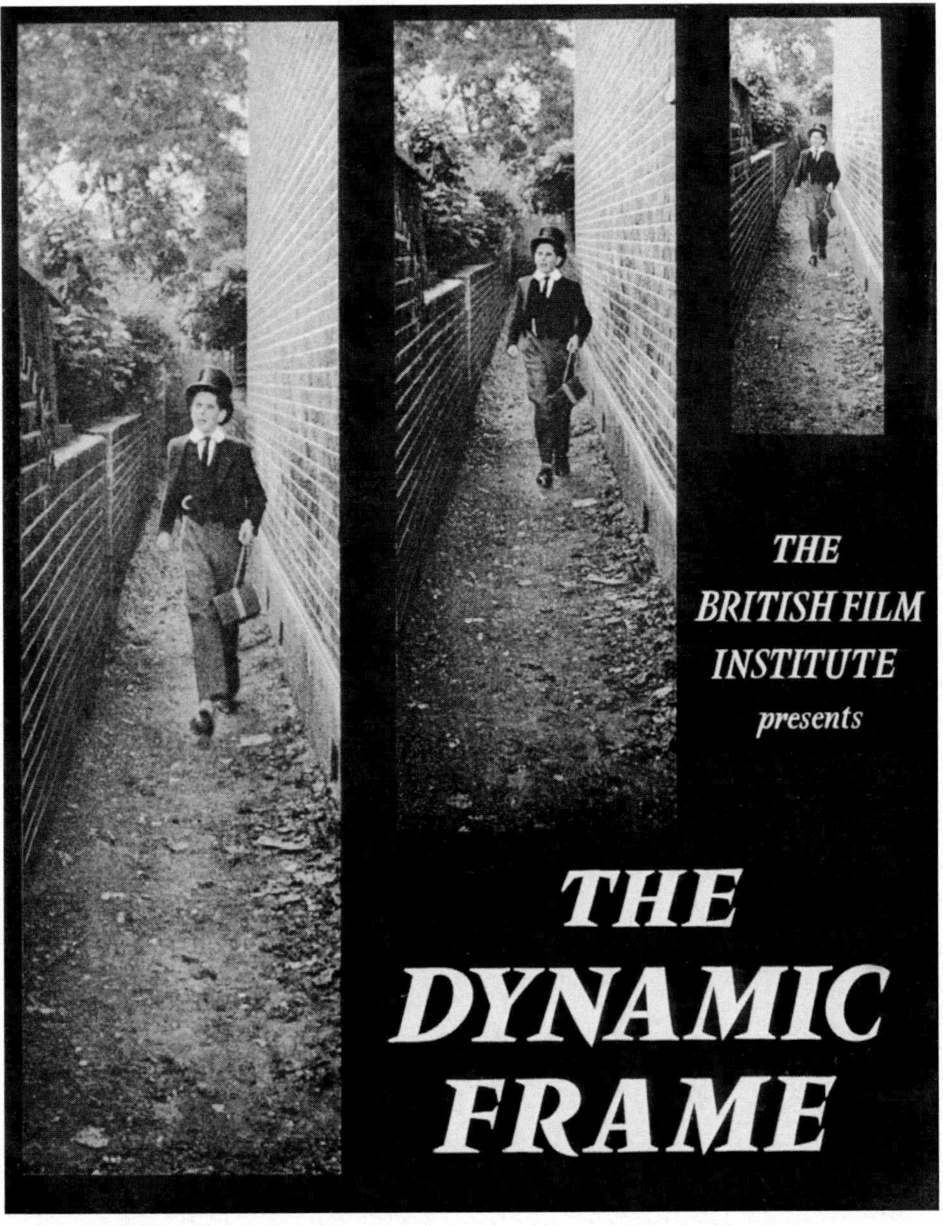

Original publicity brochure for *The Door in the Wall*, featuring the new "Dynamic Frame" technique.

James Bernard told me today that he has just finished one of the oddest musical tasks of the year. Twenty-nine-year-old Mr. Bernard, former personal assistant to Benjamin Britten, has been writing music for a monster — the giant Thing, half-man, half-cactus, of *The Quatermass Experiment*, TV science-fiction serial of a couple of years ago.

Mr. Bernard has done the music for the film version. There are about 20 minutes of it and, says the composer proudly, "not a single tune from beginning to end."

> It was recorded for the picture by the strings of the Royal Opera House orchestra who produced one of the more bizarre effects by drawing their bows across taut strings on the wrong side of the bridge of their violins. "An absolutely terrible noise" is the composer's description of the result.

Paul Dehn also spoke up for the music in a syndicated review for *London Calling* (March 8, 1956):

> A subordinate contribution to my "shivers" was the incidental music by James Bernard [... who] has taken his main theme, which consists of two notes a semitone apart, from the peculiar rhythm of the monster's heartbeat.

This remains the only published explanation of the theme's origin.

The success of *The Quatermass Experiment* was to bind Bernard to Hammer Films for the remainder of the company's existence; and because of his association with horror scores, it is easy to overlook some of his rather different film projects. In 1955, for example, he was approached by the director Glenn H. Alvey, Jr., to write the music for an experimental film called *The Door in the Wall* (AB Pathé/BFI/Lawrie, 1955). Based on the short story of the same title by H.G. Wells, the film was in part financed by the British Film Institute Experimental Production Committee to give the first demonstration of what Alvey called the "Dynamic Frame Technique." This new process, originated by Alvey himself, was explained in the film's accompanying brochure:

> In *The Door in the Wall* it has been the director's intention that the size of the picture shall be limited only by comfortable viewing on the one hand and the maximum screen area on the other; the shape of the picture is continuously related to the subject matter and the position of the maximum screen area on the other; the shape of the picture is continuously related to the subject matter and the position of the picture on the screen is governed by the mood of the action of the scene. Frame changes occur both on cuts and also during a shot, generally in conjunction with the camera movements. Some effects are more successful than others, but the chief purpose of the film has been to answer such questions as the following: When is a frame change imperceptible and when is it distracting? To what extent can static frames of different proportions be intercut?
>
> And most important of all, is the dynamic frame simply a "gimmick" or can it be an important contribution to film technique?[6]

Filmed in only ten days, and lasting just under a half hour, rather more use of the dynamic frame was made than Alvey envisaged would be required in a full-length feature film, but, nonetheless, the result is startlingly original, even when viewed today. The H.G. Wells story was chosen because of the opportunity it offered to blend realism with fantasy: politician Sir Frank Wallace, played by Stephen Murray, is obsessed by a childhood dream in which a green door gives privileged access to a beautiful enchanted garden in which he felt "exquisitely glad—as only in rare moments, and when one is young and joyful one can be glad in this world."[7] Wallace spends the rest of his life searching for the door and one evening, after having told his story to a friend, he finds it again. The following morning, however, his dead body is discovered lying on derelict ground, the implication being that the world of fantasy has no place in the adult world of political intrigue and materialism. The adult must "die" before the child within can be released. One of the most effective uses of the dynamic frame technique occurs when the frame is narrowed to show only the mysterious door. When the door is opened to reveal the magic garden behind, the frame simultaneously widens, creating an oceanic sense of liberation and expansiveness.

Anne Blake, who would later appear as Rosa Valiente in Hammer's *The Curse of the Werewolf,* played Sir Frank's childhood aunt, while Leonard Sachs put in an appearance as his father, with Ian Hunter playing the role of Wallace's adult confident, Henry Redmond. The production was filmed in lush Technicolor by Jo Jago, the well-upholstered Victorian sets of Bertram Tyrer anticipating the kind of environment that Hammer's Bernard Robinson was later to make the visual trademark of so many classic horror films.

Bernard's music was scored for a modest chamber orchestra and, like the documentary about Greece, which he would later work on for Basil Wright, it anticipates some of his famous Hammer themes and atmospheres. When, for example, Sir Frank, as a child, first comes across the mysterious door in the wall, we hear an **arpeggiated** figuration on the piano, which will later develop into the music that accompanies the scene in *Dracula* (Universal-International/Hammer, dir. Terence Fisher, 1958) when Lucy prepares herself for a nocturnal visitation from the Count (see chapter five, example 23). A rather Debussy-like Arcadian atmosphere of harps accompanies shots of children dancing inside the garden, and when the boy himself enters the garden — the adventure of a life-time — we hear music that appropriately looks forward to Bernard's famous theme for *She* (see chapter 9, example 12a).

Just before the film's release in 1956, Alvey wrote to thank his composer, enclosing a check for £100 to cover additional expenses. "Please understand," he continued, "that I am delighted to have some way to show my appreciation for the excellent, really outstanding music which goes a long way to 'make' my picture."

But experimental films weren't the only alternative to Hammer facing Bernard at that time. On June 18, 1956, the Greek soprano Arda Mandikian, who was a member of the English Opera Group in which Britten was a leading light, performed a song by Bernard at the Jubilee Hall as part of the Aldeburgh Festival. Joy Boughton (the daughter of the composer Rutland Boughton) and Malcolm Williamson, who would later score several Hammer films, also appeared playing oboe and piano respectively. In Bernard's song, a setting of George Darley's "Mermaid's Vesper-Hymn," Mandikian was accompanied by the harpist Enid Simon; and Mandikian would collaborate with Bernard the following year, performing some of the music he wrote for *Across the Bridge* (Rank/IPF, dir. Ken Annakin, 1957). Bernard also turned his hand to comedy scoring for the BBC radio production of Marivaux's classic farce *Les Fausses Confidences,* starring Max Adrian and Tony Britten, and for Helena Wood's "comedy of Very High Life," *Hunt Royal,* in which David Peel once again featured in the castlist as the Duke of Angoulème. In 1956, Hollingsworth had conducted the Sinfonia of London in a performance of Bernard's music for a radio adaptation of Sir John Burgoyne's *The Heiress* in which the role of Lady Emily was played by Ursula Howells. Bernard's old professor, Herbert Howells, therefore had two reasons for tuning in: to hear the incidental music of his former pupil and also to listen to his daughter's performance. He wrote to give Bernard his verdict:

3 Beverley Close
Sunday 11 P.M.
16th Dec 56

My Dear Jim

I've just been listening to "The Heiress" which had a double attraction for me — Your music enchanted me. Not for a long time have I been more happy about "incidental" music. It's a difficult art. Your special gift for it is beyond doubt ... and I feel very content on that ground as long as you'll see to it that it doesn't steal too much of your time and energy for the other things you want to write.

I hear of your meeting Ursula at rehearsals — I'm glad of that.

Have a good Christmas: and look in at R.C.M. one day and let me hear of your works. I'd much like to see you.

Yours ever

Herbert

Ursula Howells went on to make a celebrated appearance as a female werewolf in *Dr. Terror's House of Horrors* (Amicus, dir. Freddie Francis, 1965), though on that occasion the score was composed by Elizabeth Lutyens. Later, Ursula Howells would appear in another Amicus film, *Torture Garden* (Columbia/Amicus, dir. Freddie Francis, 1967), sections of which were scored by Bernard.

Nineteen fifty-six was also the year that Britten and Pears embarked on their tour of Japan and the islands of Bali, a trip that was to have an important musical impact on Britten's ballet *The Prince of the Pagodas* and his chamber opera *Curlew River*, based on the Japanese Noh drama *Sumidagawa.* Bernard wasn't forgotten by the couple all those miles away; Britten sent him a postcard from the "Junidanya" Restaurant in Tokyo where they had enjoyed a "delicious" meal and had been reminded of their young friend's culinary expertise. Later, Pears sent a copy of the recipe of his favorite dish: *mizudaki* beef with goma-seed sauce, invented by a certain Mr. Nishigaki.

Bernard may not have been able to enjoy the delights of the Orient in person at that time but he did have an opportunity that same year to enjoy the scenery of the islands of Samoa in his next film commission. This was *Pacific Destiny* (Wolf Rilla, 1956), which was based on the reminiscences of Sir Arthur Grimble, the colonial administrator, writer and broadcaster whose book *A Pattern of the Islands* had started life as a series of very popular talks for BBC Radio. James Lawrie, the producer of this independent feature, was a Scottish banker who had also helped to finance the English Opera Group, and therefore had connections with Britten, which in turn led to Bernard's involvement. Starring Denholm Elliot as Grimble, the film was shot on location at the island of Upolu in Western Samoa and tells the story of Grimble's British colonial civil servant coming to terms with both the climate and the somewhat irascible character of his superior, played by Michael Hordern. Most of the film's music is either authentic native Samoan folk music or takes the form of guitar solos (performed by Julian Bream), which Bernard based on the Samoan folk idiom. There are plenty of opportunities for the inhabitants of Upolu to demonstrate their musical and choreographic skills in the colorful dance sequences, but little of the music was actually by Bernard himself. The most impressive part of the score occurs in the opening section set in London. Very much in the tradition of Max

Steiner, who often referred to national anthems in his film music, Bernard quotes *Rule, Britannia!* to reinforce the location—and simultaneously paid homage to his relative, Thomas Arne, who had originally composed the song.

Cutting to Denholm Elliot's wedding celebrations, Bernard obliges with a snatch of Mendelssohn's wedding march and then, in an effective musical transition from England to Samoa, the last notes of *Rule, Britannia!* are repeated on Bream's guitar, lending a suitably exotic timbre to that imperial tune. Later in the film, *Rule, Britannia!* is sung by a chorus of Samoan children in Grimble's honor, and Bernard was also able to pay homage to his favorite composer Debussy, by having Grimble play that composer's Prelude "*La fille aux cheveux de lin*" ("The girl with the flaxen hair") on the distinctly out-of-tune piano that follows him to his island paradise.

A much more important feature film occupied Bernard later that year. This was *X—The Unknown* (Exclusive/Hammer, dir. Leslie Norman, 1956), his second film for Hammer, which was released on September 21. Following the success of *The Quatermass Experiment, X—The Unknown* capitalized on Cold War fears of atomic war. A seemingly unstoppable blob-like monster emerges from a fissure in the ground that appears without warning during an army training session. One of the soldiers is killed. The unseen monster later kills a small boy and a radiographer by literally melting the flesh from their bones. More victims are claimed while the film's scientific hero (played by Dean Jagger) sets to work to defeat the monster with its own weapon: radiation.

Unexpectedly, one of the most striking moments of Bernard's music for this film is its absence during the opening credits. These are introduced by five bars of music consisting of rising chromatic scales interspersed with string **tremolos**. The scales are placed an **augmented fourth** (or **tritone**) apart from each other in the first and second violins. So, too, are the scales of the violas and cellos, and the final chord on which the music comes to an abrupt end emphasizes this tritone relationship:

James Bernard, *X—The Unknown* 1M1, bar 5

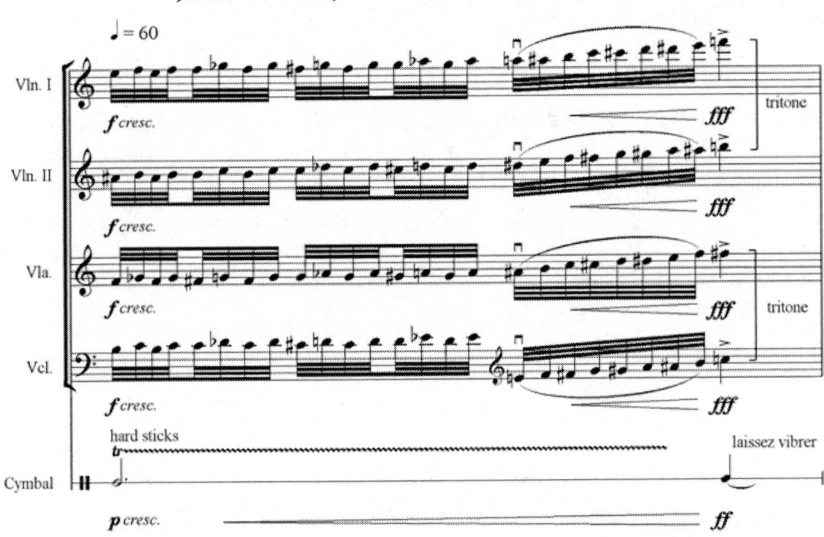

Example 5

Of all the intervals that James Bernard was to exploit in his subsequent scores, the tritone is by far the most important, because of its ready-made connotations of evil, terror, fear, ambivalence and, most importantly, the Devil. Indeed, the mediaeval name for the tritone was *diabolus in musica*—"the devil in music." Its use in ecclesiastical music from the fourth to the sixteenth centuries was actually forbidden as it was regarded as the most discordant of all intervals, and it is the tonal ambivalence of the tritone that gives it its special quality. **Augmented fifths** convey a similar sense of tension as we shall see, but the augmented fourth, because of its wealth of association with evil, is by far the most powerful.

A particularly impressive nineteenth-century example of the diabolic connotations of the tritone can again be found at the opening of a piano piece by Liszt. His "D'après une lecture du Dante: Fantasie, quasi Sonata," from the second book of *Années de Pèlerinage* (composed between 1839–49), begins with an imposing series of tritones played in octaves in a passage that is one of the many nineteenth-century forerunners of Bernard's later *Dracula* theme. Tritones also feature in the famous "mystic" chord created by the Russian composer Alexander Scriabin, where they are mixed with augmented and **perfect fourths**: (example 6).

Alexander Scriabin, "Mystic Chord"

Example 6

This mixture of different kinds of fourth has a strange, disturbing quality that Scriabin often used for music associated with Lucifer, Satan and Prometheus— mythological beings who, in that composer's mind, were symbolic bringers of knowledge and therefore ultimately the benefactors of mankind; but knowledge is an ambivalent force that can be used for good or evil, and there is nothing more ambivalent in music than an augmented fourth.[8]

The departure of the music (leaving merely the desolate sound of curlew calls during the remainder of the main title) anticipates the emotional contribution of the "sound designer" in later twentieth-century films, but it wasn't Bernard's idea:

> I wasn't allowed to have ideas! It would probably have been Tony Hinds and John Hollingsworth between them who would have made that decision. I was very young and very much a novice at the whole thing, so I kept quiet most of the time. If I said anything, I was not taken much notice of—in a kindly way; but Tony used to be very helpful musically, not when I was actually composing, but he clearly had a strong musical feeling and appreciated the music very much. I think this is shown by the fact that he was willing to employ somebody young and unknown like myself. He was willing to take risks and to find interesting talent, and was very acute at feeling where the music was needed. If the dialogue

and acting was strong, both he and John Hollingsworth were keen not to have music. That way the music is much more effective when it does make an appearance.

Ostinati also feature through the score: short, insistently repeated phrases or rhythms that create a great sense of tension. Right at the beginning, Bernard combines a **dotted rhythm** with a falling semitone and harmonizes it with a Scriabin-like chord of augmented and perfect fourths. The effect perfectly compliments the tension of the soldiers on their exercise:

James Bernard, *X—The Unknown* 1M1(a), bar 3

Example 7

An even simpler, though no less effective ostinato occurs in the first reel, when the earth begins to move and the mysterious hole in the ground first appears. Trills accompany a four-note ostinato in the cellos and basses:

James Bernard, *X—The Unknown* 1M2, bars 15–17

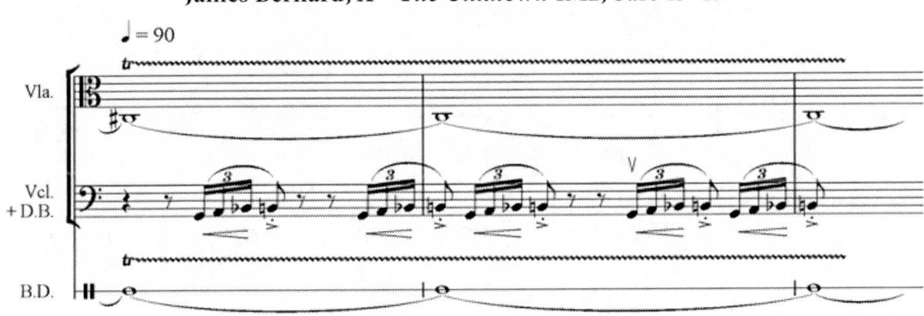

Example 8

For a subsequent shot of the mysterious hole, Bernard exploits the tension of the augmented fifth. Like the augmented fourth, this interval, particularly when used as part of an **augmented triad**, has a long connotative history. Wagner, for example, frequently resorted to the augmented triad for moments of anxiety or tension, such as for Brünnhilde's battle cry in *Die Walküre (The Valkyrie,* first performed in 1870):

Richard Wagner, *Die Walküre,* Act II, scene 1, "Brünnhilde's Battle Cry"

Example 9

For the appearance of the sinister hole in *X— The Unknown*, Bernard creates the enharmonic equivalent of two tonally unrelated augmented fifths:

James Bernard, *X—The Unknown* 2M2, bars 1–2

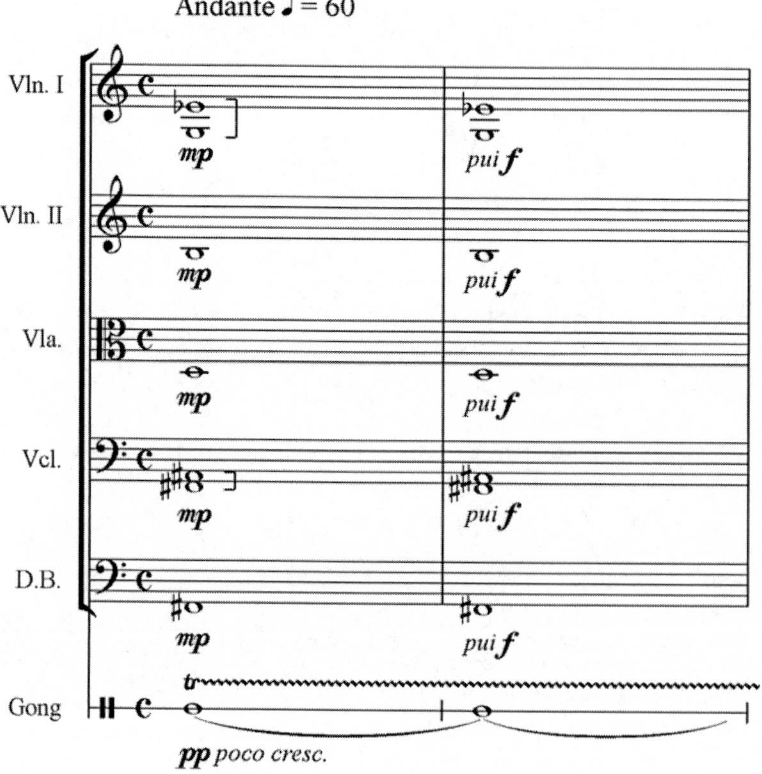

Example 10

Later on, in reel six, Bernard actually calls for the kind of string **glissandi** that Bernard Herrmann went on to use in the famous *Psycho* shower scene. Bernard's glissandi create a very acerbic effect when playing tone clusters created by **divided strings.** No other English film composer was writing effects like this for British films in the mid–1950s:

James Bernard, *X—The Unknown* 6M4, bars 10–11

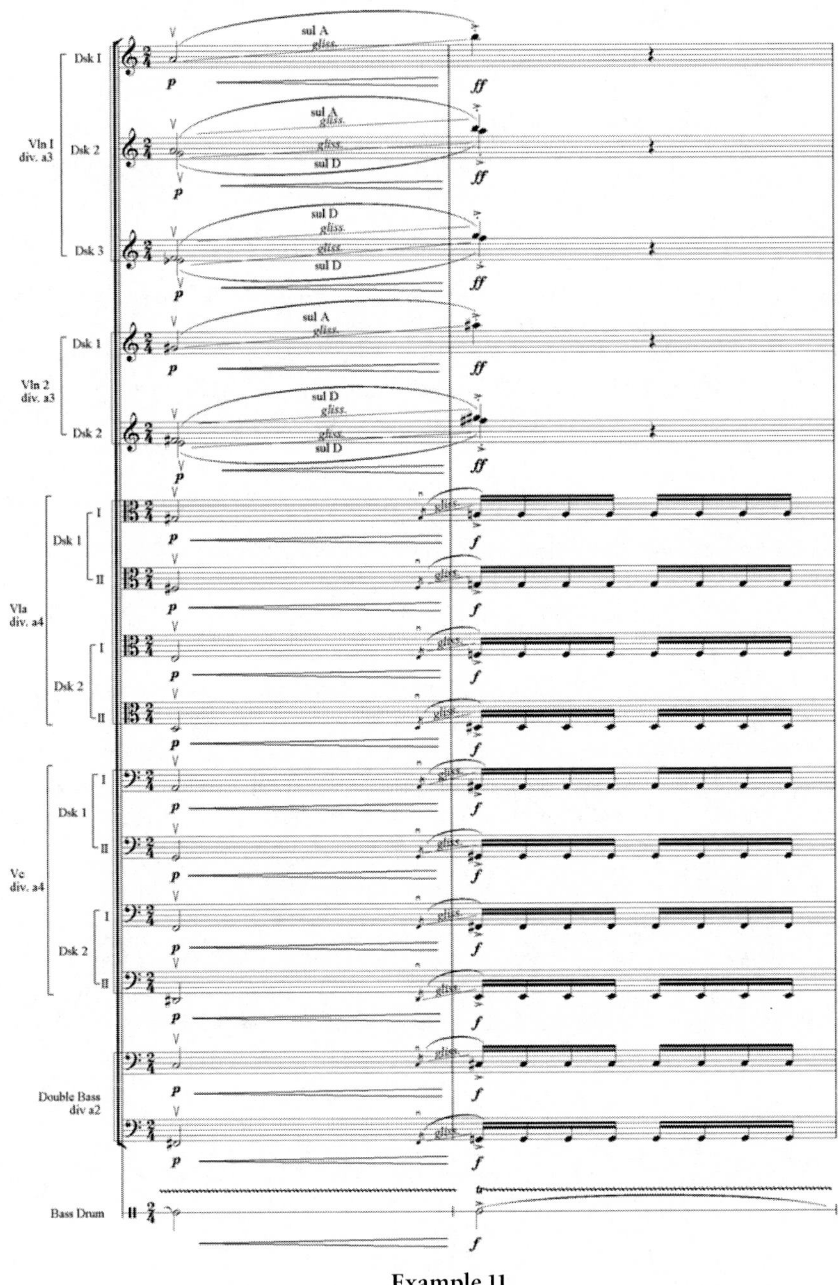

Example 11

In all his scores, Bernard was always alert for any opportunity to insert some lyricism or pathos. The death of the boy in *X— The Unknown* is accompanied by the first of Bernard's many moving string laments. This brief little Requiem is based on a three-note theme that descends by semitones. Again, the material could hardly be simpler but in its emotional use of **appoggiatura**, it creates a highly emotional effect:

James Bernard, *X—The Unknown* 4M2, bars 8–11

Example 12

Even before *X— The Unknown* had been released, Hammer had started work on a sequel to *The Quatermass Experiment,* economically entitled *Quatermass 2.* In this adventure, Prof. Quatermass investigates a sinister government research plant. Modeled on the Professor's own plans for an installation that is capable of supporting life on the Moon, the plant turns out to be the nerve center of an alien invasion. Having arrived on this planet in a shower of meteorite-like pods, the aliens soon take over the bodies of high-ranking government officials and set about the manufacture of a deadly toxin, with a view to world domination.* The final showdown, set against the backdrop of the Shell Haven oil refinery on the Essex coast, takes place to some of the most exciting music James Bernard ever wrote, even though it is sadly obscured by a hail of machine-gun ricochets on the soundtrack.

For this score, the percussion section was expanded to include a piano and the characteristic Bernardian timbre of the vibraphone, as well as timpani, cymbals, side drum, bass drum, tenor drum, gong and xylophone. The prologue plunges us immediately into an action sequence: A young couple are driving along a country road. The young man has been infected by the alien force and narrowly avoids a collision with Prof. Quatermass. A simple four-note motif is presented in **canon**, and **sequenced,** creating a furious, buzzing effect, which also anticipates Herrmann's use of driving ostinati in *Psycho*:

James Bernard, *Quatermass 2* 1M1, bars 10–13

Example 13

**The plot bears some similarities to* Invasion of the Body Snatchers *(Allied Artists, 1956), which was released the previous year.*

Again, this anticipates Herrmann's use of driving ostinati in *Psycho.*

The prologue leads to the main title where, after a rising chromatic scale in the strings, the principal theme of the film is fully stated. Even simpler than that of *The Quatermass Experiment,* this section consists merely of a rhythmically propelled falling semitone, given an added emphasis by the piano which plays along in unison in a similarly high register: (example 14).

The first shot of the falling meteors introduces the vibraphone, quietly accompanying the main theme in minor seconds. Later, during Quatermass' first journey to the plant with his assistant (Brain Forbes), the film's second major theme is introduced: another four-note motif of rising and falling semitones, presented as a **syncopated** canon.

James Bernard, *Quatermass 2* 1M1, bars 149–150

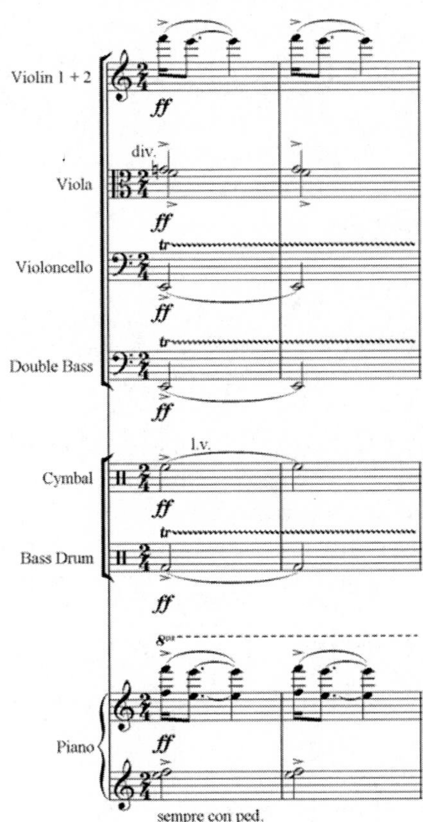

Example 14

James Bernard, *Quatermass 2* 2M1(a), bars 6–8

Example 15

Inevitably, tritones have already appeared but when the alien plant guards march off Quatermass' assistant, Bernard creates an appropriately brutal accompaniment with a chord again constructed from perfect and augmented fourths. (Herrmann was to take a similar approach when motorist Janet Leigh is tailed by a patrol car along the highway in *Psycho):*

James Bernard, *Quatermass 2* 2M1(b), bars 35–39 (reduction)

Example 16

In fact, Stravinsky beat both Herrmann and Bernard to this effect in "The Dances of the Young Girls" from *The Rite of Spring* (first performed in 1913), where the same chord (actually very similar in construction to Bernard's) is repeated insistently for many bars.

A tour of the sinister plant is arranged; Quatermass is present in the company of the concerned MP, Broadhead. This scene contains a good example of how music can be used to increase excitement by means of acceleration. During the first half of the scene, the pace is a sustained ***andante*** (crotchet=60) but when Quatermass escapes through a door inside the dome and runs away from the rest of the inspection party, the music speeds up, and by the time we see him running away from the dome the pace has increased to a lively ***presto*** (crotchet=192). Broadhead, who has also broken away from the main group, now appears at the top of the "food" dome, screaming in agony to the accompaniment of another advanced tone cluster that effectively slides down chromatically, propelled by a syncopated rhythm that cleverly imitates his lurching gait. Such falling chromatic scales will accompany the many deaths and disintegrations of Dracula in Bernard's future scores, his penchant for taking a single chord and sequencing it chromatically, like this, growing out of his boyhood interest in Debussy, who often did much the same thing.

In complete contrast to all that, Bernard then provides us with a classical Irish jig for the dance organized by the inhabitants of Winnerton Flats; but for the alien monster, revealed towards the end of the film as Quatermass infiltrates the "food" dome, string glissandi rise and fall, the harmony emphasizing suitably discordant minor seconds:

James Bernard, *Quatermass 2*, "Monster" music (reduction)

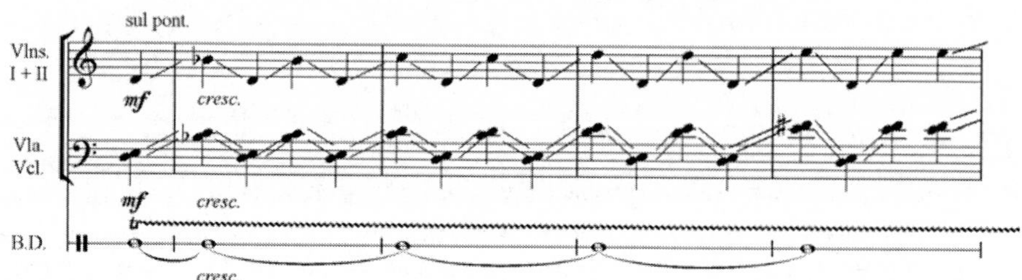

Example 17

That effect is also to recur in scenes featuring other monsters in subsequent films, particularly when a giant spider materializes in *The Devil Rides Out* (Warner/Hammer, dir. Terence Fisher, 1968), and also when Dracula prepares to sink his fangs into the neck of Tania (played by Anoushka Hemple) in *Scars of Dracula*.

For the grand finale, featuring a running gun battle with the guards, Bernard returns to the mood of the film's opening sequence. A stomping ostinato accompanies a variant statement of the main theme, continually rising in pitch and volume:

... while a simple **semiquaver** oscillation (example 19) foreshadows the music that underscores Dr. Ravna's attempt to lure Marianne back to his chateau towards the end of *The Kiss of the Vampire* (see chapter 8, example 20).

James Bernard, *Quatermass 2* 7M1, bars 9–13

Example 18

The stage was now set for Bernard's first musical encounter with full-bloodied Gothic horror and the beginning of his long association with Count Dracula.

James Bernard, *Quatermass 2* 9M1, bars 83–84

Example 19

5

Things Rank and Gross

"I am Dracula; and I bid you welcome, Mr. Harker, to my house."

Count Dracula in Bram Stoker's *Dracula*[1]

At the same time as working for Hammer, Bernard also scored three feature films for Rank. He suspected that good old-fashioned snobbery was the reason for his not having been asked to do more: "I have this theory that Rank dropped me, that they disapproved of Hammer's gory horrors and shockers and thought, 'Oh, we don't want to be connected with that!'"

However, Rank in fact distributed several early Hammer films, perhaps undermining such a conspiracy theory. The first of Bernard's three films for Rank was *Across the Bridge.* Based on a story by Graham Greene, it is basically a chase movie in which a corrupt German financier, Carl Schaffner (Rod Steiger), escapes from his creditors and the law. He attempts to murder a man on a train and subsequently adopts his victim's persona as well as the man's faithful dog, Dolores. Later, he discovers to his horror that his victim was a ruthless assassin called Paul Scarff who is wanted by the Mexican authorities. A much worse revelation follows when Schaffner learns that Scarff has survived. Schaffner then escapes across the border into Mexico where he confronts an equally corrupt chief of police (played by Noel Willman, who would later appear as Dr. Ravna in *The Kiss of the Vampire).* The police chief naturally believes Schaffner to be the assassin with a price on his head. After proving his real identity, Schaffner is then ostracized by the inhabitants of the Mexican village. Now penniless, he is eventually redeemed by the compassion he feels for the faithful hound, Dolores. But she is abducted by a British policeman (played by Bernard Lee) and tied to the bridge as bait. Unable to endure her pitiful howling in the night, Schaffner tries to rescue her but falls into the trap that has been set to catch him. He is pursued by the police as soon as he unties the dog and in a final irony is hit by a police car, falling to his death over the white line that marks the border.

For the first time in his career, Bernard based the main title music of this score on the syllables of the film's title, an approach that was later to become something of a personal trademark. It, and the music for the furiously paced opening sequence in which Schaffner realizes that his fraudulent schemes have been discovered, have a Quatermass-like intensity, exploiting the timpani to highly dramatic effect along with a **triplet** theme that Bernard would later use for vampire bats in several Dracula films (see chapter 13, example 13). Another theme also anticipates the "Undead" motif of *Dracula* (see example 15 below). During a montage of newspaper headlines, which reveal that Schaffner has escaped from the law, the "Undead" and "Vampire Bat" themes are combined over another pounding timpani **ostinato**.

Bernard also successfully imitates the rhythm of the train on which Schaffner drugs his victim, and, as with many a catastrophic fall or disintegration in later Hammer pictures, a string **glissando** accompanies the moment when Schaffner throws Scarff out of the window.

Noel Willman was not the only member of the cast to appear later in Hammer films: Bernard Lee would make a brief appearance in *Frankenstein and the Monster from Hell* (Avco/Hammer, dir. Terence Fisher, 1973), and Marla Landi would play the role of Cecile in *The Hound of the Baskervilles* (United Artists/Hammer, dir. Terence Fisher, 1959).

Both Julian Bream and Arda Mandikian performed on the soundtrack. Bream played Bernard's suitably Mexican theme (with its echoes of Rodrigo's Guitar Concerto and Chopin's D minor Prelude, Op. 28, No. 24) and Mandikian sang the lament that accompanies the funeral of Paul Scarff. The lament is loosely based on an inversion of the main title theme and it creates a similar effect to "*Vissi d'arte,*" the aria in which the eponymous heroine laments her fate in Puccini's opera *Tosca* (first performed in 1900).

The main theme of the film was later published as a song with lyrics by John Michael and Neville Philips, and recorded by Dame Vera Lynn as well as the Charles McDevitt Skiffle Group. To Bernard's delight, it averaged two or three broadcasts a week, as well as appearing on the Continental and American radio.

In his review of the film for the *News Chronicle* (August 2, 1957), Paul Dehn was particularly impressed by Dolores the dog:

> ... a mournfully unthoroughbred spaniel [...] who was discovered in Battersea Dogs' Home and groomed specifically for co-stardom with Mr. Steiger by her trainer, Allen Percival. St. Sebastian never gazed skyward with so monumental a look of martyrdom as Dolores in her final anguish. Landseer never found a sitter whose nose was more moist with devotion.
>
> Had the film been a silent one, she might have queened it over all comers; but though she can snarl and yelp and whimper as evocatively as any exponent of The Method, she cannot speak — and here Mr. Steiger has the measure of her.
>
> His voice has as many stops as a cathedral organ and he selects them impeccably.

Dehn also drew attention to the "haunting motif in a fine score by James Bernard," but Bernard's finest score was yet to come.

If *The Quatermass Experiment* marked the beginning of Hammer's international success, *The Curse of Frankenstein* created the winning formula for the company's series of gothic horror films. *Frankenstein,* however, is technically a science fiction tale, and therefore a quite logical continuation of Hammer's earlier science fiction products. Loosely based on Mary Shelley's novel, Jimmy Sangster's screenplay describes how Baron Frankenstein creates what Hammer preferred to call "The Creature," rather than a monster. The Baron then marries his childhood sweetheart, Elizabeth, and later resurrects the Creature after his horrified assistant, Krempe, has killed it. A complication ensues when Frankenstein confesses that he has no intention of marrying the maid with whom he has been enjoying a casual romance. The maid decides to take her revenge and one night breaks into the Baron's laboratory to find incriminating evidence. There she falls victim to the Creature, who later attacks Elizabeth. Frankenstein hurries to the rescue and shoots the Creature, but Paul has alerted the authorities. There is no evidence of the Creature because it fell into a vat of acid, but Frankenstein, accused of murdering the maidservant, is condemned to death.

In this first color film version of Shelley's classic tale, Peter Cushing starred as the dedicated Baron. Christopher Lee also began his association with Hammer as the misshapen Creature; but it would be quite some time before Bernard would actually meet those two stars in person. As for Terence Fisher, the director whose name was similarly to be associated with gothic horror, Bernard recalled:

> I knew him but I never got to know him well. He was a rather shy, modest, retiring person. I did once ask him, "Terry, don't you ever want to come to any music sessions?" He said, "Oh, no, I don't know anything about music. I'm much happier to leave it to you lot." It's sad. There are so many people I'd have liked to have known more. Maybe if they'd had get-togethers one might have got to know the people more. Maybe they did have end of production parties when they were wrapping up the film on the floor but then, obviously, I was at home composing so I wouldn't have gone, even if they had invited me. I would be at panic stations!

Even so, Bernard did receive a special invitation, apparently from Baron Frankenstein himself, to "meet the Creature" at the Warner Theater, Leicester Square, on the evening of May 2. Printed in flowing copper-plate, the invitation card suggested that "funeral" would be the appropriate dress code. Hammer was to make this sort of gimmick a speciality of the house, but an invitation from the Baron was rather tame in comparison to the more outrageous publicity ploys of later films. Another Hammer gimmick began with the first of Bernard's many syllable-inspired themes for the company:

> People think it's peculiar, but [if] you take a song by Schubert, to take a very high example; obviously he gets the idea for a tune from the opening lines of the poem he's setting. I would have imagined that's what would have happened. And so I find it often works extremely well, like *Taste the Blood of Dracula* or *Frankenstein Must Be Destroyed.* They give you a sort of rhythm and they give you something to start with.[2]

In fact, this method of theme generation was later used in the James Bond films. However, the main title theme of *The Curse of Frankenstein* had actually appeared some years earlier in Bernard's music for the BBC Radio production of *The Duchess of Malfi.* In that context it had been sung by the chorus of madmen in Act IV, scene 2 of the play, by which time the Duchess of Malfi has been put in prison by her tyrannical brother, Ferdinand. The madmen emerge from their cells singing a text to what Webster describes as "a dismal kind of music"; part of Bernard's "dismal music" became the main theme of *The Curse of Frankenstein.* (It is even in the same key.) Appropriately, the film's opening scene is also set in a prison, in which the Baron, like the Duchess before him, is being held captive.

James Bernard, *The Dutchess of Malfi* M22, "Mad Song"

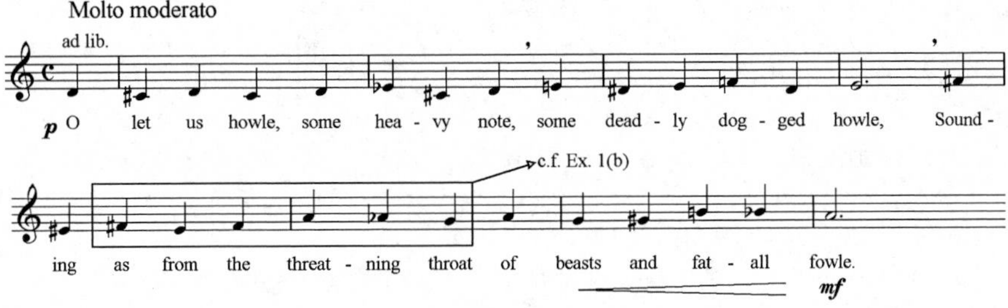

Example 1a

To correspond with the fact that *The Curse of Frankenstein* was Hammer's first color film, the orchestral forces available to the composer were expanded from the modest string and percussion forces of Bernard's earlier science fiction films:

James Bernard, *The Curse of Frankenstein* 1M1, opening title music

Example 1b

> Of course, John Hollingsworth knew from experience that I could write for strings and percussion quite effectively but I did say to him, "On this one, surely now you must upgrade my orchestra and let me have some brass!," and he said, "Oh, yes, of course you shall—and some woodwind too!"

The supporting harmony of the main theme is based on **consecutive minor triads**, while the **perfect** fourths of the higher registers are given a discordant harmonic seasoning of **minor** and **major seconds**:

James Bernard *The Curse of Frankenstein* 1M1, bars 10–11 (strings only)

Example 2

In complete contrast, the next section of music is a pastiche of Schubert that underscores the early scenes in the film up to the dialogue between the young Baron (played by Melvyn Hayes) and his teacher, Paul Krempe (played by Robert Urquhart). Scored for string orchestra alone, the Schubert pastiche was originally intended to continue under the remainder of the dialogue between Hayes and Urquhart but was finally omitted from this later section.[3] Later, a genuine extract from Schubert's incidental music for *Rosamunde* (first performed in 1823) accompanies the wedding reception of Frankenstein and his bride, Elizabeth.[4]

The next important theme accompanies the resuscitation of the dead puppy, which constitutes the Baron's first successful experiment. Appropriately, this "Resurrection" theme bears a close resemblance to one associated with the state of being "Undead" in *Dracula* (see example 15). In both cases, the themes signify a return to life:

James Bernard, *The Curse of Frankenstein* 2M1, bars 1–3

Andante ♩ = 60

Vln. I

Vla.

Vcl.

Example 3

In reel two, another premonition of *Dracula* occurs at the beginning of the scene in which Frankenstein cuts down a corpse from a gibbet. The music opens with a ***fortissimo*** statement of what will eventually become Bernard's famous "Dracula chord" (consisting of a **tritone** combined with a minor second). This chord may well have its origins in the music of Debussy, who used a transposed version of it in the first bar of his piano Prelude, "*Les sons et les parfums tournent dans l'air du soir*" ("Sounds and perfumes revolve in the evening air," composed between 1909–10).

James Bernard, *The Curse of Frankenstein* 2M2, bar 1 (reduction)

Example 4a

Claude Debussy, *Preludes*, Book 1, No. 4, *Les sons et les parfums tournent dans l'air du soir*, bar 1

Example 4b

The "Dracula chord" is followed by a rather jaunty metamorphosis of the "Syllable" theme. This is played on a bass clarinet as Frankenstein climbs the gibbet and cuts down the corpse. Because this jaunty theme will also accompany the intrusion of Frankenstein's maid into his laboratory, it is appropriate to label it "Trespass." The dotted rhythm here lends a certain humor to the scene but the use of sinister bass clarinets ensures that it is macabre humor. The "Trespass" theme continues during the grisly operation scene that follows, this time scored for trombones, violas, cellos and double basses:

James Bernard, *The Curse of Frankenstein* 2M2, bars 54–56

Example 5

With the exception of the "Schubert" theme, all the material introduced so far (the title theme, and the "Trespass" and "Resurrection" themes) is combined in a short sequence that accompanies the Baron's journey to the Municipal Charnel House, where a pair of not-so-sparkling eyes are awaiting collection. The "Resurrection" theme also accompanies the murder of Prof. Brandt, the distinguished scientist whom Frankenstein invites to his home and then pushes to his death from the landing at the top of the stairs. This might not initially seem the most appropriate theme to use at this point but as the Baron will later resurrect Brandt's brain in the skull of the Creature, it actually makes perfect sense.[5]

Later, in the Frankenstein family crypt, we watch the Baron at work removing Brandt's brain, accompanied by another appearance from the bass clarinet. Towards the end of the section, the action cuts to a shot of Elizabeth lying in bed, and the music that covers this cut is a good example of what Wagner had referred to as "the art of transition."[6] Indeed, Wagner was particularly proud of this particular aspect of his art, which took two basic forms. The first anticipates the cinematic "dissolve" in its seamless transition from one scene to another (often quite different in mood and content).[7] The second anticipates the cinematic "cut": an abrupt change from one scene to another.[8] It is the second kind of transition that we encounter in *The Curse of Frankenstein* with the shot of Elizabeth lying in bed. A solo violin takes over from the bass clarinet and viola, playing a modified version of the "Syllable" theme. The change of timbre indicates a change of location as well as signifying the presence of an endangered female, and the last note of the violin is emphasised to indicate Elizabeth's anxiety when Paul knocks on the door. After she calls out, "Who's there?," the "Syllable" theme is further metamorphosed during her conversation with Paul. He is now violently opposed to Frankenstein's project, and pleads with Elizabeth to leave Frankenstein forever. The music here is reminiscent of a melody in Beethoven's Op. 13 *Pathétique* Piano Sonata in C minor (composed between 1798–99):

James Bernard, *The Curse of Frankenstein* 5M1, bars 19–23

Andante ♩ = 60
Più mosso ♩ = 69
Solo Vln. I
Gli altri
Vla.
Vcl.
D.B.
mp
sfp
p
pp

Example 6a

This theme will appear again, in slightly altered form, in *Scars of Dracula* (see chapter 13, example 19) when the pathos of its Beethovenian connotation will be exploited. Here, it is really best regarded as a development of the "Syllable" theme, its sense of urgency created by the slightly increased pace.

We now come to the film's central and most effective moment:

Ludwig van Beethoven, *Sonata Pathétique*, Op. 13, 1st movement, bars 141–142

Allegro molto e con brio

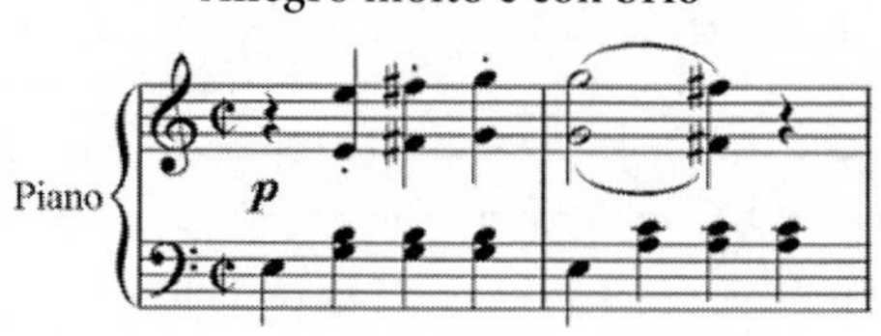

Example 6b

the unveiling of the Creature. Bernard accompanies this with another tone cluster, to which the piano makes an important textural contribution. An impressive example of his skill at constructing a leitmotif from a single chord, this idea is given a sequential treatment, rising chromatically, as well as being rhythmically articulated:

James Bernard, *The Curse of Frankenstein* 6M1, bars 8–13

Example 7

The "Creature chord," in a similar presentation, later accompanies the Creature's attack on a blind man. When Paul shoots the Creature, high-pitched strings and woodwind screech an ironically distorted version of the "Resurrection" motif:

James Bernard, *The Curse of Frankenstein* 6M4, bar 7

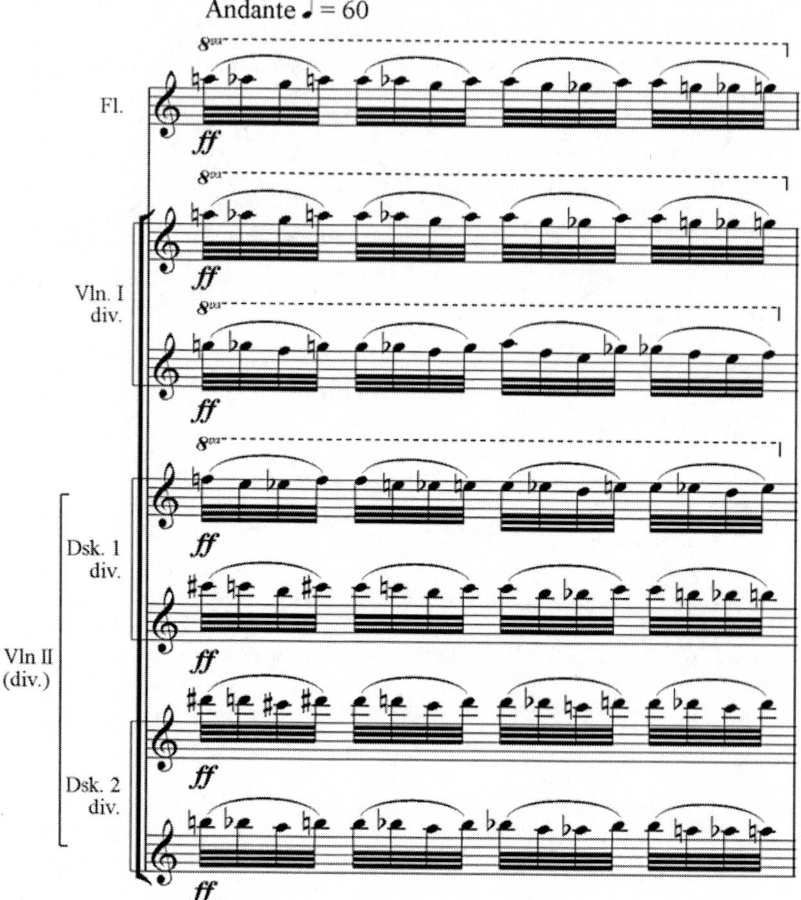

Example 8

The Creature is buried, but that is not the end of the story, of course. Without telling Paul, Frankenstein exhumes the body and vows to give it life again. Not surprisingly, the "Resurrection" motif returns in an unmodified version as he speaks.

Requiring incriminating evidence to put her blackmail plan into action, Frankenstein's maid creeps up to the laboratory, accompanied by the "Trespass" theme, (example 9), with string writing reminiscent of the prologue in *Quatermass 2.*

James Bernard, *The Curse of Frankenstein* 7M1(a), bars 50–52

Example 9

When the maid watches the light go out from under the door of the Baron's study, a bar's silence points up her anxiety far more effectively than any musical effect. A sudden *lack* of music is, after all, not quite the same thing as having no music at all. This silence is "framed" by music and is thereby invested with dramatic meaning.

The final music section accompanies Frankenstein's procession to the guillotine. A muffled bass drum summons memories of the "March to the Scaffold" from Berlioz *Symphonie fantastique* and the end title indeed presents the "Syllable" theme as a somber march. In a final **coda**, Bernard brings back the falling **semitone** of the main theme of *The Quatermass Experiment,* thus providing a musical link between the two films, and the score ends on a dark, brooding D minor chord.

The Curse of Frankenstein was almost universally despised by the critics of the time ("For sadists only" was the famous response of Campbell Dixon in *The Daily Telegraph*, May 4, 1957); Paul Dehn was virtually a lone voice of approval for the film.[9] Despite the critics, however, *The Curse of Frankenstein* was a huge box office success and Hammer realized that its future lay in gothic horror. Bernard, however, was keen to continue his diverse career, having no idea at that time that his name would later be inextricably linked to Hammer horror films. Rank commissioned another score from him for the film adaptation of Joy Packer's novel *Nor the Moon by Night* (Rank, dir. Ken Annakin, 1958). This tells the story of an African game warden (played by Patrick McGoohan) who falls in love with an Englishwoman (played by Belinda Lee). As soon as her aged mother dies, she hurries to join her penpal-cum-fiancé in the wilds of Africa where she is met at the railway station by McGoohan's assistant (played by Michael Craig). On the long journey to McGoohan's isolated home, she falls in love with the Michael Craig character instead.

Bernard's score is memorable mainly for the title song, with lyrics by Jack Fishman, which was sung on the soundtrack by Frank Holder to atmospheric marimba accompaniment. Marimbas returned later in the score along with bongo drums to create the tribal atmosphere that Bernard would again find useful for Hammer's *The Plague of the Zombies* (Seven Arts/Hammer, dir. John Gilling, 1965) and *She* (particularly in the scene when the Amahagger people prepare to sacrifice Leo Vincey).

For several years, the composer was puzzled when receiving money from the Performing Rights Society for a film called *Elephant Gun,* only later discovering that this was the American release title of *Nor the Moon by Night.* There is indeed one very impressive sequence when an elephant stampede threatens to flatten McGoohan to a pulp. Elephants charge towards the camera to music that could well have been conceived for the climax of *Quatermass 2,* the elephants themselves being characterized by scalic passages on trumpeting brass. For a subsequent, highly convincing attack on McGoohan by a lion, Bernard again takes a single chord and presents it sequentially, in much the same way, though nowhere near as effectively as he would do for his next Hammer film, *Dracula.*

But before that seminal cinematic event, he completed his third and final film for Rank. This was *Windom's Way* (Rank, dir. Ronald Neame, 1957), in which Peter Finch played Dr. Alec Windom, a GP in Malaya who tries to prevent a native uprising against the unfair working conditions of Michael Hordern's unsympathetic plantation manager,

Patterson. The musical supervisor and conductor for this film was Muir Mathieson, of whom Bernard, unlike many other composers, has fond memories:

> Muir was the tsar of music for British films. If you wanted to write music for films at that time, you really had to be "in" with Muir. He also had a famous lady secretary, known as Dusty. She was really very nice but you had to charm her because she was one of those ladies who could be a total dragon and you had to get through that and then everything was fine. Everything was referred to Dusty before it went to Muir, who was charming. He was quite Scottish in manner—a family man with a wife and seven children, and he became quite a good friend of Paul and myself. I do remember on *Windom's Way* he came round to our house in Bramerton Street to check that I was doing the right thing. He didn't quite like all my harmonies! Apart from that, I found him very easy to work with and we had a very friendly relationship.

However, in a letter to Britten on March 5 the following year, Bernard confessed that he was "furious at the way they mucked up the music in the dubbing."

The music for the opening titles imitates the sound of an Oriental gamelan orchestra, an idiom that had influenced Bernard's favorite composers Debussy and Ravel, as well as Britten, in his ballet *The Prince of the Pagodas* and the opera *Death in Venice;* but Bernard's use of gamelan textures in *Windom's Way* was certainly unusual, if not unique for a British film at that time. Paul Dehn, writing in the *Rotherham Advertiser* (November 16, 1957), felt that the music deserved a special mention:

> It is music that captures every mood, every variation of this fascinating film. Much of the music is local, as befits the story. Malayan music using flutes and drums is ingeniously welded with the full dramatic tones of Western orchestral music. James Bernard, now 32, is making a great reputation for himself as a writer of film music.

In fact, there isn't a great deal of music in this film, though a waltz theme, which originally accompanied the scene in which Windom and his wife bathe in a river, was published as "The Waltz from Windom's Way" for piano solo. It is in a similar mood to the waltzes Bernard would later score for the ball scenes of *The Kiss of the Vampire*, one of the host of vampire movies that followed in the wake of Hammer's most celebrated film, *Dracula.*

"There's no question but that when an actor's fantasy collides with a certain fated role," Christopher Lee wrote in his autobiography, "there's a relocation of the atoms of his professional life, akin to a change of state in chemistry."[10] Lee found it difficult to shake off his association with Dracula after the amazing success of that film, and Bernard found himself in a similar situation, though with none of the reluctance and reservations of the actor.

Universal Studios had emphasized romance when promoting their original version of *Dracula* (Universal, dir. Tod Browning, 1931). It was released on St. Valentine's Day and advertised as "The Strangest Love a Man Has Ever Known." Hammer, on the contrary, focused uncompromisingly on horror and sex, fully aware that everyone in the audience would know, by then, who and what Dracula really was. Their publicity tag was "Who Will Be His Bride Tonight?" and the difference of approach is manifest from the very first bars of the opening music of each film. The 1931 film had used a romantic theme from Tchaikovsky's ballet *Swan Lake*. In complete contrast, Bernard wrote a somber march, which leaves one in no doubt as to the kind of story that is about to unfold. Accompanying majestic shots of the castle exterior and its foreboding Teutonic stone eagles, the music aims to terrify overtly.

19 Brammerton Street, London: the house where the "Dra-Cu-La" theme was born.

Bernard clearly recalled the day on which he first thought up his famous "Dra-Cu-La" theme:

> I'd be working on one floor of our house. Paul had been working on another upper floor, tapping away on his typewriter at whatever he was doing, and I shouted up, "Paul, do you think this is too obvious to just try and say 'Dracula' in the music?" He was very musical. He could play the piano and had a nice light tenor voice, so I valued his opinion. He said, "No! No! That's it! Use it! Don't be shy! You've got it!"[11] He was very encouraging. So that was it: "Dra-Cu-La!"—and then the next bit was, "Beware of Dra-Cu-La! Dra-Cu-La! DRA-CU-LA! Watch out for DRA-CU-LA!"—terribly childish!

But it is not quite as simple as that. To understand fully the astonishing effectiveness of Bernard's theme, one must explore its musical genealogy. Like John Williams' theme for *Close Encounters of the Third Kind* (Columbia/EMI, dir. Steven Spielberg, 1977), the "Dra-Cu-La" theme draws upon some powerful musical archetypes. The *Close Encounters* theme manages to convey a mythological resonance because, like so many of Wagner's leitmotifs for the *Ring* cycle, it is no more than a rumination on a **major third,** a **fifth** and an **octave** (which together constitute a **major chord**).[12] These intervals are the DNA of Western musical tradition and, despite a century of atonality and serialism, are still immensely powerful in the hands of a skilful composer.

Similarly, the evocative octave of the "Dra-Cu-La" theme has a musical lineage as long and distinguished as Dracula's. Octaves have often been used to create a sense of urgency and excitement. Vivaldi, for example, was extremely fond of pounding octaves and used them liberally in his *Gloria* in D major:

Antonio Vivaldi, *Gloria*, "Gloria," bars 1–3 (reduction)

Example 10

There is nothing diabolic about Vivaldi's octaves, but there is certainly a sense of nobility and energy here. They are also elements of Dracula's character[13]; but it was Beethoven who invested the octaves of Vivaldi with a sense of daemonic energy in the **Scherzo** of his Ninth Symphony (first performed in 1824). For the first time in a symphonic work, Beethoven used timpani as an integral rather than merely decorative element, when they hammer out the angry octaves of this very dark musical "joke":

Ludwig van Beethoven, *Ninth Symphony*, "Scherzo," bars 1–5

Molto vivace (𝅗𝅥 = 116)

Example 11

Building on this heritage of octave symbolism, Wagner later employed octaves for his *Ring* cycle motif known as the "Oath of Fidelity." It accompanies Fricka's dialogue in *Die Walküre* when she insists that Wotan must uphold the law of marriage, and it returns to devastating effect at the end of Act II of *Götterdämmerung* (first performed in 1876) when Brünnhilde is virtually raped by Siegfried who, in the guise of Gunther, breaks all the vows of fidelity in one blow and injects an element of brutality into the symbolism of the demonically energetic octave:

**Richard Wagner, *Götterdämmerung*, end of Act II,
"Treueschwur" motif ("Oath of Fidelity") (reduction)**

Sehr lebhaft
Full Orchestra
ff
3
3
3

Example 12

Perhaps it was this theme that inspired that arch–Wagnerian Anton Bruckner to create an astonishing octave theme in the first movement of his Ninth Symphony in D minor (left unfinished on the composer's death in 1896). Bruckner's octave theme is scored for a gigantic orchestra and given a somber momentum by the kind of dotted rhythm that had long been associated with funeral marches. Robert Simpson has described Bruckner's Ninth as "dark to the pitch of blackness,"[14] and compared its "furious, titanic ... tramping and heaving towards a truly seismic eruption" to Milton's description of Satan in *Paradise Lost*:

Forthwith upright he rears from off the pool
His mighty stature; on each hand the flames
Driven backwards slope their pointing spires, and rolled
In billows, leave i' the midst a horrid vale.
Then with expanded wings he steers his flight
Aloft, incumbent on the dusky air,
That felt unusual weight; till on dry land
He lights—if it were land that ever burned
With solid, as the lake with liquid fire,
And such appeared in here as when the force
Of subterranean wind transports a hill
Torn from Pelorus, or the shattered side
Of thundering Etna, whose combustible
And fuelled entrails, thence conceiving fire,
Sublimed with mineral fury, aid the winds,
And leave a singèd bottom all involved
With stench and smoke. Such resting found the sole
Of unblest feet.[15]

Every night
he rises from
his coffin-bed
to silently
seek
the
soft
flesh,
the warm
blood
he needs
to keep
himself
alive!

Original publicity brochure for Hammer's 1958 *Dracula* (a.k.a. *Horror of Dracula*).

Anton Bruckner, *Ninth Symphony in D Minor*, 1st Movement, bars 61–71

Example 13

Satan's "unblest feet" are now ready to stride out to Bernard's Dracula march, which retains Bruckner's dotted rhythm and adds a demonic tritone and clashing major second to the harmony: truly the culmination of three centuries of octave signification. Bernard's orchestration is also very important, emphasizing, as Bruckner and Wagner had done before him, the equally demonic timbres of the brass, particularly the trombones, which Berlioz once famously described as "majestic, formidable and terrible."[16] As Philip Martell, later, somewhat prosaically remarked, "On horrors as a rule you need a lot of brass."[17]

The reiterated statements of the "Dra-Cu-La" theme are linked by an idea that will later evolve into the main title theme of *Dracula Has Risen from the Grave* (Warner–Seven Arts/Hammer, dir. Freddie Francis, 1968):

James Bernard, *Dracula* 1M1

Example 14a

James Bernard, *Dracula Has Risen from the Grave* 1M1

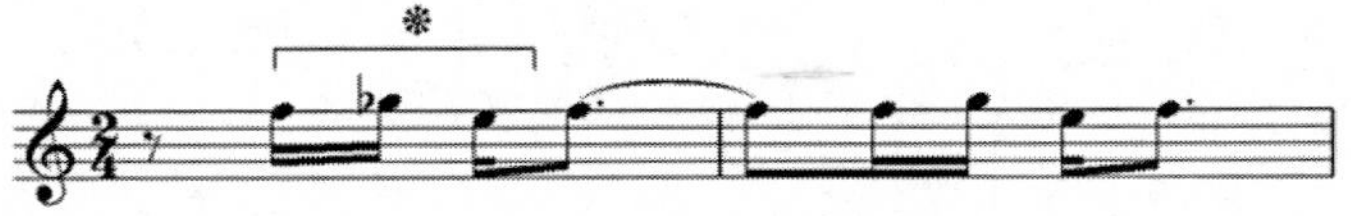

Example 14b

An important secondary theme is also introduced in the Dracula march. Whereas the first theme refers specifically to Dracula, this second theme, featuring another tritone relationship and accompanied by ***martellato*** assaults from the snare drum, has a more general application and is associated with the condition of actually being "Undead":

James Bernard, *Dracula* 1M1, "Undead" theme

Example 15

After the main title, a new theme is immediately introduced by the violins. It underscores Jonathan Harker's commentary and is to be associated with him throughout what follows. In Jimmy Sangster's screenplay, Harker, though apparently a librarian, is in fact a vampire hunter, fully aware, like the 1958 cinema audience, of Dracula's true nature. As such he is quite different from the Harker of Bram Stoker's original novel. Stoker's Harker survives, but Sangster's becomes a victim and is later dispatched. Given his ultimate fate, it is highly appropriate that Harker's theme is actually related to the "Undead" motif:

James Bernard, *Dracula* 1M2, bars 6–16

Example 16a

Harker's theme provides further evidence of Bernard's fascination with the music of Liszt and Debussy. The last three bars of example 16a echo the final bars of Liszt's *Valse oubliée No. 1* (composed in 1881), a work which, as we shall see, also informs Bernard's "Vampire Rhapsody" in *The Kiss of the Vampire*. The opening of the "Harker" theme is also reminiscent of Debussy's "*Pour invoquer Pan, dieu du vent d'été,*" the opening piece of that composer's *Six Épigraphs Antiques* (1914):

Franz Liszt, *Valse oubliée No. 1* (final bars)

Example 16b

Example 16c

Whereas Liszt's *Valse oubliée* is **pentatonic** merely in *feeling*, "*Pour invoquer Pan....*" is technically pentatonic in its opening bars, and the first two bars of Bernard's "Harker" theme might be said to echo it. The *Six Épigraphs Antiques* were actually reworkings of earlier orchestral pieces, which Debussy had composed in 1900 for recitations of and mimes inspired by the *Chansons de Bilitis* prose poems of Pierre Louÿs. Significantly, Bernard's fascination with the symbolist aesthetic of Debussy and Louÿs goes back to his school days at Wellington College:

> We had a music society. Boys were allowed to read a paper. I chose Debussy and Ravel. I didn't know a great deal about Debussy then but I'd read that he'd set some songs to rather risky, sexy words and I made a point of reading out a translation of one of these very erotic songs [from the *Chansons de Bilitis*]. I deeply shocked one of the master's wives!

It is therefore logical that the shades of Debussy and Louÿs should return in Bernard's score for the most erotic and shocking British horror film ever seen by audiences at that time. While there is no evidence that Debussy actually read Stoker's *Dracula*, he was certainly a fervent admirer of the horror tales of Edgar Allan Poe and spent a great deal of his time on an unfinished operatic project based on "The Fall of the House of Usher." Gothic atmospheres, premature burials and vampiric *femmes fatales* were all part of the symbolist aesthetic out of which Debussy's style and tastes evolved.

Inside Castle Dracula, the "Harker" theme is quietly elaborated by a body of strings, interspersed with statements of the "Dracula chord":

James Bernard, *Dracula* 1M2, bars 62–67

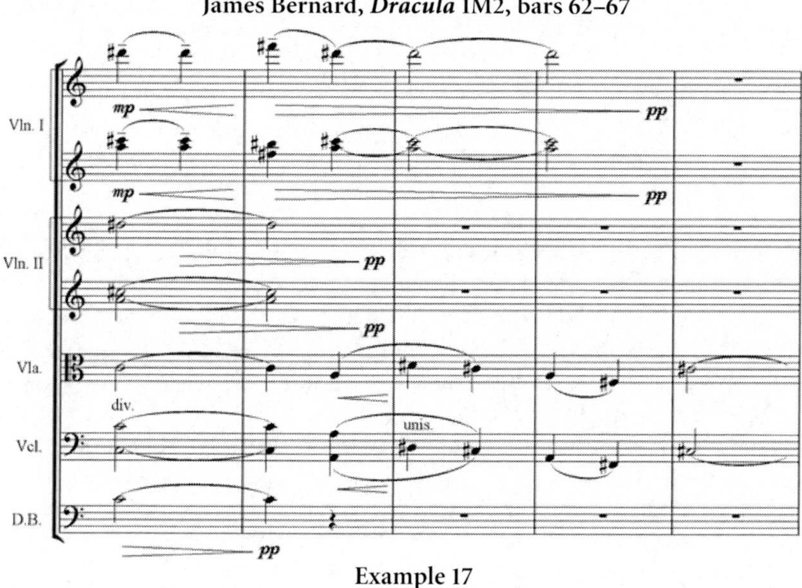

Example 17

Together, these musical effects create a muted sense of unease that is matched by the well-ordered, tidily arranged but utterly deserted hall in which Harker now finds himself. Perhaps we expected a cobweb-infested vault. Instead, Hammer's resident art director, Bernard Robinson, created a much closer equivalent to Stoker's description of "a well-lit room in which a table was spread for supper, and on whose mighty hearth a great fire of logs flamed and flared."[18] As Harker reads the letter left for him by the Count, a trumpet intones the "Dra-Cu-La" octave theme, which is then repeated on strings as the camera pans to the Count's coat of arms over the fireplace.

The "Dracula chord" is then elaborated as Harker moves the dishes of his meal to one side, accidentally causing one of them to clatter noisily to the floor. Falling tones in the strings suggest that the castle itself is whispering a warning:

James Bernard, *Dracula* 1M2, bars 109–112 (strings only)

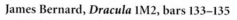

Andante ♩ = 60

Dsks. 1, 3 Violin I Dsk. 2 — Dsk. 1 Violin II Dsk. 2 — Dsk. 1 Viola Dsk. 2 — Vcl. — D.B.

Example 18

As Harker stoops to pick up the plate, we see the lower portion of a shell-pink dress appear behind him. This is worn by Dracula's first vampire bride (played by Valerie Gaunt) but as we don't know who or what she is her theme isn't heard yet. Instead, Bernard cleverly develops the "Harker" motif with string tremolos that rise and fall through a chord based on a **minor triad** with an **added seventh**. This is the kind of "alert" chord that Mahler often used in music associated with death. (In the first movement of Mahler's *Third Symphony*, first performed in 1902, the deadly forces of Winter are indeed characterized by a horn call based on this very chord.)

James Bernard, *Dracula* 1M2, bars 133–135

Example 19a

The vampire woman asks Harker to help her but her expression rapidly changes and she hurries away to the sound of agitated strings and flute playing another minor triad with an added augmented fourth. A variant of this "Flight" motif will return later in the film:

Gustav Mahler, *Third Symphony*, 1st Movement (reduction)

Example 19b

James Bernard, *Dracula* 1M2, bar 144 (flutes and violins only)

Example 20

Harker turns to see the tall silhouette of Dracula standing at the top of the stairs, accompanied by his octave theme, and Christopher Lee speaks his famous first lines as Dracula, bidding Harker welcome to his home. The understated nature of Lee's performance here is deliberately at odds with the music, which has set up expectations of a terrible monster. Instead we are introduced to an imposing but courteous and well-spoken aristocrat, apparently quite human.

After being shown to his room, Harker realizes with a resigned smile that he has been locked in. A trumpet quietly plays his theme as he walks over to the desk to write up the day's events in his diary. We now learn of his mission to destroy the vampire, and in the manner of an operatic orchestral recitative, Bernard's music underscores Harker's voice-over with sustained string chords, filling in the pauses at the end of each phrase with quiet statements of the octave theme. After a death-like sleep, Harker awakens to the sound of his door being unlocked. He goes downstairs to the library, accompanied by the "Dracula chord" on high strings. The oily timbre of the bass clarinet here echoes Wagner's use of that instrument in the last scene of *Götterdämmerung* when Gutrune wanders about the deserted Gibichung Hall and peers into Brünnhilde's empty room. The bass clarinet motif in *Dracula* is the first manifestation of what will eventually become a rising three-note theme to be associated with Lucy. (At the moment it is a *four*-note rising theme with a final falling semitone.) As we shall hear, all of Lucy's music is based on a rising three-note theme. But she is the second of Dracula's brides. The first is associated with the bass clarinet theme, which we will call the "Vampire Bride" motif (example 21).

James Bernard, *Dracula* 2M2, bars 1–3

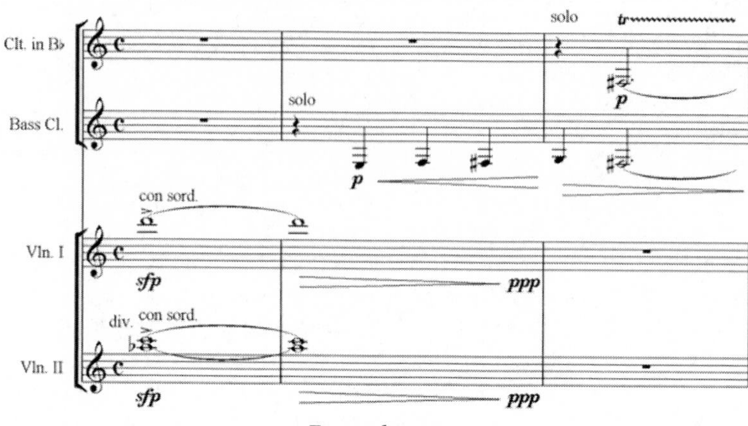

Example 21

Harker walks into the library where the vampire woman is waiting for him. Originally their dialogue was to be entirely underscored with the metamorphosis of Harker's theme based on the Mahlerian minor seventh chord mentioned above. In the event, however, this motif appears only as the vampire woman puts her lips to Harker's neck. With the appearance of Dracula, the octave theme returns.

Awakening in his room, Harker realizes he has been bitten. The music emphasises his shock: trills on E natural rise up through the strings and wind, and at the climax of Harker's realization of the truth, an F joins the E, creating a characteristic Bernardian minor second, but only for a quaver beat. Silence follows, and low strings and somber brass then reflect on Harker's predicament (their sudden descent in pitch symbolizing both a literal and metaphoric fall).

As mentioned earlier, there is an echo of Stravinsky's *Rite of Spring* in Bernard's music for *Quatermass 2*. In *Dracula*, the high-pitched bassoon, which is heard as Harker records the devastating news in his diary, is also reminiscent of the very opening of Stravinsky's ballet. Though the melody is different, the timbre is almost identical and creates a similarly desolate mood to Stravinsky's musical depiction of a wintry pagan landscape. Again, Harker's voice-over is supported by the "Dracula chord" on hushed strings, and the end of each of his sentences is punctuated with the octave theme.

Harker now sets about destroying Dracula and the woman in his power. He makes his way to the mausoleum, accompanied by the "Undead" theme, but this time that theme is given a particularly gruesome twist by being played ***sul ponticello*** on strings (with woodwind above). For the first shot of Dracula in his coffin, the pitch of the "Undead" theme is raised and the snare drum emphasizes the rhythm. Harker makes the fatal mistake of choosing to dispatch the female vampire first. He raises his stake and hammers it home to repeated statements of the "Undead" theme in strings and wind.

Major thirds have long been used in erotic contexts and are often tinged with a sense of decadence or danger. Monteverdi was one of the earliest composers to exploit this association to the full at the end of his opera *L'incoronazione di Poppea* (*The Coronation of Poppea,* first performed in 1642) when Emperor Nero and the courtesan, Poppea, having murdered their way to the top, rejoice in their love of each other. Their duet is festooned with strings of seductive major thirds, and in *Dracula* they also signify eroticism and death. They are first heard in this mausoleum sequence, sliding down **chromatically** as darkness descends and Dracula awakes, but these major thirds (played by the violins) are contaminated by note clusters in the woodwind, as well as rising major thirds, major seconds and tritones in the brass. Together, such clashing intervals combine to create a perfect musical metaphor of sexual allure and demonic horror. When Dracula eventually appears at the top of the mausoleum steps he is, of course, accompanied by his octave theme played by the entire orchestra in an imposingly resonant orchestration; but the last statement of the theme is interrupted by a slight pause before the Count slams the door behind him on the last chord: a simple but brilliantly effective way of emphasizing Harker's demise.

After the musical box that introduces the scene in which Peter Cushing's Van Helsing enters a garlic-festooned inn, the next music we hear is a solo trumpet quietly intoning the "Harker" theme as Van Helsing makes his way to Castle Dracula in search of his colleague. A hearse rushes past him, as violins and flutes play a variant of the "Flight" motif, ending with the "Dracula chord" to let us know, should we be in any doubt, who is lying in the coffin.

In the fourth reel, the thematic relationship between the "Undead" theme and "Harker" is made fully apparent when both are presented side by side. The "Harker" theme accompanies a shot of Harker lying in his coffin, while the "Undead" theme accompanies a shot of the vampire woman who has now been transformed into the hideous corpse of an old hag. These themes alternate throughout the rest of this section.

There is no more music until the end of the fourth reel when Lucy prepares herself for one of the Count's nocturnal visitations. A gentle lullaby introduces us to Lucy who lies ill in bed. However, as mentioned earlier, this lullaby, which seems so innocent and sweet, is actually related to the "Vampire Bride" motif:

James Bernard, *Dracula* 4M3, bars 1–4

Andante ♩ = 66

Vln. I (Dsk. 1) — *p con tenerezza*

Vln. II (Dsk. 2) — *p con tenerezza*

Vla. (Dsk. 1) — *p con tenerezza*

Example 22

Lucy removes her crucifix, opens the French windows and reclines on her bed, full of expectation. For the following classic example of horror film scoring, the vibraphone is combined with the celesta, an instrument that made its first appearance in Tchaikovsky's "Dance of the Sugar Plum Fairy" from *The Nutcracker* ballet (first performed in 1892) and which has ever since had magical or supernatural connotations. The sweetness of the sugar plum fairy is certainly present in this scene but as Bernard has himself explained:

> I tried to get a kind of theme which was meant to be sweet in a nasty way. They were being dragged into this kind of act which is sex, really, only it was being aimed at the neck instead of lower down; but they felt the evil too.

It is now that the dangerous allure of major thirds is felt to the full. The vibraphone presents a flurry of oscillating major thirds while the celesta plays equally unnerving whole-tone triplets (again in the manner of Debussy):

James Bernard, *Dracula* 5M1, bar 3

Moderato ♩ = 90

Clts. I, II; Vibes; Celesta (L.H., R.H.; *poco cresc.*); Vla. (div.)

Example 23

This little ostinato continues while clarinets, violas and cellos transform what seemed so innocent in the previous lullaby (three rising notes) into something seductive yet simultaneously appalling. Whereas in the lullaby the three notes rose in a major key, they now rise chromatically (a worrying sign that Lucy has been sexually aroused). They are given a further sense of unease by the **trill** on the first note of each three-note group, as well as the dotted rhythm that also appears. The rhythmic impetus of this dotted rhythm adds to the excitement as the orchestral texture thickens and the pitch rises.

Terence Fisher was always a stickler for scenic details and made sure that a few (but not too many) autumn leaves fluttered about in the gathering wind outside Lucy's bedroom to herald Dracula's arrival. Bernard picks up on this with fluttering **sextuplet** chromatic scales in the woodwind that rise higher on each repetition as the storm gathers momentum and the wind begins to howl. Later, when Lucy lies gasping for breath in her bedroom surrounded by garlic flowers, Bernard provides a musical equivalent of her restless breathing. This is basically a rising semitone with a trochaic rather than iambic stress:

James Bernard, *Dracula* 6M1, bars 7–9

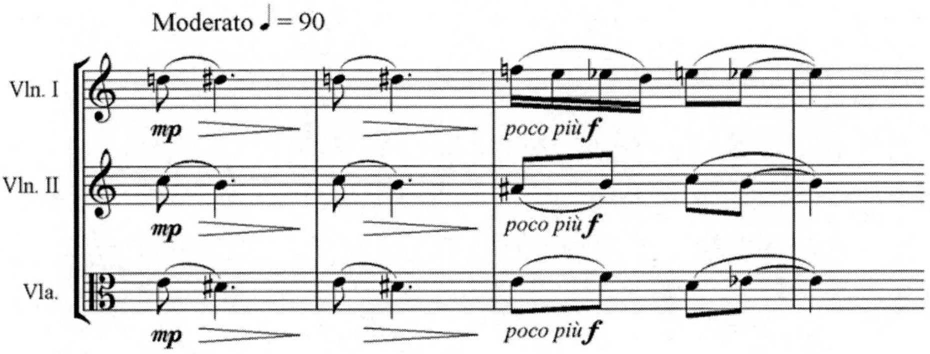

Moderato ♩ = 90

Vln. I
Vln. II
Vla.

mp
poco più f

Example 24

Richard Strauss had taken a similar approach in the opening passage of his tone poem *Tod und Verklärung* ("Death and Transfiguration," first performed in 1889), the opening bars of which imitate the gasping of an artist struggling for breath on his death bed. Bernard's theme has a wider signification, however, for it later recurs during what Stoker's novel refers to as the "bloofer lady" episode. During that scene, a little girl (called Tanya in the film) encounters the undead Lucy on Hampstead Heath. (The actual location of Hammer's *Dracula* isn't so specific, having a vague Middle European locale.) The breathless semitone motif should therefore be called "Fear in the Night" (though it has nothing in common with the quite different Hammer film of that title). "Fear in the Night" also accompanies Arthur's watch of the house during Dracula's attack on Mina, and it is finally speeded up in the climactic chase sequence at the end of the film. All these are indeed scenes of nocturnal fear, but they also have an increasing breathlessness about them.

Van Helsing's subsequent staking of Lucy is covered by twelve bars of highly emotional music conveying the redemption of her soul. The music is constructed from **chromatically altered chords**, which Wagner had also employed for similarly "redemptive" effects. For example, at the end of Wagner's *Parsifal* (first performed in 1882), the eponymous hero restores order to the Grail community to just such an effect:

Richard Wagner, *Parsifal*, end of Act III (reduction)

Sehr langsam und Feierlich

(Kundry, with her gaze uplifted to Parsifal, sinks slowly lifeless to the ground. - Amorfas and Gurnemanz kneel in hommage before Parsifal, who waves the Grail in blessing over the worshipping Knighthood.)

Example 25a

Bernard follows Wagner's example, even writing the music in the same "redemptive" key of D flat major. The result perfectly complements the sensitive performance of Peter Cushing as well as the elegiac autumn leaves that fall outside the crypt in the emerging dawn:

James Bernard, *Dracula* 7M1, bars 2–5

Andante ♩ = 60

Vln. I — *p sost.* — *poco cresc.*

Vln. II — *p sost.* — *poco cresc.*

Vla. — *p sost.* — *poco cresc.*

Dsk. 1 Vcl. — *p leggiero* — *poco cresc.*

Dsk. 2 — *p sost.* — *poco cresc.*

Figure 25b

With the shot of Lucy's tranquil face now finally at rest, the "Undead" theme loses its final, troubling tritone, and is replaced by a soothing **perfect fifth.** (The implicit tritone between the first and third notes of the motif remains however: Lucy is dead, after all.)

The next important music section occurs in the eighth reel during the scene in which Dracula assaults Mina while Van Helsing and Arthur are outside guarding the house. As Dracula climbs the stairs, his octave theme pounds away, interspersed with dramatic pauses. In between the end of a previous statement of his motif and the beginning of the next one, he then slams the bedroom door behind him. The music therefore helps to articulate the action, emphasizing the effectiveness of James Needs' editing of this sequence. Indeed, these two Jameses — Needs and Bernard — are largely responsible for the overall pacing of the classic Hammer films.[19]

Bernard's great love of Verdi informed the exhilarating chase music that propels us to the climax of the film. Here the "Fear in the Night" motif is speeded up and sequenced in much the same way that Verdi brings Act I of *Rigoletto* to such an exciting conclusion. In that opera, the hunchback jester, Rigoletto, realizes that his beloved daughter, Gilda, has been kidnapped while he has been blindfolded. Verdi's stage directions for this scene are just the kind of thing a silent film director would have bellowed through a megaphone to the perspiring actor:

> He tears off his bandage and mask, snatches up a lantern left by one of the courtiers and by its light recognizes the scarf; rushes into the house — returns, dragging forth Giovanna, at whom he stares in bewilderment, he tears his hair, tries to cry out but can't.

Giuseppe Verdi, *Rigoletto*, end of Act I (reduction)

Example 26a

Bernard's chase music takes a similar approach:

James Bernard, *Dracula* 9M2, bars 17–26 (reduction)

Example 26b

For the final showdown between Dracula and Van Helsing, the rhythm of the music again emphasizes the choreography of the scene. As Dracula starts to strangle Van Helsing, Bernard reduces the rapid **semiquaver** movement to **minims**. The struggle is also reflected by the iambic stress at the end of each minim group, and **syncopation** is introduced as Dracula appears to gain the upper hand:

James Bernard, *Dracula* 9M2, bars 48–52 (strings only)

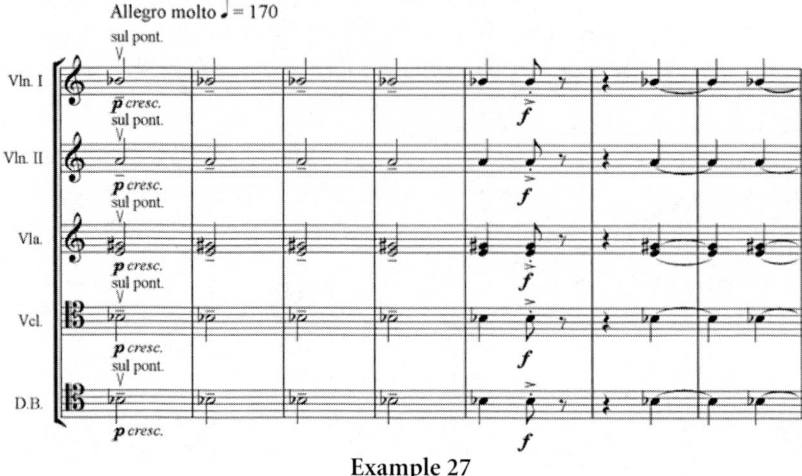

Example 27

Van Helsing plays dead but suddenly he opens his eyes and takes Dracula by surprise. Flurried statements of "Fear in the Night" accompany Van Helsing's escape, followed by the hiatus of a **crotchet** rest as both size each other up. Then, more syncopation reflects their respective maneuvering for position, leading to the inspired moment when Van Helsing runs along the refectory table and pulls down the curtains to admit the light of day. This action is accompanied by more flurried statements of "Fear in the Night," the effect of the sunlight atomizing the theme and dispersing the forces of darkness, as Dracula disintegrates to descending chromatically sequenced statements of his octave motif.

Outside in the castle grounds, the wound caused by the crucifix on Mina's hand heals, and the "Undead" theme again replaces its final tritone with a tranquil fifth, this time played by a romantic solo violin. Back in the castle, we are shown a pile of Dracula's ashes as a flute imitates the gust of wind that blows them away.*

James Bernard, *Dracula* 9M2, bars 159–162

Example 28

**John Williams used a similar effect at the end of John Badham's* Dracula *(Universal/Mirisch, 1979) when Frank Langella's Count is quite literally hoist with his own petard and his cloak flutters, bat-like, into the sky at the end of the film.*

The end title triumphantly intones the redeemed version of the "Undead" theme, ending on the rhythm of the "Dra-Cu-La" motif but omitting its descending octave. (Each note of the theme is played on the same pitch.) An ascending octave would have been inappropriate: the Count's soul has presumably not ascended into Heaven, but a descending octave would emphasize too strongly his more likely destination. At this stage we are now more concerned with those left on earth, poised between these metaphysical opposites. A final comparison with Wagner's *Parsifal* lies in the fact that that opera and Bernard's score both come to a redemptive end in D flat major.[20]

Just as Miklós Rózsa was responsible for the classic sound of the Biblical epic in his film scores for *Quo Vadis* (MGM, dir. Mervyn Le Roy, 1951) and *Ben-Hur* (MGM, dir. William Wyler, 1959), so James Bernard's score for *Dracula* defined the sound world of the gothic horror film and has yet to be surpassed.

6

Hounded

"Sometimes the chords were sonorous and melancholy. Occasionally they were fantastic and cheerful."

Dr. Watson on the violin improvisations of Sherlock Holmes in *A Study in Scarlet* by Sir Arthur Conan Doyle[1]

With Dracula dispatched, for the time being at least, Bernard now turned his attention to other projects. As well as getting to know Erwin Stein at Boosey and Hawkes, he had also become quite friendly with Alan Frank, the head of music publishing at the Oxford University Press. At this time Bernard still had ambitions to write a serious orchestral piece and was thinking about a concerto grosso for percussion and orchestra. Frank expressed enthusiasm but nothing came of the project. However, OUP did publish Bernard's *Three Mediaeval Poems*: choral settings of two anonymous texts, "The Falcon" and "Maiden in the Moor," along with Chaucer's "Now Welcome Summer." A Britten-like simplicity characterizes the first one with its **minor-key** version of "Three Blind Mice" presented in **canon**:

James Bernard, *Three Mediaeval Poems*, "Maiden in the Moor," bars 1–2

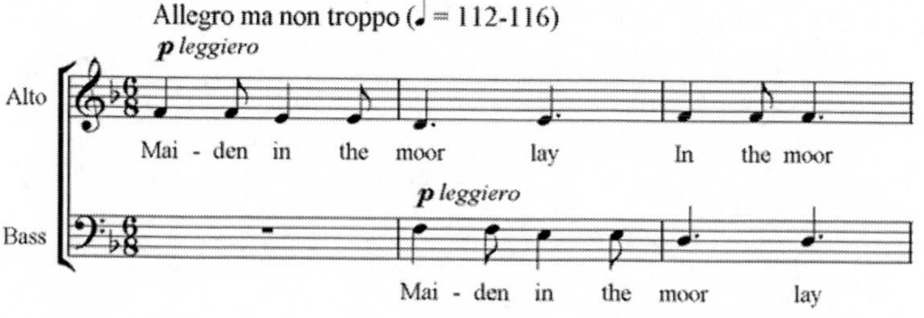

Example 1

The second is even simpler, scored for a mezzo-soprano over a tenor and bass choir in a gently rocking 6/8 meter:

James Bernard, *Three Mediaeval Poems*, "The Falcon," bars 1–8

Example 2

"Now Welcome Summer" is the most complex, in which soprano and alto parts are divided, with some lively syncopations:

James Bernard, *Three Mediaeval Poems*, "Now Welcome Summer," bars 1–3

Example 3

The Oxford Music Bulletin for January-May 1958 described these pieces as "most imaginative settings which will be enjoyed by more advanced choirs. They are the first works to be published by this gifted young composer." Bernard appropriately dedicated them to his mentor, Imogen Holst, who conducted the Purcell Singers in a performance of the Chaucer setting in October the following year. She immediately sent a reply to Bernard in her typically exuberant handwriting:

20 High Street
Aldeburgh
March 6 58

Dear Jim

VERY many thanks for the songs—I'm delighted to have them and immensely proud of the dedication! BLESS YOU.

It was good to hear your news, and I'm *terribly* impressed by your gramophone sales!! It would be lovely to see you both—I shall hope that it won't be in the too distant future!

Very much gratitude.

Love from Imogen

The "gramophone sales" referred to the song that had been based on Bernard's guitar theme from *Across the Bridge.* Britten also sent his congratulations and was particularly pleased to hear that his protégé had been commissioned by Wellington College to write an opera as part of its centenary celebrations:

Red House
26th March 58

My Dear Jim

I am sorry not to have written before and thanked you for your nice long letter, and for sending your first published opus, but I have only just returned from a long tour on the Continent, and found them waiting for me. I do hope you have a great success with the Mediaeval poems; you should because they look easy and grateful to sing, and have very characteristic moods—something for the singers to get hold of. I am also glad that the Oxford Press shows interest in other of your connections with the Press.

Thank you for writing so fully about your activities. I am really extremely glad that things are going so well with you. It is fearfully difficult to get started as a composer, and I think you have done splendidly—a real example to other young composers who are often too grand (or too incompetent) to accept commissions of the sort that you have always done. I must confess I particularly look forward to the Wellington opera. I have just finished a new piece of that kind, which will be done at Aldeburgh this year, with about 200 local children taking part, but thank God I have not got to control them myself.[2]

Much love to you and Paul

Yours ever

Ben

Alan Frank next suggested that it would be a "good thing" for Bernard to compose a Sonatina for clarinet and piano as there was a dearth of works for this combination of instruments. Bernard immediately set to work on one which was duly published by OUP in 1958 and sold for the princely sum of eight shillings and six pence. Dedicated to his mother, the Sonatina's first movement is entitled "Mattinata," the second "Notturno" and the third "Danza." The opening movement is based on a simple rocking theme that actually foreshadows the love theme from *Dracula Has Risen from the Grave*:

James Bernard, *Sonatina for B♭Clarinet and Piano*, "Mattinata," bars 1–2

Example 4a

James Bernard, *Dracula Has Risen from the Grave* 5M1, bars 7–8, "Love" theme

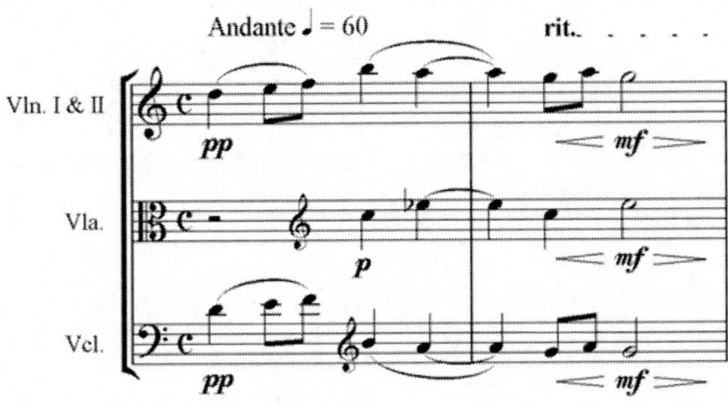

Example 4b

The lively, syncopated third movement, featuring some very Bernardian **major seconds** in the piano part, brings the work to an exuberant conclusion. Alan Frank had high hopes for a successful first performance:

O.U.P.
44 Conduit Street
London W1
13th May 1958

Dear James

You'll be glad to hear that I sent your Clarinet work to Gervase de Peyer,[3] and have just heard from him. He likes it very much indeed, and says he will look for opportunities to play it next season. Of course, I shall be in touch with the BBC at the right time, and we are thinking about a first public performance.

Yours

Alan (Frank)

Unfortunately, success eluded the piece and Bernard put the failure of his Sonatina down to the prevailing fashion of the time when, as he put it, composers "had to be post–Schoenberg to be taken seriously at all." Later, he would try his hand at serial style, but while finding the discipline stimulating, it never came naturally to him. Meanwhile, another film project came to the rescue, not from Hammer Films but from the documentary director Basil Wright, who had just completed filming his travelogue *Greece, the Immortal Land* (Marsden Film Productions [Gladys and Basil Wright], 1958). Wright had been trained by John Grierson for the GPO Film Unit in the 1930s, and had been one of the directors of that unit's 1936 documentary *Night Mail,* for which Britten had composed the music in collaboration with the poet W.H. Auden. With the coming of the second World War, the GPO Film Unit had been reorganized as the Crown Film Unit, producing such propaganda films as *Men of the Lightship* (David MacDonald, 1940), with music by Richard Addinsell, as well as *Target for Tonight* (Harry Watt, 1941), scored, as mentioned before, by the man who had conducted some of Bernard's radio work, Leighton Lucas, and conducted on the soundtrack by John Hollingsworth. Indeed, Britten's *Young Person's Guide to the Orchestra* had originally been commissioned for the Crown Film Unit's 1946 documentary, *Instruments of the Orchestra*, directed by Muir Mathieson.

Wright had been friendly with Dehn and through him he now approached Bernard to compose the score for this independent production financed by Wright and his mother Gladys. Bernard worked in close collaboration with Wright and his editor, Adrian de Potier, who had been faced with the task of cutting some 20,000 feet of Eastmancolor film. Wright himself explained in the publicity leaflet for the film:

> Right from the start we decided that we did not in any way want to make either a travelogue or a documentary, but rather perhaps something in the nature of a poetic meditation about the land of Greece and its people as seen by someone coming from outside and, as it were, falling in love with them. The clue to this approach seemed to us to be the extraordinary and unique sense of the co-existence of the past and the present which we found everywhere in Greece, and we attempted to construct the film entirely around this idea. All the images were shot with this mood in mind; all the words, music, and sound effects were similarly treated. Whether the film is a success, or a failure, my mother and I at least have the satisfaction of knowing that, on a completely independent basis and without any outside interference or influence, we have made a film we wanted to make in exactly the way we wanted to make it.

As well as commissioning Bernard's music, Wright involved the actors Michael Redgrave and John Gielgud, both of whom became personal friends of the composer. Redgrave recited passages from Thucydides, while Gielgud intoned poems by George Seferis, who, when not writing poetry, was the Greek Ambassador to London. The film opened on October 24, 1958, at the London Film Festival, sharing the program with *Smultronstället* (*Wild Strawberries*) (Ingmar Bergman, Svensk Filmindusti [Allan Ekelund], 1957). Seferis later wrote to Wright conveying his "sincerest congratulations to yourself, your Mother, screenwriter Rex Warner and all those who took part in the making of the film." Bernard's score was again conducted by Muir Mathieson, on whom the composer remembers paying a social call:

> Muir was very friendly, from long before we knew him, with Basil Wright. Basil invited Paul and me for the weekend and it wasn't very far away from where the Mathiesons lived, so we all went over for drinks one Sunday evening to Muir's house.

> I listened to a lot of Greek music for *Greece—the Immortal Land.* I remember Arda Mandikian, who was awfully nice and sweet, lent me a book of Greek folk songs when I met her for the "Mermaid's Vesper Hymn" which she performed at Aldeburgh. I never did give it back and she died when she was quite young.

The music for *Greece—the Immortal Land* is again interesting from the point of view of Bernard's subsequent Hammer scores, in particular *She*, for which *The Immortal Land*, might well be said to be a study. The film opens with a modal melody very much in the style of Miklós Rózsa's Biblical epic style, and Bernard also quotes the Greek National anthem; but the anticipations of *She* accompany shots of olive groves when we hear an embryonic form of the "Ay-E-Sha" motif (see chapter nine, example 12 a), accompanied by very *She*-like harp **arpeggios**. The influence of Debussy's piece for solo flute, *Syrinx* (composed in 1913), can also be felt in the oriental flute melody that accompanies shots of Greece's arid landscapes. Bernard's flute melody here is very similar to the music he later wrote for the flashback scene in *She* when Kallikrates is observed in the arms of a beautiful woman just before he is murdered by the jealous Ayesha. The opening nightclub music of *She* is also prefigured in the music Bernard wrote to cover shots of Greek coopers at work in the brilliant sunshine.

Other themes for future Hammer films also have their origin in *Greece—the Immortal Land.* A quiet timpani roll under Gielgud's reading of Seferis' poem leads to shots of ancient Greek statues, which Bernard juxtaposes with the alternating **consecutive triads** that are eventually to be used to symbolize the "Power of Good" in *The Devil Rides Out.* Bernard also places very sinister **chromatic** timpani **trills** under an impressive reading in the original language (by Katina Paxinou and Alexis Minotis) from Sophocles' *Oedipus Rex*, a device which will also return in *The Devil Rides Out.* And another motif from *Greece—the Immortal Land* went on to form part of Bernard's next score for Hammer, *The Hound of the Baskervilles*:

James Bernard, *The Hound of the Baskervilles*
3M3, bar 1, "Abbey" theme

Example 5

The commission to compose *The Hound of the Baskervilles* arrived at the same time that Bernard was working on his Wellington College opera *Music from Mars*; "a nuisance, in a way," he confessed to Britten on November 19, "but alas, the Wellington job only provides rewards on the higher plane!" Britten replied:

Red House
Nov. 26. 58

My dears, Paul and Jim

Forgive the joint letter, but I do think of you together, and not only do I want to thank you for the nice letters you both wrote about the Fludde[4] but to wish you jointly the best of luck for the Wellington piece. I look forward to it with impatience—when are the dates?—do you think I should be allowed in if I can manage to get there? *Don't* make it too difficult, Jim, will you? I am so pleased you are doing this piece; it is a very wise operatic start for you, and we hope for great things in that direction from you (this is for Jim, this bit).

I think I shall be in London in Dec. and Jan. a bit so can I do what I've always wanted, asking myself to see you? Peter's in Germany or otherwise would join in sending love.

Yours ever, Ben

In the event, Britten didn't attend any of the three performances of the piece conducted at Wellington College by Maurice Allen on the 15th, 16th and 20th of June 1959, but Arthur Fox-Strangeways, another old Wellingtonian, did write a review of the proceedings for *The Times* (June 18, 1959):

> *Music from Mars* depicts the unexpected adventures of three boys and a master "at any boys' school in England but Wellington"—it couldn't happen here—rehearsing for the school concert. The part-song, composed with the aid of a dream in order to gain the extra marks for an original composition in the inter-house competition by a slip in the cog of time-and-space machine lands the singers on Mars, whose inhabitants understand English only if it is sung. This last condition, induced by radio listening, allows a new distribution of recitative, aria, and spoken dialogue, and another of Mr. Paul Dehn's happy ideas in his libretto is to assign two voices (with but a single thought) to the Martian High-Master, who sings in octaves, treble and bass. All this makes for very good fun to be obtained from the modest resources of boys' unstable voices and an orchestra of piano, strings and percussion apt to depict space-travel. Mr. Bernard is fertile in thinking of figures that will become significant with repetition, in writing *aria parlante,* and in providing something lightly lyrical of simple charm, such as the lullaby needed to put one of the sleepless Martians into coma.
>
> If the music was simple, the *décor,* by Timothy O'Brien, was terrific: there is nothing now that half a dozen electricians, such as flourish in every school laboratory, cannot do with a few strands of wire, a few bulbs, and a radio set. Mr. Britten's example in his *Let's Make an Opera* is thus being fruitfully followed in hitherto unexpected quarters.

The Times Educational Supplement (June 19, 1959) added:

> Mr. Paul Dehn's libretto has many felicitous touches, and his comedy holds just the right balance between directness and sophistication. The music forms an effective counterpart to the words, with a refreshing freedom of style in the touches of jazz, the lunatic ditty for the Prologue and Epilogue, and the percussive music for outer space. There is not, of course, much opportunity for extended vocal writing; one of the few places, a song for the treble Martian in Act one, suffered from the hazard of first night nerves. But what the music lacked in line it made up for in pace and vitality.

The Master of Wellington, Graham Stainforth, sent Bernard and Dehn a congratulatory letter, remarking that the opera was the "most successful and possibly the most remarkable of our Centenary Celebrations." Bernard now rather hoped that *Music from Mars* would find its way to being published and looked again to Britten for help. A disappointing reply arrived from Aldeburgh:

Nov. 3rd 59

My dear Jim,

It didn't need a chance glimpse of you in Sloane Street the other day to remind me I hadn't written to you about, nor yet returned, "Music from Mars." It has been on my conscience a long time — altho' there's an extenuating circumstances [sic] like a really tremendous pressure of work, writing and performing since you came back from your holiday, and then a long visit, also working hard, to Italy from which Peter and I only got back last week. All the same I know I should have written before, altho,' I fear, what I want to say isn't easy.

I don't honestly feel I can recommend your and Paul's piece to Boosey and Hawkes. You know, I'm sure, how very sympathetic I feel towards you and the kind of music you write, and I'd love to have you published by them — but I don't feel that it is suitable work to start off with, and if I am going to introduce you to them it must be with something in which I am completely confident.

It would take a long time to tell you exactly my reactions. Most likely they would bore you, especially as you've had the work done, and most likely were very pleased with it, and judging by the photos you sent you should have been pleased with the *look* of it. But were you honestly pleased with the *sound*? Did the young people *really* make an effect with their voices — didn't you really want more power and incisiveness than they could give you? You have written some technically *very* difficult stuff, and must have had some very special children if it really worked. From my experience in giving young people stuff to sing, I've come to the conclusion that the music must be lyrical (not only a dramatic expression), well boiled, ideas clear and precise — o, and many other things too long to go into now. I feel it is all a bit too complicated, elaborate for young people. This is, anyhow, what *I* feel — many people I am sure may feel differently, and I see no reason at all to try B+H off your own bat, and, of course, Jim, I wish you, sincerely, luck with it! Another thing which, alas, may fight a bit against it is its very particularly public school background — it does all seem a bit too "Wellington" for the bulk of the schools who do this kind of thing — alas, practically no public or private schools.

I wish I could say this rather than write it — only life is so difficult, if I'm in London I'm up to the eyes with dreariness, otherwise it's work and travel. But one day we *must* meet, and you tell me you forgive me for being difficult, narrow-minded, short-sighted — but at least honest?

Much love to you both

Ben

Bernard's response to this letter was understandable:

I tried to make it not too difficult for boys, though Ben rather annoyed me, good friend though he was. I was frightfully cross with him because it didn't seem any more difficult than lots of things he'd written for the young — and the boys had performed it without any problems, in fact brilliantly.

Fortunately, Hammer was more enthusiastic about commissioning Bernard to compose the score for *The Hound of the Baskervilles.* At the end of Conan Doyle's original tale, Holmes suggests to Watson that they unwind by going to see Meyerbeer's opera *Les Huguenots*. However, for the main "Syllable" theme of Hammer's version of the tale, Bernard, instead of Meyerbeer, again looked to Scriabin's "mystic chord"[5] (see chapter 4, example 6). More of a harmonic than melodic idea, this theme is based on a Scriabinesque collection of **perfect** and **augmented fourths**, but Bernard added a note that isn't present in Scriabin's chord. In the example below, it is the A, which creates a typically Bernardian clash of a **major second** with the G that immediately precedes it (third stave down).

James Bernard, *The Hound of the Baskervilles* 1M1, bars 7–9 (short score)

Example 6

This "Syllable" theme actually takes six false starts before being fully stated in the seventh bar, when it coincides with the main title projected on the screen. Scored for resonant brass and strings, it is perhaps one of Bernard's most impressive themes (*Dracula* notwithstanding). Sometimes, Bernard will simply present the chord without breaking it up, associating the harmony with the Hound itself.

The main title music also introduces two other themes. The first of these is associated with the ruined "Abbey" that is supposed to be haunted by the terrible Hound of Hell (see example 5 of this chapter). The second is the motif for Sir Hugo Baskerville, the aristocrat whose wicked ways were the cause of the legend back in the eighteenth century.

James Bernard, *The Hound of the Baskervilles* 1M1, "Sir Hugo" theme

Example 7

The next music section is one of the few occasions where a track from one of Bernard's previous scores was reused in a different film. It occurs in the lavishly mounted and beautifully photographed eighteenth-century prologue during the sequence when Sir Hugo, drunk with lust, wine and rage, chases an unfortunate girl who has managed to escape from his clutches. As Sir Hugo mounts his horse, sets loose the hounds and pursues the girl over the moor, we hear the music that so effectively accompanied Van Helsing's pursuit of Dracula in the final section of Bernard's previous Hammer film. It is just as effective in this new context but also acts as an unintentional reminder that both Baskerville Hall and the set for the ruined abbey are actually re-dressings of sets that had previously appeared in *Dracula*. Bernard was unhappy about this reprise because he had in fact written music especially for this chase. The only part of it we do hear is derived from the "Sir Hugo" theme, and in its dotted rhythm and rising pitch it also resembles the moment in Act II of Wagner's *Parsifal* when the wicked magician, Klingsor, summons his army of slain, but now reanimated zombie warriors:

James Bernard, *The Hound of the Baskervilles* 1M2, bars 4–5 (reduction)

Example 8a

Richard Wagner, *Parsifal*, Act II, scene 1 (reduction)

Example 8b

When Sir Hugo arrives at the brooding ruins of the abbey on the moor, we hear a flute play the "Abbey" theme. It is there that Sir Hugo murders the girl and soon after meets a grisly end, accompanied by the terrifying "Hound chord."

The scene now moves to the Baker Street chambers of Sherlock Holmes (played by Peter Cushing); the famous detective is being told the legend of "The Hound of the Baskervilles" by Dr. Mortimer (Francis De Wolff). Under Mortimer's commentary we hear the "Syllable" theme stated quietly by a bassoon. Mortimer suspects that the recent death of Sir Charles Baskerville was somehow connected with this legend. The truth of the matter is that a poor relation of Sir Charles, Clive Stapleton (Ewen Solon), has used the legend to cover his own murderous tracks. He keeps a dog starved of food in a disused mine and uses it to attack his victims in the hope of eventually inheriting the Baskerville estate. Now, only Sir Henry Baskerville (Christopher Lee) stands in his way.

Sir Henry might well have fallen victim to Stapleton's next murderous scheme had it not been for Holmes' quick thinking. During a meeting between them at Sir Henry's London hotel, a tarantula emerges from Sir Henry's tobacco pouch and crawls up the sleeve of his jacket. In the music that accompanies this scene, Bernard returned to the clashing major seconds on ***sul ponticello*** strings that had been so effective in the Quatermass films. After Holmes, Watson and Mortimer kill the spider, we hear a new idea (again harmonized in major seconds), which forms the basis for a motif that will be associated with moments of "Danger" in subsequent scenes:

James Bernard, *The Hound of the Baskervilles*
3M1, bar 27, "Danger" motif

Example 9

Watson later meets Stapleton's daughter Cecile on the moor, but she runs away when he explains that he is staying at Baskerville Hall. Bernard provides her with "Running" music, which has the same sort of urgency and energy as the string and glockenspiel passage of Wagner's music for Siegfried's Rhine Journey in *Götterdämmerung*:

James Bernard, *The Hound of the Baskervilles*
4M1, bar 5, "Running" motif

Example 10a

Richard Wagner, *Götterdámmerung Vorspiel*, "Siegfried's Rhine Journey" (reduction)

Example 10b

Watson pursues her and falls victim to the treacherous Grimpen mire. As he struggles to escape being sucked under, we hear a variant of the "Danger" motif on cellos and basses. The low register and contrary motion, together with the clashing harmonies, create a graphic musical image of Watson's struggles:

James Bernard, *The Hound of the Baskervilles* 4M1, bars 20–21

Example 11

Later that night, Watson and Sir Henry see a light from a lantern being used as a signal on the moor. This is symbolized musically by two flutes sustaining an augmented fourth. They rush out to investigate, accompanied by a "Pursuit" motif that elaborates the **tritone** tension of the "Lantern" chord (example 12).

James Bernard, *The Hound of the Baskervilles* 5M1, bars 1–4 (reduction)

Example 12

When Holmes explores the mine another new idea is introduced. Holmes realizes that Stapleton keeps the Hound in the mine, a location that accounts for the fact that the sound of the dog's howls seems to come from the bowels of Hell. The "Syllable" motif accompanies the opening shots of this section, followed by the "Danger" motif, which, this time, is propelled by a characteristic Bernardian snap rhythm:

James Bernard, *The Hound of the Baskervilles* 7M1, bars 13–14 (reduction)

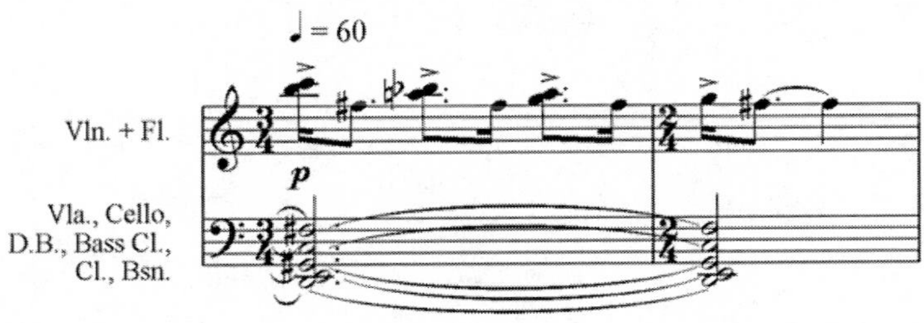

Example 13

(This rhythm had, incidentally, been used before by Britten not only in *Peter Grimes* but also in the rather different context of "The Splendour Falls" from the *Serenade for Tenor, Horn and Strings.*)

Bernard's motifs continue to appear in the manner that Debussy once ironically described as "visiting cards"[6] when discussing Wagner's leitmotif system, and the film is brought to a rousing conclusion by a recapitulation of the opening title music. Despite a rather disappointing Hound, which Christopher Lee claimed "made a nonsense of the story,"[7] the film served Conan Doyle well in its convincing recreation of Victorian England. Andre Morell's performance also ensured that Watson would no longer be portrayed as the bumbling idiot of Nigel Bruce in the Universal *Sherlock Holmes* series. Although Bernard's music was not so crucial to the film's success as it had been in *Dracula* and *The Curse of Frankenstein,* it nonetheless consolidated Hammer's muscular and immensely popular approach to horror subjects.

7

Serial Killers

"Have you ever had your bones scraped, Captain?"

Chung King (Christopher Lee) in *The Terror of the Tongs* (Columbia/Hammer, 1961)

At the end of 1959, Bernard found himself involved in the first of what were eventually to number four scores for oriental Hammer adventures. Two of them exploited the murderous activities of Indian and Chinese cults, another constituted Bernard's only score for a war film, set in Japan, and the fourth turned out to be Hammer's final vampire movie, which relocated Count Dracula in China for *The Legend of the Seven Golden Vampires* (Hammer-Shaw, dir. Roy Ward Baker, 1974).

The Stranglers of Bombay was based on the real-life atrocities of the "Thuggees" who worshipped and murdered for the Indian goddess, Kali. Sensationally, if absurdly, advertised as having been shot in "Strangloscope," the film starred Guy Rolfe as Lewis, an English Army officer who uncovers an unholy alliance between one of his fellow officers and this murderous organization. Fresh from his villainous role in *Windom's Way,* Marne Maitland aided and abetted the devilish doings of the cult's high priest (played by George Pastell), while the mutual friend of Britten and Bernard, David Spencer, appeared as Gopali, the treacherous brother of Lewis' Indian servant, Ram Das.

For both *The Stranglers of Bombay* and *The Terror of the Tongs* Bernard again made effective use of percussion instruments. In *Stranglers,* many of the scenes played out by the followers of Kali beneath the shadow of her huge statue are accompanied by the kind of native drumming that would feature in Bernard's scores for *She* and *The Plague of the Zombies.* The main title, however, consists of two ideas. The first exploits the tension of the **tritone** as well an energetic rhythm. The second constitutes the film's "Syllable" theme:

James Bernard, *The Stranglers of Bombay*, main title themes (transcription)

Example 1a and 1b

The first idea is later greatly slowed down and syncopated when Lewis' arrogant fellow officer, Connaught-Smith (played by Allan Cuthbertson), is murdered and his body is dragged to a ritual pyre by the Thuggees.

Another theme also recurs throughout the film; Bernard was to use it again in slightly modified form for *The Kiss of the Vampire.* It is first heard when Lewis tries to discover who is responsible for the abduction of his faithful Indian servant, Ram Das, and consists of a rising **minor triad**, the top note of which falls by a **semitone**. Significantly, there is no music at all for the film's most sadistic scene, in which Lewis is spread-eagled by the Thuggees under the blazing sun while a snake is let loose to kill him (he is saved by a mongoose at the last minute). The only music to accompany the fight between the two animals is again native-style drumming.

Music for a rather different film came next. *A Place for Gold* (British Lion, 1960) was another documentary directed by Basil Wright, this time with a script by Paul Dehn. It had been commissioned by the Worshipful Company of Goldsmiths, whose publicity brochure described how the film follows "a young silversmithing apprentice, from his 'binding' in the traditional ceremony at Goldsmiths' Hall to his 'freeing' there as a qualified craftsman at the age of 21. There are shots of this historic building, of some of the fine collection of antique and modern plate there, and of pieces from the British Museum and the Victoria and Albert Museum. The film describes some of the present and past activities of the Worshipful Company of Goldsmiths, shows how a silver jug is made by hand from a flat sheet of metal, and visits some of the leading British silver factories and shops. It is a unique blend of history and art both old and new."[1] Opening at the Warner Theater in London, *A Place for Gold* rather uncomfortably shared a program with the highly influential "kitchen sink" melodrama, *Saturday Night and Sunday Morning* (Bryanston/Woodfall, dir. Karel Reisz, 1960), the photographer of which, Freddie Francis, later became a well-known Hammer director.

Hammer soon beckoned Bernard back to the fold. *The Terror of the Tongs* was set in Hong Kong rather than India but was nonetheless very much the same kind of story as *The Stranglers of Bombay.* Christopher Lee played Chung King, the leader of the infamous Red Dragon Tong, while Marne Maitland appeared as a crippled freedom fighter. Geoffrey Toone, a long-standing personal friend of Bernard, made his only Hammer appearance as Capt. Jackson Sale, who joins forces with Maitland after the murder of his own daughter by the dreaded Tong assassins. Eventually, their struggle proves successful and Lee is sent to another ignoble death.

Bernard's score is again terse and to the point, consisting of a handful of Oriental themes and plenty of tuned percussion along with tam-tams and cymbals. The main theme is, in fact, no more than a cycle of **perfect fifths**:

James Bernard, *The Terror of the Tongs*, main title themes (transcription)

Example 2a and b

Accompanied by resonant tam-tams, this simple idea nevertheless conveys a powerful sense of oriental mystery. A secondary idea is based on a **pentatonic** scale (see example 2b on page 108).

Capt. Sale's daughter, being a true English girl, is represented by an "occidental" **major**, sometimes **minor arpeggiated triad.** But a pentatonic theme returns for the music that accompanies scenes in the casino which is run by the Red Dragon (example 3).

James Bernard, *The Terror of the Tongs*, "Casino" theme (transcription)

Example 3

The love theme that accompanies the scenes between the half-caste girl, Lee (played by the very French Yvonne Monlaur), and Toone's rugged captain is also pentatonic:

James Bernard, *The Terror of the Tongs*, "Love" theme (transcription)

Example 4

Debussyian **whole-tone scales** also appear in the music for scenes set in the opium den, which Sale visits as part of his search for the headquarters of the Red Dragon Tong.

Modest though his musical contribution was for this equally modest film, Bernard received a rare official letter of thanks from executive producer Michael Carreras, who complimented him on his "excellent" music which "certainly has given the picture a tremendous 'lift.'" The conductor on both films was, as usual, John Hollingsworth, who had by now developed the friendly habit of driving Bernard to the recording sessions at Anvil Studios in Beckonsfield. Bernard recalled:

> I used to take a taxi over from our little house in Chelsea in Bramerton Street on the morning of a recording at the crack of dawn because we were starting at nine or something hideous, and would arrive outside John's flat in Latimer Court, ring the bell and either go up or he'd come down and then we would embark in his little red MG. He liked little dashing, low sports cars. On the way home we'd always stop off at a particular pub and have some drinks with great relief that all had gone well. He was a great giggler and such fun.
>
> I never actually questioned John about his association with Hammer. I think he was quite happy. Otherwise he'd never have stayed as long as he did. When people have died you think, "Oh, I wish I'd asked him more about that," but he wasn't a person who exactly invited heart-to-heart chats.

John had a charming sense of humor. The old Gainsborough films used to be introduced by a lady in lovely period dress with a big hat. She would turn and smile; that was the logo for Gainsborough films. John called it a "picture hat." So, when we'd come to a bit in the middle of all this dramatic Dracula stuff or Frankenstein stuff where I got a chance to have my little romantic bit, he would turn to me and say, "What? Have you got your picture hat on, dear?" before he started conducting. So we always had nice little jokes like that.

In those days I was usually able to do all the composing before I started orchestrating, which is what I still prefer to do. We used a copyist called Phil Jones. He looked rather like a Roman Emperor. He was a tall, florid man and we used to call him the Emperor Jones. I think he lived in Emperor Gate — that's why! His wife often used to come and collect my scores and take them back to Phil. Presumably he would then do photocopies and let John have them but John never used to say, "Jimmy, when can I have the score?" To all intents and purposes, as far as I was concerned, he hadn't seen anything until the day before the recording because sometimes I only finished the score, in those early days, during the night before the recording and I would take the last two or three scores down to the studio with me. Phil Jones would come down to the studio and be copying the parts for the afternoon during the morning session, doing it all by hand. So, John seemed not to need a great deal of time to prepare. He picked up things extremely quickly. He was obviously highly musically talented.

Ken Cameron and Eric Tomlinson, who used to run the Anvil Studios, were extremely efficient. We had to have the film projected so we could see if the music was fitting the images; and there used to be time to stop if we were not sure if something had worked.

When the lunch break came, John and I would always go off to a pub. I think we used to get about an hour and a half, so there was plenty of time to get some lunch; but Tony Hinds always vanished during that time. He never said, "Shall we go and have lunch together?" Where he went I don't know. I remember saying to John, "What does Tony do?" and he said, "I don't know." Tony had a slight remoteness about him, and yet I remember many years later in 1976, when Paul Dehn had died and we had a memorial service for him in St. Martins-in-the-Fields, somebody looked out from a pew and said, "Oh, Jimmy, you probably don't know who I am. It's Tony Hinds," and I thought, "How sweet of him to have taken the trouble!"

Unusually for a producer, Hinds attended nearly all of Bernard's recording sessions during his time with Hammer. An amateur cellist himself, Hinds enjoyed the whole process but rarely interfered. In fact, the only time he remembered having made a composer rewrite something (not Bernard, he hastened to add) was when the score in question (he couldn't remember which) came to an end with a major chord. Hinds felt this sounded too happy for a horror film, and insisted on a minor chord to bring the film to a close instead.[2]

Around this time, Bernard was also involved in several West End theater productions. Marne Maitland appeared (as "Mr. Sharma") in one of them, Peter Mayne's *The Bird of Time* at the Savoy Theater in the Strand. The action was set in Kashmir and the music was appropriately performed by members of the Asian Music Circle. Mayne was another of Bernard's wide circle of friends and wanted him to be involved with the music, though Bernard didn't actually write any original material for it: "I think I just sort of advised the Indian players," he recalled.

In 1959, thanks to his friendship with Jeremy Spencer, the brother of David Spencer, Bernard had written a song called "Ben's Blues" (about which the composer can remember nothing at all) for the Arts Theater Club production of Andrew Sinclair's play *My Friend Judas,* in which Spencer had played the role of Winkie Lloyd-Limsden. Michael Redgrave went on to employ Bernard for his 1959 adaptation of Henry James' short story *The Aspern Papers* at the Queens Theater. This starred Redgrave himself in the role of "H.J.," Beatrix Lehmann as "Miss Bordereau" and Flora Robson as "Miss Tina." Concerning the attempts of a literary historian to prise from an old woman the letters that were sent to her from a fictional American poet called Aspern, the play required music for a poem especially written for the production by Redgrave himself. It was called "The Green Hussars" and Bernard was only too happy to oblige. He received a letter of congratulation from Flora Robson, who performed the song on stage:

> 18 Milner Street
SW3
Aug 21st 1959
>
> Dear Mr. Bernard,
>
> Please forgive me for being so long in thanking you for your kind wishes on the first night. I am very shy about the song, as it is so long since I sang in public, but the cast adore it, and Michael particularly. We have done everything to stop applause, as it creates the atmosphere so well for the scene, but at the matinee yesterday it broke out willy-nilly.

Bernard sent her flowers and she wrote again with the news that Noël Coward had attended one of the performances and had "loved the song," which apparently all the stagehands were whistling as well. Redgrave was delighted with the music: "your song has all the effect I had hoped for," he wrote in a letter to Bernard. "It is really a beautiful moment."

In 1961, Bernard went on to provide the songs and incidental music for the Old Vic's production of *Twelfth Night*, which starred several actors who would later leave their mark on Hammer horror films as well: Joss Ackland, Barbara Jefford and Alec McCowen.[3] However, it was the strictly non–Hammer Tom Courtenay, who played Feste the clown, who had most to do with the music. There were more opportunities for musical revue as well. Bernard had followed up his contribution to *At the Lyric* in 1953 with *Going to Town* at the St. Martin's Theater in 1954. In 1961, Joan Heal, Beryl Reid and George Rose[4] starred in *On the Avenue* at the Globe Theater in Shaftesbury Avenue; Bernard provided music for the numbers "Bertie and Gertie" and "Who Goes Home?," both setting lyrics by Dehn. Much of the remaining music for the Revue was by Richard Addinsell, with whom Bernard also became acquainted, though, as he recalled:

> We never knew him well. His longtime friend was a very well known haute couturier called Victor Steibel. We went to their house once. They lived in Victoria Road, Kensington, or just off, where Hardy Amies also lived. (He was another friend of ours.) I remember going to the house once and Richard Addinsell was playing a record of Nat King Cole playing the drums! Funny the odd things one remembers. They were tremendous opera fans. They always had the same seats (in row E in the stalls) and we often saw Richard and Victor coming in.

Addinsell had enjoyed a long-standing working relationship with Joyce Grenfell and she became a much closer friend of Bernard and Dehn:

> We had a cozy dinner in our very small house in Bramerton Street and invited the Grenfells and some friends, Lord and Lady Huntingdon with their two daughters.[5] After dinner we were sitting in our very small drawing room having after dinner chat and I or Paul asked Joyce to do a sketch, explaining that the girls might not have seen her perform before. She said, "Yes, of course," and without any fuss she got up and did about two numbers, which were just as funny as when she was on stage.

Much as he enjoyed working in the theater with actors, and writing film scores, Bernard was still trying to make his mark as a concert composer. Alan Frank at OUP next suggested that he might care to write a piece for the Scandinavian concert saxophonist Sigurd Rascher.[6] Bernard agreed and Rascher came to see him. The result was Bernard's only music to have been composed using Schoenberg's **serial** system. Coincidentally, that same year saw the release of Hammer's *The Curse of the Werewolf,* with its innovative serial score by Benjamin Frankel. Though Bernard was never to employ serial techniques in any of his own film scores, the opening notes of his Passacaglia seem to be a mirror image of the opening bars of his score for *Dracula Has Risen from the Grave*:

James Bernard, *Passacaglia for E♭ Saxophone and Piano,* bars 1–8

Example 5a

Example 5b

The main theme of the Passacaglia is also virtually identical to the four-note "Syllable" theme for *Nosferatu,* which was to be written some thirty years later:

James Bernard, *Nosferatu*

Example 5c

Also, the piano part of the Passacaglia's eleventh variation resembles the music that accompanies the awakening of the Baron's brain transplant patient in *Frankenstein Must Be Destroyed* (Warner-Pathé/Hammer, dir. Terence Fisher, 1969).

James Bernard, *Passacaglia, Variation 11,* bar 1

Example 6a

James Bernard, *Frankenstein Must Be Destroyed*
9M3, bar 37 (reduction)

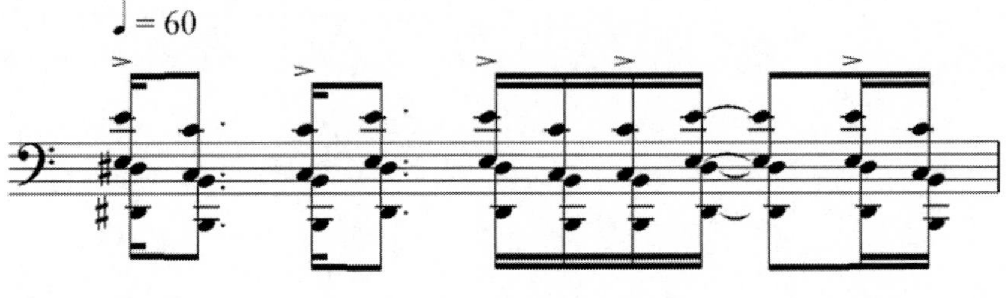

Example 6b

Bernard provided two pages of typescript analysis for his complex saxophone piece and hoped that by following Schoenberg's example he might attract the favorable attention of fashionable critics. This was, after all, the period when the total-serialism of Pierre Boulez and his followers maintained a stranglehold on art music:

> The Passacaglia is built on a slow ground of 8 bars, containing all 12 notes of the chromatic scale. The basic rhythm is 3/2 and the basic tempo 𝅗𝅥 = 54, though these are frequently subdivided into smaller and quicker units.
>
> The ground is repeated 13 times, though not always in the bass—at Figs. 7, 8, 9, 10 and 11 in its retrograde inversion. The first time, it starts on the note G flat and ends on G natural a semitone higher; the second time, it begins on G natural and ends on A flat a semitone higher; the third time, it begins on A flat (G sharp) and ends on A natural—and so on, till it has been played at every level of the chromatic scale. The 13th time, like the first, it begins on G flat and ends on C natural.
>
> The saxophone announces the ground unaccompanied. The piano then takes it up and repeats it 6 times at chromatically rising levels, as already explained, and

decorated in various ways. The saxophone then accompanies it with 6 variations of the inversion of the ground. There is then a short cadenza, after which the piano resumes its decorated and chromatically rising repetitions of the ground, but now in its retrograde inversion. This retrograde inversion is played 5 times, while the saxophone plays five variations of the direct retrograde form of the ground.

Finally, at the 13th repetition of the ground, it is played (as at the beginning) by the saxophone and in its original form. The piano right-hand also plays the ground in octaves with the saxophone while the left-hand plays, note-for-note, its inversion.

A later addition to the manuscript records that Bernard thought it all "far too cerebral!" Britten, who was duly informed of the project, also expressed some doubts:

Red House
[undated]

My dear Jim,

Thank you for your nice letter (please forgive this hasty p.c. in reply to it)—I was glad to hear your news, and to know that things are going so well with you. I hope to see Colin's[7] *12th Night*—and I hear he's very pleased with your music. I was, frankly, a bit surprised about the 12-tone adventure, but one can only judge for oneself and I find it terribly inhibiting and academic. But for goodness' sake don't forget the *performers* point of view and the natural technique of the instruments! I'm interested to hear of Paul's idea for Lennox[8]—that sounds fine.

Love to you both

Ben

Rascher, on the other hand, was most enthusiastic about Bernard's serial piece and performed it widely throughout Canada and the United States. He wrote Bernard several letters charting audience reaction:

July 8 61

Dear Mr. Bernard

Finally a word from that far-away Saxophone player across the water!

During the last 2 months I gave the Passacaglia a good deal of treatment and found it to be thoroughly playable. Not only the "easy" sections, but the others as well [...]. All sections are good, and can be played in proper time. Moreover, I found the work to be well organized, possessing a clear structure and the sequence of metamorphosis is logical.

[...]

I gave the premiere a week ago in Kansas [June 27, 1961]. At the Emporia College there have been for the last 10 years a few summer concerts—chamber music one evening, followed by a solo recital the next evening. It was my fourth visit to this college in 10 years—and I was glad to be able to bring so outstanding a program.

[...]

P.S. There were *no* reviews!

Sadly, Rascher didn't feel that there was any great chance of the work being published as "there are as yet not enough saxophone players who play such music (and *can* play it—your piece is really not very easy!)" That passing comment virtually killed the piece, and after a while both the Passacaglia and Rascher disappeared from view. "That's why I gave up writing concert music," Bernard explained, "because nothing seemed to happen."

But a great deal more was just about to happen, and not just in the gloriously gory world of Hammer horror. The spirit of musical comedy was in the air.

8

Virtue and Danger

"I bleed, I die, I faint, I fall."

Lord Foppington in "Hurry Surgeon!"
from *Virtue in Danger*

As a change from the horror of Hammer films, Bernard now enthusiastically acted on a long-standing ambition to write a musical in collaboration with Dehn. The idea was to adapt Sir John Vanbrugh's 1696 restoration farce *The Relapse; or Virtue in Danger* for the musical stage. It was an ambitious undertaking. Eighteen numbers in all were required, many of which were inspired by lines from the original play such as "Fortune, thou art a bitch!" and "Stand off old Sodom!" As the original program notes explained:

> The composer (apart from one uninhibited salute to Handelian oratorio in "Hurry, Surgeon!") has tried to avoid period *pastiche* by restricting 17th century influence solely to a song's melodic line, on which astringency of harmony and flexibility of rhythm can make their modern comment.
>
> But both the author and composer of the adaptation felt that it would be madness to stand too far back from the play's full restoration flavor and therefore, just as no words have been used in the lyrics which might baffle Vanbrugh's eye, so no instruments are used in the 11-piece orchestra (harpsichord, harp, wind and drums) which could offend his ear.
>
> Vanbrugh is buried not far from the Mermaid Theatre at St. Stephen's Walbrook; and (though every effort has been made to preserve the cream of his dialogue in this two hour adaptation) he will undoubtedly turn in his grave if *all* the dialogue is attributed to him.[1]

Of course, the score took a while to write, and meanwhile there were plenty more commissions from Hammer. Bernard's first film of 1961 brought him into contact with the American director, Joseph Losey:

> He was the only director I worked with who took a deep interest in what I was going to do. When Hammer suggested me to him, I don't think he knew anything about me. So I was summoned to meet him before I definitely got the job. At that stage he was living in a very comfortable house or apartment in Montpellier Street

Double Act: Paul Dehn and James Bernard at work on *Virtue in Danger*, 1962 (photograph Julieta Preston).

> in Knightsbridge—apparently alone. I got on very well with him, although other people have found him difficult. It's all to do with how one approaches people, isn't it?—and always trying to see the good things in people rather than the bad. I was a bit daunted because I'd read the script and he'd said something like, "Well, how do you visualize the music?" That's a question which it's almost impossible to answer. At any rate, I said something. I should think I talked absolute balls. But whatever I said it must have gone down all right because after that one meeting it was agreed I should do the score. Then he pretty much left me and John Hollingsworth to do it, though he did come to the recording session.
>
> Paul and I went on being friendly with Joe. We saw him from time to time. We never became on the terms of asking him to come to dinner but he would ask us to come to something that he was involved with like a press showing of a film. He was a rather interesting man. I'd love to have known him better.

Based on an obscure novel by H.L. Lawrence called *The Children of Light*, *The Damned* (Columbia/Hammer-Swallow, dir. Joseph Losey, 1963) is Hammer's most overtly political film and was appropriately filmed in the same year that Dehn's volume of satirical anti-nuclear verse *Quake, Quake, Quake* (Hamish Hamilton, London, 1961) was published.[2] With the Cuban missile crisis only just over a year away, Oliver Reed recalled that during the shooting of *The Damned* Losey "used to take the cast out to dinner and preach anti–Bomb stuff to them. He was very left of centre...."[3] Anticipating many of the motifs in later films such as *A Clockwork Orange* (Warner/Polaris, dir. Stanley Kubrick, 1971) and *Apocalypse Now* (Omni Zoetrope, dir. Francis Coppola, 1979), *The Damned* tells how a wealthy American, Simon (played by Macdonald Carey), is mugged by leather-clad teddy-boy hooligans. However, his encounter with mindless violence in the streets of Weymouth pales into insignificance when later, in the company of Joan (Shirley Anne Field), he discovers a secret government establishment inhabited by radioactive children. These are "the damned" of the title and are being trained by a scientist, Prof. Bernard (Alexander Knox), to inherit the world after the "inevitable" catastrophe of nuclear war. An attempt to liberate the children fails, by which time Simon, Joan and King are all contaminated with radioactivity themselves.

The movie was set on the south coast of England (the bleak landscape of Portland Bill adding much to the general sense of isolation and paranoia), so Bernard was now given his first opportunity to compose sea music. Not until his score for *Nosferatu* in 1998 would he have such an opportunity again. The opening establishing shot of a deceptively tranquil seascape is accompanied by three flutes playing the film's main motif. Bernard then introduces the "modern" timbre of the alto saxophone, though this was actually Hollingsworth's idea. As well as connoting modernity, the alto (and later tenor) sax also contribute a melancholy and desolate atmosphere, perhaps inspired by Debussy's Rhapsody for Saxophone (composed between 1903–05). Bernard's main motif is based on alternately falling and rising **major seconds** and **perfect fourths**. The fourths expand into **fifths**, then **sixths** and ultimately into **sevenths**, before returning to fourths, thereby creating an effective musical metaphor for rising and falling waves.

The melancholy quality of falling seconds and fourths had been exploited by Chopin in his D minor Prelude (Op. 28, No. 24, composed between 1831–39):

James Bernard, *The Dammed* 1M1, bars 13–20

Example 1a

There are also Wagnerian echoes. Charles Rosen has pointed out Wagner's debt to Chopin for much of the "characteristic" harmony of *Tristan und Isolde*.[4] An element of *Tristan* he does not mention, however, is the Chopin-inspired cor anglais melody

Frédéric Chopin, *Prelude Op. 28, No. 4*, bars 8–10

Example 1b

played by the shepherd at the beginning of Act III. Tristan, mortally wounded, lies in the grounds of his castle in Brittany, while the shepherd, posted on the battlements, looks out over the deserted sea for a glimpse of Isolde's ship. Indeed, Wagner's description of this scene is similar to the opening shot of *The Damned*: "The situation is supposed to be on rocky cliffs; through openings one looks over a wide sea to the horizon." Wagner's melancholy cor anglais melody therefore looks back to Chopin and forward to *The Damned*.

Richard Wagner, *Tristan und Isolde*, Act III, Vorspiel (reduction)

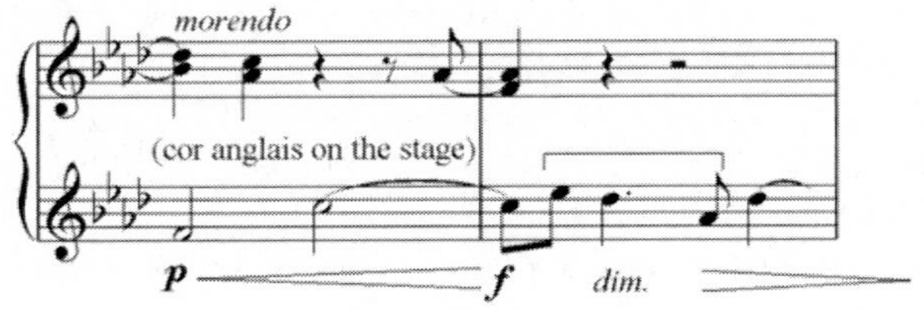

Example 1c

Britten had also exploited Wagner's combination of Chopinesque melancholy with sea imagery in *Peter Grimes*, and experience of that opera had no doubt influenced Bernard in *The Damned*. The connotative history of these maritime fourths certainly helps to account for the peculiarly evocative power of so simple an idea. A little later on in reel one, the quietly intoned **tritones** of the first and second trombones further unsettle the apparently tranquil seascape (and are again reminiscent of passages in the sea interludes of *Peter Grimes*):

James Bernard, *The Damned* 1M1, bars 9–10

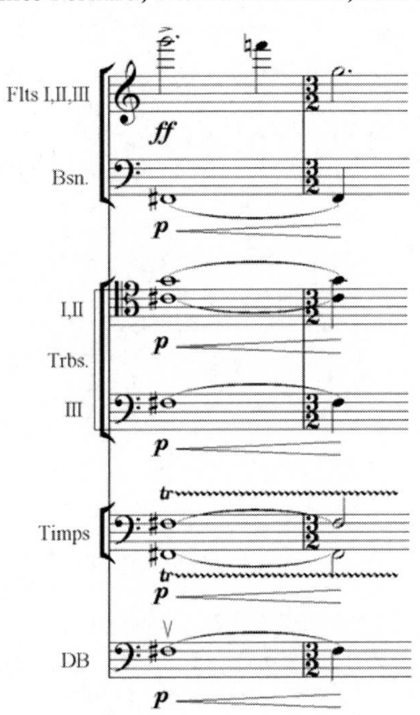

Example 2

The troubled image of a lonely ocean is then rudely interrupted by the appearance of the leather boys with Joan. They are loitering in sunny Weymouth by a nineteenth-century clock tower that symbolizes both a past age of security and the fact that time is running out for twentieth-century civilization. The song that accompanies this scene ("Black Leather Rock") was one of Bernard's few "pop" numbers, scored for electric guitar, tenor sax and percussion. However, as he felt inexperienced in this type of scoring, he happily entrusted its arrangement to Douglas Gamley.[5] The melody of the song is in fact related to the opening seascape motif. The second and third measures of the first bar feature a rising second and another falling fourth. However, accelerated and given a jaunty dotted rhythm, the relationship is not immediately obvious:

James Bernard, *The Damned* 1M2, bars 1–2 (tenor sax only)

Example 3

The lyrics were written by Evan Jones:

Black leather, Black leather
Smash, Smash, Smash.
Black leather, Black leather
Crash, Crash, Crash.
Black leather, Black leather
Kill, Kill, Kill
I've got that feeling— Black Leather Rock.

Jones' other draft version (with further alternatives in square brackets) wasn't used in the finished film, but it is more specific about the nihilistic, anti-militaristic stance of the film:

Black leather, black leather, stand at ease
Altogether chaps, stand at ease.
If I'm going to die tomorrow
I won't die in a [bright red coat] pin-striped suit
Let me die in a black leather jacket
With a rope around my throat.
Tomorrow perhaps
We'll be blown off the maps
[So] all together chaps
[Stand at ease]
Let's rock and roll.

Bernard may not have been familiar with how to score this type of song but the words certainly echo the premise of his and Dehn's Oscar-winning idea for *Seven Days to Noon.* Bernard remembered Oliver Reed coming to his house in Bramerton Street to learn the tune: "It always embarrasses me now because I think the lyrics are awful! Oliver was very affable. He sat by me at the piano and I played it through for him."

The scene set on Simon's boat, after Joan has escaped from her brother and the gang, begins with a falling **tone** on oboes, over which the flute plays the "Seascape" motif. This tranquil falling tone will eventually turn into a wailing **semitone** fall at the end of the film when we hear the radioactive children pleading for help after their foiled attempt at escape.[6] At the moment, however, the adventure has only just begun. The sinister trombone tritones return when Prof. Bernard arrives at the secret military establishment where the children are imprisoned. There is also an **open fifth** involved here, created by the D natural of the bass trombone:

James Bernard, *The Damned* 3M1, bars 14–15

Example 4

Open fifths have a hollow ring to them, lacking, as they do, the **third** that identifies major or minor tonality. Wagner had exploited the hollow sound of open fifths in his *Ring* cycle, where they symbolize the illusory nature of the Tarnhelm, the magic helmet that allows the wearer of it either to become invisible or to change his shape. One might also say that the appearance of an open fifth, surmounted by a tritone at this moment in *The Damned*, signifies both the artificiality and the horror of the situation.

When Simon and Joan arrive on the island where the military establishment is based, Bernard expands his "Seascape" motif with **triplet** and **semiquaver** decoration in the manner of Debussy's *L'Après midi d'un faune* (composed between 1892–94):

James Bernard, *The Damned* 3M2, bars 5–12

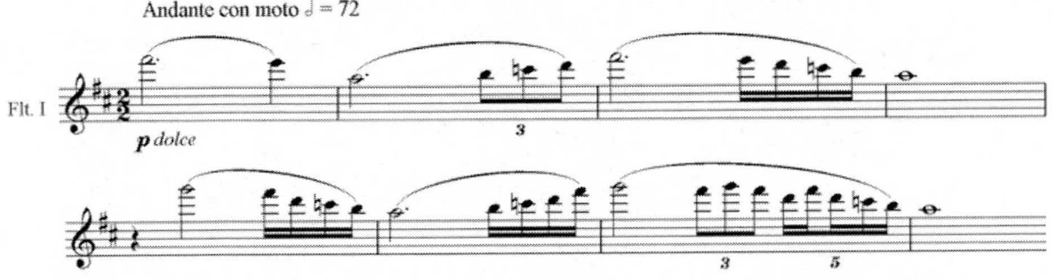

Example 5a

Claude Debussy, *Prélude à l'après-midi d'un Faune*, bars 1–2

Example 5b

Later, in the fifth reel when Simon and Joan find themselves in the cave and meet the radioactive children for the first time, the falling semitone that originally accompanied the "Seascape" motif is transferred to string orchestra, giving an elegiac suggestion of what a Bernardian string quartet might have sounded like if he had written one.

Not all of the music that Bernard composed for this film was actually used in the finished print because Losey made some changes during the final dubbing:

> I do remember at one point in the session he said he wanted something a bit different from how I'd written it, so I got into a huddle with John and we decided that I should plink the piano strings at a certain moment. When we did it, Joe said, "Yes! That's just what I wanted!" but I don't think you could hear it in the finished film!

Losey's perfectionism resulted in expenses that Hammer would have preferred not to have incurred and relations became so strained between director and producer (Hinds) that the recording session of *The Damned* was the only one of Bernard's sessions that Hinds refused to attend.

With the final shots of Simon and Joan sailing to their radioactive death over a halcyon sea, Bernard brings back the "Seascape" motif, and exploits the ethereal, other-worldly sound of string **harmonics**. As the cries of the children pleading for help emerge from their prison, the music similarly wails with the falling semitone mentioned above.

The contrast between apocalyptic science fiction and restoration comedy couldn't be greater, but as soon as *The Damned* was completed Bernard returned to *Virtue in Danger*. *The Damned* wasn't actually released until May 19, 1963, by which time *Virtue in Danger* had already been playing at the Mermaid Theater for just over a month (it opened on April 10). Bernard recalled,

> It played to packed houses, but got rather mixed reviews because it was quite frivolous and they thought some of our numbers were rather rude. People were more easily shocked back then. We were crushed flat by Harold Hobson who was then the critic of *The Sunday Times*. The critics are so unkind. Harold Hobson tore it to shreds. He thought it was indecent but most people seemed to enjoy it. We played to packed houses for two months and then because it was the policy of the Mermaid Theatre, it had to come off or be transferred to the West End. So H.M. Tennent decided they were going to transfer and the only theater which was available was The Strand. That's quite a big theater and this was really an intimate musical, which worked brilliantly in the Mermaid but it simply didn't work at the Strand. Also we coincided with a tremendous heat wave and that always empties theaters. We only survived a month. Someone remembered us though because

Derek Nimmo, I remember, chose "Wait a Little Longer, Lover," which Pat Routledge sang, as one of his Desert Island Discs.

"Wait a Little Longer, Lover" was the song that most of the critics singled out as well. Philip Hope-Wallace wrote in the *Manchester Guardian* on April 18:

> [...] Paul Dehn's rhymes are often neat and witty, and the music by Jimmy Bernard has a touch of style which is all too often wanting in this kind of thing. One tune in particular, as put over by the widow Berinthia of the play — a delightfully graceful and sly performance by Patricia Routledge — to the words "Wait a little longer, lover," would catch anyone's ear instantly. And there are three or four good numbers besides.
>
> A sterner view could be taken as well: namely that though these ditties are pleasant they add nothing whatever of intrinsic worth to Vanbrugh's old play and indeed tend rather to impede and halt its racy and ribald progress. If this be a means of introducing a new public to an old classic then it will serve. But if purists (if the word can be applied to those who fancy Vanbrugh's salty frivolities and improprieties) had their way they would probably prefer the play neat, without the musical furbelows or the kind of mopping and mowing of maids and candle carrying lackeys who infest Wendy Toye's brisk balletic production.
>
> But this formula seems popular. The bawdry is "safe," being fancy dress stuff. The music sweetens the half sexual vulgarity of the plot. Even the most respectable can sit back and smile, even tap time with the foot. It may not be "Gilbert and Sullivan" and, being a musical, it can hardly be "shocking," can it? [...]

In the July edition of *The Gramophone,* Michael Cox reviewed the Original Cast Recording:

> The lyrics are excellent and make one wish that Paul Dehn would write more often for the light musical theater. James Bernard's music shows great respect for the period of the play both in style and orchestration but fully exploits the rhythm and wit of more modern music. The romantic songs are not exactly memorable, with one exception — the duet "Wait a Little Longer, Lover" between Berinthia and Worthy (Basil Hoskins) sticks in the mind very happily. The point numbers and ensembles are very strong and splendidly performed — a cast of real actors with real voices is what every musical needs and this one very definitely has. This is undoubtedly the best English musical for many months and I strongly recommend it for its wit and originality.

James Bernard, *Virtue in Danger*, "Wait a little longer, lover," bars 3–6

Example 6

The large cast also included the Shakespearean actor, Alan Howard, Richard Wordsworth, who had starred in *The Quatermass Experiment*, and Lewis Fiander, who would later appear as Howard in Hammer's *Dr. Jekyll and Sister Hyde* (MGM-EMI/Hammer, dir. Roy Ward Baker, 1971). John Moffatt, who took the part of Lord Foppington, became another good friend of Dehn and Bernard, and he wrote them a letter after the first night:

Flat A
59 Warrington Crescent
London, W 9
11th April 1963

Dear Paul and Jimmy

I'm so tense with excitement after the first night that I can't sleep so I've huddled on me dressing-gown and am up by 3 A.M. and trying to consume me mind with other things than mere reading.

The first thing I want to do is to thank you both for the *beautiful* present you have given me. I've never had such a gorgeous first-night present before — and "come to that" I've never had such a gorgeous part. I can't tell you how much I enjoy playing it and working on it and rehearsals have been such fun and it's such a splendid company and you have both been so kind and helpful and encouraging that on occasion I've felt like bursting into tears because everyone is so nice.

I hope the show will run and run and run, and — even if in August heat-waves the weight of me costume on the one hand and the intolerable warmth of me wig on t'other destroy me constitution, I'll perish content.

Bless you both. Love

John M.

Sad to report, *Virtue In Danger* did not "run and run." The following year, in October, Moffatt was in New York where he saw Bernard's latest Hammer film, *The Kiss of the Vampire.* He duly sent a postcard of the Empire State Building:

New York
[Postmark] 10th Oct 64

Have just seen and heard "Kiss of the Vampire" at the R.K.O. Palace, Broadway. V. scary, and that piano piece nearly sent me off into catalepsy!

The piano piece to which Moffatt referred was the celebrated "Vampire Rhapsody," Bernard's gothic reply to Addinsell's "Warsaw Concerto," which had started a veritable fashion for what the American press came to label "tabloid concertos."[7] *Kiss of the Vampire*, like *The Damned*, took some time to appear. Shooting was completed in October 1962 but it had to wait until January 1964 to be released. Bernard, indeed, had had to interrupt work on *Virtue in Danger* to complete the music, much of which, including the "Vampire Rhapsody," had to be scored before shooting could begin:

I had to do the waltz sequence for the masked ball of vampires. That was all choreographed by Leslie Edwards, who was at the Royal Ballet and was an old friend

Richard Wordsworth as Coupler in *Virtue in Danger.*

of John Hollingsworth's—a charming, sweet man. The waltzes are again orchestrated by Douglas Gamley. Because the time for writing *Kiss of the Vampire* was very short, I'd written the tunes of the waltzes to be played on the piano when they were filming that sequence and I remember ringing John and saying, "John, I'm a bit desperate, and as the waltzes are very straightforward Viennese type waltzes, do you think we could get someone to orchestrate them?" He said, "Oh, yes, Douglas Gamley!" So Douglas did the excellent orchestrations of them and it was he who played the solo piano.

The Kiss of the Vampire was the last time Bernard was to work with Hollingsworth, who died of tuberculosis soon after completing the film. Bernard remembered the rather sad end of Hollngsworth's life:

> In the last few months of his life, he began to get terribly breathless—I remember that. And I also remember once taking him to Verdi's *Atilla* at Sadlers Wells opera house. Paul was working or couldn't come so I took John, and I always remember thinking, "What a fool I am!" because I'd booked seats at the front of the dress circle and I remember poor John puffing and blowing as we went up the stairs. He was very uncomplaining and just said, "Do you mind if I take it slowly?"—which we did and we enjoyed the evening but I realized that he wasn't very well.
>
> He had a very good friend who lived in the same block of flats called Terry Earle, and John let Terry have a key to his flat. Because John lived alone, I suppose it's always good to have a neighbor or a chum who's got a key. Terry often used to call by and say, "Hi, John," or tap on his door. Then, one morning, he had tapped on his door several times and there was no reply. So finally he went into the flat and found poor John lying dead, sprawled across the bed. It seems he'd died all alone in the night while trying to reach the telephone.

With Christopher Lee still reluctant to repeat his most famous role as Dracula, a different vampire character, and actor, had to be found for *The Kiss of the Vampire.* Noel Willman happily obliged and created the role of Dr. Ravna with considerable relish: "I found playing a vampire great fun," he later confessed.[8] Barry Warren played both Ravna's vampire son, Carl, and the imposing grand piano for the important scene in which he mimed not only to Chopin's D flat Nocturne, Op. 27, No. 2, but also Bernard's famous "Vampire Rhapsody." Hollingsworth gave him the necessary tuition and was well-satisfied with the result, even going so far as to suggest that he should take up the piano professionally.[9]

Title page of a piano selection of tunes from *Virtue in Danger*.

Just as Bernard's music for *Quatermass* anticipated the musical idiom of Bernard Herrmann, the action of *The Kiss of the Vampire* had several things in common with the approach of Alfred Hitchcock. The denouement, in which Ravna's vampire cult is destroyed by a squadron of bats, anticipated the climax of Hitchcock's

The Birds (Universal, dir. Alfred Hitchcock, 1963). Indeed, this was one of the reasons why the release of *The Kiss of the Vampire* was delayed. Universal, who owned both properties, gave Hitchcock priority over a low-budget British horror film. Also like Hitchcock, Don Sharp's directorial approach focused on suspense and the conflict between illusion and reality rather than straightforward horror. In so doing, he created one of Hammer's most successful vampire films, its classic status being confirmed some years later by being satirized in *The Fearless Vampire Killers, or Pardon Me, Your Teeth Are in My Neck* (MGM/Cadre/Filmways, dir. Roman Polanski, 1967).[10]

Young honeymooners, Gerald and Marianne Harcourt (played by Edward de Souza and Jennifer Daniel) are stranded in Bavaria, close by the mysterious Chateau Ravna. After being invited first to dinner (where Marianne is almost overcome by the hypnotic effect of the "Vampire Rhapsody") and later to a masked ball at the Chateau, Marianne is abducted and Gerald brusquely informed the following morning that he arrived at the chateau alone. Desperate, Gerald seeks the help of Prof. Zimmer (Clifford Evans) who reveals his plan to defeat the vampire cult that destroyed his own daughter. Gerald and Zimmer rescue Marianne and an occult invocation ensures that the forces of evil are compelled to destroy themselves.[11]

Bernard's score is again tightly constructed. All its themes ultimately derive from the opening flourish of the main title music, and it is this tautness of construction that accounts for the score's immense success.

Example 7 contains the major theme of the film, which is associated with the character of "Dr. Ravna." As is so often the case with a Bernard score, the theme is harmonized in **minor seconds**, as is the next motif, "Fear," which also grows out of the opening flourish.

The "Dr. Ravna" theme is then clearly spelled out in **crotchets** following the syllables of his name and title:

James Bernard, *The Kiss of the Vampire*
1M1, bar 3 (violin I only)

Example 7

James Bernard, *The Kiss of the Vampire*
1M1, bar 6 (violins only)

Example 8

James Bernard, *The Kiss of the Vampire*
1M1, bar 12 (violin I only)

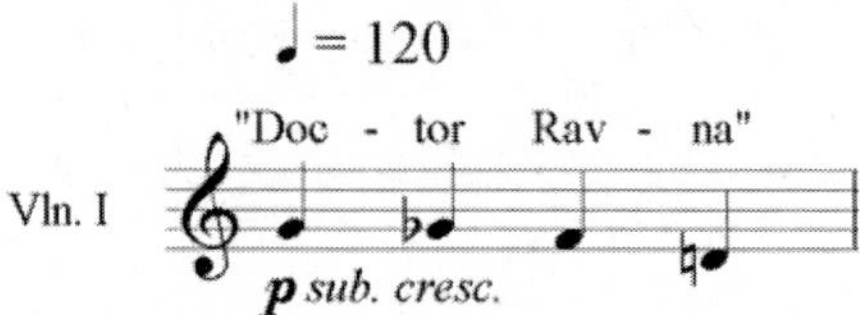

Example 9

After this has been **sequenced** for six bars, the piano makes its first solo entry with the main theme of the subsequent "Vampire Rhapsody":

James Bernard, *The Kiss of the Vampire* 1M1, bars 18–21 (piano only)

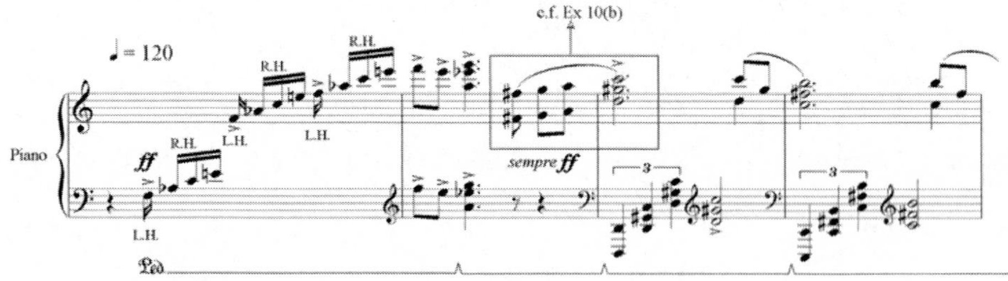

Example 10a

Again, Bernard relies on a single chord to create his harmonic effect here. Constructed from **augmented** and **diminished** fourths, it too has an affinity with Scriabin's "mystic chord" (see chapter 4, example 6). Also, Scriabin's piano piece, *Poëme Satanique*, with its markings "***dolce appassionata***" alternating with "***riso ironico***" and "***amorossissimo***," graphically suggest a diabolic eroticism with which his mystic chord, because of its inherent tritone tension, is most often associated. Indeed, in his ninth Piano Sonata, subtitled "The Black Mass," Scriabin went so far as to mark one passage "*avec une douceur de plus en plus caressante et empoisonée*" ("with a sweetness that is increasingly caressing and poisonous"):

Alexander Scriabin, *Piano Sonata No. 9*, Op. 68, bars 97–98

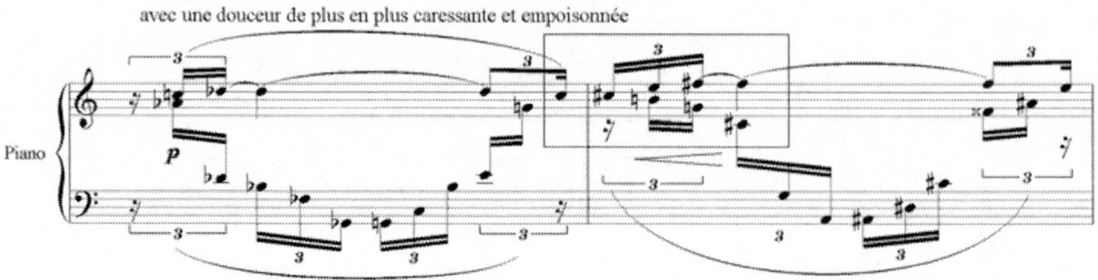

Example 10b

The outline of Scriabin's melody is also similar to that of the "Vampire Rhapsody." If Scriabin's E natural in the triplet of the second bar of example 10b was a D sharp, it would indeed be identical to Bernard's phrase. Scriabin described his music as conveying the ecstatic pleasures of erotic love, the "bite of hyenas," "the sting of serpent" and "the maggot of satiety,"[12] pleasures no doubt enjoyed to the full by members of Dr. Ravna's vampire cult. But Scriabin was not Bernard's conscious model for the music of *The Kiss of the Vampire*. Instead, he looked to Liszt, as Scriabin had done before him. The piece that particularly impressed both composers was Liszt's *Mephisto Waltz No. 1* (composed between 1859–62), with its emphasis on tritone harmony and florid virtuosity. A theme associated with Prof. Zimmer, and especially the occult ceremony over which he presides at the climax of the film, finds a parallel in Liszt's *Mephisto Waltz*, though it is somewhat disguised in Liszt's piece due to one of the notes being an ***acciaccatura***:

Franz Liszt, *Mephisto Waltz No. 1*, bars 95–98

Example 11a

James Bernard, *The Kiss of the Vampire*
9M1, bars 41–42 (vibraphone only)

Example 11b

Also, Bernard's harmony here is reminiscent (though obscured by **added notes**) of a chord at the beginning of the languorous middle section of the *Mephisto Waltz*:

Franz Liszt, *Mephisto Waltz No. 1*, bars 340–341

Un poco meno mosso (ma poco)

Example 12a

James Bernard, *The Kiss of the Vampire*
9M1, bars 15–16

Andante con moto ♩ = 72

Vln. I
Vln. II
Vla.
Vcl.
D.B.
mp

Example 12b

As mentioned in chapter five, the "Vampire Rhapsody" itself has certain things in common with Liszt's late piano work, the *Valse oubliée No. 1* (composed in 1881). Though Bernard's Rhapsody is in 4/4 rather than Liszt's 3/4, the pitch contour of Bernard's melody is indeed similar to Liszt's piece:

James Bernard, *Valse oubliée No. 1*, bars 17–18

Example 13a

James Bernard, *The Kiss of the Vampire* 3M2, bars 7–8

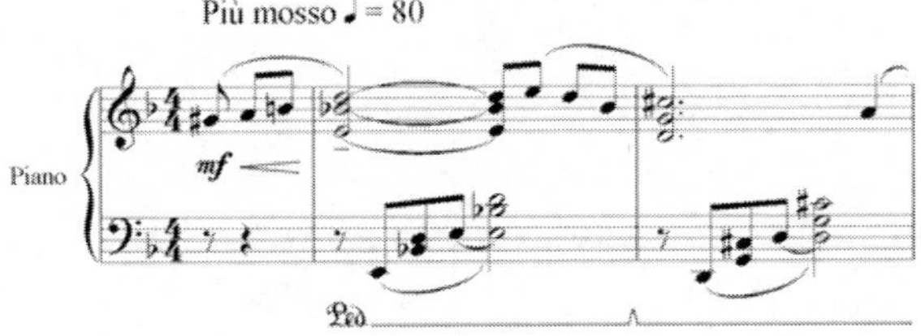

Example 13b

After the main title section, the action takes us to a forest track somewhere in Bavaria (actually Hammer's favorite forest location of Black Park, not far from Pinewood Studios in Hertfordshire). A suitably oily clarinet intones a theme associated with the Chateau Ravna, the first three notes of which are a reordering of the second, third and fourth notes of the opening flourish:

James Bernard, *The Kiss of the Vampire* 1M2, bars 1–4, "Chateau" theme

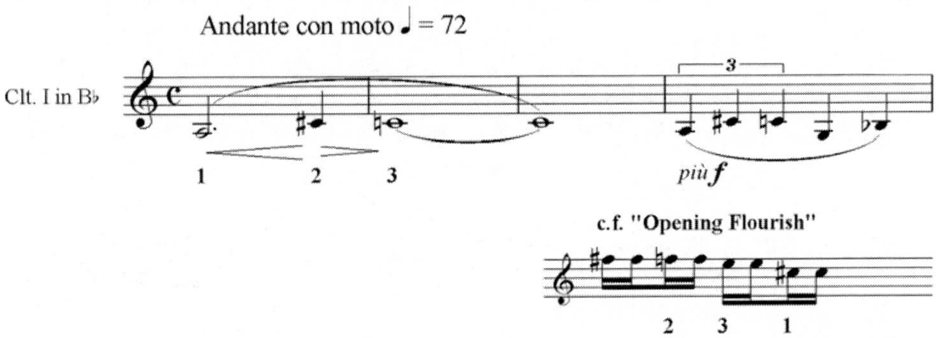

Example 14

Like so much of the material in this score, the "Chateau" theme is based on the interval of a rising diminished fourth (which Bernard sometimes spells as its **enharmonic** equivalent of a major third).

Gerald and Marianne's car breaks down and Marianne is left alone while Gerald goes off in search of petrol. The "Chateau" theme returns and tritones accompany the shot of Ravna in his turret, spying on Marianne with his telescope. As Ravna leans out of the window, the oboe introduces what will later form the second part of the "Vampire Rhapsody" (also derived from the opening flourish):

James Bernard, *The Kiss of the Vampire* 1M2, bars 20–22

Example 15a

James Bernard, *The Kiss of the Vampire*
3M2, bars 44–45, second theme of "Vampire Rhapsody"

Example 15b

A storm rises and a tree is uprooted. Marianne runs away and the "Chateau" theme is speeded up, forming a motif that will become associated with "Flight" in future scenes:

James Bernard, *The Kiss of the Vampire* 1M2,
bars 31–32 (violin I only), "Flight" motif

Example 16

This motif provides the required sense of momentum, building up to the shock of Prof. Zimmer's appearance when Marianne runs into him. Her surprise is emphasized by more clashing minor seconds. Later, after Marianne and Gerald have settled into a mysterious hotel, a carriage brings Ravna's servant with an invitation to dine at the chateau. A clarinet in its low **chalumeau** register intones the "Chateau" theme, followed by the strings with "Dr. Ravna." The Doctor may not be on screen but his presence is certainly felt in the music (one of the ways in which Bernard employs his leitmotifs in a truly Wagnerian manner).

A new theme occurs at the beginning of the third reel with the appearance of Tanya, the vampire girl. She had once been the daughter of Bruno, the hotel manager, before Ravna introduced her to his vampire cult. As Gerald and Marianne are ushered into the music room of the chateau, Tanya slips out on her mission to exhume Prof. Zimmer's daughter, whom she now believes to be one of the undead. Unknown to her, however, Zimmer has already prevented this eventuality, having driven a spade through the heart of his daughter's corpse as she lay in her coffin during the film's prologue.

Bernard marks Tanya's clarinet theme "***desolato***" and it is best described as an **atonal** rumination around another diminished fourth, having evolved out of the "Chateau" theme. One can also compare its effect to the Shepherd's tune in Act III of Wagner's opera *Tristan und Isolde*, already discussed with regard to *The Damned*:

James Bernard, *The Kiss of the Vampire* 3M1, bars 1–4

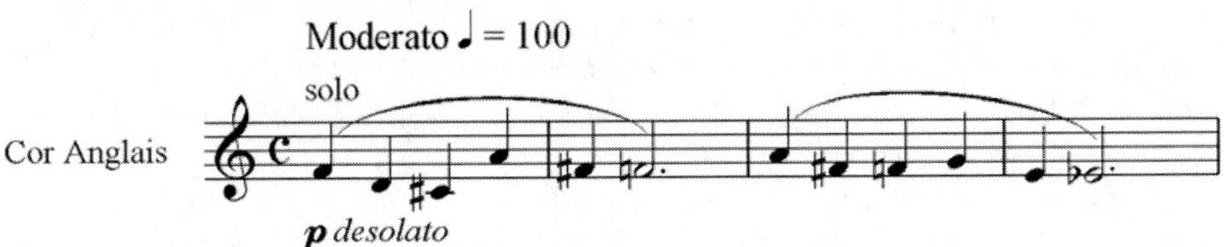

Example 17

Later, when Tanya's mother, Anna, weeps over a photograph of her lost daughter, we hear another melody for solo flute, which Bernard marks "***triste ed espressivo***." This melody is placed securely in C minor but its phrase structure is similar to Tanya's "atonal" theme. Both these wind solos could be regarded as metamorphoses of an original "Tanya" theme that we never hear, the lack of an "original" theme nicely suggesting what is missing in Tanya: her human soul.

We now come to the scene in which Carl performs the "Vampire Rhapsody."[13] The flow of the piece is interrupted by cutting to a shot of Prof. Zimmer. He has been bitten by Tanya after having interrupted her at work by the graveside of his daughter. Immediate action is called for if he is to avoid infection from the vampire's kiss, so he stokes up the fire, takes a gulp of brandy and thrusts his hand into the flames to cauterize the wound. Accompanied by pounding **crotchets** in the lower strings, we hear the "Chateau" theme once more. After a **crescendo**, there is a sudden change of **dynamic** as the strings play a suitably discordant **note cluster** (incorporating two more tritones as well as more minor seconds). Such a device increases the tension of the moment as we realize what Zimmer is planning to do. One might call this musical effect "dynamic framing"—not in the way the term was used for Bernard's experimental film *The Door in the Wall*, but rather with regard to the contrast of **diminuendo** and crescendo as a means by which to emphasize an action.

As the pitch and volume of this discord rise to ***fortissimo***, we cut suddenly back to Ravna's music room where the Rhapsody is by now in full flow. The musical spell has begun to take effect on Marianne, and Bernard reflects this by introducing string **trills** and vibraphone **tremolos**. These rise in pitch, clashing with the piano's harmonies to create a disorientating and hypnotic effect. The accompaniment rises in volume and reaches a climax when the piece is interrupted by an anxious inquiry from Gerald, who at long last suspects that not all is as civilized at it appears to be: "Marianne!" he shouts. "Are you feeling all right?" Carl stops playing but the strings continue, clashing high-pitched minor seconds against his final E minor chord. The strings are held quietly for four and a half bars to suggest the hypnosis slowly losing its effect.

After breakfast the following morning, Gerald and Marianne are told a little more about the mysterious Prof. Zimmer: He never eats with Bruno and Anna but lives instead on cognac and sour cream. Although we have already been introduced to Zimmer, this is the first time we hear his musical theme. It too can be traced back to the opening flourish, being a retrograde version of its second, third and fourth pitches (and consequently an inversion of "Dr. Ravna": the mirror image of evil, so to speak).

"Zimmer," "Dr Ravna," and the "Chateau" theme are all combined after Carl and his sister, Sabena, come to the hotel to invite Gerald and Marianne to a party at the chateau. Zimmer interrupts to inform them that the weather seems to be improving, fully aware that vampires cannot tolerate bright sunshine. The siblings hurry away and the section ends with a musical reminder of what happened to Tanya when she accepted just the same invitation: flute and oboe play her atonal "soulless" motif.

The series of waltzes that accompany the dance sequences at Dr. Ravna's party are for the most part thematically unrelated to the rest of the score, but the opening notes of the first waltz are actually the same as the "Chateau" motif:

James Bernard, *The Kiss of the Vampire* 5M1A, bars 6–9 (strings only)

♩. = 58

Vln. I + II

Vla.

Cellos

Bass.

Example 18

The third waltz has an element of **chromaticism** as well as a pitch contour that also relates to the opening flourish:

James Bernard, *The Kiss of the Vampire* 5M1C, bars 1–3 (strings only)

Example 19

The last dance is a ***galop***, marked ***Allegro con Forza***. Towards the end, Bernard superimposes the "Chateau" and atonal "Tanya" themes as Carl exchanges his mask for one that is identical to the one that Gerald is wearing. By this means he intends to lure Marianne away from the party and imprison her. The "Vampire Rhapsody" returns on the piano as he beckons her to follow him. Realizing too late that she is the victim of a trap, Marianne finds herself locked in an upstairs room.

Bernard claims not to have been particularly attracted to the organ but several of his scores contain imaginative writing for it. When Marianne is introduced to the vampire cult in reel six, Scriabin-like accumulations of fourths on the organ accompany her entrance, the solemnity of the situation being emphasized by soft strokes on a gong.

Having been thrown out of the chateau and told by Carl that he arrived there alone, Gerald now finds himself in a distinctly Hitchcockian situation. Back at the hotel, everyone denies the existence of Marianne, and Gerald begins to think he is going insane. However, just as Wagner's orchestral **leitmotifs** can provide information that is not forthcoming from the lips of his singers, so Bernard's "Chateau" theme tells us where Marianne really is. Of course, Bruno and Anna have been coerced into this conspiracy of silence by Ravna himself. Desperate, Gerald seeks the help of Prof. Zimmer who, living up to his German surname, seems to spend most of his time in his cluttered hotel room. This he has converted into an occult laboratory with the aim of eventually destroying Ravna and his acolytes.

First, however, Marianne must be rescued, during which operation the "Flight" motif plays its part. The music slows down when Gerald and Zimmer waylay the Ravnas' servant and crush him with a stone obelisk in the chateau courtyard. Tritones, again built over an open fifth as in *The Damned*, accompany the action here; and for the final incantation, Zimmer's theme is accompanied with the Lisztian harmonies discussed above. The vibraphone adds a suitably unearthly quality.

Ravna wants Marianne back, however, and summons all his willpower to force her to return to the chateau. As he concentrates, the brass intone his theme to the accompaniment of one of Bernard's very effective but equally simple **ostinati**:

Marianne forces her way through the windy forests to the "Flight" motif but is

James Bernard, *The Kiss of the Vampire* 9M2C

Example 20

prevented from arriving at her destination by Gerald and the priest he has summoned to help. They are only just in time, because Zimmer's magic is about to begin. Sensibly, there is no music during the climactic bat attack but there is plenty of flapping and screaming. Afterwards, Marianne recovers from her trance and we hear Zimmer's theme quietly played on flutes. As the bats fly away to the opening flourish, Ravna and his vampire followers lie dead in the chateau. The "Vampire Rhapsody" returns on full orchestra, now as a slow waltz (allowing us to compare it even more successfully to Liszt's *Valse oubliée*). The final bars, however, do not resolve onto the D major chord we expect. Instead we are left with a **dominant** chord, clouded by tritone harmonies above it. The resulting effect undermines our sense of triumph; and, sure enough, Hammer had plenty more vampires ready to take Dr. Ravna's place.

9

Femmes Fatales

"I heard a voice, I think the softest and yet most silvery voice I ever heard."

Ludwig Horace Holly in H Rider Haggard's *She*[1]

After completing the music for *The Kiss of the Vampire* Bernard went on an African safari in the company of his brother Bill, Bill's wife Meg and Stephen Courtauld (Meg's cousin). Bill and Meg had a house outside Salisbury (now Harare) in Rhodesia (now Zimbabwe); they later took their guests to stay with Stephen Courtauld's parents, Sir Stephen and Lady Virginia Courtauld, at their amazing treasure-trove of a house—"La Rochelle"—outside Umtali, a small town near the border with Mozambique. Sir Stephen and Lady Courtauld, incidentally, had previously lived in a lavishly decorated Eltham Palace in Kent.

So it was on the Gorongoza Game Reserve in Mozambique that the intrepid party made their safari. Bernard described the adventure in a long letter to his "darling mama," listing the many birds and animals he had seen: "20 lions, lots of elephants" and "huge herds of every kind of buck, wart-hogs with their endearingly hideous babies, hippos in soggy clusters in the river and *masses* of birds." He celebrated his thirty-eighth birthday with a picnic in "a rather burnt Mozambique forest." Courtauld had insisted on treating him to a selection of chocolate confections, most of which unfortunately melted in the heat, but some survived intact. Everything else was washed down with wine, papaws, tangerines and cucumbers.

Brother Bill also took them to the original Zimbabwe ruins, after which the country is now named. These had an extraordinary atmosphere of a lost civilization, and there was one narrow passageway along which Bernard's sister-in-law, Meg (who had strong psychic reactions to places), refused to walk, owing to the overpowering sense of evil she sensed to be emanating from it. Even so, they climbed the ruins both in the bright sunshine of the day and again after dark in the brilliant cold moonlight, and the place reminded Bernard of Rider Haggard's epic 1897 novel, *She*:

> *Kôr is fallen! No more shall the mighty feast in her halls, no more shall she rule the world [...]. Kôr is fallen! and her mighty works and all the cities of Kôr [...] are for the wolf and the owl and the wild swan, and the barbarian who comes after. Twenty*

> *and five moons ago did a cloud settle upon Kôr, and the hundred cities of Kôr, and out of the cloud came a pestilence that slew her people, old and young, one with another, and spared not.*

Appropriately, it wouldn't be long after that exciting real-life adventure that Bernard would compose the music for Hammer's film adaptation of *She*. Meanwhile, in the wake of Hollingsworth's death, Marcus Dodds was contracted to supervise and conduct Bernard's next two Hammer scores, *The Gorgon* and *The Secret of Blood Island* (Universal-International/Hammer, dir. Quentin Lawrence, 1965). Like his predecessor, Dodds had conducted ballet but Bernard never got to know him well. He remembers him as being friendly but "in a rather distant way":

> Marcus was very laid-back about it all. It was he who suggested I use a wordless voice in conjunction with a Novachord for *The Gorgon*. An **Ondes Martenot** would have been good but that would have been too expensive. I think we even considered that, but an Ondes Martenot would have had to be specially brought from France and probably played by Yvonne Loriod.[2] So, Marcus said, "You know there's really quite a good instrument. It's like an electric piano, called a Novachord." I put the voice in complete unison with the Novachord: just a single line to create the ambivalent sound we needed, so that the audience wouldn't know if it was human or inhuman.[3]
>
> I'd also written a line in the score with a lot of little crosses along a single stave and wrote the word "Hiss" over them. The master percussionist, James Blades, regarded this as a challenge, so we stopped while he tried out every effect he could think of; but nothing quite worked, so we had to abandon it. He was always so charming, like a benign gnome, and after the session he came up to me and said: "I've been asked to do some strange things, particularly by Ben Britten, but I've never been asked to produce a hiss before."

Located in the village of Vandorf, the mysterious Castle Borski is haunted by the spirit of Megaera, one of the three terrible Gorgons, who were so horrific of visage that anyone who set eyes on them was instantly turned to stone. In Hammer's atmospheric and dream-like retelling of the tale, Megaera's spirit possesses a beautiful amnesiac, Carla Hoffmann (played by Barbara Shelley). She is the assistant of Peter Cushing's Dr. Namaroff, the sinister and obsessed director of the Vandorf Medical Institution.

After the mysterious death of his son, Dr. Heitz (Michael Goodcliffe) arrives to undertake his own investigation. One night he is drawn to the castle and is literally petrified by the Gorgon. Later, his other son, Paul (Richard Pasco), continues to search for the truth and is followed to Vandorf by his university professor, Meister (Christopher Lee). Dr. Namaroff suspects the truth but protects Carla out of possessive infatuation with her. In the final scene, he too is killed by the gaze of the Gorgon and it is left to Meister in his role as a nineteenth-century Perseus to deliver the final blow by cutting off the Gorgon's head with a sword.

The main title music is based on an **augmented triad**. Liszt had employed augmented triads to horrific effect in his musical recitation *Der traurige Mönch* (published, 1860), with its piano accompaniment of a poem by Nicolaus Lenau about the Gorgon-like ghost of a monk whose face is so sad that anyone looking upon it is driven to suicide. Similarly, Liszt's *Faust Symphony* (published in 1854) opens with a sequence of **broken** augmented triads to convey the brooding, mysterious personality of Faust, a dabbler in occult wisdom. Bernard punctuates his augmented triads with chords, which pound out a typically clashing **major second** (here spelled as a **diminished third,** its **enharmonic** equivalent):

James Bernard, *The Gorgon* 1M1, bars 11–14 (reduction)

Example 1

The film opens in the studio of the young artist, Bruno Heitz. His model informs him that he is to be the father of her child. Heitz hurries off to inform her father, pursued by the girl. As he leaves, we hear a theme that conveys a powerful sense of melancholy by means of an **appoggiatura:**

James Bernard, *The Gorgon* 1M2, bars 1–3 (reduction)

Example 2

A particularly melancholy coloring of this melody occurs in reel two at the conclusion of the courtroom scene in which Prof. Heitz claims that there is a conspiracy of silence in the village of Vandorf. The melody is played by the somber timbre of a *Tristan*-esque cor anglais. Many of the early cues in this score are very short and introduce no new material, and the film's "Love" theme, associated with Carla and Paul, is not introduced until reel four. One of Bernard's most haunting themes, it is responsible for a great deal of the strangely poetic atmosphere of the film and it is interesting to compare its falling **fourth** (in the third bar of example three) with the falling fourth of the "Ayesha" theme in *She;* see example 12a later in this chapter:

James Bernard, *The Gorgon* 4M2, bars 1–6, "Love" theme (reduction)

Example 3

When Paul visits his brother's house and is caught in a storm in the garden, he catches a glimpse of the Gorgon reflected in the pond. He runs back to the house, and falls unconscious to a string glissando. Awakening in Dr. Namaroff's hospital, his delirious condition is nicely conveyed by the discordant tremolo strings playing ***sul ponticello***. After his recovery, Paul determines to exhume his father's body to discover the real cause of death. As he does so, the Novachord builds up a chord based on fourths in much the same way that Malcolm Williamson had done on the organ in his score for *The Brides of Dracula*. Whereas Williamson had paid tribute to Bernard in that film, here the roles have been reversed.

Paul is eventually drawn to Castle Borski itself. Flutes and oboe suggest a rather sinister bird song thanks to the presence of another **augmented fourth**:

James Bernard, *The Gorgon* 7M1, bars 1–9

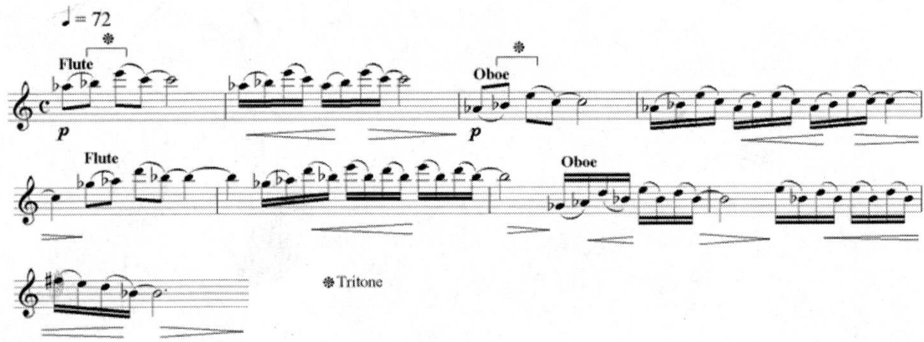

Example 4

Actually, example four is derived from the "Siren" motif usually sung by the solo soprano. All that has happened here is that the notes have been rearranged. (In the first bar of example four, the E and C have been reversed.) When Paul sees Carla sitting regally on a throne in the castle, the Novachord informs us that it is she who is possessed by the spirit of the Gorgon.

They embrace and their "Love" theme is surrounded with the kind of harp arpeggios that Bernard was later to develop for the love scenes in *She*. Carla implores Paul to take her away from Vandorf at once, but Paul insists that they wait until the mystery has been solved. Despairingly, she realizes that by then it will be too late for both of them.

The "Love" theme is impressively metamorphosed when Paul visits the castle in the final reel of the film and there encounters Namaroff, who is waiting to decapitate the Gorgon. The tranquility of the theme is suitably disrupted by more augmented triads:

James Bernard, *The Gorgon* 9M3, bars 12–15 (reduction)

Example 5

The music that accompanies the final decapitation of the Gorgon intriguingly echoes the final bars of Act II of Wagner's *Parsifal* when the enchanted flower garden of the magician, Klingsor, is spectacularly destroyed:

James Bernard, *The Gorgon* 9M3A, bars 5–7 (reduction)

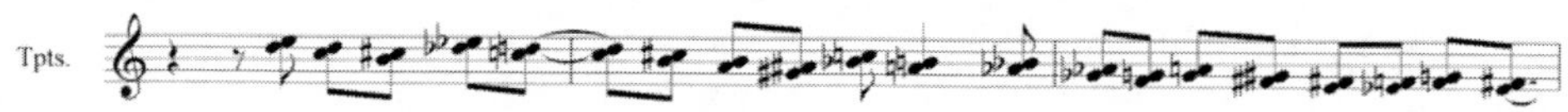

Example 6a

Richard Wagner, *Parsifal*, end of Act II (reduction)

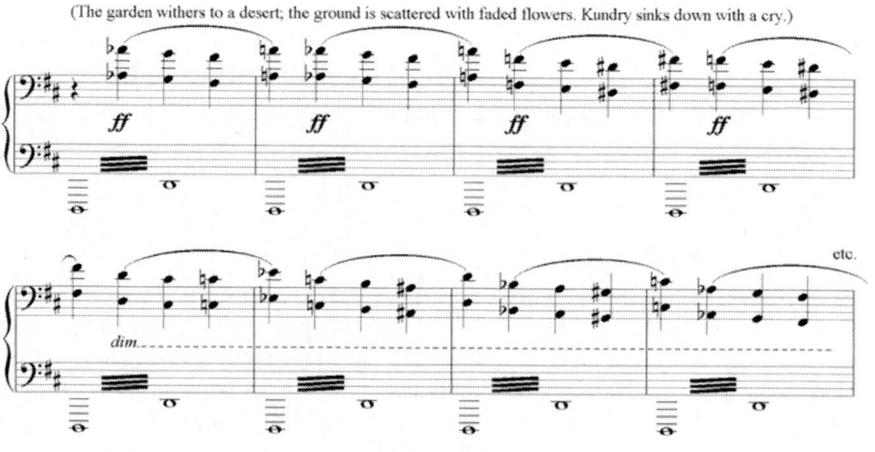

Example 6b

The Gorgon may have been destroyed, but Barbara Shelley returned as a rather different kind of potentially fatal woman in *The Secret of Blood Island*. In this prequel to Hammer's earlier *The Camp on Blood Island* (Val Guest, Columbia/Hammer [Anthony Hinds], 1958) she played a secret agent who parachutes into occupied Malaya and is shielded from discovery by British POWs. Bernard's score for this drama was the most minimal one he ever composed. As he explained:

> A lot of the score for *The Secret of Blood Island* is rather repetitive and tuneless because I was trying to depict the never-ending, grim and cruel conditions in a Japanese prisoner of war camp. Marcus didn't want to look at the score before the recording session; he was like John in that. It was Philip Martell who always wanted to see what was going on all the time.[9] But I do remember Marcus worrying that my score for *The Secret of Blood Island* looked rather too repetitive and relentless. When he saw the finished film, though, he agreed that it works really rather well.

Basically, the score consists of two themes in which rhythm is more important than melody. Indeed, the rhythms are often intoned by percussion alone, like Morse code. The first theme is introduced in the prologue in which Shelley makes her final escape (the rest of the film is told in flash back):

James Bernard, *The Secret of Blood Island*, theme 1

Example 7

This first theme appropriately spans a **tritone**, and is often played by plucked strings, which lend a further rawness to the sound. The final falling **semitone** is later presented as a theme in its own right:

James Bernard, *The Secret of Blood Island*, subsidiary falling semitone theme

Example 8

The second theme is introduced in the main title:

James Bernard, *The Secret of Blood Island*, theme 2

Example 9

There is also a motif associated with scenes of tension inside the camp, particularly when Michael Ripper's sadistic Japanese soldier interrogates the prisoners. Again, a tritone forms its most characteristic interval:

James Bernard, *The Secret of Blood Island*,
"Tension" motif

Example 10

The closing credits bring the opening motif back in slightly modified form, punctuated by resonant fifths in the brass:

James Bernard, *The Secret of Blood Island*,
end title (reduction)

Example 11

The First World War provided the historical setting of *She*, the 1965 film that introduced Hammer's most glamorous *femme fatale*. Producer Michael Carreras was of the opinion that "there's no doubt that the future lies with bigger productions."[4] Instead of vampires and monsters, he wanted to see Hammer produce more Hitchcockian thrillers and high Romantic adventure films. *She*, one of Hammer's most lavish spectacles, was one of the first results of this change of direction, and the most expensive film Hammer had yet made.

Major Holly (played by Peter Cushing) embarks on a search for the lost city of Kuma, accompanied by his valet Job (Bernard Cribbins) and his colleague Leo Vincey (John Richardson). They embark on their long journey beyond the Mountains of the Moon, encountering on their way the beautiful Ustane (Rosenda Monteros). She is the daughter of Haumeid (André Morell), the ruler of the Amahagger tribe who are slaves to the Queen of Kuma: Ayesha—She Who Must Be Obeyed (Ursula Andress). Ustane falls in love with Leo, but Leo has already been captivated by the beauty of Ayesha, who has bathed in the cold blue flame of immortal life and has been patiently waiting through the weary centuries for the return of her long lost love, Kallikrates.

On arrival at Kuma, Leo discovers that he is the reincarnation of this same Kallikrates. He also learns of the ruthless ways of the jealous queen, who puts Ustane to death and persuades Leo to join her in the flame of eternal life. He does so, but while it bestows immortality on him, it takes it away from her; and in the film's most graphic moment of horror, we watch her age and wither like one of the vampires in *Dracula,* and Leo is left to face eternity without her.

In *Ayesha — the Return of She,* his sequel to the original novel of *She,* Rider Haggard pointed out how the name of his principal character was to be pronounced:

> In response to many inquiries [I] may add that the name Ayesha — which since the days of the prophet Mahomet, who had a wife so called, and perhaps before them, has been common in the East — should be pronounced *Assha.*[5]

Understandably, no one in the film actually pronounces the name like that, and neither does Bernard's music, the main theme of which, like Dracula's, is again based on the syllables of the character's name.

Ayesha herself is an archetypal figure. In a classic Jungian sense she could be said to represent the anima, "a personification of all feminine tendencies in a man's psyche."[6]

> Many examples from literature show the anima as a guide and mediator to the inner world: Francesco Colonna's *Hypnerotomachia,* Rider Haggard's *She,* or "the eternal feminine" in Goethe's *Faust.*[7]

Seductress, siren, eternal woman — Bernard's theme for Ayesha captures all these qualities by employing equally archetypal musical symbols. It is simply constructed from a rising fifth and a falling fourth:

James Bernard, *She* 1M1C, bar 6

Example 12a

There are many nineteenth and early twentieth-century composers who explored ways of representing the "eternal feminine" and her more dangerous archetypal sister, the *femme fatale,* in musical terms. Many of these contain a falling fourth, but in the choral finale of Liszt's *Faust Symphony,* the final lines of Goethe's *Faust ("Das ewige weibliche zieht uns hinan"*—"The eternal feminine draws us onwards") are set to a melody that includes both a rising fifth and a falling fourth:

Franz Liszt, *Eine Faust-Symphonie*, "Schlußchor," bars 25–25 (tenor solo only)

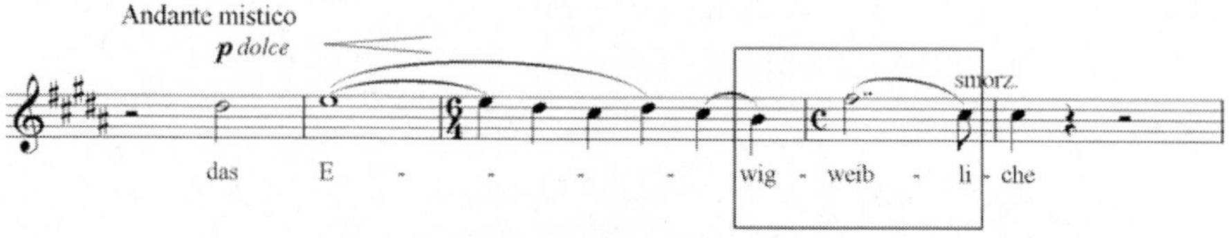

Example 12b

This is perhaps the most striking parallel to Bernard's theme, but fourths are also crucial in the seductive waltz sung by the flower maidens of Wagner's *Parsifal*:

Richard Wagner, *Parsifal*, Act II, "Flower Maiden's Waltz"

Leicht bewegt

p

Komm'! Komm'! hol - der Kna - be!

Example 12c

This "siren" fourth was further developed by Debussy, in a piece actually called "*Sirens,*" which forms the third movement of his orchestral suite *Nocturnes* (first performed in 1900):

Claude Debussy, *Nocturnes*, "Sirènes," bars 30–31 (choir only)

Example 12d

Bernard himself confesses that though he didn't realize it at the time, his "Ay-E-Sha" theme is very similar to the melody of the "Daybreak" music from Ravel's ballet *Daphnis et Chloé* (first performed in 1913), and certainly the eternal Ayesha, who bathes in life-giving flames, is a kind of sun goddess (see example 12E).

The rhythm of the "Ay-E-Sha" theme stresses the second beat of each group of four, giving the false impression of a romantic waltz. Sometimes it is harmonized with melancholy **minor triads**. At other times, however, **minor seconds** add an undercurrent of mystery and subdued menace. Ayesha is, after all, a despotic tyrant as well as a beautiful woman, representing the dangerous allure of fantasy. As a Jungian analyst, M.L. von Franz, has explained, "the anima symbolizes an unreal dream of life, happiness, and maternal warmth (her nest)—a dream that lures men away from reality."[8] Indeed, the main "Ay-E-Sha" theme is actually preceded by another important motif associated with this darker side of the anima. Representing "The Power of She" it introduces the film and will return throughout the action, often in the form of brass fanfares, whenever Ayesha demonstrates her tyrannical cruelty.

After the first statement of "The Power of She," the main title sequence alternates between the "Ay-E-Sha" theme (accompanying shots of the cavern where the flame of eternal life burns amidst exotic flowers and vines) and the rhythmic drumming of the Amahagger during one of their ritual dances. This is the only Hammer film scored by Bernard to break the main theme into segments; but there will be plenty of opportunities to hear the theme without interruptions later on. In fact, the "Ay-E-Sha" theme consists of two sections—the syllabic "Ay-E-Sha" theme and a secondary **triplet** theme that moves through another fourth:

Maurice Ravel, *Daphnis et Chloé*, 10 bars after 155 (violas, cellos and basses only)

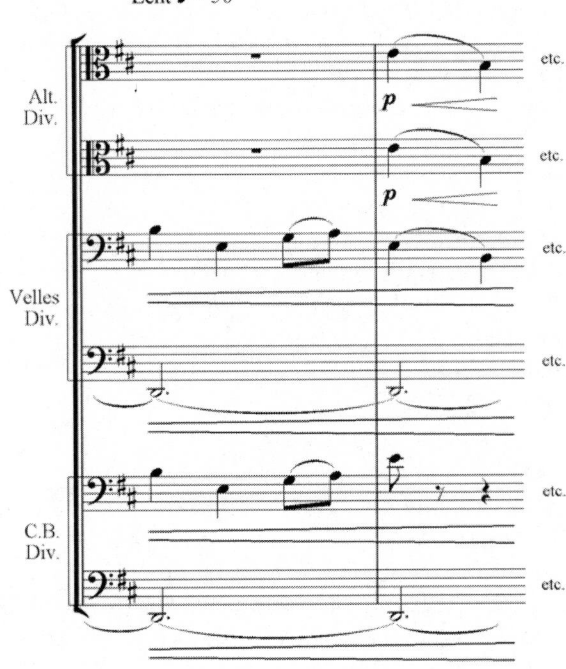

Example 12e

James Bernard, *She* 1M1C, bar (violin I only)

Example 13

Hammer's version of the tale may have sensibly ignored Rider Haggard's instructions with regard to the pronunciation of "Ayesha" but it also, perhaps less sensibly, ignored the novel's opening chapters set in England. Instead, the film condenses the information we learn there into a single scene set in an Egyptian nightclub. As a result, the sense of Kuma being at the ends of the earth is somewhat undermined. However, there is an advantage to the nightclub scene in the rare opportunity it offers to hear Bernard try his hand at exotic Arab-style music. This is scored for a flute, musette, clarinet, guitar, trumpet, Persian zither, marimba, bongo drums, Israeli drum and strings. The result is as different from the score that surrounds it as was the Irish jig in *Quatermass 2*. The Arab music exploits the "Oriental" connotation of the **flattened sixth** and **sharpened seventh** of the **harmonic minor scale**:

James Bernard, *She* "Arab Night-Club Music," bar 1 (Musette only)

Example 14

Ustane catches Leo's attention and he persuades her to leave the nightclub with him; but Ustane is merely a pawn in a far more complicated game. She has been sent to lure Leo to the house where Ayesha will later introduce herself to him. That scene does not appear in Haggard's novel either, but it was obviously felt necessary to introduce Ursula Andress fairly early on in the film to facilitate the several hallucinations of her that Leo will later experience. Knocked unconscious outside the mysterious house, he awakens to find himself in an exotically furnished room; as he looks around, Bernard's "Expectation" motif is played by clarinets and bassoons (example 15).

Ayesha then makes her entrance to a reprise of her theme. She gives Leo a ring and a map and offers him the challenge to travel to her realm beyond the Mountains of the Moon where he will be granted everything that he desires.

James Bernard, *She* 2M1, bar 2

Example 15

A new motif appears in reel three, when Holly and Job accompany Leo back to the house. It is now deserted, but Leo still possesses the ring and the map. After briefly exploring the empty rooms, Holly takes another look at the map and his enthusiasm for adventure is kindled. He confesses that the discovery of a lost city would indeed be the crowning glory of his life, and it is at this moment that the "Quest" theme is first heard. Its melodic contour is appropriately similar to that of "Ay-E-Sha":

James Bernard, *She* 3M1, bars 1–9 (horn only)

Example 16

It is also predominantly **pentatonic**, and echoes Debussy's use of this exotic scale in "*Pour invoquer Pan, dieu du vent d'été*" ("For invoking Pan, god of the summer wind") from *Six Épigraphs Antiques*; see chapter 5, example 16c. The "Quest" theme is played by the horns accompanied by string **harmonics** in fifths. Fifths have acquired an "oriental" connotation over the years, typified by their appearance in the temple scene of Verdi's *Aida* (first performed in 1871), and also in many of the Edwardian drawing room songs about the Romantic sands of the desert composed by Amy Woodforde-Finden. The first song in Woodforde-Finden's cycle, *A Lover in Damascus* (first published in 1904), was the kind of salon song that Bernard's father would have enjoyed singing, and it contains a particularly effective example of tramping "oriental" fifths:

Amy Woodforde-Finden, *A Lover in Damascus*, "Far Across the Desert Sands," bars 7–11

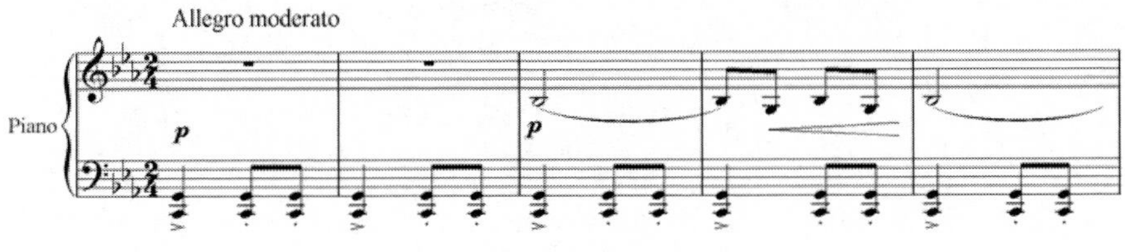

Example 17

The "Quest" theme will soon be combined with "Ay-E-Sha" as the three friends set off on their journey across the desert; but before that we hear Ustane's theme as she watches them prepare for their adventure. "Keep safe, my Leo," she whispers, fearing that he might not. Like the "Quest" theme, the "Ustane" motif has certain things in common with "Ay-E-Sha." In fact, it is a kind of mirror image of it, representing, as it does, the second lover in Leo's life. It is played by the oboe d'amore (the alto of the oboe family), and this "oboe of love" is a singularly appropriate instrument to convey not only Ustane's affectionate character but also her oriental charm. "Ustane" is melancholy whereas "Ay-E-Sha" is alluring.

The journey across the desert, which so effectively conveys the atmosphere of a mystical pilgrimage by combining the "Ay-E-Sha" and "Quest" themes, was subsequently criticized by Hammer's next musical supervisor, Philip Martell:

> I remember [Bernard] did a piece for Peter Cushing riding on a donkey that was very slow and tedious, matching the visual action but emotionally wrong. It should have been upbeat and bright. I told him, "We're not interested in the tempo of the legs. We're interested in the tempo of the heart. Just make it exciting."[9]

But perhaps it is not so much excitement that the music needs to convey here as anticipation and determination. After the initial part of the journey, the friends bivouac in an oasis. During the night, Leo experiences the first of his Ayesha hallucinations by staring into a pool of water. Her image materializes, arms outstretched and accompanied by the "Ay-E-Sha" theme, but as Leo puts his hand into the water the hallucination disappears to a gentle rippling of harps. Harps have often been used at transitional points in narrative music, and are also often employed to convey the transition between dreaming and waking. Rimsky-Korsakov employed rich harp arpeggios to support the solo violin in his symphonic suite *Schéhérezade* (composed in 1888), indicating, each time they appear, that one story is over and another is about to begin. In Wagner's *Siegfried,* Brünnhilde is awoken from her magical sleep by a similar harp effect. Eero Tarasti has suggested that "the timbre of the harp frequently has a connotation referring immediately to a mythical past."[10] Could this be due to the fact that the harp is one of the oldest and most archaic of instruments with a lineage stretching back to Apollo and Orpheus? The harps that accompany Leo's "awakening" from an hallucination are therefore a well-established musical symbol of transition from the world of dreams into reality.

The image of Ayesha beckons Leo through a heat haze, suggested in the score by high-pitched string harmonics, but the party are eventually ambushed by marauding camel thieves. For this, Bernard introduces an "Attack" theme, which is a loosely retrograde version of the earlier "Expectation" motif:

James Bernard, *She* 4M2,
"Attack" theme

Example 18

Stranded in the desert with no camels and very little water, Holly and Job are all for abandoning their journey, but Leo insists that they all press on. The "Ay-E-Sha" and

"Quest" themes are now distorted, and the wide intervals of an accompanying **ostinato** played by the double bass and harp imitate the weary footsteps of the explorers:

James Bernard, *She* 4M3, bars 1–7

Example 19

Then, in a scene borrowed from David Lean's *Lawrence of Arabia* (Colum bia/Horizon [Sam Spiegel], 1962), a tiny dot appears in the shimmering distance. Imagining that it is Ayesha who is coming towards him, Leo whispers her name as her imploring image is superimposed over the scene. **Trills**, a tritone apart in strings and vibraphone, create a musical equivalent of this mirage, over which statements of the "Ay-E-Sha" theme increase in intensity until exhaustion eventually overcomes even the determined Leo. In fact, the mysterious traveler turns out not to be Ayesha but Ustane. After restoring them with food and water, she takes the three friends to meet her father, Haumeid, who lives with the Amahagger tribe as their ruler. The Amahagger are introduced by characteristically Bernardian tritones in the trombones, and these are joined by marimba **trills**. As the Amahagger advance, the timpani intone an impressive motif that makes its one and only appearance in the film here:

James Bernard, *She* 5M3, bar 4

Example 20

The Amahagger tribesmen realize that Leo's face is the same as Kallikrates, whose features have long been used as a symbol of the power of Ayesha. A ritual dance sequence now takes place, the music of which consists entirely of native drumming and chanting. Bernard did compose a chant of his own for this but, as he explained, it wasn't used in the end:

> That was one of the occasions when I did go down to the set. I think they were filming at Elstree. We rehearsed the Amahagger war chant in an old gymnasium and we had a wonderful lineup of black drummers run by a friend of Ken McGregor, who was my friend after Paul died. It was really through *She* that I met him. He was one of the Amahaggers, and there was a man called Ginger Johnson who was Trinidadian. He had a sort of drumming group and there were about eight drummers all beating away. I'd written a very simple chant. I was standing by the pianist and Phil Martell was directing and they were working up a really good chant. I remember Michael Carreras, who loved jazz, saying, "This is my sort of stuff. I love it. We must have this!" He was really thrilled by it; but in the cutting of the film it went. You just hear it beginning and then it vanishes. I was sad about that because it was really rather powerful with a whole lineup of male singers and those powerful African type drums.

Leo is rescued from the sacrificial blade of the Amahagger by the arrival of the high priest, Billali (Christopher Lee). He is announced by the first of several regal fanfares, which later to resonate through the corridors of Ayesha's palace. They were all played on the soundtrack by instrumentalists from Kneller Hall, the home of London's Royal Military School of Music. The first fanfare is scored for trumpets. In fact, it is the same "Power of She" motif that had opened the film, and it is thematically related not only to "Ay-E-Sha," in its final fifth, but also to the triplets of the counter-melody of that theme:

James Bernard, *She*, "Fanfare No. 1" (2 trumpets)

Example 21a

James Bernard, *She* 7M2, bars 20–23, counter-melody to "Ay-e-Sha" theme (violin I only)

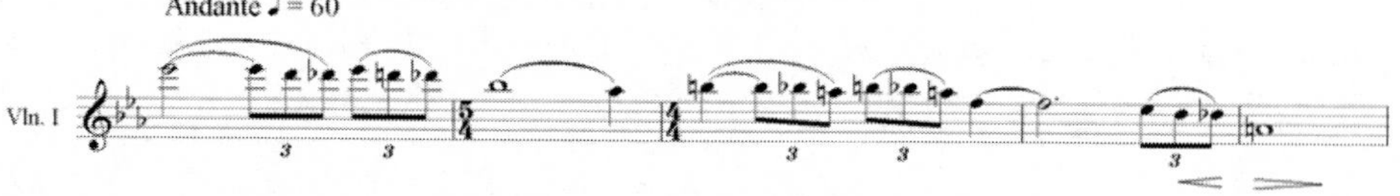

Example 21B

Billali takes some of the Amahagger back to Kuma to receive punishment for their crime of attempting to sacrifice the man who bears the features of Kallikrates, and announces that Holly, Leo and Job are to join the party. Ustane begs Billali to allow her to accompany them; her theme is woven into the following heroic march, which is for the most part in three beats in the bar. The procession then enters Kuma through the legs of a Colossus carved from the rock face. Twelve trumpets are used here, divided into three **desks**. The first intones "The Power of She," and is answered by the second desk, as though from the city itself. The third desk then plays a quiet response to this answering phrase, suggesting that the signal has been carried even further into the center of Kuma. Bernard asks the players to use mutes for this third phrase, marking the passage "***lontano***":

James Bernard, *She*, "Fanfare 2" (6 trumpets)

Example 22

Holly and Job are shown to their quarters and Leo is taken away to recover from his ordeal in a separate room. The next music section accompanies a shot of him sleeping. Harps and vibraphones oscillate on what are actually two alternating **consecutive triads**, but the oscillation is so rapid that it sounds more like a straightforward trill.[11]

When Leo has fully recovered, Ayesha pays him a visit. Her arrival is announced with a flurry of harp **arpeggios** playing an expectant **minor seventh** chord (the same Mahlerian "alert" chord discussed with regard to *Dracula* where it connoted a rather more sinister sense of expectation). At the peak of this arpeggiated chord, high-pitched strings take over with the "Ay-E-Sha" theme, creating the same sense of ethereal wonder that Wagner had conveyed with equally high-pitched strings at the beginning of the final scene of *Siegfried,* when the hero discovers Brünnhilde on her mountain peak, surrounded by the rosy glow of dawn.

Leo is now informed that he is the reincarnation of Kallikrates, and Ayesha regresses him back in time. The flashback that follows is accompanied by one of the score's most effective and beautiful moments. We observe Kallikrates with another woman in the desert of ancient Egypt. A camel train wanders out into the distance behind them and Leo remembers that "the encampment is on the banks of the Nile; the night is cool; the smell of soft perfume fills the air; the moment is one of love." The flute melody here, marked "***languido quasi improvisato***," is based on an oriental scale, once again reminiscent of Debussy's celebrated solo flute piece, *Syrinx*:

James Bernard, *She* 7M2, bars 36–37

Example 23a

Claude Debussy, *Syrinx*, bar 3

Example 23b

Quiet, low-pitched augmented triads on a resonant harp punctuate the flute and add a further sense of expectancy to the scene. The slight sense of foreboding they create is appropriate because Ayesha has been watching this assignation, just as later she is to observe Leo and Ustane in each other's arms. Wild with jealousy, she then plunges a knife into the adulterous heart of her beloved Kallikrates, as the orchestra intones a martial version of "The Power of She" played by trumpets and accompanied by a chord, which, with its tritone relationships, is very Scriabinesque (example 24A).

James Bernard, *She* 7M2, last 3 bars (trumpets 1 & 2 and strings only)

Example 24a

Later, in reel eight, when we are shown Ayesha and Leo sleeping and dreaming of each other, muted strings create a dream-like atmosphere, the rising and falling semitones in the violas and cellos suggesting their agitated breathing in much the same way that the "Fear in the Night" motif of *Dracula* had suggested Lucy's troubled sleep. Over the violas and cellos, the violins whisper the "Ay-E-Sha" theme, but it is cut off abruptly when Ayesha's soldiers awaken Leo and escort him to witness the execution of Ustane.

Alexander Scriabin,
***Piano Sonato No. 9*, bar 30**

Example 24b

The mystical phenomenon of the flame of life, which Ayesha subsequently reveals to Leo, is suggested musically by two more rapidly oscillating consecutive triads played by the vibraphones and harps. The "Ay-E-Sha" theme is then brought in underneath on violas and cellos, while shots of the flames are emphasized by means of a **crescendo** in the suspended cymbal:

James Bernard, *She* 9M1,
1st two measures of bar 28 (vibraphone and harps only)

Example 25

Two interesting modifications of "The Power of She" theme occur in subsequent scenes; first when Ayesha destroys the mummified corpse of Kallikrates:

James Bernard, *She* 10M2, bars 22–25

Example 26

... and second when Billali attempts to grab immortality himself and attacks Leo:

James Bernard, *She* 10M4, bars 4–5 (oboe I only)

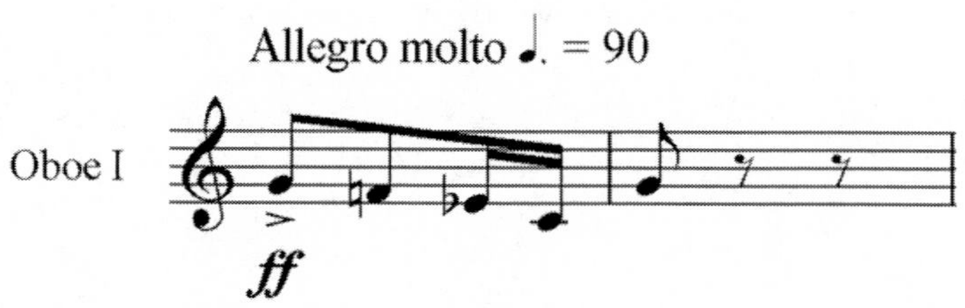

Example 27

Billali, however, is stabbed in the back by Ayesha before he can crawl into the flame of life. That privilege is reserved for Ayesha and Leo, who enter it together at the end of the film; but though the flame gives Leo eternal life, it takes back what it had once given to the immortal woman. She decays into a hideous hag before falling lifeless to the ground, and her theme disintegrates along with her body. Its beauty is destroyed by clashing minor seconds, and its original falling perfect fourth distorts into a horrifying augmented fourth: a devastating tritone. A very wide string

glissando accompanies her collapse onto the floor of the cavern and moaning minor seconds in the cellos imitate the sound of air being expelled from her lungs:

> She, who but two minutes before had gazed upon us the loveliest, noblest, most splendid woman the world has ever seen, she lay still before us, [...] no larger than a big monkey, and hideous—ah too hideous for words![12]

10

Back from the Dead

"martellato (It.; Fr., martelé*): literally "hammered"*

Collins Encyclopedia of Music[1]

She was the film that introduced Bernard to Hammer's new musical director, Philip Martell. Born in London's East End in 1915, Martell had begun his career as a promising virtuoso violinist. Entering London's Guildhall School of Music when he was only eleven, Martell had studied under the violinist and composer, Benoit Hollander.[2] A solo career failed to materialize but he soon found himself in demand as a musical director in the theater and for silent films, as well as performing in his own dance band. But then he lost everything when a German bomb hit the family home during the blitz. After the war, he experienced an equally explosive working relationship with Otto Preminger on the film adaptation of Bernard Shaw's play *St. Joan* (Wheel, dir. Otto Preminger, 1957). Although the music for this was being written by Viennese operetta composer Mischa Spoliansky, Preminger wanted Martell on the set every day even if he wasn't actually needed:

> Preminger said, "You can have a dressing room, you can have a piano in there, you can have a telephone in there..." I said, "But I don't want to stay here!" "...Or you can stay here and watch me shoot the picture. You can do what you like but I want you here." I said, "I'm sorry, Otto, I can't do that. I want to work at home. I want to start thinking about your music"—and there was a lot of music—[...] but he said, "Either you do as I want or you get off my picture. Please yourself!" So I left. Three days later, I get a phone call from his assistant saying, "What the hell do you think you're up to?" I said, "Nothing." He said, "You could be down here doing something, couldn't you?" I said, "I'm not on your picture any longer." He said, "Preminger's sacked you?" I said, "Yes." "Well, he's sacked the leading lady, sacked the leading man, half the technicians—they're all still here, so who do you think you are?" I said, "I'm not anybody!" He said, "Well, come on down and let's stop this nonsense."
>
> So I went back and started working again with Preminger. [...] One day, I was very honored and I was invited to take tea with him in the tea break along with three or four stooges: his yes-men. Preminger said to me, "Look, I want something on the soundtrack that represents the voices that Joan hears in her head, but I don't want it done with musical instruments." [...] Sitting at the table was

a man who said to me, "I'll give you a clue as to what might be useful: a syrinx." I said, "I don't even know what it is." He said, "Well, I've heard it and it's very beautiful and I think it might do as the voices." So Otto said, "Right! Go and get him!" But I didn't know where to get him, so I asked this man, "Where did you hear this?" "In Paris, at the exhibition." I said, "When?" "In 1926." So Otto said, "Go to Paris and find him."

[...] So I started hunting around and got nowhere and then I phoned the BBC record department [...] and I said, "Do you know anything about a syrinx?" And they said, "Yes." "Have you got one?" They said, "No, we had a record." [...] So they found it, I heard it and I knew this was going either to be the entire answer or part of the answer [...] but I couldn't use that record. It was old and scratchy, so I then started ringing the embassies. [...] When we got to Rumania, they sent an LP of this music, and it was just what I was looking for. I then scribbled down the theme that we were going to use and then I said to Otto's assistant, "Let's bring the man over and we'll record it." So we brought the man over from Rumania. He came into the studio on Saturday morning at Shepperton, complete with interpreter and bodyguard, and proceeded to put the music on the stand and play — and it was exactly what was on the record. I said, "Well, tell him that's nice. Can he play this?" Well, you know the answer, don't you? He couldn't read music. Not a bloody note! So I kept the man there a week. We put him up in an hotel and I taught him note by note, through the interpreter, and we got it. But Otto hated me because I didn't care if he fired me.[3]

Martell's elevation to the sought-after post of musical supervisor to Hammer Films (which he occupied until his death in 1993) came via his friendship with director Val Guest, who had previously given him his first job in sound film. Towards the end of his life, after suffering a stroke, Martell gave an interview about his fascinating career with the company and made some very cutting remarks about Bernard's approach to film composition:

I'm unimpressed. I think he has a lot more talent than he uses. He's been spoiled by being put onto picture after picture. Consequently, he thinks everybody wants what he wrote on the last picture. He does it all over again, with very slight variations. [...]

Jimmy can be a good composer, but he likes to be left alone, and not interfered with. He resents my coming late into the picture and changing what he wants to do and my telling him, "No."

Personally he is very charming and delightful; very well-mannered and intelligent. This is what bothers me about his music. He had a good background. He came up with those "DRA-CU-LA" notes on the first film, and he thought, "What a good idea!" Since then he's built up such masses of noise around them.[4]

But Bernard has only fond memories of their association:

We got on immensely well. He always appeared to like my music very much. He used me a good deal, as you know. But how can I describe Phil? He was a short little man with a great big chip on his shoulder. I know I have a very public-schooly sort of voice. I could tell he was jealous of that from remarks he made: "Of course, you with your Eton education..." I always had to tell him, "It's not Eton, it's Wellington." He said it on purpose. He'd make jokes but there was a kind of undertone of seriousness, of bitterness in them. He was jealous of my general background — middle-class to upper-class background. It was jealousy of

> that — nothing to do with the music. He wanted to show that although he was short and hadn't had much of an education and came from a family of Jewish refugees— he wanted to show despite all that he had won through and he was the master. He was like Napoleon.
>
> He loved telling stories. He would tell one endless stories in which he came out on top. One had to get quite used to that. A lot of them were very interesting: how he'd stormed out of a session, flung the baton down and just marched out. And whoever it was, the producer had had to beg him to come back. He'd had an unhappy marriage. I never met his wife because he was divorced when I first came to know him. He had a great sort of bitterness against his wife. He used to talk to me about his affairs— we were as friendly as that. I don't mean love affairs. I don't think he had any at that stage, but he said, "I know that if I were to die now, my wife would have to inherit half of what I have. I don't want her to inherit a bean." He was a disappointed, lonely man and lived alone in a rather rambling house in Highgate, which was slowly falling to bits around him. It had been very nice.
>
> I think for years he concealed his envy of me. We'd been very friendly on film sessions. He said very nice things and was always telling me how bad he thought other film composers were. He used to find Malcolm Williamson very trying and was always telling him he must re-do bits. I must say, Phil never told me I must re-do a bit. We never had any rows or cross words. The sessions all went well. We always got through in time and then we'd go out to lunch together; but he was the last to offer a round of drinks. He wasn't very keen on digging into his pocket. If you went to a pub for lunch, he'd be delighted for you to look after everything.
>
> Anyway, when that interview with Phil appeared in *Little Shoppe of Horrors* I was absolutely astonished; but by then Phil had had the first of the strokes from which he finally died. Strokes can lead to a personality change. I think that suddenly, all the pent-up envy he had of me — nothing to do with music, all to do with my background — it all came out. It came out in that bitter interview in which he said my music was far too loud and vulgar — and praised a score that Malcolm Williamson had done. To me he had always told me how difficult Malcolm was! I rang Dick Klemensen, who was the founder of *Little Shoppe of Horrors*, and said that I was amazed. He said, "We were astonished by it and we asked Phil if he wouldn't rather rethink some of the things he'd said but he said no, he didn't want to re-think anything." He attacked a whole heap of people. So he was getting a whole lot of bile out of him and it was all to do with the chip on his shoulder. I used to feel sorry for Phil in a way because he was a sad man and it came across.

Martell had a brother called Harry and it was Harry's job to fix the orchestra for the recording sessions. Star soloists regularly featured anonymously on the soundtracks of Hammer films. Jack Brymer was often first clarinettist and Leon Goossens would sometimes appear playing the oboe. Sidonie Goossens played one of the harps in *She*, the same film in which Barry Tuckwell performed the elegiac horn solos.

The trumpeters from Kneller Hall who provided the impressive fanfares for that film returned for another of Bernard's fanfares, this time written for a production of Milton's play *Samson Agonistes*, which was again directed by Michael Redgrave. The production formed part of the opening festival of the Yvonne Arnaud Theater in Guildford on June 16, 1965, a venue that was pleasingly appropriate, given Bernard's correspondence with Arnaud at the beginning of his career. Most of the music was pre-recorded but the chorus of Hebrew captives, which included Rachel Kempson and Fay Compton, had to sing a mournful dirge live on stage during each performance.

Despite the additional support of John Quentin, Ian McCulloch, Roy Purcell and Brian Poyser, the men weren't very strong musically, so, as Fay Compton had told Bernard that she could produce a convincing bass voice, he asked her to join the men. This was something she was quite used to doing, having been one of the most famous "principal boys" in the days of lavish West End pantomimes.

Another of Bernard's new acquaintances from the time of *She* was Ken McGregor, who later became his partner after Dehn's death. The first time Bernard ever saw him was at a spectacular pantomime of *Aladdin* at the London Coliseum. The genie of the lamp was played by Milton Reid, who had previously appeared as the strong man in *The Terror of the Tongs.* There were also three slaves of the lamp, impersonated by three extremely handsome black men who were rigged out in gold lamé jock straps, gold sandals and very little else.[5] One of them was McGregor, who had already appeared as a slave alongside Elizabeth Taylor in *Cleopatra* (Twentieth Century–Fox, dir. Joseph L. Mankiewicz, 1963) as well as playing one of the Amahagger tribesmen in *She.*[6]

The year before *She,* McGregor had been brought along to a party by a mutual friend of Bernard and Dehn. At first, Bernard didn't much take to this "grand, handsome man, who seemed rather standoffish." The feeling was mutual and their paths didn't cross again until the rehearsals of the war chant for *She.* Recognizing the man who had been at last year's party, Bernard went up to him during a coffee break and thought he was still rather standoffish; so the rehearsal went on and the day came to an end without any further contact. Later, Bernard drove down to the set at Elstree in the S-1 Silver-Grey Bentley, which Julian Bream had suggested he ought now, as a successful film composer, to be driving. After the day's shooting, he offered McGregor and another Jamaican dancer a lift back to London. At first McGregor refused,

Ken McGregor, June 1968 (photograph James Bernard).

preferring to use the studio bus, but when he saw the Silver-Grey Bentley waiting for him, he changed his mind. Bernard recalled the occasion very clearly:

> It was wonderful hot weather and they were all at the peak of their form because they were all body builders with rippling muscles. Ken was in a very open summer shirt and as I was driving I felt quite distracted by these rippling black muscles beside me. That was the beginning of our long friendship.

She was finally released on April 18, 1965, and by way of contrast Bernard wrote the first of what would eventually number four Christmas carols for the Oxford University Press. *Good Day!,* setting an anonymous text, is a lively work, characterized by more **open fifths**, again demonstrating Bernard's ability to create excitement with very little material. In the first eight bars, for example, the soprano and alto lines are doubled an **octave** lower by tenors and basses, so in effect there are only two lines at work here:

James Bernard, *Good Day! A Christmas Carol,* bars 1–4

Example 1

It was 1966 that Hammer's Dracula rose from the grave for the first of his eight sequels. It had taken seven years for the company to mount another Dracula film, mainly because of Christopher Lee's reluctance to repeat the role that had made him an international star. There had, of course, been two Hammer vampire films in between: *The Brides of Dracula* and *The Kiss of the Vampire*, but in both of these Dracula himself had been conspicuous by his absence. In *Dracula — Prince of Darkness* (Warner/Hammer/Seven Arts, dir. Terence Fisher, 1966) the Count remained consistently mute, due to Lee's distaste at the lines that had been written for him,[7] but the soundtrack loudly intoned the same Dracula motif that had contributed so much to the success of the original film. Bernard recalled telephoning Anthony Hinds about this and asking if he agreed with his idea of using the Dracula theme again. Hinds was very enthusiastic, realizing that it would give the sequel greater continuity; and to provide even more continuity, the final scenes of *Dracula* were shrouded in a frame of smoke and used as a prologue. For the main title that followed, Bernard provided a slightly more up-tempo version of the Dracula march without the bass drum beat that had thundered through the main title of the original film.

Not surprisingly, given the subject and the preponderance of the Dracula theme, the score for *Dracula — Prince of Darkness* has a great deal in common with that for *Dracula*, but it also has some significant differences. **Tritones** are, of course, central to the harmonic texture but so too are **whole-tone scales** (which conveniently combine with the three whole-tone span of that interval). It is this predominantly whole-tone atmosphere that accounts for the score's rather different texture, and again shows the influence of Debussy, whose harmonic idiom was to a large extent colored by that particular scale. Liszt had combined whole-tone scales with the **augmented triads** I have already discussed in connection with his musical recitation, *Der traurige Mönch*. In this, Liszt anticipated Debussy by several decades and set a precedent for that scale's association with situations of supernatural terror. Debussy's use of it was more often for exotic coloration, though he too exploited its unnerving connotations.

The first half of *Dracula — Prince of Darkness* is concerned with the Count's resurrection. Two married couples are on holiday in central Europe. Charles and Diana (played by Francis Matthews and Suzan Farmer long before the celebrated wedding of Lady Diana Spencer and the Prince of Wales) are cheerful and enthusiastic about their adventure. The prim and proper Helen and her long-suffering husband Alan (played by Barbara Shelley and Charles Tingwell) are respectfully frightened and wearily resigned at the prospect of going any further. At an inn they meet a priest called Father Shandor (Andrew Kier), who warns them not to travel to Carlsbad and on no account to visit the castle there.

Needless to say, the castle is where they end up. Dracula's faithful retainer, Klove (Philip Latham), explains that he has instructions to provide food and lodging to any travelers who happen to pass by. During the night, he lures Alan into Dracula's vault, kills him and uses his blood to resurrect the Count in the film's most impressively macabre scene.

Dracula then sets about vampirizing Helen and almost succeeds in enlisting Diana into the ranks of the undead. In the climax, Charles and Father Shandor follow the Count back to his castle. The vampire's coffin slides onto the frozen surface of the castle moat, Shandor fires his rifle to shatter the ice, and Dracula is drowned.

After the main title we are back in Black Park, again standing in for the forests of the Carpathian Mountains. A funeral procession along the shore of a lake is accompanied by another march in the traditionally somber key of C minor:

James Bernard, *Dracula—Prince of Darkness*
1M2, bars 3–4 (strings only)

Example 2

The corpse at the center of this procession is about to be staked through the heart. But before this can be accomplished, Father Shandor arrives and forbids such a barbarous act. The dead girl is not a vampire, he insists; but genuine vampires are soon to appear.

The first whole-tone theme is introduced when the four English tourists find themselves at a crossroads near the castle. The theme is subsequently always associated with "Travelling" (example 3).

James Bernard, *Dracula—Prince of Darkness* 2M1, bar 3 (clarinet I only)

Example 3

We are also introduced to a variant of the "Undead" theme from *Dracula*. To distinguish one from the other, the *Prince of Darkness* version of the "Undead" theme will be referred to as the "Vampire" motif:

James Bernard, *Dracula—Prince of Darkness* 2M1, bar 6 (oboe only), "Vampire" motif

Example 4

These two motifs are combined as the frightened coachman argues with his passengers before throwing down their luggage and hurrying away. The "Travelling" theme is now played mournfully by an oboe, whilst a new theme associated with "Anxiety" appears in the strings and wind. This consists of two **minor seconds** that rise and fall by a **tone**:

James Bernard, *Dracula—Prince of Darkness* 2M1, bars 35–36, "Anxiety" motif

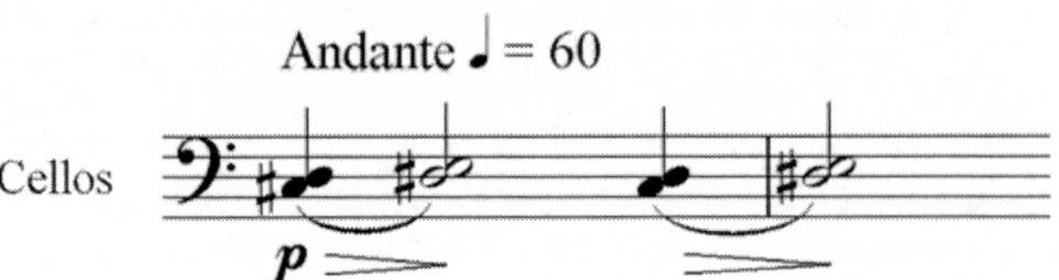

Example 5

A mysterious coach and pair now appears as if from nowhere and promptly transfers the stranded quartet to Castle Dracula. The music for this hair-raising journey is also based on the "Travelling" theme, suitably speeded up; but as the coach pulls up outside the castle, the "Dra-Cu-La" theme tells us who is waiting for them inside. The travelers hesitate before the main door, the "Anxiety" motif telling us all we need to know about how they are feeling.

During the meal served by Klove, Charles offers a toast "To Count Dracula!" No sooner has he spoken the words than a gust of wind blows through the hall and a **tone cluster** in string **harmonics** supports the appearance of a new theme on the vibraphone associated with "Evil." This is actually no more than the first three notes of the "Vampire" theme, whose genealogy we have already traced back to the "Undead" motif of the original *Dracula*:

James Bernard, *Dracula—Prince of Darkness* 4M1, bars 1–2

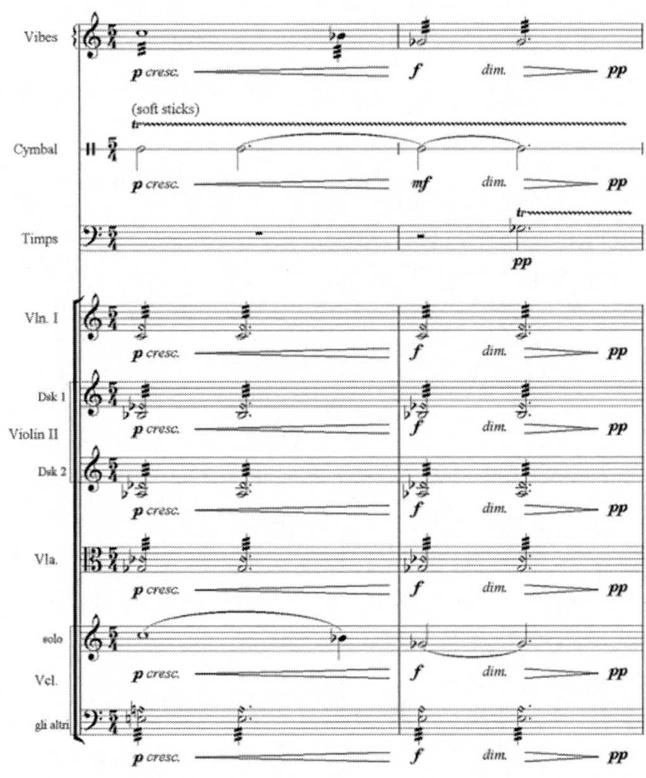

Example 6

As explained above, the *Dracula* "Undead" theme actually began life in *The Curse of Frankenstein.* Similarly, the new "Evil" theme derived from it for *Prince of Darkness* had also appeared in *The Damned,* in that score's opening melody for flute. Given the living death of the radioactive children in that film, it is appropriate to bring back a theme with such associations for a vampire film. Back in Castle Dracula, everyone retires for the night while Klove puts out the lights. The camera then pans through the deserted corridors to suggest that the restless spirit of the Count is still haunting the place. A variant of the "Vampire" theme accompanies this midnight prowl, its rhythm alternately spelled out by the timpani. Helen then has a terrible nightmare and as we watch her writhing beneath her bed sheets we hear the three-note "Evil" theme, again supported by string harmonics forming another tone-cluster. The music tells us that she is dreaming of her eventual destiny as one of the undead.

Later that night, Klove manages to dispatch Alan with a stab in the back and begins his elaborate ritual to revive the Count. Bernard once again masterfully restrains himself here to create a highly effective counterpoint to the action with the minimum of musical means. All he requires is a gong stroke to alternate with a rhythm derived from the "Vampire" theme, which is played by timpani and double basses. The resulting **ostinato** continues for twenty-seven bars.

James Bernard, *Dracula—Prince of Darkness* 5M1, bars 48–50

Example 7

Klove strings up Alan's body over the sarcophagus and slashes his throat. A torrent of blood pours over the ashes and Dracula's body is gradually reconstituted. **Trills** in the percussion, low strings and wind rise through the whole orchestra during this magical process, building up a gigantic chord that is fully the equal of Dracula's terrifying majesty, constructed, as it is, from augmented triads spread throughout the entire orchestra (example 8).

James Bernard, *Dracula—Prince of Darkness* 5M1, final bar (reduction)

Example 8

Klove now summons Helen down to the vault. The first thing she sees is her husband strung up over the sarcophagus. To accompany her horrified reaction, Bernard uses a short, two-note theme with the familiar snap rhythm, which harks back to the *Quatermass* films:

James Bernard, *Dracula—Prince of Darkness*
5M2, bar 1 (flutes only)

Example 9

After Dracula's attack on Helen, we cut to the following morning. To accompany the shot of dawn, Bernard creates a "Daybreak" theme on flutes. This is in fact a slightly altered form of the "Vampire" theme in that its fifth note rises rather than falls. It is also a good example of the stylistic continuity of Bernard's overall approach. In *The Devil Rides Out*, after one of Mocata's psychic attacks on Tanith, Bernard will employ a loosely retrograde version of the "Daybreak" theme:

James Bernard, *Dracula—Prince of Darkness*
5M2, bar 24 (flutes only)

Example 10a

James Bernard, *The Devil Rides Out* 7M2, bars 2–4 (oboes only)

Example 10b

The big set piece of reel six, in which Dracula and the now undead Helen attack Charles and Diana, brings together most of the themes discussed so far and is a splendid example of Bernard's skill at synchronization. The choreography of this scene is characterized by sudden bursts of violent activity followed by pauses as each party tries to outwit the other, and the music reflects this with its own frantic activity, interspersed with held chords or silences.

The section begins as Klove slams the castle door behind Diana. Her shock at being locked in is reflected by a ***fp*** minor second on **tremolo** strings. The strings then rapidly climb to a much higher pitch by means of a **snap rhythm** and are joined by the clarinets for a statement of the "Vampire" motif as Diana looks nervously around her. Helen then walks down the stairs looking much more voluptuous than she was in life, while string harmonics and the vibraphone usher in the "Anxiety" motif, harmonized with a note-cluster that encompasses a tritone.

James Bernard, *Dracula—Prince of Darkness* 6M3, bars 11–12 (vibraphone, violins and cello only)

Example 11

"You don't need Charles," Helen insists, and as she advances the "Evil" theme emerges on the vibraphone. She is about to "kiss" Diana when Dracula appears on the balcony, accompanied by the "Dracula chord." The tempo then increases to double speed and the snap rhythm combines with a rising **chromatic** scale as Dracula runs down some stairs and lunges at Diana with two statements of the "Dra-Cu-La" motif.

Charles shouts, "Let her go!," and the hiatus in the music reflects Dracula's surprise. Helen then advances towards Charles and we hear the "Evil" motif as fangs protrude through her smile; but Charles throws Helen back, accompanied by a tritone in the strings. Trills in the wind then float over a rapid rising string passage as Dracula advances upon Charles. The snap rhythm combines again with the "Dracula chord" during their struggle. Another hiatus follows; it is reflected by anticipatory trills in the lower strings and timpani. Dracula looks down imperiously at his victim with a quieter statement of the "Dra-Cu-La" theme; but Charles then notices two crossed swords on the wall and realizes he has a chance. As he rushes to grab one of these weapons, another rapid chromatically rising passage in wind and strings accompanies him, followed by yet another hiatus. The strings trill on tritones as the opponents size each other up and begin to fight to a sequenced presentation of the "Dra-Cu-La" theme. Dracula has the upper hand and snaps the sword in two before beginning to strangle Charles.

When all seems hopeless, Diana wrenches herself free from Helen but as she does so the crucifix she wears around her neck swings against the bare flesh of Helen's arm. She shouts out in pain. This distracts Dracula and the struggle is again interrupted by another punctuating "Dracula chord" from the brass. Expectant trills in the wind and strings then carry us forward to the next section when a bell, signifying the forces of good, accompanies a close-up shot of the wound on Helen's arm caused by the crucifix. (Tritones in the timpani rumble underneath.)

As mentioned in the previous chapter, Bernard often uses **dynamics** to frame the emotions of a particular moment: a sudden diminuendo in the bells followed by a rapid increase in volume reflects Helen's (and Dracula's) feelings of shock, realization and anger.

The "Anxiety" motif is now speeded up and given a rhythmic impetus. Played on strings and wind, it rises through whole-tone steps, combining with the bell and timpani as Charles grabs the shattered sword and positions the two halves together to create a makeshift crucifix. Powerless against this potent symbol, Dracula and Helen cower at the other end of the room; but Klove is waiting at the door. The "Vampire" motif is sequenced as Diana shouts out a warning to Charles. He manages to overcome the servant and escapes with Diana to the "Travelling" motif that had brought them to the castle in the first place. Charles drives the carriage so fast that he has an accident and is forced to carry Diana to safety in his arms. Bernard nicely catches the sense of exhaustion by slowing down the "Travelling" theme and harmonizing it in minor seconds.

The rest of the film concerns the hunting and destruction of Dracula. Less music is required here, and no new themes are introduced.

With Dracula dispatched for the second time, Bernard started to think about taking a holiday and it was during his time on the Island of Ischia the following summer that he met an unexpected admirer of his famous "Dra-Cu-La" theme. On that occasion he and Dehn were the guests of the playwright Terence Rattigan, who had been a close friend of Dehn for many years and was at that time renting one of the holiday homes on the island, owned by composer William Walton and his wife Susana. Walton had fallen in love with the area many years earlier while visiting the Bay of Naples with the Sitwells and had eventually built a villa on Ischia, which lies some ten miles off the coast of Naples. He called the villa *La Mortella*, and moved into it in July 1962. Lady Walton described the property at great length in her memoirs:

> We had carpets woven in Sardinia, and had brought wrought-iron door handles and locks in England. My mother had been busy painting doors, copying designs we had found in the bishop's palace in Forio. From Bolanzo we had ordered handmade majolica stoves to heat the house and dry the salt-laden air that winter storms enveloped us in; in Vetri we had bought stone steps and the stone floor of our entrance hall. From Taormina came inlaid marble tables, majolica sconces, pelmets, and antique pillars.[8]

The Waltons built not only *La Mortella* but also several other villas on the hillside leading down to the sea and liked to lease them to favored friends. Rattigan always took the villa they called *Christabella* and it was there that Dehn and Bernard spent three very happy holidays. *Christabella* was situated at the opposite end of *La Mortella's* garden, so it was no effort to walk over to the Waltons' house for meals and cocktail parties; and it was in this way that Bernard got to know Walton. Walton would often come over to *Christabella* on his own because, although he himself wasn't gay, he enjoyed being in the company of "the boys," as Bernard put it. The Waltons entertained some very famous names in this idyllic island setting. Julian Bream also stayed at *Christabella*. On another occasion, Ralph Vaughan Williams and his wife Ursula came to visit; and the pianist John Ogden and his wife Brenda Lucas were guests of the Waltons at the same time that Dehn and Bernard were enjoying the hospitality of Terence Rattigan:

> One night we were up there for drinks at the Waltons' house and William said, "Oh, our guests will be down in a moment: John Ogden and his wife." They duly appeared and as soon as I was introduced to him he said: "DRA-CU-LA! Dum-Da-Da!! I love it!" And I thought, "John Ogden is my favorite pianist from now on." That was the only time I ever met him but as soon as he heard my name, he knew. I thought that was wonderful — and very flattering!

Susana remembered Dehn as "delightful company"[9] and it wasn't long before Walton suggested they should collaborate on an opera. This eventually became *The Bear,* a comedy based on the one-act farce of the same title by Anton Chekhov. It was first performed at the Jubilee Hall in Aldeburgh in 1967, sharing the program with the premiere of Lennox Berkeley's opera *Castaway*, which also had a libretto by Dehn. Walton had had to interrupt work on the composition of *The Bear* due to an unexpected illness. Since the autumn of 1965 he had been suffering from influenza which he couldn't shake off, and after subsequent attacks of breathlessness he had visited a heart specialist who diagnosed that the underlying problem of all these ailments was lung cancer. Like Dehn, who would later succumb to the same illness, Walton had been a heavy smoker, a pleasure he immediately forswore, much to Susana's delight. Bernard recalls an occasion around this time when Walton paid them a visit at his home in Bramerton Street:

> There was a ring on the doorbell but we weren't expecting anyone. Paul went down and who should be standing on the doorstep but William Walton. He said, "Oh, Paul, I'd love to come in and have a chat with you." Paul said, "Well, of course, my dear, come right in." William wanted to have a private chat with Paul as he'd just been to have a check-up after having had the cancer operation and they thought there might be secondaries. That was before he had the deep-ray therapy which cleared them all up; but I do remember his calling on us just out of the blue like that, which shows how fond of Paul he was. He badly needed someone to pour it out to.

The deep-ray treatment, when it came, exhausted Walton. Susana recalled, "He became so weak that he could hardly walk. The treatment also upset his stomach, so he could hardly eat."[10] Finally, it was decided to double the dose of rays and this had the desired effect. Not long after his cure, when Walton was recuperating at The Savoy Hotel, Bernard and Dehn decided to give him a treat:

> We rang up and said, "William, dear, shall we come to the Savoy to see you, because we would like to give you and Susana dinner." They said that would be lovely and so we went up to the Suite and had drinks and then went down to the Savoy grill for dinner. I suppose they thought Paul was earning a fortune, because he had become a highly paid film writer, and I always remember they chose caviar to start with. Paul didn't turn a hair!

But hairs would rise and stomachs would churn when Bernard's next Hammer film forced its way out of the grave in the shape of *The Plague of the Zombies*. Cornwall has long been associated with Arthurian legend and pagan religions but Hammer were perhaps the first to introduce voodoo to the county. According to *The Plague of the Zombies* it was imported there from its native Haiti by a certain Squire Hamilton (played with ice-cold courtesy by John Carson), who then set about forcing his undead slaves to extract tin from a mine. It would be unwise to approach this film as a Marxist allegory but it is safe to say that the zombies keep Hamilton in the comfort to which he has become accustomed and to which the luxurious interiors of his manor house, furnished by Hammer's resident art director, Bernard Robinson, attest. In fact, the exterior of the Squire's home was provided by Oakley Court, the romantic mansion on the banks of the river Thames close to Bray Studios, which is now a luxury hotel.

No one is safe from Hamilton's voodoo menace. Alice (played by Jacqueline Pearce) is the wife of Dr. Peter Tompson (Brook Williams). She has already succumbed to lethargy and listlessness after cutting her wrist in a minor domestic accident, an accident that had actually been carefully arranged by the wicked Squire. Back in his cavern, Hamilton anoints a voodoo doll with Alice's blood, and then uses it to bring about her destruction and subsequent resurrection as one of the living dead. But Alice's zombie existence doesn't last for long because Dr. Tompson's old professor (played by André Morell) comes to the rescue and swiftly decapitates her. Then, in the film's most visually imaginative and much discussed section, Tompson dreams that he is surrounded by zombies, who force themselves out of their graves and stagger towards him through pools of blood.

The professor's daughter, Sylvia (Diane Clare), who has accompanied her father on the trip to Cornwall, very nearly goes the same way as Alice. Hamilton visits her when she is alone in the Tompsons' home. He asks for a glass of water, contrives to break the glass and sees to it that the girl cuts her finger with it. Then he returns to his mansion with a drop or two of her precious blood in a flask and sets to work. But Hamilton's scheme is soon discovered. His collection of voodoo dolls catch fire in a climactic conflagration, and the zombies go up in flames. The mine collapses and Hamilton's reign of terror crashes to a suitably cataclysmic conclusion.

Bernard's score for this film is hardly complex but it nonetheless provides an effective contribution to the action. The film opens with a ritual in Hamilton's voodoo cavern, accompanied by the kind of African drumming Bernard had composed the previous year for the tribal dance scenes in *She*. This time, the main orchestral theme, which emerges out of the drumming, is based not on the syllables of the film's title but on those of the incantation intoned by Squire Hamilton as he officiates at his voodoo ritual: "*Cada Nostra, Cada Estra.*"

James Bernard, *The Plague of the Zombies* 1M1, bars 2–3
(bass clarinet and bassoons only)

Example 12

As can be seen, this theme is again harmonized in minor seconds and features another diabolic tritone. Vibraphones add a characteristic sense of unease and the marimba lends a primitive connotation to the whole. During this opening sequence, we cut from the drumming natives in Hamilton's cavern to shots of Alice asleep in bed, murmuring the hypnotically induced "*Cada Nostra*" incantation as her wound bleeds. Eventually, she wakes up and screams.

The "*Cada Nostra*" theme is now worked up into a furious ***presto*** during the main title, accompanied by equally furious drumming from the bongo drums and timpani.

As Bernard knew all too well, a composer can often add more to a scene by keeping a low profile than by making his contribution felt by being more intrusive. In reel two, Bernard simply takes the "*Cada Nostra*" theme and plays it quietly on vibraphone: first, when Prof. Forbes re-reads his pupil's letter informing him of trouble in Cornwall, and second, when the Prof. and Sylvia arrive at Tompson's house to be greeted by the sickly Alice. Nothing could be simpler than the music in this section but the dramatic effect is just what is needed to create the feeling that amidst all this apparent normalcy something is wrong.

Another theme appears here, which derives its rhythm from the originally furious bongo drumming of the main title. Again featuring tritones in its harmonization, it consists merely of two alternating **semitones**, initiated by the vibraphone, then taken up by the marimba and later played by violas and cellos.

James Bernard, *The Plague of the Zombies*
2M2, bar 8 (marimba only)

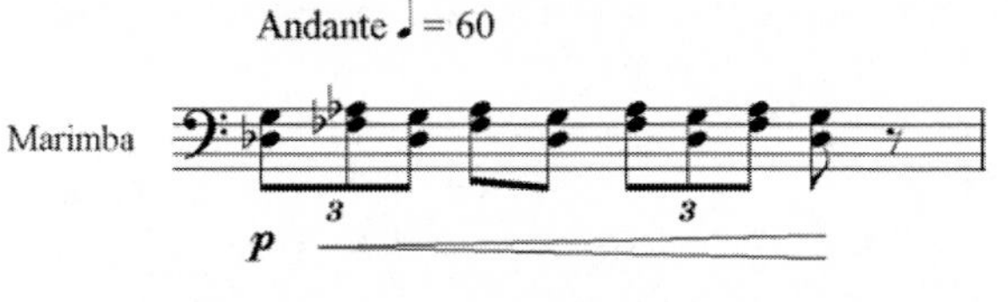

Example 13

The "Semitone" and "*Cada Nostra*" themes return when, before settling down for the night, Alice and Sylvia discuss how handsome the Squire is; but Alice doesn't stay in bed for long. Soon she is sleepwalking down the moonlit street towards the deserted mine, as a clarinet develops the "Semitone" theme into a motif associated with "Mystery":

James Bernard, *The Plague of the Zombies* 2M3, bars 22–24 (clarinets only)

Example 14

A single chord is frequently all that Bernard needs to emphasize a particular shock or point up a single action, as with the discovery of Alice's blood stained corpse in reel four. All that happens here is the presentation of a simple minor second spread through the entire orchestra.

The next important cue begins when Hamilton attacks the village priest. The priest has joined forces with Prof. Forbes and Dr. Tompson to help trap whoever is responsible for this zombie plague. They lie in wait in the graveyard but the priest is tired and goes home alone. Disguised in his voodoo robes, Hamilton attacks the priest in order to distract Forbes and Tompson. They run off to help, and as soon as the graveyard is deserted Hamilton sets about raising Alice's corpse from her grave. The rhythm of the "Semitone" theme is now combined with tritones on the timpani, and this simple material is then carried into the wind and strings, leading to a change of tempo when Alice's corpse actually turns into a zombie. As her flesh turns gray, violas, wind and marimba play a descending chromatic scale, again harmonized in minor seconds, while tritones in the cellos also slide down by chromatic steps. As Alice snaps open her zombie eyes, another loud minor second is distributed throughout the orchestra; then the process is reversed, with an ascending chromatic scale, as she advances towards the Professor and his horrified protégé.

Alice's decapitation is too much for Dr. Tompson. He faints, and the famous dream sequence begins. For this, Bernard draws on the device he had used in the *Quatermass* films. Strings are instructed to play on the wrong side of the bridge, "to make a grotesque squealing noise throughout," while the vibraphone plays an ostinato consisting of chromatically rising semiquavers. As the zombies emerge from the earth, cellos and basses play a simple figure of two rising semitones, which are later emphasized by the bassoons. Eventually the trombones join in with this simple idea and the section builds to a crescendo, ending ***fff*** as Tompson wakes up and screams.

James Bernard, *The Plague of the Zombies* 7M2, bar 12

Example 15

The horror is only just beginning for Dr. Tompson but Bernard required no new musical ideas to accompany the film to its gruesome conclusion.

11

Black and White Music

"But the music which they made was like no other Rex had ever heard before,"

Dennis Wheatley, *The Devil Rides Out*[1]

The title of *Frankenstein Created Woman* (Warner/Hammer–Seven Arts, dir. Terence Fisher, 1967) had been thought up by Anthony Hinds as a satirical response to Roger Vadim's *And God Created Woman* (Iëna-Hodu/UCIL/Concinor, dir. Roger Vadim, 1957). In Vadim's film, Brigitte Bardot had notoriously stripped off her bikini on a St. Tropez beach and became an international star on the strength of what she revealed. Hammer's riposte was much more decorous. There was plenty of murder but no extreme nudity. Perhaps as a consequence, it failed to elevate its female star, Susan Denberg, to quite such dizzy heights of celebrity as her French rival.

In its somewhat complicated and metaphysically rather intriguing plot, Frankenstein manages to capture the soul of a young man called Hans, who had been falsely accused of murder and executed. The Baron transplants this soul into the dead body of Christina, the girl Hans loved. Thanks to the Baron's surgical genius, Christina is not only restored to life but her deformity is rectified. Things inevitably go wrong when the transplanted soul compels Christina to kill the three youths who were actually responsible for the murder for which Carl was mistakenly taken to the guillotine. Full of remorse for what she has done, Christina hurls herself over a cliff.

Bernard's score begins with trombones intoning another "Syllable" theme. The "Frank-En-Stein" part descends by a **minor third** followed by a **tritone**, and actually follows a similar pitch contour to Wagner's motif for the evil sorceress, Ortrud, in *Lohengrin* (first performed in 1849). This is an appropriate echo due to the fact that Frankenstein is now dabbling in the transference of souls, and is therefore even more of a scientific sorcerer.

In this film, Frankenstein also resembles the Mephistopheles of Goethe's *Faust* in his aim to ensnare a particular soul. It is therefore equally appropriate that after the three rising tones which follow the syllables of "Cre-A-Ted," it is the "devil in music" that spans the syllables of "Wo-Man." When the Baron was playing God, in *The Curse of Frankenstein,* the main theme interestingly contained no tritones.

James Bernard, *Frankenstein Created Woman* 1M1, bars 2–7 (trombones only)

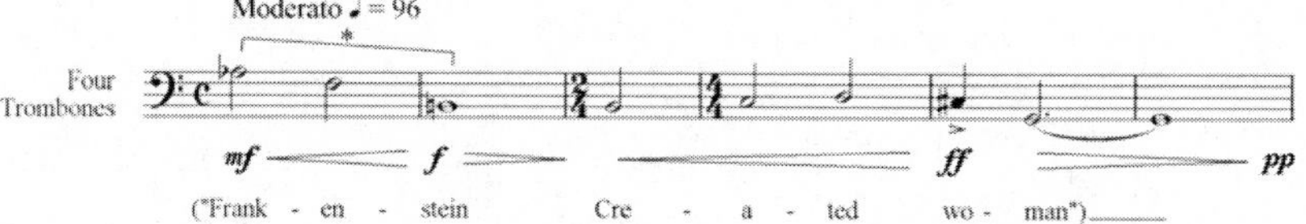

Example 1a

Richard Wagner, *Lohengrin*, Act II, Prelude, bars 13–14

Example 1b

After this somber introduction, played against a vertical shot of a guillotine, Bernard indulges in some rather elaborate writing for a quartet of timpani. Berlioz had been the first composer to create chords for differently tuned timpani in his *Symphony fantastique* (composed between 1828–30), where they imitate the sound of distant thunder. Bernard's timpani accompany the prologue to similarly threatening effect in a sequence that shows the execution of Hans' father. The first theme we hear is associated with the "Father" and consists of a rising and falling **chromatic** theme, harmonized in **major seconds** (example 2).

James Bernard, *Frankenstein Created Woman* 1M1, bars 14–15

Example 2

The next theme is associated with "Death" (example 3).

1M2, bar 1 (oboe only)

Example 3

As the blade of the guillotine is winched up, ascending trumpet chords mimic the action (example 4).

James Bernard, *Frankenstein Created Woman* 1M2, bars 14–15 (trumpets only)

Example 4

The main title music not only presents the "Syllable" theme on four trumpets, four trombones and four timpani, with string **tremolos** beneath, but also introduces the motif associated with "Christina." This is combined with the "Syllable" theme on trombones, cellos and double basses:

James Bernard, *Frankenstein Created Woman* 1M3, bars 6–10 (strings only)

Example 5

By way of experiment, the Baron has deliberately frozen himself to death but has prevented his soul from leaving his body. Now he must be revived and it is during this process that we first encounter Dr. Hertz (played by Thorley Walters). He and Hans subject the Baron's inert body to increasingly powerful electric shocks; with each flick of the switch the string **trills**, which successively rise by **tones**, contribute a great deal to the increasing tension of the scene. As the Baron is revealed, we hear the "Syllable" theme and when he finally opens his eyes a C minor chord on the vibraphone suggests the return of his soul to his body.

Later, three ruffians, long in the habit of mocking Christina's deformity, break into her father's inn for a late-night drinking session. The influence of Debussy is again apparent in the music here with the appearance of descending **whole-tone scales**. These are intoned by the brass and strings after the ruffians have been discovered by the landlord, whom they then beat to death. An important **semiquaver** figure is also introduced in this scene and will recur in later scenes of tension:

James Bernard, *Frankenstein Created Woman*
4M1, bar 18

Example 6

When the body of Christina's father is discovered, Hans is immediately blamed for the murder. The courtroom scene that follows is again accompanied by the quartet of timpani, though it is difficult to hear that they are actually playing minor seconds, being so subdued under the dialogue. The effect, however, is just what is required here, providing a sinister pulse to the proceedings. When the sentence is passed and Hans is found guilty, the timpani thunder out the "Father" motif, while cellos and double basses loudly intone the "Death" theme.

Hans is duly executed and soon afterwards Frankenstein manages to capture Hans' soul. When we are shown this mysterious phenomenon, Bernard creates one of his most astonishing musical sound effects. It is achieved by combining high-pitched **octave** oscillations on vibraphones with equally high-pitched string **harmonics**, oscillating in semitones. The vibraphones and strings then combine to create a complex **tone cluster**:

Bernard himself was never sure quite how such effects would sound in reality, and certainly no mere analysis can give an adequate suggestion of its effect.

After Christina's operation, Hertz explains to her that she was once hideously deformed. Christina's motif punctuates statements of the main "Syllable" theme, which is then developed in a manner that makes it even more reminiscent of Wagner's "Ortrud" motif from *Lohengrin*:

James Bernard, *Frankenstein Created Woman* 7M3, bars 1–5

Example 8

Bernard next distorts Christina's theme by changing one of its intervals from a minor third to a **diminished fourth** and instructing the strings to play in **harmonics**. In this modified form it now accompanies the scene in which Anton, one of the three ruffians, encounters Christina in a street and is persuaded to join her. If, like the cinema audience, he could hear Bernard's music at this moment, he would realize that he is walking to his death:

James Bernard, *Frankenstein Created Woman*
8M2, bar 20 (violin I only)

Example 9

The same music will accompany the seduction of Christina's second victim. Indeed, Bernard is able to base all the subsequent sections of his score on existing thematic material. When, for example, the Baron rushes off in pursuit of his creation in the final reel, the "Syllable" theme is speeded up and **syncopated** to exciting effect:

Opposite: Example 10

James Bernard, *Frankenstein Created Woman*, 6M3, bar 1

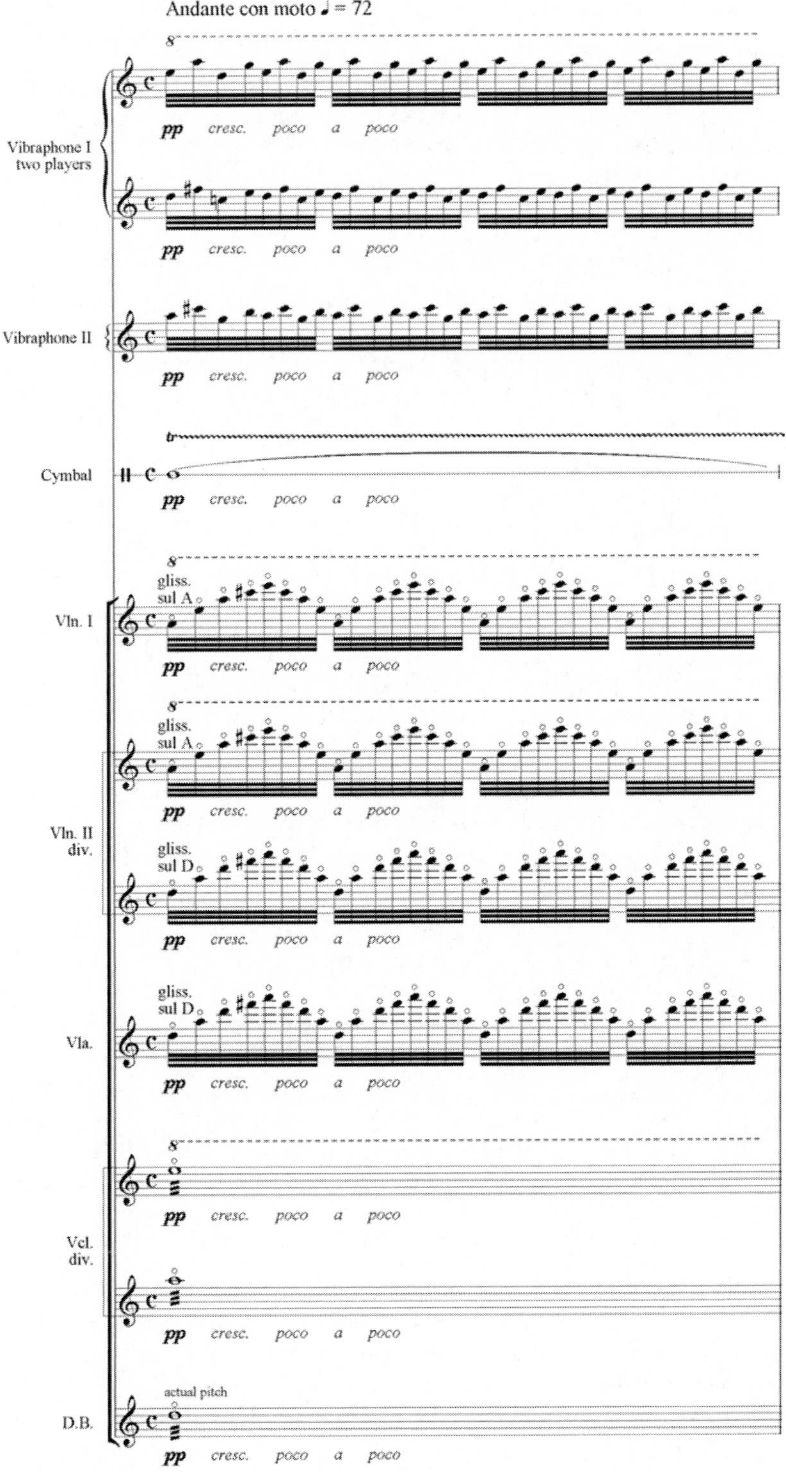

James Bernard, *Frankenstein Created Woman*
9M4, bar 1 (strings only)

Example 10

While working on the score of *Frankenstein Created Woman*, Bernard composed two more carols, for the Oxford University Press, this time to anonymous fifteenth-century words. These were dedicated to Walter Hussey and John Birch, the choirmaster of Chichester Cathedral where Hussey was now Dean. "Be Merry!" is a calypso carol with jaunty syncopations, anticipating Bernard's musical *Battersea Calypso* (see chapter 15) and his long period in Jamaica during the 1970s.

James Bernard, *Be Merry! A Calypso Carol*, bars 5–8

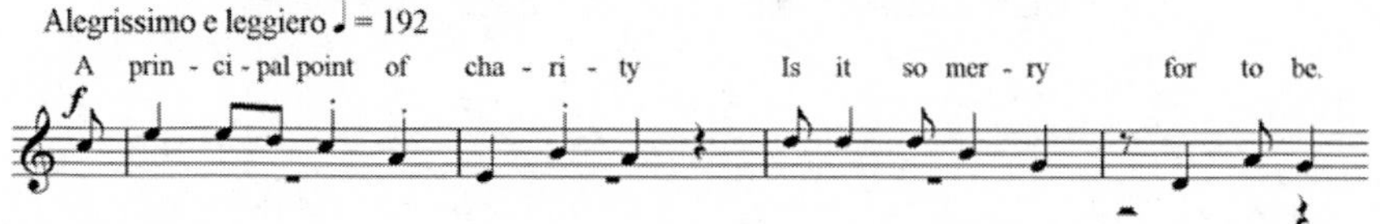

Example 11

"Jesus Is His Name" is a lullaby carol based on a "sighing" falling tone sung by the basses, with **consecutive triads** in the soprano and alto lines. These consecutive triads, with their sacred connotation, will return in the score for *The Devil Rides Out* when Christopher Lee's Duc de Richleau hypnotizes Simon Aron before placing a crucifix around his neck:

James Bernard, *Jesus Is His Name, A Lullaby Carol*, bars 11–12

Example 12

Bernard's rather more ambitious *Magnificat and Nunc Dimittis* for choir and organ was composed in 1968. Dedicated once again to Hussey and Birch, it was first performed at the Southern Cathedrals' Festival at Chichester that year. In an interview for an item in *The Times* Diary entitled "Black and White Music," Bernard explained what it was like to compose sacred and profane music simultaneously:

> It's rather schizophrenic—in one half of my mind I'm thinking of the *Magnificat*, in one half of orgies and black masses. I've just done the *Magnificat*, today I'm recording the music for a Satanic orgy that they're filming in a few days' time; and then I'll be going back to the *Nunc Dimittis*.[2]

Bernard's penchant for harmonic textures built on different kinds of fourths in the manner of Scriabin is again evident in the *Magnificat*:

James Bernard, *Magnificat and Nunc Dimittis*, bars 16–18

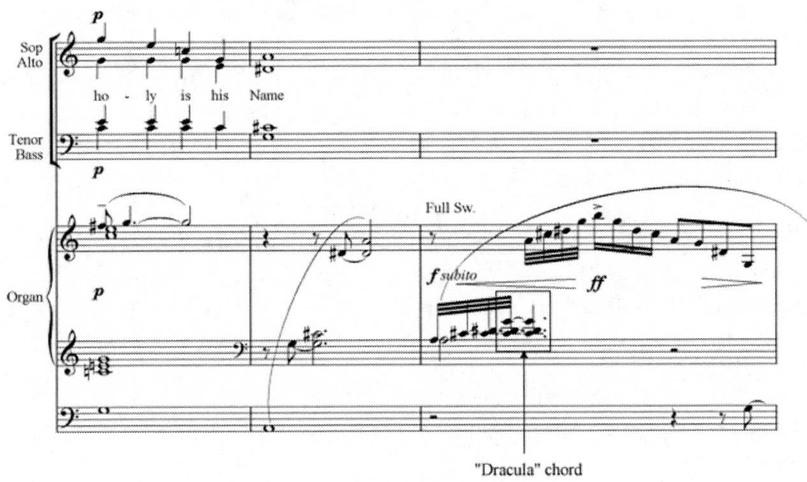

Example 13

Hussey failed to mention Bernard's piece in his memoirs, devoting his attention instead to the much better-known *Chichester Psalms* of Leonard Bernstein; but he does record how later, in 1975, he asked Bernard and Dehn to help him secure the services of William Walton for the 900th anniversary of the founding of Chichester Cathedral:

> I decided to have a try and got an old and close friend of mine, James Bernard, to mention it when the Waltons were having a meal with him. Walton's reply was, "Oh, yes. Anything to put off getting on with the Third Symphony."[3]

"Walter was very loyal," Bernard recalled, "but he wasn't really a movie person. I don't think he ever saw my films." It was through his friendship with Hussey that Bernard got to know the artist Graham Sutherland, with whom he remembers having spent a very happy evening while on holiday in Venice, and whose paintings he collected to decorate the walls of his various homes over the years. Hussey had commissioned Sutherland to paint *The Crucifixion* that still hangs in St. Matthew's Church, Northampton, opposite Henry Moore's sculpture of the Madonna and Child. Bernard was also introduced to Ceri Richards, the Welsh artist who had designed the costumes for Britten's *Noye's Fludde,* and who went on to design Hussey some very elaborate ceremonial robes, which in the event were hardly ever worn. Over the years, Bernard purchased several of Richards' paintings, some of which were inspired by an enthusiasm he shared with Bernard: the music of Debussy.

Before writing the score of his next Hammer project, Bernard was approached by Hammer's most powerful British rival, Amicus Films, to collaborate on the score of a compendium film called *Torture Garden* (Columbia/Amicus, dir. Freddie Francis, 1967). Bernard shared the composing honors of this with Don Banks, contributing music for two of the stories. Many of his familiar techniques are to be found here. In the scenes that link the stories together, we are introduced to the sinister Dr. Diabolo (played by Burgess Meredith), who invites a group of strangers into his fairground fortune-telling booth. As the strangers successively stare into the shears of the Goddess of Fate before discovering their respective destinies, Bernard reused the effect he had created for *The Kiss of the Vampire* when Prof. Zimmer had performed his occult ceremony. In the first story, Bernard looks back to the example of Saint-Saëns's *Danse Macabre* (first performed in 1877), using a xylophone to accompany the discovery of a witch's skeleton in a cellar. String **glissandi** in the manner of Bernard Herrmann's *Psycho* score accompany shots of a malevolent black cat, the witch's diabolical "familiar"; and when the cat begins to hypnotize its unfortunate victim, vibraphone tremolos anticipate one of the effects in Bernard's next score for Hammer.

The Devil Rides Out was released in the same year as another seminal devil-worship movie, *Rosemary's Baby* (Paramount/William Castle, dir. Roman Polanski, 1968). Both films marked a shift in public taste away from gothic horror towards black magic subjects, though Hammer failed to capitalize on the trend until it was too late.[4] On viewing the rough cut of *The Devil Rides Out,* Hammer executives had been very worried indeed:

> "It was terrible!" remembers [Anthony] Hinds. "However, with a bit of revoicing, some minor editing and a good meaty score, it really turned out to be quite good."[5]

Bernard's score is certainly meaty, not so much dripping with blood as rippling with muscular demonic energy. Building on the style he had developed in the past, he also incorporated some new orchestral timbres and effects, particularly in the percussion department. Faithfully adapted from Dennis Wheatley's 1934 novel, *The Devil Rides Out* tells how the Duc de Richleau (played by Christopher Lee) saves his young friend Simon Aron (Patrick Mower) from the clutches of the black magician, Mocata (Charles Gray). Caught up in all of this is a girl called Tanith (Niké Arrighi) who is also about to receive her Satanic baptism. She is rescued from this terrible fate at the eleventh hour, and during the film's most impressive scene, De Richleau, his niece Marie Eaton (Sarah Lawson), her husband Richard (Paul Eddington) and Simon spend the night inside a magic circle, while Mocata subjects them to a series of terrifying conjurations. When the Angel of Death is finally sent to claim them, De Richleau desperately intones the words of the Sussamma Ritual, which can alter time and space. The Angel of Death is banished but at the dreadful price of Tanith's life. Mocata then abducts Peggy, the Eatons' daughter, whom he intends to sacrifice so that Tanith may be restored to him. Richleau and the friends summon Tanith's spirit to tell them where Peggy has been taken, and in the climactic showdown the power of good finally defeats the forces of evil.

Influenced by Maurice Binder's sophisticated title designs for the James Bond films, which were at the height of their popularity at that time, the main title sequence of *The Devil Rides Out* was one of the most elaborate Hammer ever produced. Swirling red smoke drifts around various occult and astrological symbols as the credits roll; but it is Bernard's music (fully the equal of, if not more powerful than his *Dracula* march) that is the most important element at work here. Actually, the "Dra-Cu-La" theme makes a guest appearance in this section, falling by an augmented fourth rather than its usual octave. Indeed, this music is a veritable orgy of diabolic tritones. Bernardian major and minor seconds add to the characteristic harmonic fingerprints, which are amplified by a large orchestra with plenty of brass.

James Bernard, *The Devil Rides Out* 1M1, bars 1–2

Example 14a

Example 14b

Another idiosyncrasy to return in this score is the use of **double-dotted** rhythms. These are introduced in the main title music and, as with the *Dracula* march, snare drums emphasize the rhythm. Bernard's shuddering tam-tams create a much larger and more frightening sound than the rather smaller gongs of *The Gorgon* and the more straightforwardly "oriental" signification of the gongs in *Terror of the Tongs.* The main theme again conforms to the syllables of the film's title, and all these elements combine to create a truly sublime evocation of Miltonesque evil.

An important new theme is introduced when Richleau and his friend, Rex van Ryn (Leon Greene), arrive unexpectedly at Simon's house. An occult meeting is just about to take place there, presided over by Mocata, and they are asked to leave. Before they go, however, Richleau asks to see Simon's observatory, correctly suspecting that in reality it is an occult temple. They all climb the stairs, accompanied by a motif on piano and vibraphone that is related to the "Syllable" theme. Whereas Bernard himself had called the main title theme "The Power of Evil" when it was released on a CD in 1996, this second theme might well be called "The Fear of Evil," quietly implying, as it does, a sense of shuddering unease (example 15).

Example 15

The combination of piano and vibraphone playing in unison here creates an unnervingly resonant effect, as if the piano is being played in a vast echoing chamber.

Simon refuses to be persuaded that he is embarking on a "desperately dangerous adventure" and resists Richleau's impassioned plea to leave the house with him immediately. The music starts when Richleau knocks Simon unconscious and takes him away by force, infuriating Mocata. Their escape is accompanied by the "Fear of Evil" theme, speeded up and played by ***col legno*** strings (a grotesque effect, which Berlioz, again, had used in the similarly macabre fifth movement of his *Symphonie fantastique).* The "Mocata" theme, accompanying a close-up of Charles Gray's face at the end of this scene, is also derived from the "Power of Evil" motif.

James Bernard, *The Devil Rides Out* 2M1, bar 30 (trombones only)

Example 16

Richleau takes Simon back to his own residence, rouses him with smelling salts, and then proceeds to put him into a deep hypnotic trance. For this section, Bernard employs the alternating consecutive triads that had appeared in his carol "Jesus Is His Name." Such triads are similar in effect to the **chromatically altered chords** heard during the redemption of Lucy in *Dracula,* and had already been explored by Debussy in his piano prelude "*La cathédrale engloutie*" to create the disorientated, watery sound of a bell tolling deep beneath the ocean. Bernard increases their sense of shimmering dreaminess by scoring them for vibraphone, and then further confuses the tonality by adding tone clusters on the piano, along with several obscuring percussion effects, involving tubular bells, cymbals and tam-tams. He has explained this kind of effect as "often rather ... repetitive ... It's just a sort of noise, which slowly increases in intensity."

James Bernard, *The Devil Rides Out* 2M2, bars 1–2

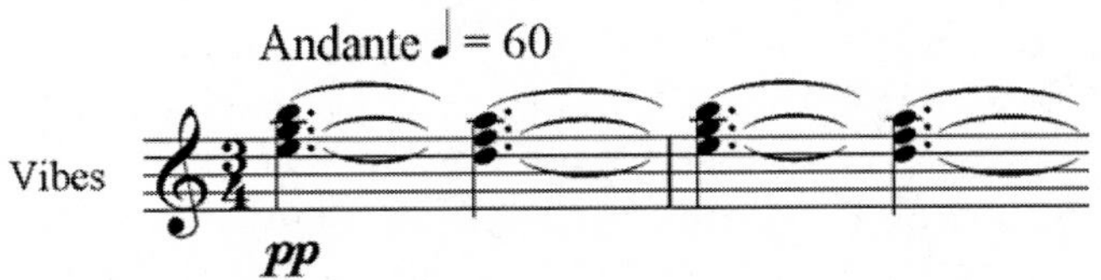

Example 17a

Claude Debussy, *Préludes,* Book 1, No. 10, *La cathédrale engloutie*

Example 17b

Richleau and Rex break into Simon's house to see what they can discover. Here, sound effects combine with the score to create a particularly unnerving atmosphere. The chimes of a clock combine effectively with the quietly clashing minor seconds of the clarinets. Then, the "Fear of Evil" theme returns as Richleau climbs the stairs to the observatory. As he opens the door, Bernard heightens the sense of expectation by momentarily reducing the orchestration to piano and vibraphone alone. All seems deserted, but after a few moments they are confronted by a terrible demon with burning eyes. For this scene, Bernard brought back the highly effective device he had first tried out in *Quatermass 2* in which string **glissandi** slide up and down the compass of a tritone with chordal punctuations from the brass. Rex is about to succumb to the terrible demonic gaze but Richleau manages to resist and throws a crucifix into the diabolical materialization. As they escape, the "Fear of Evil" motif is greatly speeded up and played by full orchestra.

Later on, the riotous orgy of Satanists features a **syncopated** version of the "Mocata" motif accompanied by an impressive battery of percussion (including marimba, tam-tams, bass drum, African drum and conga drum). Originally, the producer, Anthony Nelson-Keys, had hoped for a naked orgy but the morality of the time put a stop to that. Bernard's music, however, fully makes up for anything that prudery might have denied from a visual point of view.

Another interesting percussion effect accompanies the rescue of Simon and Tanith. A timpani **trill** rises through a thundering chromatic scale as Richleau and Rex drive their car, headlamps blazing, towards a manifestation of the Goat of Mendes. The unfortunate initiates are just about to be forced to kneel in submission before this monstrosity but are saved from their satanic baptism in the nick of time. However, the danger for them and their friends has in fact only just begun. They all return to the Eatons' home in the country, and during Richleau's temporary absence on a research trip to the British Museum, Mocata pays Marie a visit, presenting the musical calling card of his motif as he arrives. The "Fear of Evil" motif to which "Mocata" is so closely related also returns during the following scene in which Marie finds herself subjected to the hypnotic power of Mocata's will. An oscillating semitone on piano and vibraphone, with rolls from the suspended cymbal, suggests the penetrating gaze of Mocata's steel-blue eyes.

This diabolical hypnosis session is interrupted by Peggy, and Mocata is shown the door. Foiled in his first attempt to get back Simon and Tanith, Mocata next sets about fulfilling his promise that "something" will come for them in his place. That night, Richleau and his friends stand in the magic circle that has been prepared in the Eatons' living room. The principal chord of this music section, which links the major events together and is used as the scene's heartbeat, appropriately contains yet another tritone:

James Bernard, *The Devil Rides Out* 8M1, bars 37–38 (piano only)

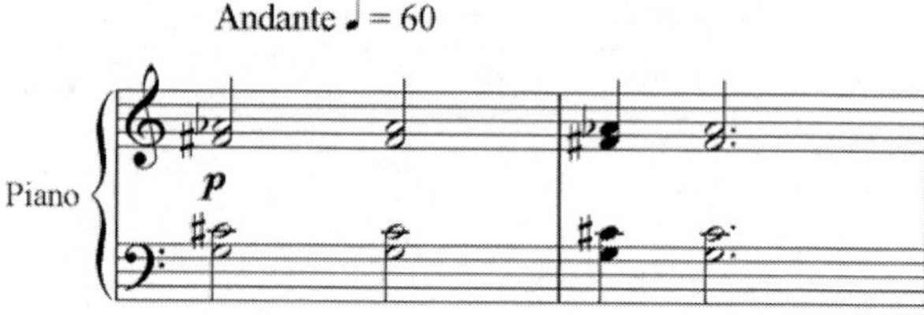

Example 18

This "Heartbeat chord" pervades the first half of this section. The "Magic Circle" motif, which punctuates it, is again derived from the original "Power of Evil" theme, being merely a rearrangement of that theme's first three notes (examples 19 a, b)

James Bernard, *The Devil Rides Out*
8M1, bar 43 (violin I only)

Example 19a

James Bernard, *The Devil Rides Out*
1M1, bar 1 (horns I & II only)

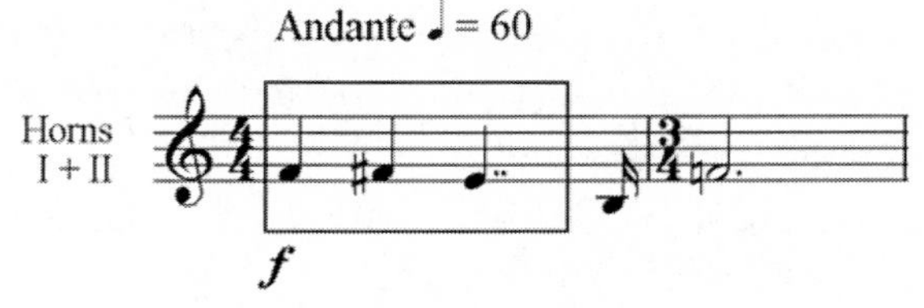

Example 19b

Bernard is careful to point up the significant moments of this scene. The first is a sudden *forte* as Simon asks for a glass of water. It tastes disgusting, so Richard Eaton volunteers to get some fresh, but Richleau points out that this is a trap set by Mocata. The lights then begin to dim and again Bernard emphasizes the action with an increase in the **dynamic** of the "Magic Circle" motif. A wind blows through the room, accompanied in the score by trills on the strings, vibraphone and, later, wind instruments, all of which grow quieter as the wind dies down. Next, Rex's voice can be heard outside but again it is only another hallucination. The "Magic Circle" theme returns, joined by trills on the marimba; then the music, like Rex's phantom voice, fades away. Two beats rest are then followed by the appearance of Mocata's most terrifying conjuration: a giant spider. Bernard's musical equivalent for this again looks back to *The Quatermass Experiment* where the strings played rising and falling **consecutive open fifths, *sul ponticello***. Here, **stopped horns** are also brought in to emphasize the horror with rising chromatic minor seconds. The music reaches a devastating climax when the apparition of Peggy appears at the door and cringes before the rearing monster. For this, Bernard brings in all his brass and horns, their minor seconds struggling to rise through a chromatic scale while the strings and wind interrupt with **chromatically sequenced** statements of the "Magic Circle" motif. Bernard's favorite snap rhythm screws up the tension as Richleau lifts a bowl of holy water and with an incantation hurls it at the hideous manifestation. The spider disintegrates to the grotesque shrieking of violins, again playing *sul ponticello*.

However, the horrors of the night are not over yet. Simon tries to leave the magic circle but Richleau restrains him. Again, Bernard heightens the tension with a simple "Action" theme consisting of a chromatically sequenced chord of a **minor seventh** (it also includes the anxious harmony of an **augmented triad**):

James Bernard, *The Devil Rides Out* 8M2, bar 8 (flutes and oboes only)

Example 20

A little later on after the defeat of the Angel of Death, a string glissando accompanies Tanith's collapse. Rex brings her body to the main house, accompanied by a tragic version of the "Fear of Evil" theme (example 21).

James Bernard, *The Devil Rides Out* 8M2, bars 80–81 (violin I only)

Example 21

Towards the end of the section, a new theme grows out of the above idea, associated with Rex's love for Tanith (example 22).

James Bernard, *The Devil Rides Out* 8M2, bars 97–98

Example 22

The second phrase of this "Love" motif (bar two of example 22) is next made to sound very agitated when it is discovered that Peggy has been abducted by Mocata (example 23).

Without telling anyone, Simon drives to Mocata's house hoping to be able to rescue her. There is only one way to find out where Peggy has been taken. Richleau hypnotizes Marie and induces her to act as a medium for the spirit of Tanith. As Richleau intones, "The sign of Osiris slain; the sign of Osiris risen," trills on the strings are accompanied by an effect unique in Bernard's music to suggest the shimmering descent of Tanith's spirit into Marie's body. It is created by a quartet of suspended hand-bells playing a simple E major chord, accompanied by trills on celesta and high-pitched violins. The violin trills give the impression of there being an added sixth (C sharp) on top of the E major **triad**, connoting the kind of mystical atmosphere exploited by Olivier Messiaen, who was fond of chords of the added sixth:

James Bernard, *The Devil Rides Out* 9M1, bars 10–11

Example 23

James Bernard, *The Devil Rides Out* 9M1, bars 44–45

Example 24

Reel nine introduces us to a motif associated with "The Power of Good." It is derived from the "Hypnosis" motif and will eventually accompany the film's final scene:

James Bernard, *The Devil Rides Out* 9M1, bars 56–61

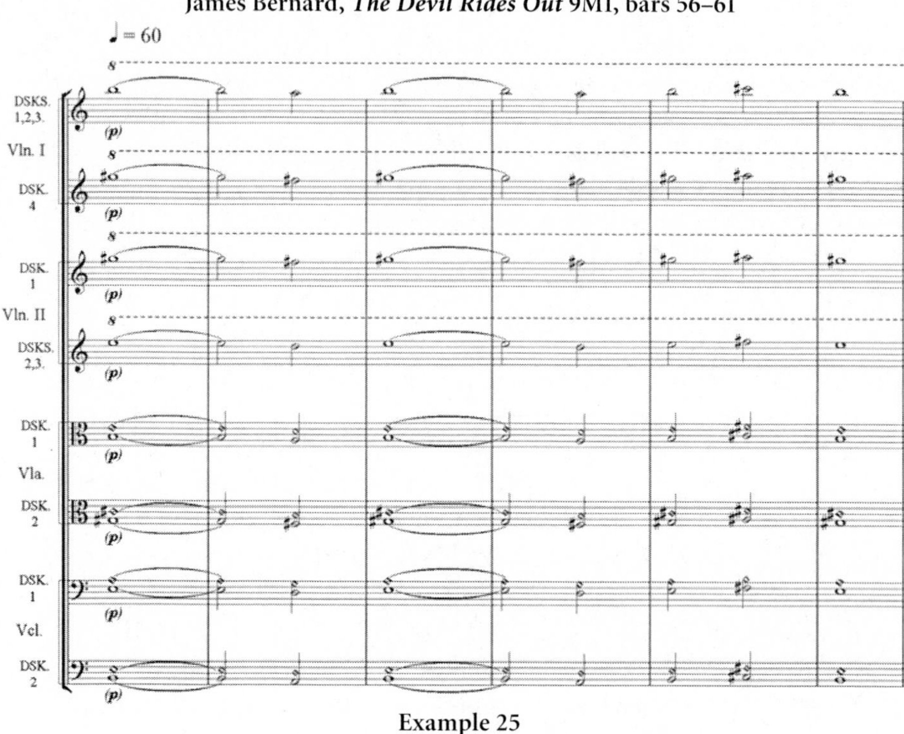

Example 25

Harmonized with consecutive triads and quietly stated by **divided strings** under Richleau's interrogation of Marie/Tanith, it again helps to create an oceanic, mystical atmosphere. Unfortunately, the only information that Tanith is able to impart is that "a winged serpent guards the way." She is too terrified to reveal more; trills on vibraphones, marimba and timpani suggest her growing anxiety. Concerned by the increasing distress of Tanith's voice and the effect it is having on his wife, Richard Eaton interrupts the ceremony. Marie screams and a gigantic string glissando passing through three octaves accompanies her collapse to the floor. (Bernard would use a similarly impressive string glissando for the death of the young girl at the end of the *Dracula* LP.) Fortunately, Marie has not been harmed by her ordeal and Rex recalls that the gates of the house he had visited earlier in the film were guarded by sculptures of just such "winged serpents." So the chase is on.

As Richleau and the others arrive outside this house, we hear tremolo strings playing the "Fear of Evil" motif. Inside, Mocata is already at work and preparing to sacrifice Peggy while the orchestra gives a somber rendition of "The Power of Evil." But just as Mocata begins to lower the knife, the spirit of Tanith again descends into Mrs. Eaton, who utters: "Only those who love without desire shall have power granted them in their darkest hour." Powerless against her, the members of the coven make way for her as she advances towards Peggy, who lies outstretched on the Satanic altar. "The Power of Good" returns with its accompanying consecutive triads.

Peggy sits up and repeats the words of the Sussamma Ritual. The temple is spiritually cleansed in a climactic cataclysm and, rising out of the noisy sound effects, Bernard brings back "The Power of Good" in an orchestral **tutti**.

The final scene begins where the magic circle scene in the Eatons' living room had ended. The "Love" motif introduces a shot of Rex and Tanith walking hand in hand through the garden. Richleau smiles and explains, "Time itself has been reversed for us ... all these things happened but now they have not happened." Bernard quietly reprises "The Power of Good" in a classic example of his serene string style. "The Angel of Death, once being summoned cannot return empty-handed," Richleau continues. "The age-old law demands a life for a life, a soul for a soul and there is only one man in all this world who can replace her life, her soul: the man who invoked the Angel of Death. Mocata is dead."

"Thank God," says Simon.

"Yes," Richleau replies, "He is the one we must thank."

The "Power of Good" theme now climbs to a pitch it has never been allowed to reach before, creating just the same effect as Wagner's use of pitch-ascent at the end of *Parsifal*. The opening theme of Wagner's Act I Prelude has always fallen by a semitone, representing man's fall from grace. At the end of the opera, however, it rises to the **tonic** note an octave higher than the one with which it began, thus representing humanity's redemption through the agency of Christ. Similarly, Bernard's "Power of Good" theme rises to the triumphant pitch always denied it before, signifying that the forces of evil have been well and truly defeated.

James Bernard, *The Devil Rides Out* 10M2, bars 23–25

Example 26

Richard Wagner, *Parsifal*, end of Act III (orchestral reduction)

Example 27

The end title places "The Power of Evil" into an optimistic **major key** and ends with a final triumphant statement of "The Power of Good."

12

Assorted Aristocrats

"Here's to the best man who can drink the most of us,
there'll be a maiden waiting in his bed."

Students Beer Song (words by Tony Colton)
from *Dracula Has Risen from the Grave*

After *The Devil Rides Out*, Bernard would work on nothing but Dracula and Frankenstein features for Hammer, though not all of Hammer's films based on these characters were scored by him. The music for *The Horror of Frankenstein* (EMI/Hammer, dir. Jimmy Sangster, 1970) was composed by Malcolm Williamson, and the two modern-dress Dracula films, *Dracula A.D. 1972* (Warner/Hammer, dir. Alan Gibson, 1972) and *The Satanic Rites of Dracula* (Warner/Hammer, dir. Alan Gibson, 1973) had music by Mike Vickers and John Cacavas respectively.

Though he never actually met a Transylvanian count or a Swiss baron, Bernard did become friendly with an Italian aristocrat who rejoiced in the rather operatic name of the Duke of Verdura. They met while Bernard was on holiday in Sicily with Paul Dehn. One of Dehn's old school friends, who was the son of the ghost-story writer Oliver Onions, had married a Sicilian *principessa*, and he now wanted Dehn to meet his new wife. When Bernard and Dehn checked into their hotel just outside Palermo, they found a note from Onions welcoming them and explaining that a car would be collecting them later that evening. Tired, and longing to lie down, they barely had time to change before the car arrived to whisk them off to a rather grand villa filled with the buzz of Italian voices. After a while, one of these voices came up behind them and said, "Golly Gum Drops!" They turned, to put a face to the voice, and there stood a short little man with an aristocratic, rather hooked nose and a very brown complexion. This was Fulco Santostefano della Cerda, Duke of Verdura, Marquess of Murata la Cerda, one of the many acquaintances of the *principessa*. A highly cultured and well-connected man, Fulco was also a friend of Cecil Beaton, who mentioned him in his diaries:

> This year [1956] instead of staying in the cushioned unreality of a luxury hotel, I rented the apartment of a Sicilian friend, Fulco Verdura: unkind friends said that in taste it was Poor Man's Charlie Beistigui. To me it was extremely pleasant, with avalanches of good art books and long-playing records of the classics; a mix-

> ture of Mannerist paintings, 17th and 18th-century engravings, and sketches by Bérard; nice bits of china, palm trees and dark green walls, an effective if slightly sketchy attempt at interior decoration.[1]

Fulco had also been acquainted with Marie-Laure de Noailles, whom Luchino Visconti's biographer, Laurence Schifano, described as "the high priestess of the Paris *beau monde*":

> In her celebrated salon on Place des États-Unis, the destitute Duke Fulco della Verdura, now reduced to designing bracelets for Channel, rubbed elbows with Russian grand duchesses and princesses washed up by the Revolution and surviving as models or workroom supervisors in the big fashion houses.[2]

Fulco now found himself rubbing elbows with two friendly English visitors and it wasn't long before he volunteered to guide them around the churches of Palermo. In the end he took them both under his wing for the whole of their two-week holiday. He soon became a great friend and every time he came to London, Dehn and Bernard would make a point of meeting him. Bernard recalled:

> At that stage he was living in New York. He had jewelry showrooms in New York, Paris and Rome. Two of his greatest friends were the Cole Porters. When Cole Porter had a new show opening, Mrs. Porter used to ask Fulco to design a first-night present for her husband. On one occasion, Fulco made a beautiful ruby-encrusted cigarette case, which I later saw in an exhibition of jewelry in London. In later years, Fulco gave up New York and came to live in London.

Fulco was also very fond of music, as he described in his own memoirs:

> Music lulled me into daydreams or, if lively, made me want to dance. My emulating stimulus did not get very far but to my great astonishment, I found that I could pick up tunes by ear and play them on the piano with one hand. This made me very proud but, since there wasn't the slightest chance of my being taught music as it wasn't considered suitable for boys, I had to content myself with a rendition of *The Pink Lady*, the *Chocolate Soldier* or very ambitiously, *Clair de Lune*. Then came the fateful day when I was taken to a matinee of *Aida* and completely and literally lost my seven-year-old head.[3]

Fulco's love of Verdi was shared equally by Bernard, who soon found out that they had many other things in common. Indeed, Fulco's description of his ancestral home bears a certain resemblance to the castle of the world's most infamous vampire:

> The staircase of Casa Verdura was rather imposing but, in spite of two enormous mirrors, marble steps, glazed stucco walls, a vaulted ceiling and a life-size, half-naked, seated female holding an urn on her knees, looking at you with a soulful air, it all suggested the adit to some strange mausoleum rather than the entrance to a house where people were supposed to live. [...] Father's part of the house [...] echoed the funereal atmosphere of the stairs: marble floor, glazed stucco, marmoreal walls and huge inlaid stalls from some chancel that should have been in a church.[4]

Bernard Robinson, Hammer's set designer, might well have been inspired by this description but Hammer wasn't able to reveal the interior of the vampire Count's castle in their next Dracula spectacular, *Dracula Has Risen from the Grave*. In this film, Dracula is prevented from entering his home due to a huge crucifix that has been attached to his front door. Instead, he spends most of his time in rented accommodation — principally the gothic cellar of an inn run by Hammer stalwart Michael Ripper. *Dracula Has Risen from the Grave* was typical of the company's growing penchant for lengthy titles, a development that Christopher Lee was reported to have disliked: "I think it's a very bad title. Why not something like 'Dracula Arisen?'"[5]

But Bernard found lengthy titles with plenty of syllables rather useful when it came to thinking up musical themes, and *Dracula Has Risen from the Grave* was no exception. With this film, Hammer's exploitation of Christian imagery reached a new level. In the previous sequel, Dracula had been presented merely as "The Prince of Darkness." Now he was depicted as an inverted Christ figure, and from its Messianic title onwards, *Dracula Has Risen from the Grave* is packed with religious imagery.

The forces of Christianity are upheld by the Monsignor (played by Rupert Davies) who makes a pastoral visit to his priest (Ewan Hooper). None of the priest's flock in the tiny village of Keinenburg will attend Mass any more as the shadow of Count Dracula's castle touches the church in the evening. The Monsignor promptly sets about exorcising the castle by securing a huge golden crucifix to the main entrance. But a storm causes the priest, who has been waiting a little lower down the mountain, to stumble and fall. His head hits the ice of a frozen stream, and the blood from his wound revives the Count, who has been preserved there since the end of the previous sequel.

Up and running again, Dracula enslaves the priest and sets about revenging the desecration of his domain. His ultimate goal is to enroll the Monsignor's niece, Maria (Veronica Carlson), into the vampiric faith. On the way he feasts on a serving maid called Zena (Barbara Ewing) before instructing the priest to incinerate her body, Auschwitz-style, in the ovens of a bakery; and it is in the cellars of this bakery that the Count sets up his temporary, rather uncomfortable headquarters.

The bakery belongs to a cafe owned by Michael Ripper's Max, and it's here that the film's young hero, Paul (Barry Andrews), earns his living. He is in love with Maria but has some difficulty persuading her uncle to allow the romance to blossom after he confesses that he is an atheist. Towards the end of the film, after Dracula has attacked Maria several times, Paul tracks down the Count and stakes him through the heart; but because Paul is unable to pray, this usually fail-safe method of dispatching the undead fails to work. Dracula removes the stake and hurries off to grab Maria.

The final scene takes place outside Dracula's castle. Maria is forced to remove the large crucifix and hurl it over the castle ramparts. It falls down the cliff side and ends up standing, ready to impale the vampire like a moth on a pin when he is finally defeated by the hero. The priest mutters an appropriate prayer and Paul is converted to the faith as Dracula, weeping tears of blood, perishes for the third time in Hammer's continuing saga.

In a laudable attempt to ring the changes, Bernard refrained from using his original "Dra-Cu-La" theme for this film. Instead he developed the short passage that had previously linked statements of that theme, thereby creating a new motif symbolic of the "Wrath of Dracula":

James Bernard, *Dracula Has Risen from the Grave*
1M1, bar 10 (flute only)

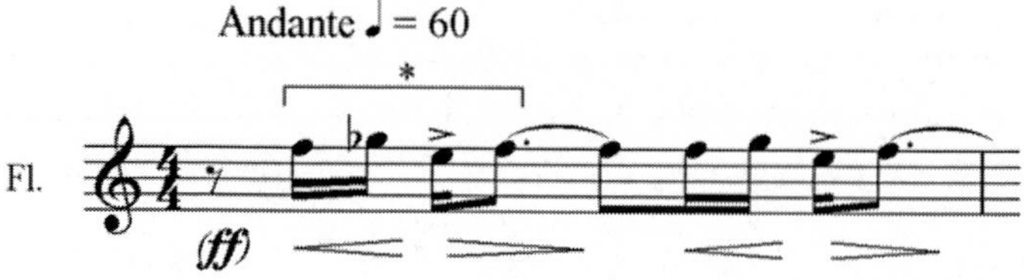

Example 1a

James Bernard, *Dracula* (title theme)

Example 1b

Scored for a large orchestra including four horns, three trumpets, three trombones and one tuba (but omitting the bassoon from the wind section), the music for *Dracula Has Risen from the Grave* is particularly resonant. It vibrates in a sonorous acoustic, investing the images on screen with a monumentality they would not be able to achieve on their own. A reverberant acoustic implies a large space. Thus, Dracula's rather confined quarters in the cellar of Max's cafe are made to seem much larger that they really are.

Bernard's main title music defines the sound world of Hammer's middle period. It begins with the sepulchral timbre of **stopped** horns, muted tuba and lower strings, intoning a theme associated with the shadow of Count Dracula's castle. It is a long shadow, stretching out over scenes that are meant to take place some distance away, and it falls over all the members of the cast. As is so often the case with the most effective of Bernard's themes, mere analysis of this simple "Castle Shadow" motif fails to convey its haunting effect. It is, in fact, no more than a rising **major third** which then falls by a **semitone**. The overall contour of this idea is similar to the threatening motif of Holst's "Mars" from *The Planets* but Bernard is able to make his idea sound sinister without recourse to the implied **tritone** of Holst's idea:

James Bernard, *Dracula Has Risen from the Grave* 1M1, bar 2 (cellos only)

Example 2a

Gustav Holst, *The Planets*, "Mars," bars 3–5 (bassoons only)

Example 2b

After three statements of the "Castle Shadow" theme, each rising in pitch, Bernard then expands its **intervals** to metamorphose it into his response to the syllables of the film's title. In the way Bernard presents this "Syllable" theme, he demonstrates how powerful a simple idea can be made to sound merely by making the entire orchestra play it in unison, without any underlying harmony (see example 3 on pages 198 and 199).

This impressive introduction prepares the ground for the "Wrath of Dracula," again scored for full orchestra but this time harmonized with a slightly altered version of the old "Dracula chord." (Instead of a **minor second** and a tritone, it is now a ***major* second**—but the "devil in music" is still there.) Another echo of the original Dracula march can be found in the snare drum that emphasizes the rhythm, along with shivering splashes of sound from the cymbals. A timpani solo then hammers out a series of unadulterated tritones, and ushers in a contrasting section for horns, brass and strings, symbolizing the act of "Exorcism" and the forces of good. Here the musical reference is to the time-honored plain chant setting of the *Dies Irae*, the text of which has been set in many a Requiem Mass. However, the original melody of the chant has also appeared

MUSIC BY
I.M.I
JAMES BERNARD
Andante
a 2
stopped a 4
mp cresc.
con sord.
a2 con sord.
S.D.
CYMB.
soft sticks
p cresc.
fp cresc.

Example 3

Example 3

as a sinister *memento mori* in a host of secular works including Rachmaninoff's *Isle of the Dead* (first performed in 1907) and *Rhapsody on a Theme of Paganini* (first performed in 1934), Respighi's *Impressioni brasiliane* (first performed in 1927) and Berlioz's *Symphonie fantastique*, to name but three examples. Other composers who worked for Hammer, including Harry Robinson and David Whitaker, also drew on the associations of the chant, respectively in *Lust for a Vampire* (EMI/Hammer, dir. Jimmy Sangster, 1971) and *Vampire Circus* (Rank/Hammer, dir. Robert Young, 1972).

Bernard refrains from quoting the *Die Irae* note-for-note, but sufficient elements of it remain for this motif to resonate with the appropriate associations. His

James Bernard, *Dracula Has Risen from the Grave* 1M1, bars 16–19 (reduction)

Example 4a

"Dies Irae" chant

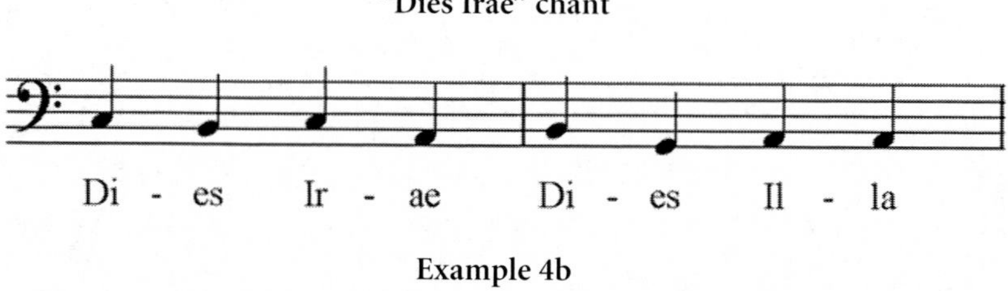

Example 4b

version of what translates as God's "Day of Wrath" therefore provides a suitable counterpart to the "Wrath of Dracula" motif. The simple supporting harmony of alternating **minor thirds** also creates, at certain points a sepulchral, rather archaic-sounding **open fifth** (in the example below between F sharp and B natural):

After this "Exorcism" passage, a final statement of the "Wrath of Dracula" brings the main title to an end.

In the next music section, a connection is made between the "Castle Shadow" motif and the evil deeds of the vampire Count whom that shadow signifies. The opening scene takes place before Dracula was destroyed at the end of the previous film. A mute altar boy discovers blood dripping from a bell-pull in the church. He climbs into the belfry and discovers the dead body of one of Dracula's female victims. Bernard accompanies the mounting tension of this eventual discovery with sequenced statements of the "Castle Shadow" motif, which gradually rise in pitch, alternating between the flutes and the strings, clarinets and oboes. The full orchestra then accompanies the awful discovery with violently oscillating minor seconds.

The "Castle Shadow" motif also underscores the conversation between the Monsignor, his priest and the customers of the village inn. When the Monsignor is told that the shadow of the castle touches the church, the "Dracula chord" appears with its restored minor second, so we know exactly who is being talked about.

Before setting out to exorcise the castle, the Monsignor takes down the crucifix that hangs over the church altar, while the strings quietly play the "Exorcism" motif. Because we are inside the church at this point, the motif sounds much more serene than it did in the main title music, with the supporting harmony moving between *major* rather than *minor* thirds. As the two men climb the mountain, however, the minor third is reinstated and the "Exorcism" motif is presented in counterpoint with the "Castle Shadow" theme. Bernard confessed that counterpoint never came easily to him:

> I can do counterpoint when it has a special purpose: when I have a theme representing Dracula and another representing Mina, for example, and they go against each other. Then the counterpoint has a point to it and it just has to work. But I'm hopeless at writing *abstract* counterpoint, which has no dramatic program to it—for instance, writing a fugue just for the fun of it. I simply don't think I can do that!

This long passage may not be a Bach fugue but it is nonetheless a masterpiece of atmospheric film scoring, drawing, as it does, on the merest of material: two symbolically laden themes, which are combined in continually higher pitches. To reflect the increasing exhaustion of the priest and the Monsignor, Bernard adds his favorite snap rhythm to the "Exorcism" motif:

James Bernard, *Dracula Has Risen from the Grave* 2M1, bars 26–27 (violin I only)

Example 5

The priest stumbles again, his action emphasized by another loud minor second, and the Monsignor allows him to remain behind. The Monsignor carries on alone and as he draws nearer to the castle, the brass threateningly take over the "Castle Shadow" theme from the wind section. Bernard also exploits the jarring effect of **false relations** here:

James Bernard, *Dracula Has Risen from the Grave* 2M1, bars 75–78 (reduction)

Example 6

After the exorcism, we cut back to the castle where the Monsignor attaches the crucifix to the door. The sacred connotation of the bells we hear at this point is emphasized by the **consecutive major thirds** they play. These create much the same effect as the **consecutive triads** heard during the sacred moments of *The Devil Rides Out.* The crucifix has the musical effect of inverting the "Castle Shadow" theme and replacing its minor second with a major second, suggesting that the exorcism has had a positive effect:

James Bernard, *Dracula Has Risen from the Grave*
2M1, bars 104–105 (reduction)

Example 7

Meanwhile, a little further down the mountainside, Count Dracula has been revived by the priest's blood, and the "Castle Shadow" theme returns to its normal shape on terrifying horns and brass. As Dracula rises from his watery grave, we appropriately hear the last three notes of the main "Syllable" theme:

James Bernard, *Dracula Has Risen from the Grave*
3M1, bars 1–2 (reduction)

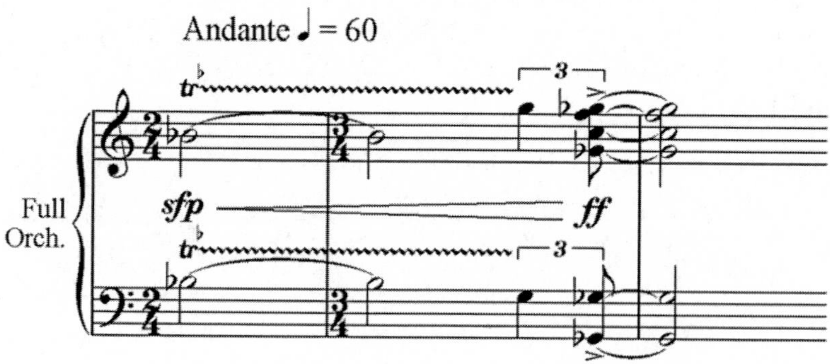

Example 8

As we have seen, Bernard often creates thematic unity in his scores by fragmenting his main syllable themes and extracting independent motifs from those fragments. The overall contour of the above theme, along with its falling semitone, is related to the "Castle Shadow" motif; but whereas the "Castle Shadow" rose by a minor third, the fragment of the "Syllable" theme in example eight rises by a **major sixth**. This major sixth will later recur when Dracula seduces Maria, and it therefore implies rather more than just the concept of resurrection. One could go so far as to invest such a rising sixth with a phallic resonance: the raising of sexual desire. Rising sixths have an interesting symbolic history, often having been associated with male heroism and erotic power. The Finnish semiotician, Eero Tarasti, has pointed out that many of Wagner's themes contain a "rising heroic sixth as the core of the leitmotif" and that "it is not without interest to notice that this ascending sixth, so characteristic of Wagner's thematics, is found even in the main theme of Richard Strauss's *Heldenleben*."[6] The heroes of Wagner and Strauss are frequently defined in terms of sexual power, and that is even more the case with Count Dracula, an erotic anti-hero *par excellence*. It therefore seems reasonable to label the motif to which Dracula is resurrected, "Phallic." It appropriately returns whenever Dracula and Maria are together, and in reel nine it is played by a pastoral oboe over a shot of the dawn, suggesting that the erotic forces of the night have been temporarily subdued.

Whatever the homoerotic undertones of Stoker's original novel, Hammer's approach to Dracula was, however, strictly heterosexual. As Dracula stares into the priest's eyes, we hear a strident version of what will later be made to sound seductive when the Count is applying his hypnotic powers to female victims. This "Hypnosis" motif is no more than a rising and falling **tone**, harmonized with another minor second and a tritone.

Another interesting thematic connection can be found in the accompanying major thirds of the film's brief love theme. These relate it to the "Exorcism" motif, which is, after all, concerned with the love of God:

James Bernard, *Dracula Has Risen from the Grave* 5M1, bars 1–5

Andante ♩ = 60 — accel.

Vln. I — *p dolce* — *poco cresc.*

Vla. — *p dolce* — *poco cresc.*

Vcl. — *p dolce poco cresc.*

Example 9

Later, Zena, the maid at Max's cafe, walks home through the forest. Dracula appears before her with the "Syllable" theme, and as he stares into her eyes we hear the rising tone of the "Hypnosis" motif. This is now soft and seductive and made all the more alluring by the **acciaccatura** before the second chord; but it is also frightening due to the supporting harmony of **augmented triads** and a shivering **trill** on the suspended cymbal:

James Bernard, *Dracula Has Risen from the Grave* 5M2, bars 126–129 (reduction)

Example 10

By this stage in the film, all the principal motifs have been introduced. Bernard does, however, continue to develop them for certain scenes. In the final section of the film, for example, which shows Dracula and Maria making their way back to the castle, the opening notes of the "Syllable" theme are presented in **canon** between strings and wind:

James Bernard, *Dracula Has Risen from the Grave* 10M1, bars 1–2 (violin I only)

Example 11

After the destruction of Dracula, the film ends with the "Exorcism" theme transposed into a major key, with a bell adding a suitable sense of benediction:

James Bernard, *Dracula Has Risen from the Grave* 10M2, bars 4–5

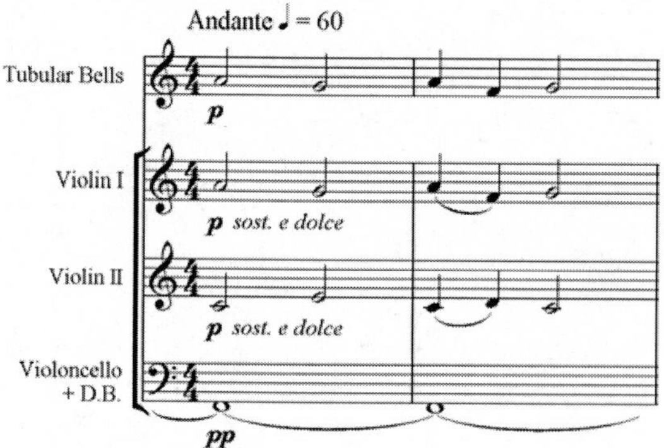

Example 12

No sooner had Dracula been dispatched than Hammer announced that *Frankenstein Must Be Destroyed* as well. The film of that name was the fifth of Hammer's Frankenstein series, and Bernard's third Frankenstein score. The Baron, still played by Peter Cushing, was at his most sadistic in this sequel: charming and urbane as ever, but revealing a much nastier ruthlessness and, in the notorious rape scene, a sexual violence that many thought out of place.

In an attempt to cure the insanity of his one-time colleague, Prof. Brandt, Frankenstein abducts him from a lunatic asylum only to induce a heart attack in his patient. Desperate to keep Brandt's brain alive (the Baron is greedy for the medical secrets it contains), he transplants it into the body of another man, Prof. Richter (Freddie Jones). The hybrid result of Frankenstein's experiment then sets about destroying his creator in a fiery finale. Caught up in the plot is Anna Spengler (Veronica Carlson), at whose boarding house Frankenstein has taken rooms. The hospital treatment of Anna's mother is being financed by Anna's boyfriend Karl (Simon Ward) who has been getting the necessary money by stealing cocaine from the lunatic asylum at which he works, and selling it on the black market. Frankenstein finds out about this and uses the knowledge to blackmail the couple into helping him. After removing Brandt's brain, Frankenstein buries the body in Anna's back garden. In a spectacularly macabre scene, a water main bursts, exposing the arm of the corpse, which waves gruesomely from the saturated rose beds.

Bernard recalled having visited Bray Studios, where the film was being shot, to discuss his music with producer Anthony Nelson-Keys:

> He was a charming man, and he said to me, "Jimmy, I'd like you to come down. I want to hear what your ideas are," which was rather unusual for a producer. So I went down and plonked out the music on some terrible old upright at Bray Studios after which he gave me lunch, apparently satisfied with what I'd come up with. So there were occasions when I went to Bray but, alas, I never saw any of the filming there, nor did I get to meet the actors.

During the opening credits, Bernard again takes advantage of the film's lengthy title to write another "Syllable" theme. Again based on Lisztian **augmented triads**, it continues beyond the rhythm of the title words with a subsidiary phrase. After the main theme has "set" the words "Frank-En-Stein Must Be Des-Troyed," this extra phrase suggests the additional words "Utt-Er-Ly Des-Troyed":

James Bernard, *Frankenstein Must Be Destroyed* 1M1, bars 7–8 (reduction)

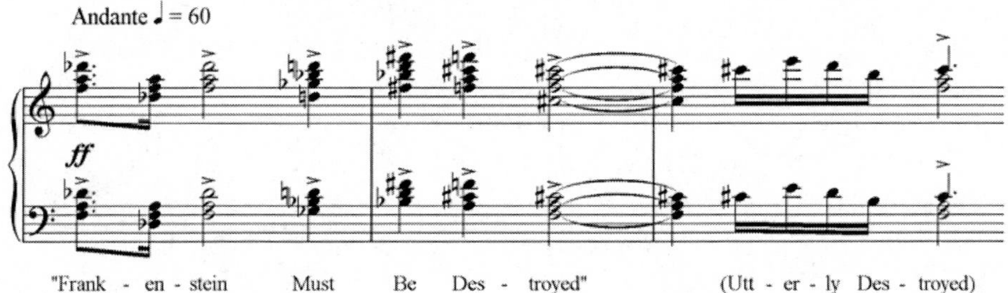

Example 13

The opening scenes of the film achieve an atmospheric texture unsurpassed by any of Hammer's other Frankenstein features. They are eloquently lit, and employ a hand-held camera; Fisher's visual style here achieves an intensity and involvement that reflects the director's own comments about the story:

> Freddie Jones plays a man who has his brain transplanted to a new body by Frankenstein, and he goes to visit his wife who fails to recognize him and rejects him. I loved that subject, which I thought was a most difficult one to portray, and I thought about that film more than any other I've done because of this element."[7]

The opening street scenes are accompanied by a Zither (an instrument suggested to the composer by Philip Martell). Indeed, the images and the music owe something to *The Third Man* (British Lion/London Films/David O. Selznick/Alexander Korda, dir. Carol Reed, 1949), Bernard's dreamy zither waltz echoing the famous "Harry Lime" theme of Anton Karas. A man is being stalked through these deserted streets. Eventually, his head is cut off with a sickle by his pursuer, a murder that is musically covered with two bars of effectively orchestrated chromatic scale. We are then introduced to a burglar who breaks into a mysterious house. All Bernard needs to increase the tension of this scene is to sequence a **triplet** theme (another of the themes he later incorporated in the score for Hammer's *Dracula* LP):

James Bernard, *Frankenstein Must Be Destroyed*
1M3, bars 31–32 (reduction)

Example 14

The orchestra, quietly playing the "Syllable" theme, tells us who is living in this house. The burglar has indeed stumbled on Frankenstein's laboratory. A struggle between the Baron and the burglar ensues, the accompanying "Fight" motif exploiting the familiar snap rhythm that Bernard often uses for scenes of violence. Minor seconds are here as well, along with **tremolos** on the xylophone, and these rise chromatically to suitably clattering effect:

James Bernard, *Frankenstein Must Be Destroyed*
1M3, bar 88 (reduction)

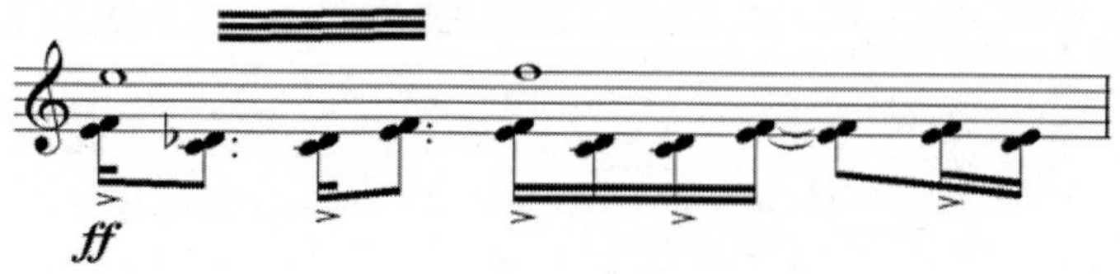

Example 15

Having blackmailed Anna and Karl, Frankenstein sets about his abduction of Brandt. During the subsequent operation on Brandt's brain, oscillating minor seconds on vibraphones create a cushion of eerie sound, under which the rising semitone figure discussed in the previous example is brought in. Again, a great deal of atmosphere is achieved with very little material here. It proved so successful that it too found its way into the *Dracula* LP.

Anna has her own theme, again based on a rising semitone, which is harmonized with a falling minor third. Its short linking passage is derived from the "Utt-Er-Ly Des-Troyed" phrase:

James Bernard, *Frankenstein Must Be Destroyed*
5M2, bars 3–5 (reduction)

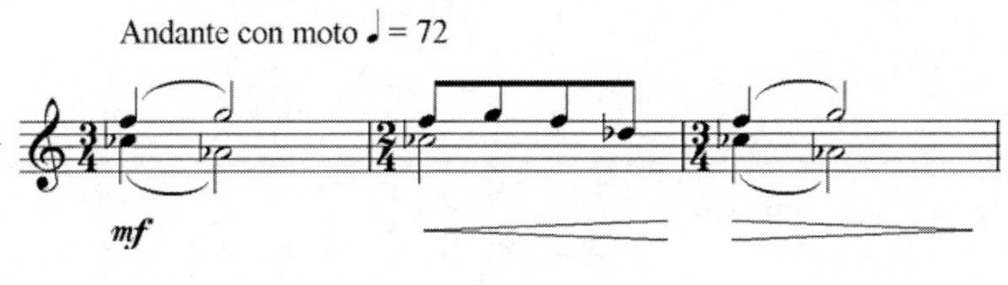

Example 16

Anna cannot sleep after her ordeal, so she gets up and walks out into the garden. In her garden shed she comes across Karl guarding the unconscious Professor. The "Scream" motif that accompanies her shocked reaction to this comprises a *fortissimo* **augmented seventh**: exactly the same interval used by Bernard Herrmann eight years earlier for the famous shower scene of *Psycho*. The James Bernard-Bernard Herrmann relationship has now come full circle.

After the controversial rape scene that follows,[8] the Baron is now ready to undertake the brain transplant. In his notes for the CD reissue of the *Dracula* LP, Bernard explained, "just before Bill Mitchell begins to speak, a sustained vibraphone tremolo is introduced and continues behind the voice, with soft interjections from muted horns and trumpets. This is derived from the accompaniment to one of Peter Cushing's highly intricate brain operations on poor Freddie Jones. Is it too far-fetched to suggest that here we are trying to implant intimations of fear in the listener's brain?"[9]

The vibraphone tremolo to which Bernard refers is based on two superimposed tritones a minor second apart, under which the "Syllable" theme is softly intoned:

James Bernard, *Frankenstein Must Be Destroyed* 6M2, bars 30–34 (reduction)

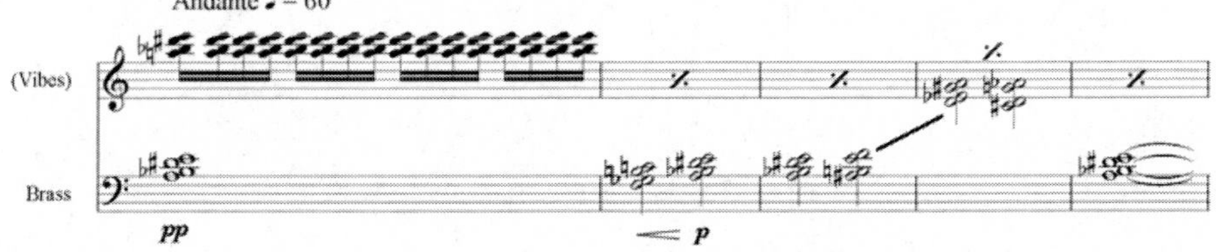

Example 17

Frankenstein is now the chief suspect of a murder inquiry, and during the police search of Anna's boarding house the "Dracula chord" is sustained for bar after bar, accompanied by a four-note rising figure, which perfectly complements the tension of the scene. However, a far more dangerous situation occurs later when the water main bursts in the garden. As Anna screams, and desperately drags the revealed corpse to a hiding place in the adjacent shrubbery, the previously troubled tranquility of her own motif is made to shriek by harmonizing it with the augmented seventh "Scream" interval:

James Bernard, *Frankenstein Must Be Destroyed*
7M4, bar 6 (reduction)

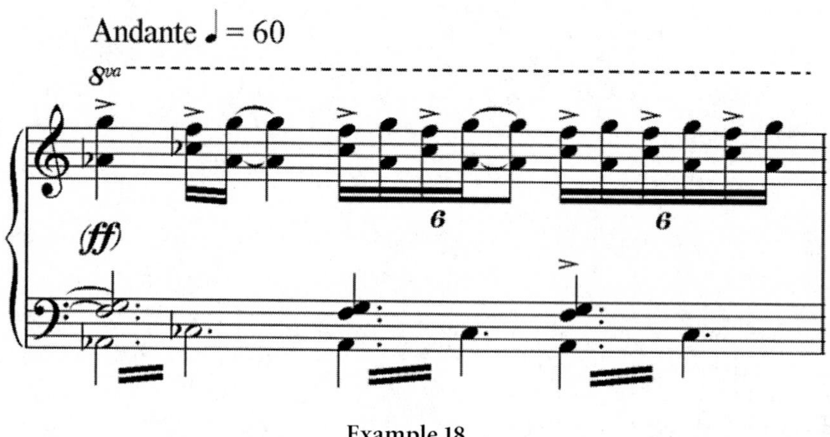

Example 18

In this score, Bernard continues to demonstrate his ability to generate new ideas from existing themes. When Richter/Brandt visits his wife at her home, the music reflects his tragic situation with a **pianissimo** transformation of the "Utt-Er-Ly Des-Troyed" phrase:

James Bernard, *Frankenstein Must Be Destroyed* 10M2, bars 51–53 (reduction)

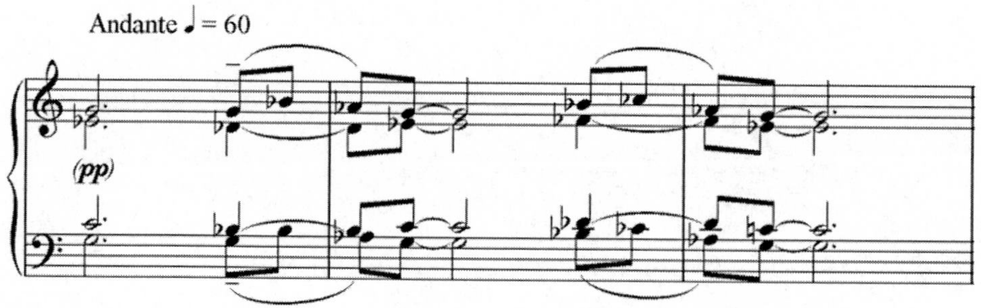

Example 19

The "Utt-Er-Ly Des-Troyed" phrase is further metamorphosed for the film's climax when it represents the fire:

James Bernard, *Frankenstein Must Be Destroyed* 11M2, bar 52

Example 20

The film ends with an elaborated statement of the "Syllable" theme in the form of a lugubrious waltz, echoing the dreamy zither waltz with which the action of the film began. The final bars reiterate the "Utt-Er-Ly Des-Troyed" phrase but in fact Hammer's Baron was to return for one more film before suffering that irreversible fate.

13

Kapellmeister to Count Dracula

"Master, did I do well? Did I please you?"

Lucy Paxton (Isla Blair) in *Taste the Blood of Dracula* (Warner/Hammer, 1970)

Taste the Blood of Dracula Hammer's fourth Dracula film, faithfully took up the story from the end of the previous sequel. A dealer in curios, Weller (Roy Kinnear), finds himself abandoned in a lonely Carpathian forest. To his horror, he witnesses Dracula's death but retains sufficient presence of mind to gather up the vampire's ring, cloak and powdered blood. These unholy relics find their way back to London where they are eventually purchased by three decadent Victorian pleasure seekers: Paxton (played by Peter Sallis), Secker (John Carson) and Hargood (Geoffrey Keen). All three have by this time become the disciples of a devil worshipper, Lord Courtley (Ralph Bates). At a ceremony in a deserted church (the only occasion when Hammer made use of the ready-made Gothic atmosphere of London's Highgate Cemetery), Courtley swallows the reconstituted blood and is transformed into the arch-vampire himself. Dracula then sets about destroying the families of the three men before being overcome by the religious imagery of the ruined church in which he has taken up residence. Falling to his death, he becomes a writhing sacrificial offering on a Christian altar.

The producer of this film, Aida Young, let it be known that she had found Bernard's previous Dracula score "too discordant." Bernard at first felt rather put out: "'How dare she!' I thought—but then I reflected that as she was the one who was paying me, I had better do what she wanted." The result was one of the most lyrical of all Bernard's melodies (with the possible exception of the love theme from *Scars of Dracula*); but the film opens with another impressive "Syllable" theme scored for somber brass, violas, cellos and basses. This rises and falls through a **tritone** and is answered by the violins (see example 1 on page 211).

Simple **minor thirds** underscore the opening scene set in a coach in which Weller encounters a lunatic fellow-passenger. The lunatic lunges at one of Weller's wares, a struggle ensues and Weller is thrown to the ground. Again, Bernard economically

James Bernard, *Taste the Blood of Dracula* 1M1, bars 1–8

Example 1

bases the passage that accompanies this fall on an accelerated version of the "Syllable" theme. Tritones on timpani and slowly moving strings accompany Weller's frightened wanderings through the wood, along with **trills** from the clarinets in their sinister **chalumeau** register.

After Dracula's blood-curdling screams, Bernard then employs **consecutive tritones** in a manner that was later to be used ironically by composer Howard Shore in his score for Tim Burton's film homage to the Z-movie director, *Ed Wood* (Tim Burton, Touchstone/Buena Vista [Denise di Novi, Tim Burton], 1994. Shore emphasized their effect with the weird timbre of the electronic **Theremin,** thereby adding a further connotation of science fiction horror):

James Bernard, *Taste the Blood of Dracula* 1M2, bars 22–24 (trumpets only)

Example 2

On the Beach: Paul Dehn and James Bernard on holiday, April 1970 (photograph James Bernard).

When we are introduced to Dracula on screen, the original "Dra-Cu-La" theme returns in the brass. The prologue now over, the main title can proceed. Coincidentally, the "Love" theme that underscores this sequence can be made to conform to the syllables of the film title, though this was not consciously intended by the composer:

James Bernard, *Taste the Blood of Dracula* 1M2A, bars 8–13

Example 3

The main title is superimposed over action in which the Paxton, Secker and Hargood families are seen leaving church after a Sunday morning service. Dialogue and church bells obscure the quiet entry of Bernard's clarinet melody but the result is just what Aida Young had asked for: an understated sequence that seems far removed from a typical Hammer horror film. The sequence therefore has the effect of undercutting our expectations, and in this, Bernard again set a precedent for future Hammer horrors. David Whitaker's score for *Dr. Jekyll and Sister Hyde*, for example, begins with a Romantic waltz, as does Christopher Gunning's main title music for *Hands of the Ripper* (Peter Sasdy, Rank/Hammer [Aida Young], 1971). Bernard's "Love" theme, however, is closely related to the "Dra-Cu-La" theme. When Weller contemplated Dracula's blood at the end of the prologue, the "Dra-Cu-La" theme was compressed into an **augmented fourth**. A rising F and G then led to a repetition, as follows:

James Bernard, *Taste the Blood of Dracula* 1M2A, bars 2–4 (horns only)

Example 4a

By transposing and rearranging the notes of the second bar of the above example, we arrive at a troubled version of the "Love" theme that later appears in reel nine when the young hero, Paul, goes in search of his abducted fiancée, Alice:

James Bernard, *Taste the Blood of Dracula* 9M4, bars 1–2 (timps and violin I only)

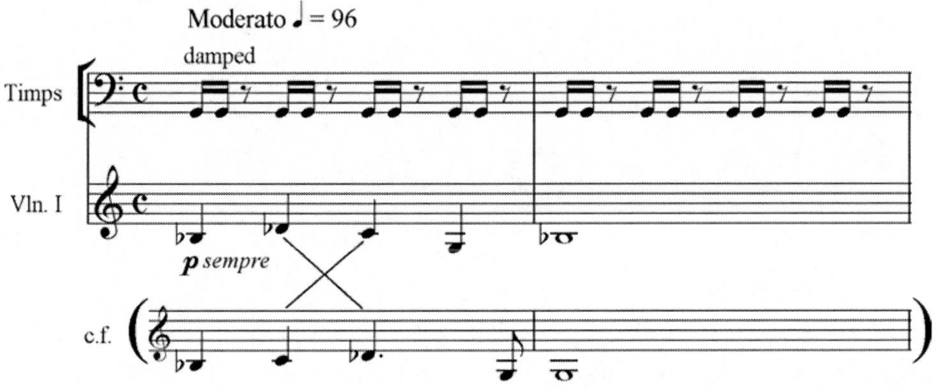

Example 4b

By simply raising the D flat in the violin line of example 4b by a tone (to E flat), the "Love" theme here is revealed in all its original tranquility. This is another example of Bernard's organic and economical approach to the generation of themes, an approach that accounts for the unity not only of each individual score but also of his entire output. The flute and first violins take over for the second repeat of the melody line, and for its final statement, strings, clarinet and flute combine to play it together. The final bars remind us that all is not as normal and happy as it seems: the final falling **fourth** of the melody becomes an ominous tritone on equally ominous **tremolo** strings.

Soon after the beginning of the film, Paxton, Secker and Hargood visit a brothel where they are entertained by an erotic snake dancer. An oriental melody line for oboe was originally intended to accompany this scene but in the event only the accompanying rhythm track was used. At the end of this section of his score, Bernard simply wrote "*Da Capo Ad Nauseam!*" perhaps reflecting something of the boredom of the three degenerates who are longing for something *really* exciting to happen. They don't have long to wait.

Hargood refuses to allow his daughter, Alice, to attend a party with Paul Paxton, the son of his fellow debauchee; but she disobeys him and later that night slips out unnoticed. Like Maria in *Dracula Has Risen from the Grave*, Alice often has to climb out of her bedroom window to reach her boyfriend. As she does so, the "Love" theme is interspersed with figurations from two flutes that romantically imitate both the sound of a nightingale and the evocatively photographed plume of the moonlit fountain in the garden below. This figuration is rather in the manner of Wagner's Wood-Bird from *Siegfried*. Indeed, the flute actually plays the first four notes sung by Wagner's Woodbird (though the pitches are rearranged and, in this example, **transposed** down a **semitone**), and it is accompanied by strings playing ***sul tasto***:

James Bernard, *Taste the Blood of Dracula* 3M1, bars 1–5

Example 5a

The romantic idyll is again undermined by a tritone that disrupts the flow of the theme just before the strings take over with a repeat.

The three men have by now encountered the devil worshipper, Lord Courtley, who has persuaded them to purchase Dracula's conveniently powdered blood and

Richard Wagner, *Siegfried*, Act II, scene 2

Example 5b

other personal effects. As Weller shows them these unholy relics, Bernard combines the "Hypnosis" motif from *Dracula Has Risen from the Grave* with another tritone, creating a hushed sense of dread and latent evil with only strings, brass and a shivering cymbal.

Having purchased Dracula's blood from Weller, the three men then make their way to a ruined church for the ceremony. Their journey (an indispensable coach ride) is a classic example of Bernardian **chromatic sequencing**. The main idea for this is merely a speeded-up version of the first four notes of the "Syllable" theme, accompanied by a pounding **ostinato** rhythm on the timpani and lower strings. The choice of theme is not only economical, it is also highly appropriate due to the fact that Lord Courtley will soon be asking all concerned literally to taste the blood of Dracula.

Towards the end of this Highgate Cemetery section, a tam-tam is synchronized with a cut to the interior of the church where we first of all focus on a flaming torch. Originally, Bernard intended to continue the music after this point with tremolo string **harmonics** over the "Syllable" theme on cellos and basses, later to be joined by ***pianissimo*** horns, but this music was omitted in favor of much more atmospheric silence, as the three men make their way through the derelict church.

Courtley is waiting for them, and wastes no time in setting to work. He distributes a portion of Dracula's dried blood into three glass goblets and a silver chalice before slashing the palm of his hand with a sacrificial blade. The blood from the wound reactivates the powder and thick magenta gore rises magically from within. During this grisly ritual, Bernard exploits the sepulchral timbre of the organ, an instrument he had used before in the *Magnificat and Nunc Dimittis*. Indeed, that Anglican church music has, ironically, several things in common with the "Black Mass" of *Taste the Blood of Dracula*. The *Magnificat* opens with a cluster of notes, which can be analyzed as a C major chord with an **added fourth** and **sixth**. The "Black Mass" similarly employs added notes; in example 6b, Bernard adds a sixth to an **augmented triad**.

James Bernard, *Magnificat and Nunc Dimittis*, bars 1–3 (organs only)

Example 6a

As we have seen, added sixths were a

favorite coloration in the ecstatic music of Debussy and Messiaen, and the music for the Black Mass might be said to demonize their magical/sacred connotation.

The Black Mass organ music also incorporates the "Syllable" theme, as well as introducing some fairly advanced cluster chords as the reconstituted blood begins to rise in the crystal goblets. The clusters are based around augmented and **perfect fourths**, which again account for their rather Scriabinesque quality. In the example below, the notes to the right of the stem in Bernard's chord for the rising blood create a series of **augmented** and **diminished fourths**; the notes to the left (omitting the E natural bass note) form augmented and perfect fourths. Each chord also encompasses a major seventh. Along with the overall texture of fourths, Bernard's music here echoes the trill theme from Scriabin's "Black Mass" piano Sonata (Op. 68), the right hand line of which also encompasses a major seventh (examples 7a, b)

As a mark of its effectiveness, Bernard drew on this effective organ music for the scene set in the vault of Castle Dracula towards the climax of the story on the *Dracula* LP.

As in *Dracula, Prince of Darkness*, the Count's eventual regeneration is accompanied with rising trills in the strings. Dracula is introduced with his old theme,

James Bernard, *Taste the Blood of Dracula*
4M2, bars 47–48

Example 6b

James Bernard, *Taste the Blood of Dracula*
4M2, bar 65

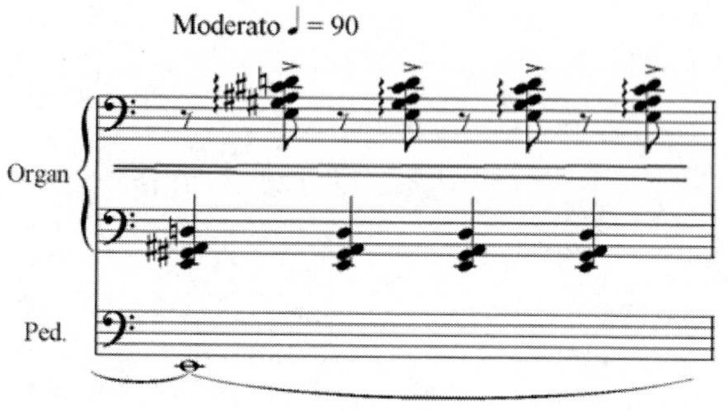

Example 7a

Alexander Scriabin, *Piano Sonata No. 9*, bar 25

Example 7b

but in its new augmented fourth version. His dialogue ("They have destroyed my servant ... they will be destroyed") is set in the manner of an operatic recitative, which Christopher Lee, who always wanted to be an opera singer rather than film star, would no doubt have preferred to sing.

Alice returns from the party to be confronted by her father. Terrorized, she runs out into the garden where Dracula puts her under his influence to the rising tones of the "Hypnosis" motif from *Dracula Has Risen from the Grave*. Alice is not actually vampirized at this point but instead becomes Dracula's servant. She takes a spade and smashes it against her drunken father's head. "The first!" Dracula intones in the same way that countless opera singers have shouted "*Eins*!" after forging the first magic bullet in the "Wolf's Glen" scene of Weber's *Der Freischütz*. Again, the operatic conventions of Hammer dramaturgy are to plain to see. All that is missing is the singing (though in the above mentioned scene from *Der Freischütz*, Weber specifically asks for the words to be spoken or shouted as melodrama and definitely not sung).

Paxton is convinced that Lord Courtley has come back from the dead and is responsible for Hargood's murder, so he and Secker return to the church to find out if this is true. They cannot locate Courtley's body but during the course of their search they do discover Lucy, who has already been vampirized by the Count. Bernard's atmospheric accompaniment to this scene was so effective that, again, he reused it at the beginning of the *Dracula* LP (when the coach breaks its axle on the "rock strewn and deeply rutted" road):

James Bernard, *Taste the Blood of Dracula* 8M1, bars 10–12

Example 8

The "Dra-Cu-La" motif is now further compressed. It no longer spans even an augmented fourth and is now reduced to a minor third, played in **harmonics** by **muted strings**, but it provides just the right suggestion of Dracula's unseen presence.

By now, Lucy has been vampirized, and she in turn contaminates Secker's only son, Jeremy, who promptly stabs his own father to death. After that, the only person left to redeem the situation is Paul. Before his murder, Secker (always the more warm-hearted and philosophical of the three debauchees) left instructions telling Paul what he must do. Paul immediately sets off for the ruined church. His journey begins with the tragic version of the "Love" theme mentioned earlier. It is accompanied by a pounding **ostinato** rhythm on the timpani to suggest the urgency of his mission ("Find her, Paul" Secker's narration insists. "Find her before it is too late!")

As soon as the narration is over, an even more agitated ostinato in the strings accompanies the tragic "Love" theme, which is now played by the wind. This reaches its peak when Paul discovers Lucy's now well-and-truly dead body in a lake. Here, Bernard metamorphoses his "Love" theme in a truly Lisztian fashion, widening the **intervals** and giving it a new rhythmic propulsion, thereby investing the scene with an epic grandeur that the live action alone is unable to convey:

James Bernard, *Taste the Blood of Dracula* 9M4, bars 41–46 (strings only)

Example 9

Inside the church, Paul reconsecrates the altar and encounters Alice, who is still under Dracula's influence. During the battle that follows, Dracula is forced up into the organ loft, where, with inspired symbolism, he wrenches organ pipes from the disused instrument and hurls them like phallic javelins onto the terrified couple below. This was one of Hammer's most explicit references to Dracula's basis in the historical figure of Vlad the Impaler. But Dracula is eventually overcome and the film ends with a triumphant metamorphosis of the "Love" theme. Placed in a major key, it is in fact based on the same kind of cadence structure found at the end of many a Bach chorale:

James Bernard, *Taste the Blood of Dracula* 10M2, bars 4–5

Example 10

Bernard's penultimate Dracula score, *Scars of Dracula* marked a turning point in Hammer's presentation of the its most bankable character. After *Scars of Dracula*, Christopher Lee's Dracula would no longer stride through opulent nineteenth-century settings. Proving his immortality, he would materialize in two films set in not-so-swinging '70s London. After that, the character would make his last Hammer appearance, played by John Forbes Robertson, in *The Legend of the Seven Golden Vampires*.

But all that lay in the future. *Scars of Dracula* was an attempt at a fresh start and a return to certain neglected aspects of the original novel. The Count was portrayed once more as an icily courteous host and was also shown scaling the walls of his castle as described in chapter three of Stoker's book; but as Christopher Lee himself put it:

> *Scars of Dracula* was truly feeble. It was a story with Dracula popped in almost as an afterthought. Even the Hammer makeup for once was tepid. It's one thing to look like death warmed up, quite another to look unhealthy. I was a pantomime figure. Everything was over the top, especially the giant bat whose electrically motored wings flapped with slow deliberation as if it were doing morning exercises.[1]

However, Bernard rose above the visual limitations and provided yet another sonorous score that pumped up the film's rather sluggish blood pressure. Ironically, he saved one of his most beautiful love themes for this late vampire entry, and later made sure it featured in Hammer's subsequent *Dracula* vinyl disc.

Screenwriter "John Elder" (Anthony Hinds) made no attempt to continue the story from the end of *Taste the Blood of Dracula*. Instead, as Christopher Lee pointed out, a rather obviously artificial bat is responsible for reviving the Count after an unspecified staking. After the bat has dribbled some blood onto the powdered remains, Dracula is back and terrorizing the villagers. Perhaps by way of revenge for having been overcome by the religious iconography at the end of *Taste the Blood of Dracula,* the vampire wastes no time in vilely desecrating the village church, before taking a more personal interest in some of its inhabitants.

In a town not far away, Sarah (played by Jenny Hanley) is enjoying her birthday party in the company of her fiancé, Simon (Dennis Waterman). Simon's brother, Paul (Christopher Matthews), is a little late, due to an all-night engagement with a lady-friend who happens to be the Burgomeister's daughter. Caught in the act, Paul manages to escape but is pursued by the Burgomeister's lackeys to Sarah's party. Leaping from a window like Shaw's Chocolate Soldier, he falls into a waiting carriage and soon finds himself traveling on the bumpy road to Castle Dracula. There he meets Tania (Anouska Hempel), who introduces him to her master. Paul is given a bed for the night and has another encounter with Tania (who attempts to vampirize him). After Dracula's sadistic attack on the beautiful bloodsucker, he tries to escape. His attempt, however, is foiled and he ends up on a meat hook in Dracula's crypt.

Meanwhile, Sarah and Simon go in search of Paul. They eventually arrive at the castle and, after some narrow escapes, including drugged soup and midnight visitations from the resident vampires, they are saved in a *deus ex machina* finale as Dracula is struck by lightning and goes up in spectacular flames.

For *Scars of Dracula,* Bernard eschewed the "Dra-Cu-La" theme altogether. Instead, he created a new Dracula motif that is stated at the very outset of the film, covering a shot of Dracula's castle:

James Bernard, *Scars of Dracula* 1M1, bars 1–3

Example 11a

This idea later forms part of the film's "Syllable" theme, and is played in unison by the whole orchestra during the main title:

James Bernard, *Scars of Dracula* 1M2, bar 5 (flutes only)

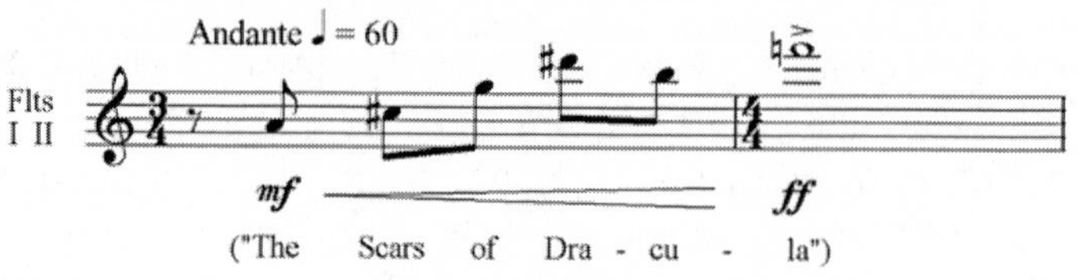

Example 11b

The next music section begins with an idea that is associated with "Pathos." (It first accompanies a traveling shot of a peasant carrying his dead daughter.) The theme is actually related to the main "Love" theme and it alternates with the "Syllable" theme:

James Bernard, *Scars of Dracula* 1M2, bars 1–2

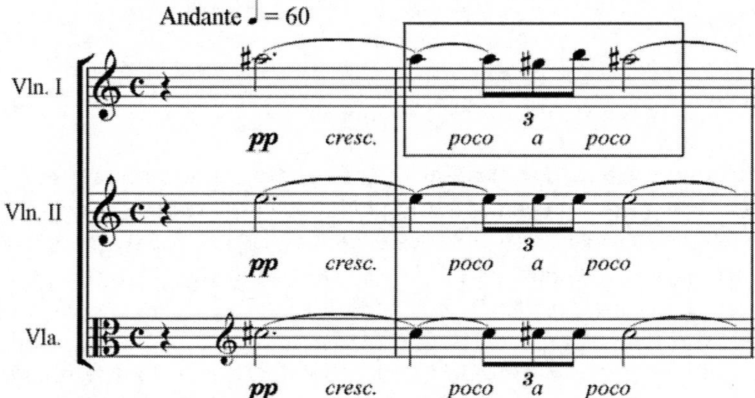

Example 12a

cf. Love Theme:

Example 12b

Another theme makes an early appearance in the film and is associated with the "Vampire Bat" that is responsible for reviving Dracula. Its screeching call is imitated by high-pitched chromatic **triplets** in the woodwind and strings:

James Bernard, *Scars of Dracula* 1M1, bar 16

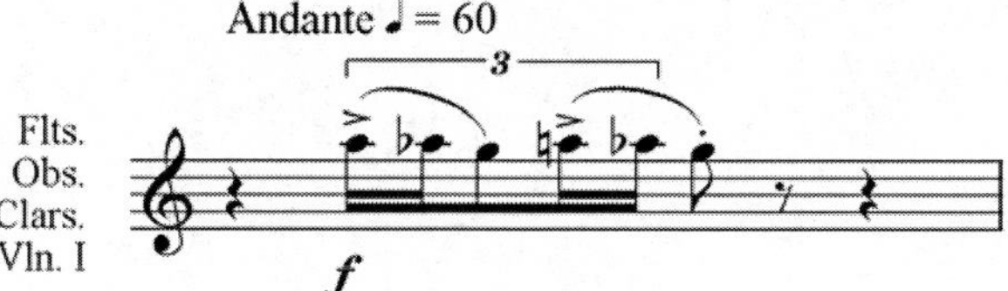

Example 13

After the desecration of their church, the villagers decide to storm the castle and burn it down. Their progress is accompanied by a straightforward but vigorous march that is repeated in continually higher pitches:

James Bernard, *Scars of Dracula* 1M3, bars 1–4 (strings only)

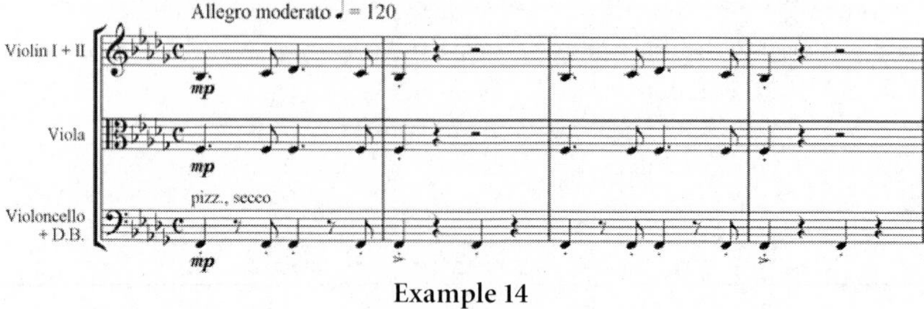

Example 14

The villagers return to the church where they expect to find their womenfolk, but instead they discover that a massacre has taken place. The horrible discovery is punctuated by a rising whole-tone scale, each new atrocity emphasized by a successive tone, played ***sforzando***. The "Pathos" theme then takes over to cover the reaction of the men (particularly the innkeeper, again played by Michael Ripper).

The two bars that introduce us to Paul lying in bed with the Burgomeister's daughter comprise one of Bernard's shortest-ever cues. It lasts only four seconds but is a rare example of his approach to comedy scoring. It was originally written for solo clarinet; Philip Martell added a piccolo to heighten the effect. This scene and the one that follows (in which Bob Todd's apoplectic Burgomeister discovers what as been going on) is far more like a *Carry On* movie than a Hammer horror film.

James Bernard, *Scars of Dracula* 2M2

Example 15

The "Love" theme first appears as Sarah and Simon are left alone together after the party. Sarah is worried about what might happen to Paul but Simon is confident that will be able to look after himself. Scored for harp and strings, the theme carries an echo of Mahler's famous Fifth Symphony ***Adagietto***, which is scored for the same forces:

James Bernard, *Scars of Dracula* 3M1, bars 1–4

Example 16

Paul eventually finds himself at Castle Dracula; Bernard effectively points up his near-fatal stumble on the steps of the castle's ramparts with a characteristic ***fp*** snap rhythm on the strings and bass clarinet. But even more effective is the musical metaphor of vertigo. For this, **minor seconds** again play a central role but the effect is really created by the disposition of pitch and timbre. Paul nearly falls over a sheer drop that plunges into the valley below. To match this giddy terror, minor seconds on trumpets "stumble" down a semitone, then low ***fortissimo*** trombones join in, followed by more minor seconds in a contrastingly high pitch in the strings. The combined effect is one of Bernard's most successful musical metaphors—a musical equivalent, indeed, to Hitchcock's use of a simultaneous forward zoom and reverse tracking shot in *Vertigo* (Paramount, dir. Alfred Hitchcock, 1958):

James Bernard, *Scars of Dracula* 3M2, bars 66–69

Example 17

No sooner has Paul recovered from his attack of vertigo than a bat attacks him, accompanied by its **triplet** theme. The bat retreats and the figure of Tania appears through the swirling mist to a serene but somehow rather disturbing **dominant seventh** chord on the harps. (This has a similar effect to the augmented triads played by the harp in *She*, when Ayesha regressed Leo back to his former life as Kallikrates.) The harp chords are integrated with the new "Dra-Cu-La" theme as Tania invites Paul into the castle. After a brief conversation, she goes off to have a room prepared for him.

Paul looks around on his own until the owner of the castle at last appears to the "Dracula chord." The Count persuades him to stay the night. As soon as Paul has gone upstairs Tania steps forward and bares her neck for a good night "kiss" from her master. The music for this seduction scene takes us back to the string **glissandi** Bernard had used to depict the monster of *Quatermass 2*. In *Scars of Dracula*, though, the strings are joined by glissandi in the harp and trills in the vibraphone. For the bite itself, the flutes, horns and brass join in with descending chromatic scales.

It isn't long before harps usher Tania into the room and a sex scene is soon underway in which the "Love" theme is eroticized. This section is another good example of Bernard's skill at thematic metamorphosis. The last three notes of the "Love" theme consist of a semitone rise followed by a falling fourth. Bernard builds on this by widening the pitch contour and expanding the intervals as follows:

James Bernard, *Scars of Dracula* 4M2, bar 39

Example 18a

James Bernard, *Scars of Dracula* 4M2, bars 40–43 (viola only)

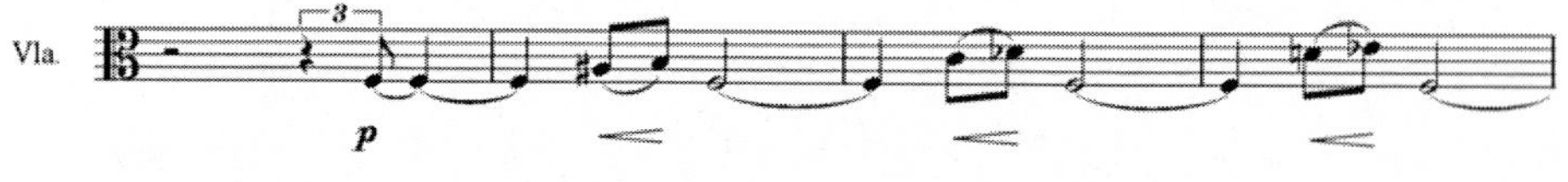

Example 18b

The strings then take this up, omitting the first note of each group of three:

James Bernard, *Scars of Dracula* 4M2, bars 51–55 (violin I only)

Example 18c

This is then elaborated with semiquavers:

James Bernard, *Scars of Dracula* 4M2, bars 56–57 (violin I only)

Example 18d

... and then a new erotic theme appears that squeezes a descending chromatic triplet in between the original descending fourth of the love theme. It is also combined with a version of the "Vampire Bat" motif on the harp:

James Bernard, *Scars of Dracula* 4M2, bars 63–64 (strings and harp only)

Example 18e

The love theme returns while Simon and Sarah walk through a sunlit wood on their way to the castle to rescue Paul. A secondary theme is also introduced, similar to an important tune in the introduction of Beethoven's "*Pathétique*" Piano Sonata, mentioned in chapter five. It will return several times during the remainder of the film to create a sense of urgency when Sarah's life is put in danger. It serves the same dramatic function as the tragic version of the love theme in *Taste the Blood of Dracula*:

James Bernard, *Scars of Dracula* 6M1, bars 6–10

Example 19

The remainder of the film introduces no significantly new musical material; after his immolation, Dracula plunges to his death accompanied by a cascade of chromatic scales.

14

Sunset in the East

"I shall cook sweet noodles for you and sing you the songs of Szechwan."

Miao Kue (played by Pik-Sen Lim) in the soundtrack album of *The Legend of the Seven Golden Vampires*[1]

The major film event of 1971 was the release of Luchino Visconti's *Morte a Venezia* (*Death in Venice,* Warner/Alfa, dir. Mario Gallo). Dehn, who had been on friendly terms with Dirk Bogarde, sent his congratulations to the star of the film who was by then living on the Continent. Bogarde, who had always been grateful to Dehn for his supportive criticism of his work and had wanted to collaborate on a film with him, wrote back with the news that most of his beautiful eighteenth-century Meissen statuettes of exotic birds had been smashed during the move from England and wondered who was going to mend a splintered skylark and a crimson parrot. Dehn, a keen ornithologist, had greatly admired this impressive collection when he and Bernard had visited the actor at Nore, his home at Hascombe in the Surrey hills. In the same letter, Bogarde also included a brief account of his approach to the portrayal of Gustav von Aschenbach, the hero of his latest film: "It is so terribly easy to stick on a false moustache and a pair of old Grannie Glasses and shuffle about a beach," he explained, "...and that was what I did not want to do."[2]

In stark contrast to *Death in Venice,* the following year saw the release of *Frankenstein and the Monster from Hell.* Venice may have been a long way away in this, the last of Hammer's Frankenstein cycle, but there was certainly plenty of death. Perhaps the result of so many electric shocks in the past, Peter Cushing's Baron had now become a blonde. The actor confessed that the wig he wore made him look rather like Helen Hayes,[3] but the lighter color somehow emphasized not only the Baron's age but also his patent yet rather endearing insanity. Cushing's portrayal of the character expunged the ruthless sadist of *Frankenstein Must Be Destroyed* and reinstated the old mixture of steely charm and single-minded dedication. As Terence Fisher explained:

> You've had so many monsters by then that at last you say where this monster has come from. He comes from Hell, from Evil, from Frankenstein's mistaken belief that he is the creator of man, which of course he isn't, and will never succeed in being.[4]

Frankenstein, though confined to a lunatic asylum, has managed to blackmail its corrupt and ineffectual director into allowing him to run the institution himself under the assumed name of Dr. Victor. His latest project is a Neanderthal hulk (played by David Prowse), assembled from various parts of the other inmates. The hands come from a sculptor (played by James Bond's "M," Bernard Lee) and the brain is courtesy of an Einstein-like, violin-playing mathematical genius called Dr. Durendel (Charles Lloyd Pack). When young Dr. Simon Helder (Shane Briant) is committed to the asylum for attempting Frankenstein's experiments himself, "Dr. Victor" naturally employs him as his assistant.

Unfortunately, the monster's psychopathic body soon gains control of the implanted brain and Frankenstein decides on his most outrageous experiment: to mate the monster with a beautiful mute girl called the "Angel" (Madeline Smith). Her real name is Sarah and it is later revealed that she is the daughter of the asylum's director, who lost the power of speech after her father attempted to rape her. Durendel, like Frankenstein, has found out about this and maintains an affection for her that will later prove very poignant when Durendel's brain ends up in the ugly monster's body.

Before Frankenstein can put his grotesque plan into action, however, the monster is shot and torn apart by the inmates. The Baron, by now utterly insane, vows to start again, but this was the end of the line for Hammer's Frankenstein, as well as for Terence Fisher. Cushing also gave one of his best performances in what should have been his Hammer swan song. In his review of the film for *The Evening Standard* (May 2, 1974), Alexander Walker wrote, "The end hints at more to come.... 'We shall need new material, naturally,' says Mr. Cushing, sweeping up the remains of the last experiment. Something no one would dream of saying at Hammer Films, naturally." He did, however, single out Bernard's score as "a prime cut above the average Music to Dismember By." Bernard's usual techniques prevail here but they are appropriately understated to match the restrained, rather claustrophobic mood of the action. There is no real "Syllable" theme but instead a motif based on Frankenstein's name that echoes the main motif of Liszt's third Symphonic Poem, *Les Préludes* (first published in 1848):

Franz Liszt, *Les Préludes*, bars 3–5 (violin I only)

Example 1a

James Bernard, *Frankenstein and the Monster from Hell* 1M1, bars 1–4 (horns I & II only)

Example 1b

The title of Liszt's piece had been drawn from Alphonse de Lamartine's *Méditations Poétiques,* from which Liszt also quoted in his preface to the score:

> "*Notre vie est-elle autre chose qu'une série de Préludes à ce chant inconnu dont la mort entonne le première et solonnelle note? [...] quelle est la destinée où les premières voluptés de bonheur ne sont point intrompues par quelque orage [...]?*" ("What is our life but a series of preludes to that unknown song of which the first solemn note is sounded by Death? [...] who is lucky enough not to have his first delights of happiness interrupted by some storm [...]?)[5]

The associations of Liszt's musical theme are highly appropriate when one considers the constantly striving and embattled Baron, who indeed regards life as a series of preludes to a life yet to come — admittedly not in Lamartine's sense but what else are Frankenstein's monsters if not perverted attempts at achieving immortality? Bernard's "Frank-En-Stein" theme pervades the score often in conjunction with its preliminary passage that is associated with "Horror," and which consists of two groups of rising **semitones.**

The film's "Monster" theme is also introduced in the main title, quietly at first, but later it will appear ***fortissimo*** with an urgent rhythm, often in the brass. It consists simply of a rising and falling semitone, and it is appropriate that we hear it during the opening scene in which a corpse is being dug up because Dr. Helder will soon be using the corpse for his own attempt at monster-making. In this, its initial statement, the "Monster" motif is elaborated by two unnerving **acciaccatura:**

James Bernard, *Frankenstein and the Monster from Hell*
1M1, bars 12–14 (oboe only)

Example 2

There is also an echo of "Dr. Ravna" from *The Kiss of the Vampire* when the following version of the "Monster" motif is later introduced by the following descending phrase:

James Bernard, *Frankenstein and the Monster from Hell*
1M1, bars 23–26 (violin I only)

Example 3

A policeman is alerted to what has been going on and pays a visit to Helder's makeshift laboratory. The tension of the scene is heightened by a **semiquaver** device that grows out of the **major third** in the second bar of example three:

James Bernard, *Frankenstein and the Monster from Hell* 1M3, bar 1 (clarinet I, bass clarinet and contra-bass clarinet only)

Example 4

This idea is sequenced in the usual way; a nicely gruesome visual moment follows when the policeman upsets a jar full of eyes that roll over the floor of the laboratory like marbles.

There is no love interest in this film but Bernard was able to write a romantic melody for Dr. Durendel's wistful violin improvisations. For these scenes, Martell lent his own violin to the actor, Charles Lloyd Pack, whom he also instructed in the correct way to hold the instrument. The opening phrase of the melody is actually related to the "Frank-En-Stein" motif (and more accurately echoes its Lisztian model):

James Bernard, *Frankenstein and the Monster from Hell* 4M1, bars 1–4

Example 5

Even more than in his previous scores, Bernard is able to create atmospheric effects here with hardly any material at all. The passage for strings in example seven, which accompanies Helder's intrusion into Frankenstein's laboratory, is based on an alternation between the **tritone** relationship in the first chord and the **augmented triad** in the second. The effect, combined with the oscillating rhythm, creates exactly the right atmosphere of anticipation.

James Bernard, *Frankenstein and the Monster from Hell*
5M4, bars 18–19

Example 6

This "Mystery" motif often returns for similar situations. The operation scene in which the monster is given a new pair of eyes (and also a later scene in which Dr. Durendel's brain is transferred into the creature's skull) is scored for the characteristic combination of **minor seconds** played in **harmonics** by strings and oscillating vibraphones, both of which are softly punctuated with chords from the horns. The result is a typically Bernardian musical sound effect.

When the monster wakes up after its eye operation, Bernard is able to create an effective musical accompaniment merely by employing a rising **chromatic** scale, and during the monster's struggle with Helder, the "Monster" motif is harmonized with tritones and intoned by the brass (four horns, three trumpets, three trombones and tuba) to a percussive rhythm that reflects the creature's brute strength:

James Bernard, *Frankenstein and the Monster from Hell*
6M3, bars 13–14

Example 7

The monster goes on the rampage, digging up graves in a desperate attempt to find the corpse of its brain donor, Dr. Durendel. When it does so, the violin theme returns but in a suitably strident and melodically distorted version in the wind and strings:

James Bernard, *Frankenstein and the Monster from Hell*
9M2, bars 65–66 (strings only)

Example 8

The excitement is then maintained but slightly subdued when the asylum director orders his staff to shoot the monster. Bernard's skill at responding to slight changes of mood (indeed in *creating* those subtle changes) is in evidence here when he harmonizes the "Monster" motif in minor seconds, and scores it for fairly high-pitched but quiet violins, while the timpani continue to pound underneath. This brings out the feeling that the horror is happening all around the asylum director but hasn't yet impinged upon him personally. It isn't long before it does arrive, however, and soon afterwards the monster is shot. As with so many of Bernard's death scenes (particularly the disintegrations of Dracula), the monster's immolation is accompanied by a falling theme that is sequenced in increasingly lower pitches. The theme itself is particularly agonized due to the **false relations**, clashing minor seconds and tritones created by the brass here:

James Bernard, *Frankenstein and the Monster from Hell* 10M1, bars 21–24

Example 9

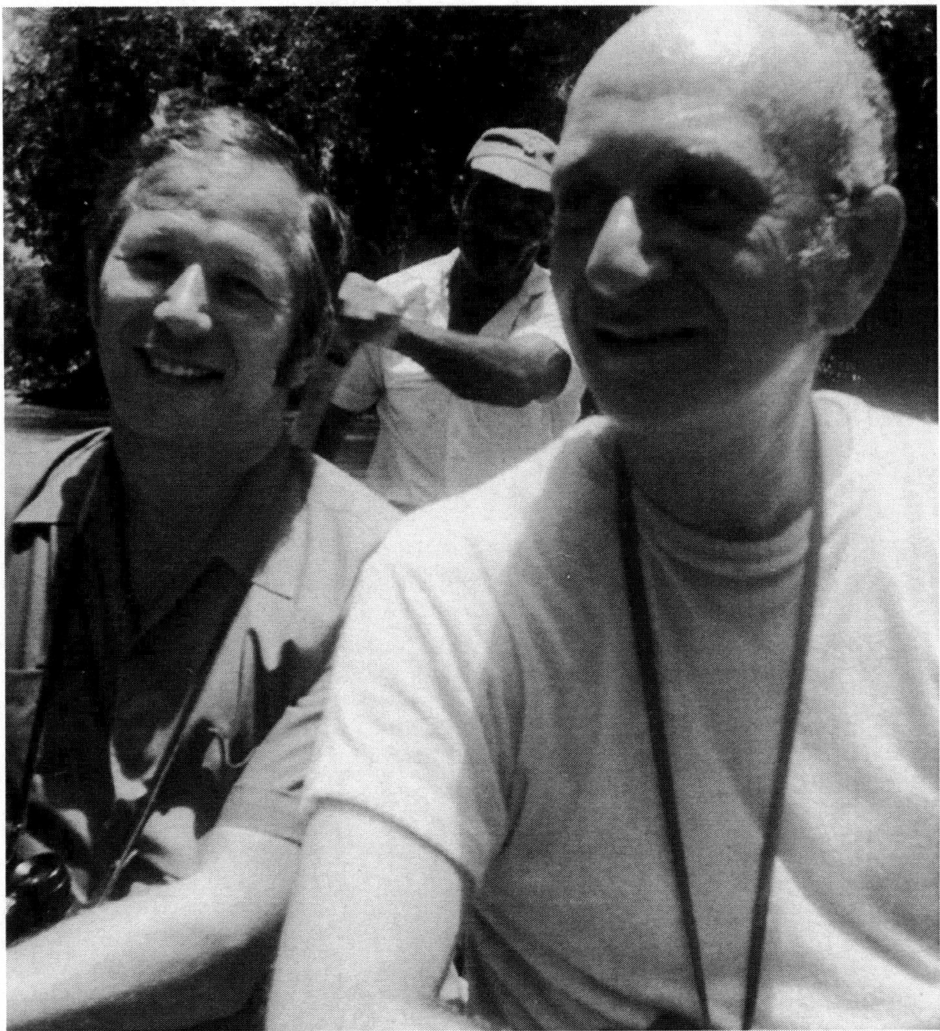

On Safari: James Bernard and Paul Dehn in South Africa, 1973 (photograph James Bernard).

As the monster dies, gazing piteously at Sarah, the violin theme appears for the last time before the mob tears his body to pieces. The assembled madmen rather resemble the madmen of the *The Duchess of Malfi,* bringing, one might say, Bernard's involvement with composing music for Frankenstein films full circle.

The score is brought to a conclusion with the rhythmic version of the "Monster" motif, this time harmonized with augmented triads. It alternates between the speeded-up version of the "Horror" theme and its "Frank-En-Stein" appendages, bringing Hammer's venerable Frankenstein saga to a close in somber A minor.

Bernard's last film for Hammer was *The Legend of the Seven Golden Vampires,* a curious and not wholly comfortable blend of Chinese Kung Fu with a traditional Dracula tale, which attempted to exploit the then-current vogue for Oriental martial arts. Ka, High Priest of the Temple of the Seven Golden Vampires, travels to Transylvania where Dracula takes on his form. Returning to China, Ka/Dracula resurrects the Seven Vampires and proceeds to terrorize the small village of Ping Kuei. Years later, Peter Cushing's Dr. Van Helsing travels to China to explore the myth of the Golden Vampires. He is received with skepticism by the academics of the University of Chungking but does manage to attract the attention of a young warrior priest called Hsi Ching, whose own grandfather had been killed by one of the vampires. Financed by a Swedish adventuress, Mrs. Buren (played by Julie Ege), Van Helsing and his son Leyland (Robin Stewart) set out with a protective bodyguard of Hsi Ching's brothers and sister. There are numerous opportunities for displays of Kung Fu during their journey to Ping Kuei, leading to the climactic confrontation between Van Helsing and his arch-enemy.

Bernard's old "Dra-Cu-La" theme was resurrected for the last time in this film and dressed in some very sonorous orchestrations, as was the **triplet** "Vampire Bat" theme of *Scars of Dracula.* Indeed, the only element that makes his score for *The Legend of the Seven Golden Vampires* different from the approach of his preceding Dracula films (apart from the fact that it was recorded, rather unnecessarily, in quadrophonics) is the use of oriental harmonic coloring. Bernard had indeed entered this territory before in *The Terror of the Tongs* but for *The Legend of the Seven Golden Vampires* he made use of many more traditional Chinese musical instruments: Chinese tom-toms, Chinese cup-cymbals, tuned gongs, plucked string instruments such as the Yang-Chin and, of course, themes based on **pentatonic** scales. The Yang-Ching, for example, is associated with Ka, whose theme is pentatonic in feeling if not in actual fact. It is first heard in the main title music:

James Bernard, *The Legend of the Seven Golden Vampires* M3, bars 1–5

Example 10

To accompany a scene set in the elegant surroundings of the British Trade Consul in Chungking, Bernard employs a Chinese flute and marimba playing a duet reminiscent of another marimba-accompanied theme in *The Terror of the Tongs*:

James Bernard, *The Legend of the Seven Golden Vampires* M7, bars 1–4

Example 11

Example 11 is actually the main "Love" theme of the film, associated with Mrs. Buren and Hsi Ching as well as Leyland Van Helsing and the warrior maiden, Miao Kue. It is later scored for Chinese flute and another plucked string instrument, the Cheng, before wordless female voices join in.

The score's third Oriental theme is associated with the seven brothers of Hsi Ching. Again, it is pentatonic in feeling, though not strictly speaking restricted to that scale:

James Bernard, *The Legend of the Seven Golden Vampires*, "Overture," bars 1–2 (reduction)

Example 12

Again, highly effective orchestral effects are often created with the minimum of means. A single line for the violins is quite sufficient to create the required atmosphere:

James Bernard, *The Legend of the Seven Golden Vampires* M21

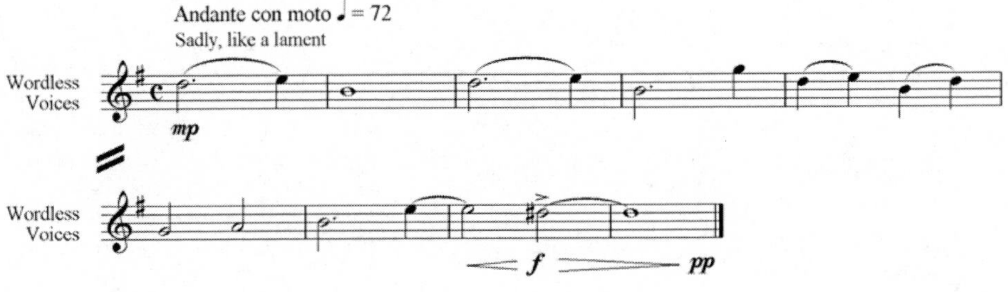

Example 13

Bernard's skill at creating musical sound effects is again much in evidence in *The Legend of the Seven Golden Vampires.* Example 14 demonstrates how a simple semiquaver pattern, consisting only of an oscillating semitone, can be elaborated by means of orchestration and **crescendo** to a searing climax (see example 14 on page 236).

James Bernard, *The Legend of the Seven Golden Vampires* M1, bars 19–25

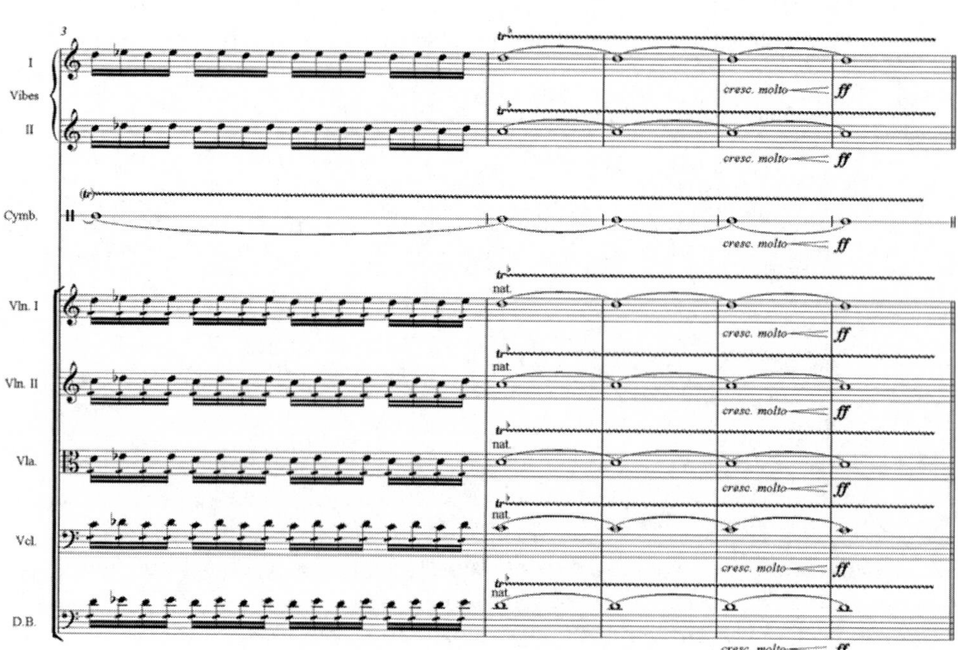

Example 14

Similarly, Bernard can turn a simple **whole-tone scale** into a looming musical monolith, redolent of supernatural terror. Accompanied by a persistent dotted rhythm in the lower strings, the first violins and flutes trill each note of the rising whole tone scale, while minor seconds in the brass simultaneously rise in pitch, accompanied by crescendi on timpani, bass drum and tam-tam:

Example 15

The Legend of the Seven Golden Vampires proved to be the last Hammer feature film that Bernard was to score. The next two attempts at reviving Bram Stoker's long-suffering character would be set in 1970s London, a period for which time Bernard's nineteenth-century Gothic style was no longer deemed appropriate (though *Dracula A.D. 1972* did use the "Dra-Cu-La" theme to accompany the opening Warner Bros. studio logo, without crediting Bernard, as a kind of unofficial studio fanfare). Carelessly, the main title credits of *The Legend of the Seven Golden Vampires* misspelled Bernard's name, but Michael Carreras did send him a letter in which he sincerely congratulated him on his score: "It is of extremely high quality and excitingly atmospheric," he wrote, and his high opinion of the score was no doubt behind the decision to release a soundtrack LP of the music, suitably rearranged and blended with spine-chilling sound effects from the film, to support Peter Cushing's beautifully delivered narration of the plot. Carreras even invited the composer to the gala opening of the film at the Warner Rendezvous on August 29, a rare honor for Hammer's most celebrated composer but one that came rather late in the day.

For Bernard, it had all been even harder work than usual and he was looking forward to a well-earned break. Unfortunately, his exhaustion prevented him from accepting yet another horror opportunity from producer Kevin Francis:

> Kevin Francis, the son of Freddie Francis, had always liked my music and he did ask me to write the music for a film of his called *The Ghoul.* It came hot on the heels of my just having nearly killed myself doing *The Legend of the Seven Golden Vampires,* which we had to do in two weeks. Anyway, he rang me up just as I was thinking, "Thank God, I can relax!" I got this message asking if I would do this new film. I said, "How long would I have for the music?" and he said, "Well, I'd really want to have it written in the next three weeks." I said, "Oh, Kevin, I'm sorry—I just *couldn't*!"

The Ghoul (Tyburn, dir. Freddie Francis, 1975), a film containing one of Peter Cushing's most moving performances, was eventually scored by Harry Robinson instead.

Hammer's long road of success, which had begun with *The Quatermass Experiment,* was now running into a dead end. The other film co-financed in the deal with the Shaw brothers was a contemporary thriller called *Shatter* (Hammer/Shaw, dir. Michael Carreras, 1974). It proved to be an unmitigated disaster. Carreras so hated the experience that he vowed never to direct or produce a film again (though he did go on to co-produce an enjoyable, but financially unrewarding remake of Hitchcock's *The Lady Vanishes* (Rank/Hammer, dir. Anthony Page, 1979). The music supplied by the Shaw studios for *Shatter* had originally horrified Philip Martell, who remembered that it was "without exaggeration, unbelievable. Unbelievable. If you'd hit anything on any keyboard, on any percussion instruments or anything at all and just shoved it all together, it would have been just the same. It was absolutely appalling."[6] What had happened was that the studio in Hong Kong had superimposed two library records one on top of the other, creating a complete confusion of sound. When the Performing Rights Society heard about this, it refused to allow the film to be released until a new score had been composed, a process that also expensively involved redubbing the entire film. But there was no other way out.

Martell therefore approached David Lindup, who would later be involved with one of Bernard's rather different musical projects, to compose original music for this final, sad film from the House of Hammer.

With the sun setting on Hammer's once glorious empire, Bernard went in search of a rising sun elsewhere. In Jamaica it would shine on him for twelve years before being eclipsed by a terrible tragedy.

15

Danger in Paradise

"They were hacked and slashed and left to die in pools of their own blood."

Lawrence Van Helsing (Peter Cushing) in the soundtrack album of *The Legend of the Seven Golden Vampires*[1]

"I know I'm not going to make old bones," Dehn confessed very early on in his relationship with Bernard. "I think I'll probably die when I'm in my sixties." And that is precisely what happened. A heavy smoker, consuming up to sixty cigarettes a day when working on his screenplays, Dehn was diagnosed with lung cancer in 1974 just after having completed the screenplay for *Murder on the Orient Express* (for which he was later Oscar-nominated). He did his best to persuade the film's director, Sidney Lumet, to hire Bernard to compose the score for this all-star Agatha Christie whodunit, but Lumet was determined to use Richard Rodney Bennett, the composer whom Bernard had met all those years before at the recording session of *The Quatermass Experiment.* Nonetheless, Bernard did attend the Royal Gala premiere of the film with his partner, and remembers seeing Dehn standing between Lauren Bacall and Ingrid Bergman in the lineup. It was very hot due to the barrage of television lights and Bacall gasped, "I wish I had a fan." "But you do," Dehn replied. "He's standing right beside you!"

Dehn was eventually admitted to the Royal Brompton Heart and Chest Hospital where the operation went very well, so well in fact that the surgeon didn't think it would be necessary to follow up the operation with the deep-ray therapy that had been required by William Walton. Unfortunately, by December of that year a lump had appeared in Dehn's throat, and cancer of the lymph gland was diagnosed. The gland was removed but by that time the disease had spread. A course of deep ray therapy then followed but soon afterwards Dehn started to suffer from stomach pains. These grew worse during a subsequent holiday in Jamaica, where he and Bernard were staying at the home of Dorothy Hammerstein, wife of the famous lyric-writer, Oscar.

On his return to England, Dehn went back to hospital where a camera was lowered down his throat and he was able to watch his growth on a TV screen in front

Partners in Crime: at the premier of *Murder on the Orient Express*, 1974. Meg Bernard, James Bernard, Paul Dehn, Bill Bernard (Wendy Hiller in the background) (photograph Bernard Estate).

of him. It was the ultimate horror movie, but like all gothic horror it had a strange kind of beauty. Bernard asked what the growth looked like and was told that it resembled a lily bud, "just like the ones you're always arranging." Deep-ray therapy removed the growth, but the cancer then invaded his brain and, Baron Frankenstein no longer being available, it became impossible to save him.

Around this time, a letter arrived from Dehn's old friend Terence Rattigan, who was also facing up to his own struggle with illness (he died in 1977):

> The London Clinic
> 22nd Aug '75
>
> Dear Paul + Jimmy
>
> Many thanks for your delicious vin du pays—polished off nightly by a drunken Irish night-nurse and myself.
>
> They still haven't found my buggette or bijou bug—but with about 16 of the *buggers* (at 50 gns a touch) you can't say they're not trying.
>
> They're giving me pills for the next 7 days that they say will make me very queer indeed, but *lovely* afterwards—if I'm not they're giving me huge dollops of cortisone, and I'll be even queerer, but *much gayer*, and also lovely afterwards

Above and opposite: At home at Tite Street, London (photograph James Bernard).

And if *that* doesn't work I suppose they'll put me down, because they need the bed.

Anyway much much love

Terry

One day not long after receiving Rattigan's letter, Bernard heard a frightening crash coming from Dehn's bedroom. He rushed upstairs to find that Dehn had lost his balance, fallen into the mirror and was sprawling on the floor, surrounded by hundreds of shards of broken glass. This broken mirror couldn't have brought worse luck. Realizing that the end was nigh, Bernard set about fulfilling his long-standing plan of buying a large house in Tite Street, where Oscar Wilde had once resided, and which was also not far from St. Leonard's Terrace, where the house occupied by Bram Stoker still stands. Bernard and Dehn's new home had everything, including a spacious music room with parquet flooring and a big book-lined study. Dehn's bedroom had its own small terrace with French windows so that he could enjoy the sunshine of the hot summer weather and the sound of the birds (he was still an enthusiastic ornithologist). In the evenings, they watched television together. The last program Dehn ever saw was a production of Wilde's story *The Picture of Dorian Gray*, starring his old friend John Gielgud. Soon afterwards, he slipped into a final coma. Bernard remembers the last time his partner looked at him consciously:

> I was able to chat to him but all the time he was looking at someone standing behind me who I think must have been his mother. She had died very suddenly aged ninety-seven (but still in apparently good health and very much "all there") only three weeks before Paul. She knew he was dying, and it seemed to me that she had gone ahead to welcome him.

A few weeks after Dehn's death, Bernard had a rather curious experience. Sitting all alone in his now rather melancholy Tite Street home, he was working out the program of Dehn's memorial service. Unsure if he had selected the right pieces of music, he took a break and went to the kitchen to pour himself a glass of sherry.

After pushing the cork back in the bottle, he took a sip and felt assured that he had, after all, made the right decision. Suddenly there was a loud "pop"; he turned around to see that the cork had shot right out of the bottle. Bernard was convinced that it was Dehn agreeing with him about the order of his own memorial service. He recalled, "I can remember saying, 'Thank you, dear!'"

The Memorial Service on November 26, 1976, at St Martin-in-the-Fields, London, included an address by Arthur Marshall, another close friend of Dehn's; a reading from Wordsworth by Michael Redgrave; and a reading from Thomas Hardy by Rachel Kempson. John Birch, Master of the Choristers of Chichester Cathedral, played the organ, Michael Berkeley, the son of Sir Lennox, directed the Consort of Voices in his own setting of "Jubilate Deo" as well as Bernard's "Nunc Dimittis," while Ken McGregor sang two Jamaican Songs, accompanied by the composer at the piano.

Another death followed soon after Dehn's. Exhausted by the strain of nursing his sick friend, Bernard had taken a long holiday in the West Indies. When he returned, he received an urgent message from Peter Pears saying that he hoped that he (Bernard) would be back in time for the Memorial Service of Benjamin Britten, who had died on December 4, 1976.

> I was always so touched that Peter had remembered me. They even had a little party afterwards and they included me in that too. I was very touched and flattered, because there were only about twenty people at the party. Malcolm Williamson was there because he had been quite a protégé of Ben, and I remember having a charming and very friendly talk with him.

Having proved that he had an attractive singing voice at Dehn's memorial service, Ken McGregor was later to take the leading vocal role in a demonstration recording of Bernard and Dehn's unstaged musical project, *Battersea Calypso*. The story of a love affair between a young Jamaican man and an English girl, half the action is set in Battersea, London, and the other half in Jamaica. The music is a mixture of straightforward romantic tunes as well as songs based on Reggae and Calypso rhythms, which are definitely Jamaican in style, and a huge contrast to Bernard's often somber Hammer horror scores. The lyrics of the title song, sung at a bus stop on a rainy day in Battersea, continued the witty, ribald style of Dehn's *Virtue in Danger*:

What is this rainy place we know?
Why have we come to like it so?
No green bananas upon the tree—
Bugger it! It's Battersea!

The lyrics of another song added after Dehn's death, "I want a Jamaican banana tonight," were by Bernard himself and they speak for themselves:

All the day I'm dreaming, dreaming,
Lying in the tropic sun,
But when the lights are gleaming, gleaming,
All I want is tropic fun.
Banana, banana, Jamaican banana,
Banana, banana, banana for me,

A young one, an old one, a hot one, a cold one,
I like it for breakfast for lunch or for tea.
A big one a small one,
A short or a tall one,
I want a Jamaican banana tonight!

There is also an amusing song for Cockney chorus in the manner of Lerner and Loewe's "Get Me to the Church on Time" from *My Fair Lady*:

We never 'ear a cuckoo down in Clapham
Or if we do it's probably a clock;
But come the warmer weather
The Neighbours get together
And the wife enjoys a little bit of Cock-
ney palaver.

The cover of the double LP demo album, designed by Anthony Holland, shows hummingbirds and palm trees framing the upturned table legs of Battersea Power Station's four towering chimneys, the same famous London landmark that had featured in Bernard's very first film *The Quatermass Experiment.* Unlike in that science fiction thriller, however, palm trees were supposed to sprout from the chimneys at the end of the musical. The piece was very nearly put on in Dehn's lifetime thanks to the theatrical agent Dennis van Thal,[2] who tried to interest impresario Bernard Delfont in the project. A day was arranged when Delfont arrived in a huge Rolls

Copper Hill Calypso: James Bernard at the piano at "Copper Hill" in Jamaica, rehearsing *Battersea Calypso* with Ken McGregor standing behind him (photograph James Bernard).

Royce to hear a play-through on the piano. He listened very intently, appeared most enthusiastic, suggested that it should be a big show at the London Palladium and then drove away. Months later, after having heard nothing more, van Thal explained that Mr. Delfont had rather a reputation for this kind of thing, hating, as he did, to hurt people's feelings. Apparently building up false hopes was quite another matter.

Undeterred, Bernard asked Philip Martell if he would be his musical director for the demo disc recording.

> I asked Phil, "What will your fee be ?" and he said, "Oh, Jimmy, I'll do it for nothing as we're such old friends." Then a little while later, after I pressed him, he said, "Yes, I think I would like a fee." I remember we paid him £600 for each session, which I was very happy about.

Martell arranged to have David Lindup orchestrate the music and secured big names such as trombonist Don Lusher to make up the orchestra. Ken McGregor sang the role of the hero, Joanne Brown sang Hilly, Isabelle Lucas took the role of Ivy and Oscar James sang Dundas, with Philip Martell conducting the Westminster Sinfonia Orchestra and the Tony Mansell Singers. Bernard himself shared the narration with Barry Justice, and the whole gloriously hedonistic affair was recorded at the Anvil Studios in Buckinghamshire (where Denham Studios had once employed Muir Mathieson) by Bernard's longtime associate Eric Tomlinson, who had worked with him on so many Hammer film scores in the past. The recording was never released commercially. If it had been, Bernard might well have had another hit on his hands.

In 1980, after several holidays in Barbados and Trinidad, McGregor felt an irresistible urge to return to his native Jamaica and persuaded Bernard to join him there. They eventually settled in a house called "Copper Hill" on the south coast of the island. This had a wonderful view of the open sea to the left, stretching away towards Cuba, the whole crescent of Montego Bay immediately below, and the rolling forested hills to the right, dotted with the brilliant reds and oranges of flame-trees and poincianas. A low house with a terrace, set in about three or four acres, it had been built by Carmen Pringle, a famous Jamaican society hostess. They moved in July after selling the Tite Street property (against the advice of all Bernard's friends and relatives), and embarked on a tropical idyll that was to last twelve years. In a 1987 letter to the author of this book, Bernard described the scene from his terrace:

> We are having a most lovely summer here — temperatures mostly in the '90s, and some good bouts of rain to keep everything green. I've never seen the countryside look so beautiful — like my idea of the Garden of Eden or the entrance to Paradise. We've got a huge crop of Allspice berries in the garden — too much to pick it all, so there is plenty for the parakeets and other birds; and I've never seen the poinciana trees more brilliantly scarlet, nor eaten so many and such sweet mangoes. And now the avocados (or just pears, as they are called here) are coming in. As for pineapples, there are mountains of them for sale along the roadsides.

Bernard took the opportunity to indulge his love of acting by taking part in the productions of the Montego Bay Theater Movement that had been founded by his friend Paul Methuen. Methuen, a leading interior and garden designer, had been a great friend of the Hammersteins and Noël Coward, and had known Jamaica in its golden age when the island had been the glamorous haunt of Hollywood stars. Bernard's first role with the players was Friar Lawrence in a black-and-white production of Shakespeare's *Romeo and Juliet.* He subsequently named two of his dogs Romeo and Juliet. Juliet, appropriately, given the manner of death of Juliet in the play, later died from rat poison. One year the company put on a performance of Hamilton Deane's famous stage version of *Dracula* in which, disappointingly, Bernard did not have a role, though some of his Hammer music was used.

During his first five years in Jamaica, Bernard wrote no music at all. Hammer Films was struggling to survive under the difficult conditions of the beleaguered British film industry, and Bernard felt that his career was over. He gave up all thought of rejoining the film business, a decision he later regretted:

> I do pray a lot, and one of my regular prayers is to ask for forgiveness for having thrown away about twelve years in Jamaica and abandoning music just for a life of leisure. Ken used to say to me, "Jimmy, what are you doing just spending your time shopping and cooking for worthless people?" Well, they weren't worthless— they were our friends, but he was quite right. I was wasting my time.

In 1985, Bernard got another call from Kevin Francis of Tyburn Films asking if he would be interested in scoring a new film for television called *Murder Elite.* Bernard agreed but realized that he would have to compose it in London and would therefore need somewhere to live. Dehn's former secretary, Fenella Evans-Tipping, put an advertisement in the personal column of *The Times*: "Composer urgently needs either a flat or house with piano for six to eight weeks." A lady called Rona Lucas offered the use of her flat in Battersea, and it wasn't long before she and her husband, the painter Keith Lucas (at one time head of the British Film Institute), became two of Bernard's closest friends. So, Bernard came over to England in 1985 and wrote the score for Kevin Francis. Philip Martell proved particularly helpful, as Bernard recalls:

> There was a section of music in *Murder Elite*, where Allie MacGraw gets trampled to death in a stable. I was really stumped. I couldn't think how to do this in a different way. We had a romantic tune in that film and Phil said, "Use that tune but distort it all and have a lot of overblown horns."

When Bernard was again visiting London (three years after working on *Murder Elite*), Hurricane Gilbert swept over Jamaica with devastating force. The rain poured into all the ground floor rooms of "Copper Hill" and one of their dogs, Tybalt, died of a heart attack, but fortunately the roof wasn't blown off. Eventually everything got back to normal and Bernard was rather disappointed to have missed the experience. Little did he know it at the time, however, that far more terrifying things were about to happen.

When they had first moved to Jamaica, life there had become calm again after the wild days when Michael Manley had been Prime Minister and had flirted with Fidel Castro in Cuba. There had been great concern that Manley had wanted to turn Jamaica into a Communist state, but after he was deposed everybody was full of hope that life would now get back to normal. A number of years later, he was triumphantly re-elected; eventually, owing to the cancer from which he subsequently died, he had to hand over to his deputy Prime Minister, P.J. Patterson.

Soon after the departure of Manley, Bernard had a rather frightening experience. McGregor was away in England visiting his family and so Bernard was left alone in the house with only a young Jamaican called Kenute for company. In the middle of the night he heard his dogs barking furiously out at the back of the house where he kept his Mercedes-Benz in a garage protected by big wrought iron gates.

Two burglars had tried to break into the guest cottage where Paul Methuen was staying, but the security arrangements had foiled them. Frustrated, they had now turned their attentions to the main house, which wasn't so well protected. The noise woke Bernard. He put on some slippers and went to investigate, but Kenute insisted on going with him. Together they walked through the sitting room past its big windows that looked out onto their terrace and Montego Bay below, then through the kitchen and out into the garage. It was there that Kenute immediately saw that several masked men were trying to break in with an iron bar. Bernard was peering over the bonnet of the car when Kenute suddenly pushed him down with the most tremendous force as a gun was fired. The bullet went right through the bonnet of the car. But this wasn't a Hammer film. It was for real. They rushed back through the kitchen when another bullet hit a long fluorescent bulb, which exploded, the glass showering over them as they ran for cover into the sitting room. Having crawled on their stomachs back to the bedroom, Bernard rushed to the phone but the lines had been cut.

They now felt trapped, so Kenute gallantly volunteered to make a run for it to summon help. He managed to unlock the padlocks on the wrought iron grill door leading to the terrace, and to get out and re-lock the door without the intruders hearing (they were still at the back of the house making a tremendous battering with their iron bar). However, the two dogs, with their acute hearing, *did* hear, rushed round to the terrace and got back inside the house with Bernard just before Kenute re-locked the door. The intruders then realized something was happening and hurtled round in pursuit, firing at Kenute as he fled barefoot down the drive. He was making for the hotel down on the coast road, from where he knew he would be able to telephone the police.

The intruders returned to the house, now able to tell, from the furious barking of the dogs, in which room Bernard had taken shelter. They couldn't actually see into the room, as the strong wooden louvers on the shutters were half-closed. Meanwhile, Bernard lay down behind his bed and heard the robbers shout, "Where's the coke?" meaning, of course, cocaine.

> I said, "I don't keep coke. You've come to the wrong place." So they said, "Okay, where's the gun?" I said, "I don't have a gun either." So they said, "Okay. Give us the money!" I had big walk-in closets in our bedroom where I always kept some foreign money. So I crept into this closet and got out my little store — about £230. Then, leaving the dogs barking in the bedroom, I padded out across the sitting room, and, reaching through the grills of the door, put the money on the steps leading down to the terrace. I ran back to the bedroom and lay down again between my bed and the closet door — in fact, as far as possible from the shutters, outside which the men were waiting. From there, I shouted "If you want money, walk round to the front of the house — as you can hear, the dogs are in here with me, so they can't harm you — and you'll find some money on the steps." So, thank God they found the money and fled; but before they went they said, "We're going to fucking well shoot you before we go." I'd gone right into the

> closet, my heart beating like a madman, and they fired the gun blind through the louvers. We found the bullets on the floor later!

Kenute by this time had contacted the police, who soon arrived in large numbers—but of course too late to catch the thieves. Paul Methuen next appeared, cool as a cucumber in a dressing gown like a latter-day Noël Coward while Bernard shouted, "Quick! Pour me a treble rum! And give me one of your heart pills! I think I'm going to have a heart attack!" Then the police sat down and all wanted drinks as well.

> We came to the conclusion later that the gunmen thought that our house was a house on a hill above us which had recently changed hands and was lived in by an American so-called "doctor" and his girlfriend. They only came down from the States from time to time but Ken had heard that they were heavily into the drug business and we think that these young men thought that our house was the house that belonged to the doctor who may well have owed them money for drugs.

One or two less frightening intrusions followed and McGregor blamed Bernard for being too friendly to everybody and encouraging trouble from thieves and hangers-on.

> He said to me, "Jimmy, this is it. You've got to go home to England. I'm not having you here any longer. It's too dangerous. It's you who brings the danger." I think that was rather unkind of him. I was only trying to help people. People would always come up to me with their hard luck stories. I'd only give the equivalent of five pounds or something. Ken used to say, "Don't give so much! They won't be grateful. They'll simply expect more and more." We decided it was time to sell. Life was getting too frightening. We didn't have any security. We loved having a wild garden rather like a jungle which made it all the easier for people to hide, of course. He said, "I have a premonition. My premonitions are good. Pack up your best stuff and have it shipped to England and you go too." This was in April '91 after Ken had had his sixtieth birthday. Kenute was not there any more. He had gone to New York, for which, in view of later events, I am thankful; so eventually I left, full of sadness. I always remember Mimi, our oldest and wisest dog, looking at me. She was highly intelligent, and the day I was leaving she gave me a look—a most piercing look—which said, "You're leaving and I'm never going to see you again." I've never forgotten that. I'm sure that animals have souls. It was so human, the look she gave me.

On his return to England from Jamaica, Bernard stayed for a long time with his brother and sister-in-law in Jersey (Channel Islands) where they lived, alternating with visits to London and also to his sister Mary and brother-in-law David in Shropshire. He kept in constant contact with Ken by telephone, begging him to come back to England and growing increasingly apprehensive when Ken told him of the threatening anonymous phone calls he was receiving, apparently for no reason. Finally, Ken promised Bernard that if the house had not been sold by the end of the year, he would come back, though it would mean calling in the vet to put down their beloved dogs.

One day, however, no one answered Bernard's call. A few days later, on August 18, 1992, it was Bernard's telephone that rang, with the terrible news that Ken McGregor had been murdered, his body hacked by a machete and left on the drive of "Copper Hill," guarded by the dogs and watched by the Turkey Vultures flying overhead with their horrible red bare necks on the look out for carrion. According to the Jamaican newspaper *The Daily Gleaner*, he had been killed on the previous Sunday morning around ten o'clock in the morning:

> The body was discovered face down and chopped in the back: its bloated condition indicated that he had been dead for days. A Toyota Corolla and satellite dish equipment were stolen. Police, led by Detective Inspector Morris mounted guard at the house and the body was not removed until Monday afternoon when forensic experts had completed their investigations.
>
> McGregor was regarded as something of a recluse. Except for his two dogs, he lived alone, reading, listening to music and watching films. At the time of his death he employed no regular staff.[3]

Bernard then had the terrible job of breaking the news to McGregor's old mother Ivy, who insisted on going with him to Jamaica to sort things out. They went up to the house together and saw the stains where the body had been lying. Bernard recalled:

> He obviously had a premonition. In an odd way he had a sort of death wish. He was very sad in those last two years. He often used to say to me, "I don't mind if I go now, I've had a very good life." He used to tell me in the last phone calls I had with him, "Jimmy I want to tell you something. I've put £5000 in a separate account in your and my name, so if anything happens to me there's that extra £5000." It made a big difference. In his closet his briefcase was missing but we went into my room which was totally untouched. I opened my closet and the first thing I saw was his briefcase. We opened it. Ken loved gold jewelry. Inside was all his gold and the bank certificate saying we had this money. I gave all the gold to Ivy immediately. She gave me back one ring with a big red stone in it.
>
> I was very frightened by the thought of driving around in my own car, but Paul Methuen keeps an old, rather battered Mazda in Jamaica and he has a great friend called Francis Gibson who's also a judo champion. Francis got in touch with me as soon as he knew I'd arrived and he drove me everywhere and was by my side all the time. I think people were after me as well. The security guards, whom I employed to guard the empty house, told me that for a few days telephone calls continued saying, "Where's Mr. Jimmy? We are coming for him next."

To this day, the mystery of McGregor's murder has remained unsolved, but according to an old friend of Bernard's, it was a tragedy waiting to happen. The friend was John Guy, and he had come out to Jamaica for a holiday in 1982. At that time everything seemed quite happy and Bernard certainly had no intention of returning to England. One day, however, Guy suddenly burst out: "You must both leave here at once, or something terrible is going to happen. You *must* believe me — I know it." They were both astonished but, being busy refurbishing their home, they soon put Guy's prediction out of their minds.

Years went by and life in Jamaica gradually grew more hazardous. After the experience with the gunmen, Bernard rang Guy in England and told him that his premonition had indeed come true, but Guy replied: "No, that's not it. It isn't finished yet" — which, of course, it certainly wasn't. The murder may well have been the work of one of those Jamaicans to whom Bernard had been much more financially generous than his partner. McGregor was seen as having sent away the goose that laid the golden egg; but now, those island boys with hard luck stories had lost them both. Some months after the murder, another close friend of Bernard, Richard Page-Smith, had a very curious experience and wrote to tell him all about it:

> 12/11. 92.
>
> My Dear Jimmy
>
> Such a strange thing happened to me a few minutes ago I feel I must write and tell you about it. I was playing the piano by myself—it is about 11 o'clock in the morning—and I suddenly thought of Ken—(I remember that he used to rather like my way of playing)—and, do you know, I *swear* I saw him standing quite vividly beside me, happy, laughing and relaxed—just a second or two—enough to make me stop playing and look around—but of course then he had gone. Now you know I don't believe in the spirit world etc., but I have a feeling you do, and I feel it essential to tell you. Another thing, when I turned around I found I had tears in my eyes and they were not tears of unhappiness, but happy tears, almost as if I'd just given Ken a big hug of welcome.
>
> I find the whole thing so strangely moving, I just feel I must tell you immediately about it. You'll probably laugh and think the silly old fool's losing his marbles—maybe I am but that is what happened a short while ago—so I've told you.
>
> Much love
>
> As always
>
> Dickey

Ken would, of course, never come back in the flesh, but there *were* signs of something stirring in Dracula's coffin...

16

Resurrection

"You just can't keep a good man down!"

Publicity tag for *Dracula Has Risen from the Grave*

Bernard's last commissions for what remained of Hammer in the 1980s had been two scores for the television series *Hammer House of Horror.* "The House That Bled to Death" and "Witching Time" were first shown along with the other 11 episodes in 1980, the same year in which Bernard bought his home "Copper Hill" in Jamaica. After the second television series, *Hammer House of Mystery and Suspense,* in 1984, it seemed as if all the life-blood of Hammer had been well and truly drained. A colorful autopsy of the company appeared in 1987 when the BBC produced a documentary called *Hammer — The Studio That Dripped Blood* in which Bernard gave his first, albeit rather short, television interview. This marked the beginning of a revival of interest in the history of England's once most successful film company. Soon after the BBC documentary, David Stoner of Silva Screen records, a company that specialized in film music CDs, wrote to Bernard explaining that he had had many requests for music from Hammer films and was planning to record a CD devoted to it. Would it be possible to arrange a meeting? Bernard was delighted to agree:

> I remember we both went over to Phil Martell's house in Highgate and sat in that extraordinary little room of his filled with everything in wild heaps. Phil clearly wanted on that first record to include all kinds of music by other composers—which was a good idea — but I think that Silva Screen were particularly keen for this first one to have the scores that were already becoming quite well-known in the film world. So they were particularly keen to have largely my music, and I think this slightly annoyed dear Phil. I remember him saying he wanted to have pieces by Paul Patterson and John McCabe.[1]

Hammer had always been reluctant to reissue the original soundtrack music because of the complications of paying the original musicians, and for years Martell had been longing for somebody to ask him to make new recordings. But when the opportunity arose, he was unable to conduct, having suffered several strokes over the previous year. On the day of the recording, as he walked to the rostrum, he received an emotional round of applause from the Philharmonia orchestra, an orchestra he had conducted so many times in the past, but after only a minute or so he was forced to put down the baton and hand over to Neil Richardson. Bernard remembers how for the rest of the day "Phil sat looking so sad and glum. We went out to lunch and tried to cheer him up but he was absolutely down."

In the wake of the television documentary and the CD, Bernard now found that he was being invited to Hammer conventions organized by a new generation of fans who had grown up with Hammer horror on late night television. The first convention he attended in 1993 had been organized by a French student, Romain Hermant, at the University of Nancy. Director and cinematographer Freddie Francis and screenwriter Jimmy Sangster had also been invited and they were all greeted by a model of Frankenstein's Monster, made by the students and put on display in the main hall of the University where the walls were decorated with Hammer film posters. Astonishingly, this was the very first time that Bernard had ever met Jimmy Sangster. When they were introduced, Sangster said, "Hello, Jimmy! We've known each other for years, haven't we!" and they greeted each other like old friends. It was practically the same with Freddie Francis, whom Bernard had never met either.

In 1994, Bernard returned from Jersey to again take up residence in London, in an apartment just halfway between the two houses in which he had lived so happily with Dehn. In that same year he was invited to the American film society, Fanex, in

Lilies and Leitmotifs: James Bernard at home in Chelsea, 1997 (photograph Lionel Cummings).

Baltimore, where he met Martine Beswick, Veronica Carlson and Val Guest — again all for the first time. He also had an encounter with the director, John Carpenter who had long been an admirer of Bernard's scores and had paid tribute to him in the soundtrack recording of his music for *Prince of Darkness* (Guild/Alive, 1987).[2] In 1993, Bernard had been introduced to the film producer Joe Kaufmann while visiting his friend, the writer Gary Smith, in Hollywood. Kaufmann had produced Carpenter's early film *Assault on Precinct 13* (CKK, 1976) but had retired from the business by the time Bernard met him. However, he told the composer that Carpenter was a great admirer of his scores. A meeting couldn't be set up on that occasion, but the following year Bernard was invited to visit Carpenter, who was filming on location near San Francisco. The director, who often composes the music for his own films, immediately asked him how Bernard had achieved certain effects in *The Quatermass Experiment* and especially *Quatermass 2,* Carpenter's favorite Hammer film. Bernard began to elucidate on the mysteries of **minor seconds** and **tritones** but all too soon Carpenter was called back to the set and their discussion had to be terminated.

During that same visit, Bernard also found himself presenting an award to the composer Danny Elfman, famous for scores for Tim Burton movies and for the theme for the television cartoon series *The Simpsons.* Word had spread that Bernard was in Los Angeles and the organizers of the mini–Oscar event invited him to give the award at the ceremony at the Hollywood Roosevelt Hotel. He sat down at a table next to Alfred Hitchcock's daughter and son-in-law but was so concerned with memorizing his speech that he didn't make much conversation with them. A warm round of applause greeted him as he made his way onto the stage where he explained that, when he started his career, being a composer of film music was considered rather down-market, but in the intervening years the profession had become much more respectable.

On another occasion, he enjoyed a delicious meal at John Carpenter's Hollywood home. Having found out that their guest was a connoisseur of fine wines, Carpenter's wife appeared with a bottle of a wonderful vintage champagne, which Bernard drank while the director sipped what looked like the flattest of pub beer. Then sirloin beef with a vast bowl of fresh asparagus was served along with an appropriately velvety blood red wine. After dinner they went down to Carpenter's viewing room and watched *Quatermass 2*— this time sipping a superb vintage port.

> He asked me if I would ever write a score for him — but since then, I've been waiting. Usually he writes his own music; his father was a classical violinist. He writes his music on a little synthesizer which he showed me and then asked me to play the Dracula theme on it. I'm not used to synthesizers and lunged into the keys only to make a feeble little noise!

Bernard was also interviewed on stage by the director, Joe Dante, in front of a large audience at a Los Angeles film convention. Both men were sitting on high stools, and when Dante asked about Philip Martell's attack on the composer, Bernard replied that he thought a lot of short people, like Martell, had a chip on their shoulder. Only when they both stood up did Bernard realize that Joe Dante was perhaps even shorter than Hammer's famous musical supervisor. Fortunately, everybody laughed.

But Hammer's pulse was growing more and more animated with news that the company would be remaking its old classics, beginning with *The Quatermass Experiment.*

After a live concert at the Barbican in which Bernard's suite from *Taste the Blood of Dracula* was performed under specially dimmed lighting, Silva Screen released a CD devoted to his music for *She, Frankenstein Created Woman, The Kiss of the Vampire, The Devil Rides Out,* the Quatermass films and *Scars of Dracula.* Hammer fans waited with bated breath for future developments all of which failed to materialize. But it was rather the case of looking in the wrong coffin, for the father of all movie vampires, F.W. Murnau's *Nosferatu,* was at that moment shaking off the dust and growing thirsty for music.

Soon after his return from Los Angeles in 1994, Bernard played back a message on his answer phone from David Stoner: Would Jimmy ring back to discuss a project he thought might be of interest? Silva Screen had been approached by an American video production company based in Houston, Texas, which was planning to bring out a restored version of Murnau's silent vampire classic. The first thing the Texas company suggested was to ask permission to use some of Bernard's existing Dracula music. Stoner explained that that was quite out of the question, but then told them that the composer of that music was still very much alive and would probably be willing to write a new score especially for them. They faxed back on convincingly headed writing paper with an enthusiastic agreement and on the strength of that single fax, the project was set in motion.

Bernard had never seen Murnau's film before, so the company sent him a video copy and he started work on the music in January 1995. But, as he recalled, it wasn't quite like the old days at Hammer:

> I was rather flummoxed because I don't read German. All the intertitles were in Gothic script so I went out and bought a school dictionary of German and tried to translate my way through the film! There seemed to be something about menstruation, but I must have got that one wrong! I sat down for three solid days stopping and starting the film, planning how I could divide it up into different sections because I'd never done a silent film before. I wrote down the whole story in longhand for myself and worked out basically that I could do it in twenty-six sections of music. It actually came out in twenty-seven sections.
>
> It took five months to write and orchestrate the score. We needed four trombones and four trumpets so I thought I could do without the horns. I love horns, but I wanted a big body of strings and I wanted double woodwind and separate bass clarinet and contra bass bassoon.

When everything was finished, he triumphantly rang David Stoner, who was delighted. The Texas company was duly contacted but there was no reply. A telephone message was left but no one phoned back. It was all rather ominous. Eventually, it became apparent that the company had vanished into thin air, rather like Count Orlok himself at the end of the film. It seemed as though all those months of hard work had been for nothing. But then in 1996, Silva Screen received a letter from Photoplay Productions informing them that they were hoping to present *Nosferatu* in 1997 as their special live presentation at the Royal Festival Hall. Silva Screen was now able to offer Photoplay a ready-made score, and that was how Bernard was brought together with Photoplay's directors Kevin Brownlow, David Gill and Patrick Stanbury. However, having watched their version of the film, Bernard realized that it was not quite the same as the Houston company's version, so when he came to analyze it, all the timings proved to be slightly different. The entire score had to be revised from beginning to end, with sections added here and other bars taken away from there. Time was at a premium (as usual) because everything had to be ready for the recording sessions in Prague in August so that the CD could be on sale for the Royal Festival Hall performance; and after the recording sessions there were rehearsals in London. At the dubbing session for the television presentation of the film, David Gill patted Bernard on shoulder and whispered, "Ben Britten would be proud of you!"

Tragically, only five days later, Gill tragically died from a heart attack.

Nosferatu was the first film adaptation of Stoker's *Dracula,* but it was very nearly destroyed by order of the author's widow, who resented the fact that Murnau had gone ahead and made the film without her permission. All the prints were put to the flames, but fortunately a negative survived. The plot follows Stoker's tale rather more faithfully than Hammer's original *Dracula,* but the names of the characters are changed in a rather feeble attempt to disguise the literary origins of the plot. Thus, Dracula is renamed Count Orlok, Harker is called Hutter, and Mina becomes Ellen. Renfield is turned into a crazed estate agent, Knock, and Van Helsing is called Prof. Bulwer (perhaps after the English novelist Edward Bulwer-Lytton, whose occult romances were very popular at that time in Germany). Bulwer's role as vampire slayer is overtaken by Ellen who, in a major alteration to the original story, voluntarily offers herself to the vampire in a rather Wagnerian finale of feminine self-sacrifice. Orlok lingers too long by her neck and the rays of the morning sun destroy him.

Bernard's score is really an extended retrospective of many of his characteristic techniques. There are two "Syllable" themes, both of which are introduced in the main title. Example 1b accompanies the title card of *Nosferatu.* Often, however, Bernard merely states the rhythm shared by both motifs, rather than their melodies.

James Bernard, *Nosferatu,* Section 1, bars 3–4 (basses only)

Example 1a

James Bernard, *Nosferatu,* Section 1, bars 35–36 (piano only)

Example 1b

These sinister themes are contrasted with the naive jollity of Hutter's theme:

James Bernard, *Nosferatu*, Section 2, bars 5–9

Example 2

The film's "Love" theme is introduced in the early scenes between Ellen and Hutter:

James Bernard, *Nosferatu*, Section 2, bars 47–51

Example 3

Another theme associated with the vampire and his domain is introduced when we first encounter the grotesque Knock. It is related to examples 1a and b:

James Bernard, *Nosferatu*, Section 3, bars 6–9 (piano only)

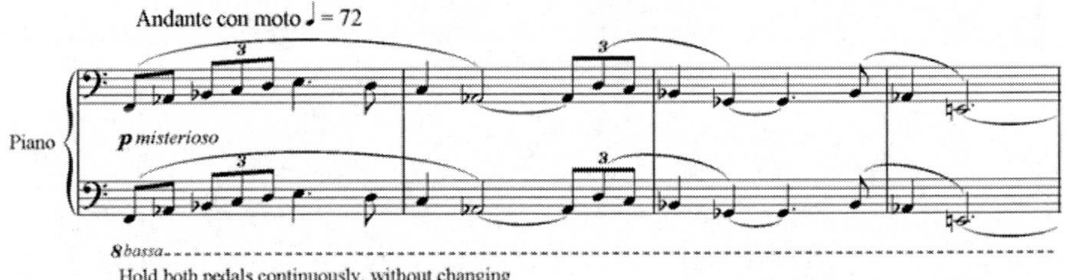

Example 4

And another theme is also introduced here, which will be used as a kind of musical punctuation mark throughout the score. The last three notes of example 5 take us back to *Dracula Has Risen from the Grave*; see chapter 12, example 1a:

James Bernard, *Nosferatu*, Section 3, bars 1–3 (cor anglais only)

Example 5

Another musical punctuation mark is first employed when Hutter spends a night in a wayside inn on his way to Castle Dracula. He horrifies the peasants by revealing his destination:

James Bernard, *Nosferatu*, Section 5, bars 30–31 (brass only)

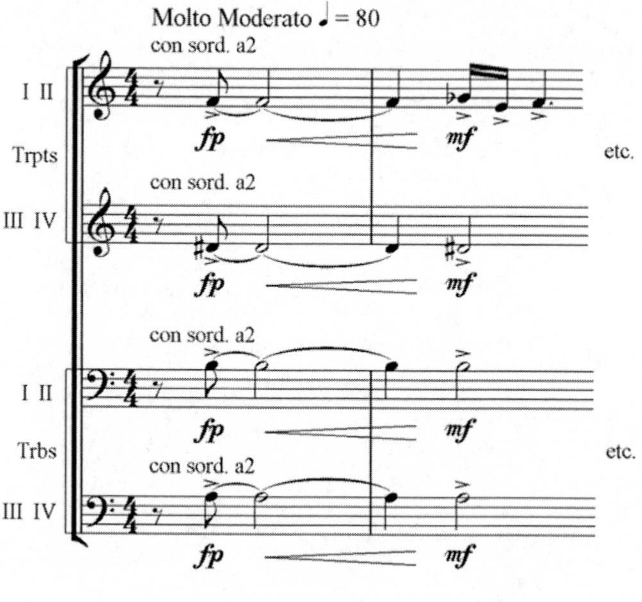

Example 6

When Hutter awakens the following morning, bird song effects, similar to the ones used in the *Taste the Blood of Dracula*, are heard. Later, Orlok's coach arrives (the sequence was shot using what, at the time, was considered the rather eerie technique of high speed stop-motion). For this, Bernard creates a similar effect to the ostinati he had used in *The Kiss of the Vampire*, when Dr. Ravna wills Marianne back to the Chateau towards the end of the film:

James Bernard, *Nosferatu*, Section 7, bars 37–28

Example 7

Whole-tone scales also make their appearance, particularly in a theme associated with impending "Danger." It is first played by plucked strings as Hutter arrives at the Castle itself:

James Bernard, *Nosferatu*, Section 7, bars 51–52 (violins I & II only)

Molto Moderato ♩ = 80 HUTTER COMES THROUGH THE CASTLE GATES...

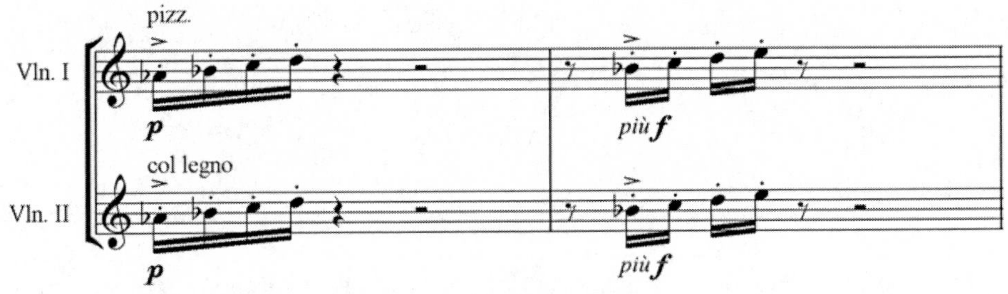

Example 8

When the "Danger" theme is later played by bassoons, while Ellen sleepwalks on the balcony of her bedroom, its ancestry in Bernard's score for *She* is made clear, for it strongly resembles the moment when Leo explores the exotic room in which he finds himself prior to his first meeting with Ayesha. Bernard's classic use of vibraphones accompanies the moment when Orlok notices that Hutter has cut himself and advances upon him. The "Hypnosis" motif of *Dracula Has Risen from the Grave* also returns during this scene.

Similarly, an echo of *The Plague of the Zombies* occurs with the tom-toms, which appear when Hutter discovers Orlok in his coffin. When Knock later eats a housefly ("The Blood is the Life!"), the music, harmonized as it is in **minor seconds**, reveals a kinship with the "*Cada Nostra*" theme from *The Plague of the Zombies*:

James Bernard, *Nosferatu*, Section 14, bars 28–29 (violin II only)

Example 9

One particularly memorable orchestral moment accompanies the harbor scene in which Orlok's coffins are being loaded onto a ship. Bernard's foghorn effect is very simply but no less effectively created by a tuba solo, punctuated by damped timpani and **staccato** piano:

James Bernard, *Nosferatu*, Section 13, bars 28–33

Example 10

Further experiments with orchestral timbre accompany the scene in which Prof. Bulwer demonstrates some peculiar biological phenomena, including the feeding habits of a Venus Fly Trap. We hear the "Nos-Fer-A-Tu" motif but it played on **muted strings** in an eerie high register. As the Fly Trap closes over its prey, a ***glissando*** effect emphasizes its grotesque efficiency (see example 11 on page 261).

Bernard's skill at writing for strings is eloquently demonstrated in the reprise of the "Love" theme that accompanies the elegiac shots of Ellen sitting on a windswept beach, longing for the return of her husband. Growing out of this is the music for

James Bernard, *Nosferatu*, Section 13, bars 78–81

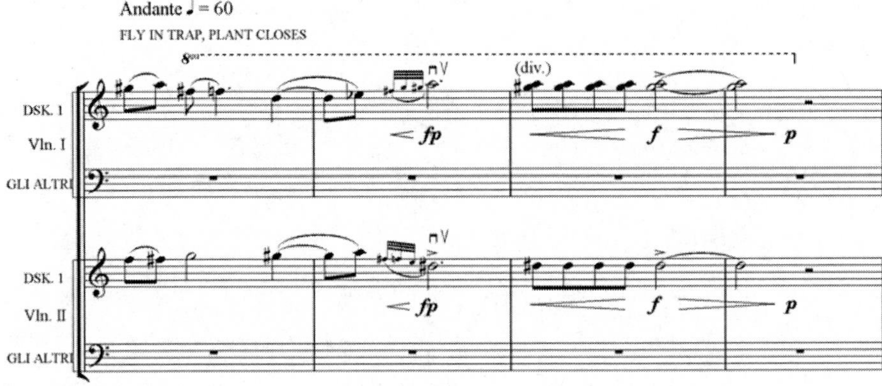

Example 11

the ship on which Orlok is traveling. A billowing **semiquaver *ostinato*** accompanies a heroic fanfare theme on brass:

James Bernard, *Nosferatu*, Section 16, bars 1–3

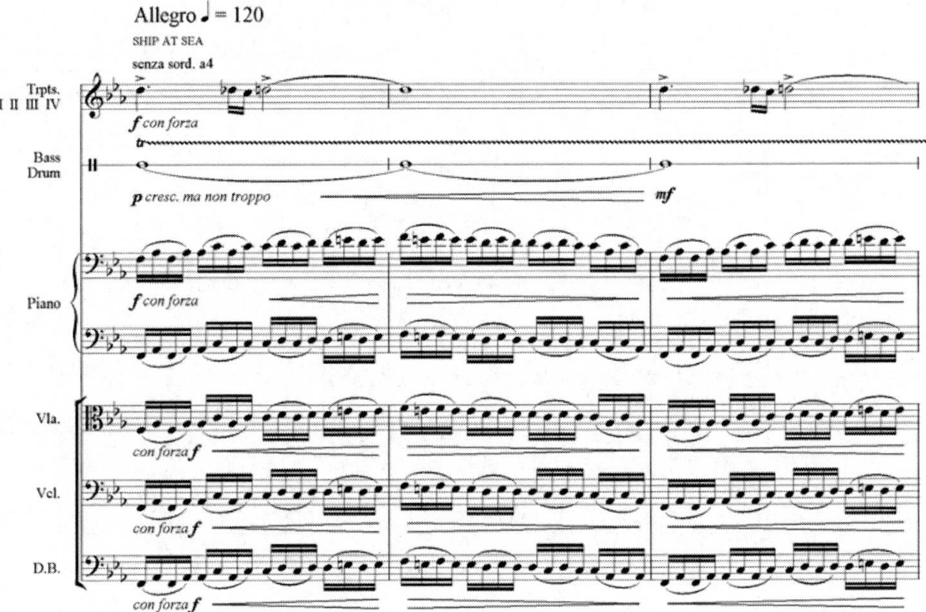

Example 12

The combination of string **harmonics** with a vibraphone **tremolo**, used to such effect in *Dracula—Prince of Darkness,* are called for again when Ellen is once more shown sleepwalking on her balcony. The "Nos-Fer-A-Tu" theme is played by oboes over the strings and vibraphones:

James Bernard, *Nosferatu*, Section 18, bars 22–24

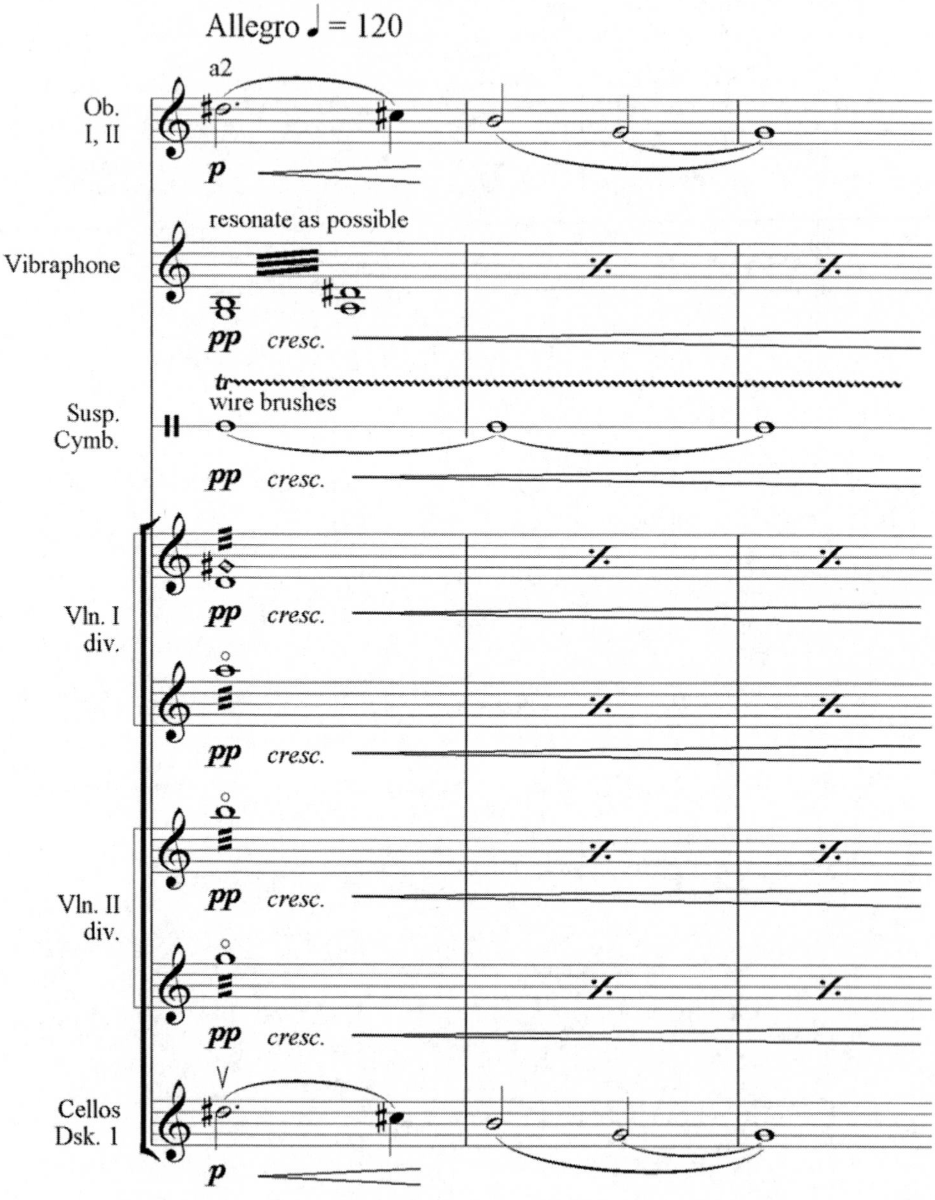

Example 13

The "Nos-Fer-A-Tu" theme is effectively speeded up during the chase sequence in which Knock is hounded out of the town. In this, the most furious section of the score, a battery of percussion accompanies a classic example of Bernardian sequencing (see example 14 on page 263).

Example 14

For the climax, Bernard again employs **consecutive triads** to create a redemptive effect. High-pitched strings play a motif derived from the "Love" theme, as Orlok is overcome by the rays of the morning sun:

25.06
25.10
25.14
25.18
FLTS. I, II
OBS. I, II
CLTS. I, II
BSNS I, II
CONTRA-BSN
WITH BSNS.
sempre ff
ORLOK STANDS, PUTS HAND TO HEART, STARTS TO MOVE. HE IS CAUGHT IN THE
TRPTS. I, II, III, IV
I, II TRBS. III, IV
TUBA
I TIMPS. II
VIBES
B.D.
PIANO
(Ped.)
VLNS. I
VLNS. II
DSK. 1 VLAS ALTRI
CELLOS
BASSES
WITH CELLOS
21
22
23
24
BOOSEY & HAWKES

Example 15

The first live performance of *Nosferatu* took place at the Royal Festival Hall on November 17, 1997, as part of both the London Film Festival and the centenary celebrations of the first publication of Stoker's famous novel. A packed auditorium received Bernard's characteristically full-blooded score with acclamation, equally impressed by Nic Raine's precisely timed conducting. Every point of synchronization slotted into place with remarkable accuracy, including such effects as the vibraphone's imitation of Count Orlok's macabre chiming clock. Bernard's music was no stranger to large audiences but this was the first time this large a gathering had heard a live symphony orchestra perform an entire film score composed by him.

Dracula might die at the end of each film but it's well-known than he can revive the fortunes of actors, film studios—and even composers. In 1998, Photoplay approached Bernard again, explaining that Universal Studios had sent them a wealth of material about their horror films for a documentary to be called *Universal Horror.* Many of the silent clips required music, sometimes in sections lasting less than a minute, which Bernard had to make sound as if they had been extracted from an entire silent film score. Other clips from sound films had their own scores so Bernard's linking music had to blend seamlessly with them. His finished score, only twenty minutes in length, was again recorded in Prague, this time in a single day.

The following year, Bernard made another trip to Jersey to visit his brother, Bill. Bill's wife Meg was in the hospital at the time, so Bill was delighted to have some company. They spent the time reminiscing, and one evening stayed up quite late before retiring for the night. When Bernard awoke the following morning brother Bill was discovered dead in his bed, having passed away quite peacefully in his sleep. It was a shock, of course, but not an entirely unexpected one, as Bill had previously suffered from a stroke. Bernard, with his customary acceptance of fate, was happy to have shared his brother's last days with him. Sorrowful though he was as he watched over his brother's body, he would have wholeheartedly agreed with what Bram Stoker had written in *Dracula*:

> ... the holy calm that lay like sunshine over the wasted face and form was only an earthly token and symbol of the calm that was to reign forever. [...] Outside the air was sweet, the sun shone, and the birds sang, and it seemed as if all nature were tuned to a different pitch. There was gladness and mirth and peace everywhere, for we were at rest ourselves on one account, and we were glad, though it was with a tempered joy.[3]

Some months after Bill's funeral, a short film, *Green Fingers,* directed by Paul Cotgrove, gave Bernard his first professional opportunity of being listed in the credits of a film featuring Hammer's most celebrated female star, Ingrid Pitt. Then Michael Berkeley, son of Bernard's friend Lennox, invited the composer to talk about his Private Passions on the BBC Radio 3 program of the same name. Bernard took great care in selecting his nine records. First was Debussy's *Syrinx,* which fitted in well with his belief in Greek myths and the supernatural, as well as having inspired certain passages of his own music. Liszt was next, Bernard's discussion of his love of piano virtuosity also bringing up the unexpected subject of tap dancing (as a boy, he had taught himself and performed while wearing Mexican costume, in the local village hall, in a dance of his own creation entitled "Tapping from Mexico"). The Liszt piece he chose was

"Les Jeux d'eau de la Villa d'Este," which he explained was the perfect expression of the combined earthiness and spirituality he perceived in Liszt's character, and with which he could so readily identify. He introduced the pieces as follows:

> Out of the fountain there seems to speak a serious voice, and I imagine the voice as speaking the words which Liszt actually attached to the piece ... from the Gospel of Saint John...: "But the water that I shall give him will become in him a fountain of water leaping into eternal life."

Third was the "Dance of the King of the South" from Britten's ballet *The Prince of the Pagodas.* Bernard described this as both "regal and savage," much admiring Britten's use of exotic percussion effects. The fourth record was the love duet from Verdi's *Otello*—an opera that was one of his very first musical memories as a child:

> It seems to me to be full of the extreme rapture of romantic love ... I love the orchestral coda, during which I can sense the balmy Mediterranean night and the smell of jasmine and tuba rose—and even hearing that gentle whirring of the cicadas in the high strings as it dies away.

Bernard also discussed his friendship with Lennox Berkeley and his memories of watching Berkeley mixing dry Martini cocktails, well iced, his *joie de vivre* in so doing being matched perfectly by the *Vivace* from Berkeley's own *Serenade for Strings.* Bernard also discussed his fascination with and love of jazz, including two numbers by black singers (Nellie Lutcher and Nat King Cole), finishing off with Joseph Suk's "Love Song" and an extract from Rachmaninoff's *Vespers.*

It seemed that Bernard was now back in demand—not that the fans had ever deserted him. Indeed, his last great tribute from them took place on Saturday, May 29, 1999. Passengers on passing river cruises must have wondered what on earth was happening at Down Place, otherwise known as Bray Studios. Long queues of people, clutching books and old LP covers, CDs and billowing posters, snaked around the lawns that sloped down the banks of the Thames. The fans were waiting for autographs from the stars of Hammer's glorious past who had gathered together to celebrate its fifty lucrative years of horror and adventure. Joining the party was Dame Thora Hird, who had appeared in *The Quatermass Experiment* as Rosie, an inebriate woman, who may well have inspired the infamous Edna of some years later on BBC television.[4] But Edna, even at her most sloshed, had never encountered a man-eating cactus.

Despite Hammer's reputation for raising the dead, nothing could be done to resurrect actor Ralph Bates, whose tragic death from pancreatic cancer led to the foundation of the research fund that was to benefit from the grand auction of Hammer memorabilia that took place on the steps of the main building. Appropriately, Bates had played Dr. Jekyll in a version of the story in which he accidentally changes sex after experimenting with female hormones in order to prolong his life and thus find a cure for all the world's illnesses.

But Julie Ege was there. She had once revealed all in the prehistoric adventure *Creatures the World Forgot* (Hammer/Columbia, dir. Don Chaffey, 1971) but had taken up a career as a nurse in Sweden and now seemed bemused that so many fans remember her. Ingrid Pitt held open house; so too did the lovely Caroline Munro,

Meeting the fans: James Bernard (right) with the author at the Hammer Reunion Day at Bray Studios, May 1999.

who once spent a much less agreeable lunchtime buried up to her neck as a severed head in *Dracula A.D. 1972*. "The crew put a tarpaulin over my head when it began to rain and then went off for beer and sandwiches," she reminisced rather ruefully. Then there was the beautiful Veronica Carlson, who had been infamously raped by Cushing's Baron Frankenstein. Francis Matthews was there too. He had been stabbed in the back by Christopher Lee's Rasputin but was now in an immaculate white suit as if nothing had happened.

There was also a chance to stand next to John Forbes-Robertson who had risen so majestically from Dracula's coffin in *The Legend of the Seven Golden Vampires*. Even without the lurid green light on his chiseled features, or the clip-on fangs, his natural-born bat-wing eyebrows still had the power to chill. And Martine Beswick, who had once stowed a stiletto in her kinky boots as the sexy sister of Ralph Bates' Dr. Jekyll, received roses and after-dinner mints from demure admirers....

But, significantly, the biggest queue of all was for James Bernard. Long before he had been able to make his way through the door, he was besieged by a respectful mob of eager fans seeking autographs. Even Wagner, who set up so many Wagner Societies in his own lifetime and decorated the ceiling of his own music room with shields representing each one of them, would have been jealous.

But the summer drew to a close and unfortunately, by the end of 1999, Bernard succumbed to the influenza from which so many people suffered during that bitterly cold winter. The illness left him feeling weak and vulnerable to medical complications—a situation that wasn't helped by the stress caused by his brother Bill's death

Old Boy: James Bernard's return to the Royal College of Music in 2000 as guest of honor at a symposium on film music (photograph Chris Christodoulou).

earlier in the year. A series of problems set in — an operation on one of his eyes meant that he had to wear an eye patch (though not, as he delighted in pointing out, quite as colorful as the ones Bette Davies had worn in Hammer's black comedy, *The Anniversary* (Hammer/Warner-Pathé, dir. Roy Ward Baker, 1968). He also suffered from osteoporosis and, latterly, a palsied vocal chord, which affected his voice and left him feeling breathless. But through it all, his spirits remained remarkably high and he was determined to keep composing.

An advertising company suggested he score a deodorant commercial inspired by

Hammer's *One Million Years B.C.* (which, perhaps for the best, failed to materialize); but he was also asked to score his first natural history television documentary—a film about blood-sucking beasts and creatures of the night, called *The Vampire Hunter*, in which the intrepid naturalist Nigel Marven subjected his body to attacks by leeches, vampire bats, fleas, body lice and other insect horrors. The best part of the film was the beautifully photographed prologue sequence in which witches, werewolves and Count Dracula himself put in personal appearances, accompanied in classic Bernardian style. This was the last time Bernard employed his famous Dracula chord, as the vampire Count leaps out of his carriage and swirls the crimson lining of his cloak in the midnight shadows. Curiously, an army of bedbugs is later seen marching over a portrait of Richard Wagner—never one of Bernard's favorite composers (although he undoubtedly influenced him); but, on reflection, perhaps Wagner's presence in the film was appropriate after all. He had indeed stolen the ideas of many other composers, including those of his own father-in-law, Liszt, so the Master of Bayreuth was a kind of musical vampire in a way. Many of the musical effects in *The Vampire Hunter* are tried and tested, including a sunrise section, which Bernard accompanied with rising major chords rather as he had done at the end of *The Devil Rides Out*; but never before had he created such an unusual effect to convey the sound of buzzing mosquito wings.

After *The Vampire Hunter*, Photoplay approached Bernard with a commission to score a documentary about the silent film horror star, Lon Chaney. He did compose several cues for this, inspired by the syllables of the catchphrase that became associated with that versatile actor: "Lon Chaney, The Man of the Thousand Faces." However, ill health prevented further work on this project, which was taken over by Nic Raine.

It seemed that Bernard's Indian summer was now drawing to a close. The medical situation grew rapidly worse, and, though well wishers filled his private room in hospital with huge bouquets of the lilies he so loved, the end was definitely in sight. James Bernard died peacefully in the Royal Brompton Hospital not far from his Chelsea home in Oakley Gardens, on July 9, 2001.

"Oh, please don't stop!," Marianne protests in *The Kiss of the Vampire;* but unlike the piano-playing vampire to whom she addresses that remark, James Bernard was not immortal. His music, however, like his infamous Transylvanian patron, lives on.

In Memoriam: A Personal Postscript by the Author

One of the happiest afternoons I spent with James was when he invited me for lunch about a year before he died. After enjoying a bowl of delicious watercress soup (homemade, of course — he was ever the accomplished chef), we sat over our cups of Lapsang tea and shared our enthusiasm for Liszt's piano music. "Au lac du Wallenstadt," "Vallée d'Oberman" and the Petrarch Sonnets from *Années de Pèlerinage* were his particular favorites— along with Liszt's Concert Study No. 3, "Un Sospiro," which I played for him on the same piano that had assisted in the composition of so many film scores.

Rather than the phrase "Mephistopholes disguised as a priest," which was how Ferdinand Gregorovious so aptly described the Abbé Liszt in the nineteenth century, one might say that James was a priest disguised as Mephistopholes, and his religious conviction is perhaps what makes his music so successful, for James always scored the films he worked on with complete conviction.

Though I could not share his Christian faith, we did both agree that Liszt's strong point as a composer was the touching honesty of his best works, virtuosic though they often are. James loved the glitter of Liszt but also the emotional core of the music, which the virtuosity sometimes seems to prevent his detractors from appreciating. Liszt's almost childlike honesty, a quality also shared by Tchaikovsky (another of James' favorites), is what characterizes the classic Bernard film scores. James believed in the fantastic stories he was telling — while he was telling them at least; and beyond that purely cinematic level, perhaps he also believed in them in a more literal sense, demonstrating, as they do, the triumph of good over evil, God over the Devil and eternal life over death. In that respect he perfectly complimented the personal outlook (and similarly touching professional ability to suspend their disbelief) of Peter Cushing and Terence Fisher.

One of Liszt's *Consolations* suitably accompanied the conclusion of James' funeral service on July 24, 2001, at Mortlake Crematorium in Middlesex, which was attended by many of his friends and family. Mortlake was rather a good place to choose for this occasion, as it had once been the home of the Elizabethan magician and alchemist

Dr. John Dee; and James was nothing if not a musical magician, often transmuting films that were occasionally of rather leaden quality into cinematic gold. With a profusion of lilies (his favorite flowers) he was sent on his way with great affection. He wouldn't have wanted anyone to have felt sad, because he knew that in the life to come he would be reunited with everyone he loved. It was appropriate that the second reading, read by his nephew Justin Lees, was John Donne's poem "Death Be Not Proud":

> Death be not proud, though some have callèd thee
> Mighty and dreadful, for thou art not so;
> For those, whom thou think'st thou dost overthrow
> Die not, poor death, not yet canst thou kill me.
> From rest and sleep — which but thy pictures be
> Much pleasure — then, from thee much more must flow;
> And soonest our best men with thee do go,
> Rest of their bones and soule's delivery.
> Thou'rt slave to fate, chance, kings and desperate men,
> And dost with poison, war, and sickness dwell,
> And poppy or charms can make us sleep as well,
> And better than thy stroke; why swell'st thou then?
> One short sleep past, we wake eternally,
> And death shall be no more. Death, thou shalt die.

James' final wish was that the last bars of his score for *The Devil Rides Out*, which he called "Awakening and Absolution," should be played to accompany his final journey. As that series of calmly stated consecutive triads led up to the transfigurative reprise of the once demonic main theme, now radiant in a major key, everyone who knew the film would have thought of the words they were intended to accompany: saved from the clutches of the Satanist Mocata, Simon Aron turns to the Duc de Richleau and says, "Thank God," to which the Duc de Richleau, lifting the little girl Peggy in his arms, replies, "Yes, Simon, he is the one we must thank." One doesn't need to believe in the film's religious message to be able to respond to the powerful emotional effect of this moment. It can be translated by anyone with an open heart into an expression of friendship, love and the transforming power of music. And that is already a truly wonderful vision.

Glossary of Musical Terms

acciaccatura—a note a major or minor second above the principal note which is struck just before or with that note and instantly released.
adagietto—a tempo indication: slightly faster than an *adagio* , meaning "slow."
added notes—added notes refer to their connection to a major or minor triad. An example of major chord with an added sixth would consist of C, E, G and A.
allegro con forza—fast with forcefulness.
andante—at a walking pace.
arpeggio/arpeggiated—when the notes of a chord are played in rapid even succession.
atonal—music which is not written in any overall key but which may nonetheless contain major or minor tonalities.
appoggiatura—In this instance, the appoggiatura functions in a similar manner to a suspension, when a dissonance is caused by suspending a tone or group of tones from one chord over a subsequent, different chord.
augmented triad—a common chord, consisting of the first, third and sharpened fifth notes of a major scale.
broken—broken chords are the same as arpeggios.
canon—the strictest form of musical imitation in which two or more parts take up, in succession, the given subject note for note.
chalumeau—the lower octave of the clarinet.
chromatic—tones foreign to the given key or chord. A chromatic ascent or descent moves by semitones.
chromatic sequencing—the repetition of a melodic motive, moving up or down by chromatic steps.
chromatically altered chords—chords which introduce notes that are not present in the given key.
coda—a passage ending a section of music.
consecutive (minor or major) triads—triads which rise or fall by steps of a tone or semitone.
consecutive fifths—Consecutive fifths may be thought of as a scale (or part of a scale) harmonized in perfect fifths.
crescendo—a gradual increase in volume.
crotchet—a quarter-note (there are four crochets to a semibreve).
demisemiquaver—There are 32 demisemiquavers to a semibreve.
diegetic—music which the characters in the film are supposed to hear as opposed to *non-diegetic* music which refers to the soundtrack underscore of which only the audience is aware.

diminished seventh chord—a four-note chord consisting of superimposed minor thirds.
diminished fourth—the enharmonic equivalent of a major third.
diminished third—the enharmonic equivalent of a major second.
diminuendo—a gradual decrease in volume.
divided strings—orchestral strings are divided into groups: first and second violins, violas, cellos and double basses. The term "divided" refers to the practice of subdividing these groups still further to facilitate greater activity amongst them.
dominant—a fifth tone of the scale, or the triad built upon that tone.
dominant seventh—a major chord built on the fifth note of a scale with an added seventh, i.e., in C major: G, B, D, F.
dotted rhythm—Placing a dot after a note lengthens its time value by half. A succeeding pulse must therefore be shortened by half.
double-dotted rhythm—Two dots after a note increases its time value by one-and-a-half. The succeeding note therefore is shortened by one-and-a-half to compensate for this.
dynamic—loudness or softness of sound.
11/8—a pulse of eleven quavers in the bar.
enharmonic—enharmonic chords differ in notation but are alike in sound, i.e., G sharp = A flat.
false relations—the chromatic contradiction of a tone : a tone and its chromatically altered octave.
fifth—There are three different kinds of fifth: perfect, diminished and augmented. A perfect fifth spans eight semitones (e.g. C–G). a diminished fifth would flatten the G, while an augmented fifth would sharpen the G.
5/8—a pulse of five quavers in the bar.
5/4—a pulse of five crotchets in the bar.
fortissimo—very loud.
fp—forte (loud), then suddenly piano (soft).
4/4—a pulse of four crotchets in the bar.
fourth—There are three different kinds of fourth: perfect, diminished and augmented. A perfect fourth consists of an interval spanning six semitones (e.g. C-F). A diminished fourth would flatten the F, whilst an augmented fourth would sharpen the F.
galop—a lively dance in 2/4 time.
glissando/glissandi—a rapid sliding of tones—a rapid scale.
harmonic minor scale—see **minor key**
harmonics—as well as the fundamental tone, a string instrument also produces a series of partial tones produced by the vibration of fractional parts of the string. Instructing a string instrument to play harmonics emphasises those partial tones.
interval—the term describing the relation of one pitch to another.
leitmotif—a melody associated with a character, idea or situation.
languido quasi improvisato—languid, like an improvisation.
lontano—literally "distant."
major chord—in C major, for example this consists of C, E and G.
major key—a key whose accompanying scale consists of three whole tones followed by a semitone, followed by three more whole tones and ending with a final semitone.
major second—an interval which spans a whole tone.
major third—an interval which spans five semitones.
major triad—in C major, for example, C, E, G.
martellato—literally "hammered."
minim—a half-note (there are two minims to a semibreve).
minor key—commonly, a key whose accompanying scale flattens the third note and sharpens the seventh.
minor second—an interval which spans a semitone.

minor sixth— an interval which spans nine semitones (e.g. C–A flat).
minor triad —a triad with a flattened third, i.e., C, E flat, G.
muted strings— a piece of metal, fitted to the bridge of a violin, deadens the sound.
non-functional harmony— harmonic structures which exist for their own coloristic effect rather than navigating a specific key.
note-cluster— a group of tones which are closely packed and cloud any clear sense of tonality.
octave— an interval which spans 13 semitones.
Ondes martenot —an electronic instrument invented in 1928 by Maurice Martenot.
open fifth —like consecutive fifths, open fifths exploit the ambivalence of key created the missing major or minor third which would make them a triad or common chord.
ostinato— an insistently repeated rhythmic or melodic idea.
pentatonic —a scale consisting of five notes, i.e., C, D, F, G, A.
perfect cadence— a harmonic closure which moves from the triad built on the fifth note of the scale to the chord built on the first note.
polymetrical— a section of music which combines differing time signatures.
presto —very fast
quaver— an eighth-note (there are eight quavers to the semibreve).
quintuplet— a group of five notes which count as one beat.
retrograde —the original note-row played backwards.
scherzo— literally a "joke." An indication of lively, energetic and frequently playful music.
semibreve —in modern music, the note of longest value (equivalent of four crotchets).
semiquavers— quarter beats.
serial/serialism— the technique of composition which dispenses with major and minor keys as its harmonic basis and instead arranges the 12 notes of the chromatic scale into a row. The row forms the new basis for melodic and harmonic structures.
sequencing— the repetition of a melodic motive, sometimes in successively higher pitches.
7/4 —a pulse of seven crotchets in the bar.
17/8 —a pulse of seventeen quavers in the bar.
seventh— an interval which spans 12 semitones (e.g. C–B).
sextuplet —a group of six notes which count as one beat.
sforzando —a sudden emphasis or stress.
Singspiel— a stage work with spoken and sung dialogue, orchestral accompaniment and often melodrama.
6/8— a pulse in which six quavers are divided into two groups of three.
sixth —an interval which spans ten semitones (e.g. C–A).
snap rhythm —a dotted rhythm in which the dotted note follows the shorter note.
staccato —a style in which the notes are performed in a disconnected manner.
stopped horns— the partial closing of the bell of the instrument by inserting the hand.
sul ponticello —in string playing, the bow is drawn across the strings very near to the bridge of the instrument.
sul tasto —"near the finger-board" of a string instrument.
syncopated —the tying-over of a weak beat to the next strong beat.
timbre —the characteristic sound of different instruments.
Theremin— electronic instrument invented by Léon Thérémin in 1920. The instrument was used extensively in the film scores of Miklós Rózsa.
third— an interval which spans five semitones (e.g. C–E). A minor third flattens the E.
3/4— a pulse of three crotchets in the bar ("waltz" time).
tone —an alternative word for note pitch.
tone-clusters —conglomerations of adjacent semitones or tones which form no recognizable chord.
tonic— the keynote of the scale.
tremolando/tremoli— an effect produced by very rapid alternation of down-bow and up-bow in string instruments.

triad/triadic harmony— harmonic structures based on common chords (which comprise the first, third and fifth degrees of a major or minor scale).

trill—the even and rapid alternation of two tones a major or minor second apart.

triplet—a group of three notes which have the value of a single beat.

tritone—the interval of an augmented fourth or a diminished fifth, so called because it comprises three superimposed whole tones.

tutti—the whole body of the orchestra.

2/4— a pulse of two crotchets in the bar ("march" time).

whole tones— pitches which rise by tones, omitting all semitone intervals.

wrong side of the bridge— in violin and viola playing, the bow is drawn over the side of the bridge closest to the player's chin.

James Bernard Filmography

For each film (listed chronologically), I have listed the director first, followed by the production company, the producer [in brackets], and the year of release.

Feature Films

The Quatermass Experiment (Val Guest, Exclusive/Hammer [Anthony Hinds], 1952).
X — The Unknown (Leslie Norman, Exclusive/Hammer [Anthony Hinds], 1956).
Pacific Destiny (Wolf Rilla, [James Lawrie], 1956).
The Door in the Wall (Glenn Alvey, Jr., Associated British Pathé/British Film Institute/Lawrie [Howard Thomas], 1956).
Quatermass 2 (Val Guest, Hammer [Anthony Hinds], 1957).
Across the Bridge (Ken Annakin, Rank [John Stafford], 1957).
Windom's Way (Ronald Neame, Rank [John Bryan], 1957).
The Curse of Frankenstein (Terence Fisher, Warner/Hammer [Anthony Hinds], 1957).
Nor the Moon By Night (Ken Annakin, Rank [John Stafford], 1958).
Dracula (Terence Fisher, Universal-International/Hammer [Anthony Hinds], 1958).
Greece, the Immortal Land (Basil Wright [Gladys and Basil Wright], 1958).
The Hound of the Baskervilles (Terence Fisher, United Artists/Hammer [Anthony Hinds], 1959).
The Stranglers of Bombay (Terence Fisher, Columbia/Hammer [Anthony Nelson-Keys], 1960).
A Place for Gold (Basil Wright, British Lion (Basil Wright), 1960).
The Terror of the Tongs (Anthony Bushell, Columbia/Hammer [Kenneth Hyman], 1961).
The Damned (Joseph Losey, Columbia/Hammer-Swallow [Anthony Hinds], 1963).
The Kiss of the Vampire (Don Sharp, Universal-International/Hammer [Anthony Hinds], 1964).
The Secret of Blood Island (Quentin Lawrence, Universal-International/Hammer [Anthony Nelson-Keys], 1964).
The Gorgon (Terence Fisher, Columbia/Hammer [Anthony Nelson-Keys], 1964).
She (Robert Day, Associated British Pathé/Hammer [Michael Carreras, Aida Young], 1965).
Dracula — Prince of Darkness (Terence Fisher, Warner/Hammer-Seven Arts [Anthony Nelson-Keys], 1966).
The Plague of the Zombies (John Gilling, Twentieth Century-Fox/Hammer–Seven Arts [Anthony Nelson-Keys], 1965).
Frankenstein Created Woman (Terence Fisher, Warner/Hammer–Seven Arts [Anthony Nelson-Keys], 1967).
Torture Garden (Freddie Francis, Columbia/Amicus [Milton Subotsky], 1967).
The Devil Rides Out (Terence Fisher, Warner/Hammer [Anthony Nelson-Keys], 1968).

Dracula Has Risen from the Grave (Freddie Francis, Warner/Hammer-Seven Arts [Aida Young], 1968).

Frankenstein Must Be Destroyed (Terence Fisher, Warner-Pathé/Hammer [Anthony Nelson-Keys], 1969).

Taste the Blood of Dracula (Peter Sasdy, Warner/Hammer [Aida Young], 1970).

Scars of Dracula (Roy Ward Baker, EMI/Hammer [Aida Young], 1970).

Frankenstein and the Monster from Hell (Terence Fisher, Avco/Hammer [Roy Skeggs], 1973).

The Legend of the Seven Golden Vampires (Roy Ward Baker, Warner/Hammer-Shaw [Don Houghton, Vee King Shaw], 1974).

Nosferatu (F. W. Murnau, Prana, 1921). Bernard's new score for this silent film received its world premiere performance in 1997 as part of the London Film Festival.

Green Fingers (Paul Cotgrove, 1999).

Bernard and Paul Dehn received an Academy Award for the original story for *Seven Days to Noon* (John Boulting, London Films [Roy Boulting], 1950).

Television

Hammer House of Horror :

"Witching Time" (Don Leaver, Cinema Arts International [Roy Skeggs, Brian Lawrence], 1980).

"The House That Bled to Death" (Tom Clegg , Cinema Arts International [Roy Skeggs, Brian Lawrence], 1980).

Murder Elite (Claude Whatham, Tyburn [Jeffrey Broom], 1985).

Universal Horror (Kevin Brownlow, Photoplay/Universal Television [Patrick Stanbury], 1998).

Bernard also appeared in the documentary *Hammer — The Studio That Dripped Blood* (Nick Jones and David Thompson, BBC, 1987).

Notes

Preface

1. *Hammer City Records Present* Dracula *with Christopher Lee*, EMI TWOA 5001, 1974.

2. *Listen to the Cinema!* was a four-part series written and presented by David Huckvale, produced by Anthony Sellors. Broadcast on February 24 and March 3, 10 and 17, 1994 (BBC Radio 4).

3. *Music Matters*, presented by Ivan Hewett, produced by Anthony Sellors. Broadcast on November 16, 1997 (BBC Radio 3).

4. Elizabeth Lutyens, *A Goldfish Bowl*, Cassell, London, 1972, p. 171.

5. Musical terms in **bold** type are clarified in the glossary. Each chapter will draw attention to them once, even if they have been highlighted in previous chapters.

6. Thomas Mann, "Richard Wagner and *Der Ring des Nibelungen*" in *Thomas Mann, Pro and Contra Wagner* (trans. Allan Blunden), Faber and Faber London, 1985, p. 187. Take, for example, the astonishing rumination on an E flat **triad** at the beginning of *Das Rheingold*, itself based on an earlier **arpeggiation** of an F major triad at the beginning of Mendelssohn's overture *Die schöne Melusine*.

7. For a more detailed exploration of this continuum, see David Huckvale, "The Composing Machine: Wagner and Popular Culture" in *A Night in at the Opera*, ed. Jeremy Tambling, John Libbey/Arts Council, London, 1994. Anselm Gerhard (in *The Urbanization of Opera*, trans. Mary Whittall, University of Chicago Press, Chicago and London, 1998) also makes many illuminating comparisons between nineteenth-century French Grand Opera, particularly the works of Meyerbeer/Scribe, going so far as to suggest that the structure of the concluding scenes of *Les Huguenots* "is more like the technique of the filmmaker Alfred Hitchcock than anything familiar from the theater of the eighteenth or nineteenth centuries" (p. 199). More sensationally, Martin Amerongen (in *Wagner—A Case Study*, trans. Stewart Spencer, Dent, London, 1983, p. 44), argues, "If Wagner had lived a century later, his home would not have been Bayreuth but Beverly Hills, and he would not have written music dramas, let alone a *Bühnenweihfestspiel*, but the soundtracks for disaster movies such as *Earthquake* and *The Towering Inferno*."

1. The Long Shadow of Castle Bernard

1. Mary Shelley, *Frankenstein*, J. M. Dent, London, 1941, p. 28.

2. See *In Ruins—The Once Great Houses of Ireland* by Simon Marsden and Duncan McLaren (Little, Brown and Co., London, 1997, pp. 22–25) for more information about Castle Bernard along with an impressive photograph of the present-day ruins.

3. From an unpublished memoir of Barthélemon in the possession of the Bernard family.

4. Unless otherwise stated, all of James Bernard's comments are drawn from conversations with the author. Similarly, all quotations from correspondence, unless otherwise stated, are drawn from previously unpublished letters in the possession of James Bernard.

5. Kentner went on to perform the the *Warsaw Concerto* on the soundtrack of the film *Dangerous Moonlight* (Brian Desmond Hurst,

RKO [William Sistrom], 1941), a piece that spawned a whole host of movie concertos— the "Vampire Rhapsody" of *The Kiss of the Vampire* being one of the more unusual contributions to that particular genre.

2. "Virtutis Fortuna Comes"

1. *St. Martin's Review*, No. 662, May 1946, p. 59.
2. Christopher Lee, *Tall Dark and Gruesome*, Victor Gollancz, London, 1997, p. 54.
3. *The Wellingtonian*, The Wellington College Press, Vol. XXXIV, No. 1, December 1942, pp. 3–4.
4. Christopher Lee (Note 2), p. 54.
5. *op. cit.*, p. 57.
6. Christopher Lee in conversation with the author.
7. *ditto.*
8. *The Wellingtonian,* (Note 3), Vol. XXXIII, No. 18, July 1942, p. 452.
9. *The Wellingtonian* (Note 3), Vol. XXXIV, No. 2, April 1943, p. 31.
10. *loc. cit.*
11. *The Wellingtonian* (Note 3), Vol. XXXIV, No. 3, July 1943, p. 52.
12. Humphrey Carpenter, *Benjamin Britten — A Biography*, Faber and Faber, London, 1992, p. 218.
13. In a letter from Britten to Bernard on Sept. 17, 1949, Britten confessed that he was "very fond" of *Spur of the Moment;* "it brings back happiest memories of a wild occasion!"
14. *The Wellingtonian* (Note 3), Vol. XXXIV, No 1, December 1942, p. 12. This review was written by a senior boy who had just left Wellington to go into the Army. He became the military historian, Prof. Sir Michael Howard, CBE, MC. Earlier, Bernard had sung treble in Howard's school madrigal group and they remained very good adult friends.
15. *The Wellingtonian* (Note 3), Vol. XXXIV, No. 3, July 1943, p. 50.
16. *loc. cit.*
17. Michael Smith, *Station X,* Channel 4 Books, London, p. 49. Gwen Davies quoted.
18. *op. cit.,* p. 88. Christine Brooke-Rose quoted.
19. This Platonic friendship was paralleled by Britten's relations with Arthur Oldham, a fellow student at the Royal College of Music: "People automatically jump to the conclusion,' said Oldham, "that because I was a young man and he was a homosexual, therefore there must have been something. That I can tell you with utter honesty there never was, and there was never any approach."— Quoted in Humphrey Carpenter, *Benjamin Britten* (Note 11), p. 213.
20. James Bernard, CD notes for *Horror of Dracula*, Silva Screen FILMCD 708, 1992.
21. Dehn's libretto for William Walton is an adaptation of Anton Chekhov's one-act farce *The Bear*, first performed at Aldeburgh in 1967. For Sir Lennox Berkeley, Dehn wrote the texts of *A Dinner Engagement* (also premiered at Aldeburgh in 1954) and *Castaway* (Aldeburgh, 1967).
22. The Hon. James Smith, of the W.H. Smith family. James Smith was a singer of German Lieder as well as being a friend of the Queen Elizabeth, the Queen Mother.
23. Walter Hussey, Patron of Art, Weidenfeld and Nicolson, London, 1985, pp. 17–18.
24. *op. cit.*, p. 19.

3. Amanuensis in Aldeburgh

1. The quotation is from Act I of *Billy Budd*, the text of which was written by E. M. Forster and Eric Crozier, after the short novel by Herman Melville. The opera was first performed in 1951.
2. This was at Crag Path before Britten's move to the Red House on the outskirts of Aldeburgh.
3. Britten's ballet, inspired by Balinese gamelan music, was first performed on January 1, 1957, at Covent Garden, London.
4. Archie White, *Sailing Ships*, Harmondsworth, Penguin Books, 1951. Dehn's and Bernard's greetings are inscribed on the cover: "Ben and Peter —/a very happy christmas/ to you both,/ with our love/ Paul. and Jim." The copy is preserved in the Britten-Pears Library at Aldeburgh.
5. Bernard and Dehn had defended *Billy Budd* against an attack by Neville Cardus, the music critic of *The Daily Telegraph.*
6. Robin Long, a twelve-year-old boy with whom Britten was friendly.
7. A protégé of Fidelity, Countess of Cranbrook.
8. Fidelity, Countess of Cranbrook, who chaired the Aldeburgh Festival Committee.
9. Billy Burrell, the young fisherman with whom Britten also became friendly.
10. Leighton Lucas had been a boy dancer with the Diaghilev ballet and later became involved scoring and conducting film music,

working with Louis Levy at Gaumont-British where he helped supervise the music for the horror film *The Ghoul,* starring Boris Karloff (T Hayes Hunter Gaumont-British [Michael Balcon], 1933).

11. Cecil Forsyth, *Orchestration,* London and New York, 1914.

12. Charles-Marie Widor, *Technique de l'orchestre moderne,* Paris, 1904, English. trans. 1906.

13. Walter Piston, *Orchestration,* Gollancz, London, 1961.

14. Gordon Jacob, *Orchestral Technique — A Manual for Students,* Oxford University Press, Oxford, 1931.

15. Formed by Boyd Neel in 1932, this orchestra pioneered the revival of Renaissance and Baroque music, which made it the obvious choice for *The Duchess of Malfi* with its use of music byElizabethan composers. It had also given the premiere in Salzburg of Britten's *Variations on a Theme of Frank Bridge* in 1937.

16. *The Turn of the Screw,* first performed in Venice in 1954.

17. Britten had been suffering from bursitis, an inflammation in his right shoulder, caused by conducting.

18. Cranko had choreographed the dances of Britten's opera *Gloriana* in 1953 and went on to provide both the libretto and choreography for Britten's only full-length ballet, *The Prince of the Pagodas* , in 1956, as well as producing the premiere of Britten's *A Midsummer Night's Dream* in 1960.

4. Trilogy of Terror

1. Peter Cushing, *Peter Cushing — An Autobiography,* Weidenfeld and Nicolson, London, 1987, p. 125.

2. Hotchkis would later score *A Man on the Beach* (Joseph Losey, Exclusive [Anthony Hinds], 1956).

3. Martell became Hammer's music supervisor in 1965.

4. Roy M. Prendergast, *Film Music — A Neglected Art,* W. W. Norton and Co., New York, 1992, p. 133.

5. Although Bernard's music often strays into atonal regions, he has never applied serial techniques to his film scores.

6. From the original publicity brochure of *The Door in the Wall* , British Film Institute, London, 1955).

7. H.G. Wells, "The Door in the Wall" in *Selected Tales,* Penguin, Harmondsworth, 1958, p. 109.

8. Carl Maria von Weber (1786–1826) so arranged the symbolism of different keys in his opera, *Der Freischütz* (1821), that C major represented what was good and holy, whereas F sharp major (a key a tritone away from that land of innocence and sanctity) defined the realm of the Devil. The interval can be somewhat tamed by grafting two of them together to make the Siamese twin of the diminished seventh chord, which went on to preside over many an operatic catastrophe. It was always effective but soon became over-exposed and is somehow never as terrifying as the hollow horror of a tritone on its own. Debussy, one of Bernard's favorite composers, exploited tritones to create unnerving effects, often combining them with **whole-tone scales** to which they are related (the **whole tone scale,** contains within it the relationship of a tritone, for example C to F sharp).

5. Things Rank and Gross

1. Bram Stoker, *Dracula,* Constable, London, 1904, p. 17.

2. James Bernard in conversation with the author for the second program in the BBC Radio 3 series *Listen to the Cinema,* first broadcast on February 3, 1995.

3. Bernard recalls how Ken Cameron, who co-owned the Anvil Recording Studios with Eric Tomlinson, was very fond of this tune and would always whistle it while wearing his kilt, whenever they met at a recording session.

4. The same Schubert extract, incidentally, returns during Countess Barscynska's soirée in *The Revenge of Frankenstein.*

5. Coincidentally, Peter Cushing's Baron will again indulge in brain transplants with another — although a presumably unrelated — Professor Brandt, in *Frankenstein Must Be Destroyed.*

6. Barry Millington (ed.), *Selected Letters of Richard Wagner* (trans. Stewart Spencer), Dent, London, 1987 (Letter to Mathilde Wesendonck, October 29, 1859), p. 475.

7. The music which links the second and third scenes in Act III of *Götterdämmerung* is a classic example of a slow Wagnerian transition that moves from Siegfried's funeral march along the banks of the Rhine to the interior of the Gibichung Hall where Gutrune anxiously wanders about awaiting the return of

Brünnhilde. The stage, in Wagner's original 1876 production, was swathed in clouds of colored steam to effect such a dissolve, while a stream of leitmotifs move through many keys in the orchestral accompaniment.

8. An example of this can be found in the *"Liebesnacht"* ("Night of Love") in Act II, scene two of *Tristan und Isolde*, when the lovers are discovered *flagrante delicto* by Isolde's cuckolded fiancé, King Mark. A **perfect cadence** is expected at the climax of the love scene but it is denied by a **diminished seventh** chord replacing the **tonic** chord — a musical metaphor for *coitus interruptus.*

9. Dehn wrote in his review for the *Daily Herald* (May 3, 1957) : "When titles like *The Curse of Frankenstein* come shuddering though the scrambled smoke, blood and flame of the Warner Theatre screen, I put on my spectacles, and spell them out and smile, and say 'Very good indeed.' [...] Monsters are my addiction and my sustenance."

10. Christopher Lee, *Tall, Dark and Gruesome,* Victor Gollancz, London, 1997, p. 184.

11. Paul Dehn's review of *Dracula* appeared in the *News Chronicle* (May 23, 1958) : "Mr. Bernard's score is a model of its kind — ranging from a sort of erotic gravy-sucking theme for strings, woodwind, celesta and vibraphone to a diabolically descending octave which is Dracula's own motif."

12. In his *Introduction to "Der Ring des Nibelungen"* (Decca Records, London, 1968), Deryck Cooke analyzed the complex network of leitmotifs in the *Ring* as an organic evolution out of the rumination on an E flat major chord in the Prelude of *Das Rheingold.*

13. Christopher Lee, *Tall, Dark and Gruesome* (Note 11), p. 184 : "There were aspects of [Dracula] with which I could readily identify — his extraordinary stillness, punctuated by bouts of manic energy with feats of strength belying his appearance; his power complex; the quality of being done for but undead; and by no means least the fact that he was an embarrassing member of a great and noble family."

14. Robert Simpson, *The Essence of Bruckner*, Victor Gollancz, London, 1992, p. 212.

15. *op. cit.*, p. 217.

16. Hector Berlioz, *Treatise on Modern Instrumentation and Orchestration,* trans. Mary Cowden Clarke, ed. Joseph Bennett, Novello, London, 1855.

17. Edward Buscombe, *Making "Legend of the Werewolf."* British Film Institute, London, 1976, pp. 10.

18. Bram Stoker, *Dracula,* Constable, London, 1904, p. 17.

19. Alfred Hitchcock stated that "film music and cutting have a great deal in common. The purpose of both is to create the tempo and *mood* of the scene." Quoted in Roger Manvell and John Hutley, *Technique of Film Music*, Focal Press, London, 1975, p. 50.

20. For further information on the vampire imagery of Wagner's Parsifal, see David Huckvale, "Wagner and Vampires" in *Wagner*, Vol. 18, No. 3, September 1997 (ed. Stewart Spencer), London, Wagner Society, pp. 127–42.

6. Hounded

1. Sir Arthur Conan Doyle, "A Study in Scarlet," in *A Treasury of Sherlock Holmes*, selected and edited by Adrian Conan Doyle, International Collectors Library, New York, 1955, p. 12.

2. The opera was *Noye's Fludde*, the costumes of which were designed by Bernard's friend Ceri Richards.

3. De Peyer was first clarinet of the London Symphony Orchestra and a founder-member of the Melos Ensemble.

4. *Noye's Fludde* was first performed on June 18, 1958 at Orford Church during the Aldeburgh Festival.

5. Towards the end of his life, Scriabin planned a large-scale musico-dramatic "event" to be called *Mystery* in which the "mystic chord" was to play a major role, hence the chord's alternative title of "mystery chord." *The Hound of the Baskervilles* is certainly a mystery, even if of a rather different kind to the one envisaged by Scriabin.

6. Edward Lockspeiser, *Debussy — His Life and Mind*, Cassell, London, 1965, volume two, p. 68: "Debussy proceeds to sling his well-known jibe at Wagner's conception of the *Leitmotiv*: 'It suggests a harmless lunatic who, on presenting his visiting card, would declaim his name in song.'"

7. Christopher Lee, *Tall, Dark and Gruesome*, Victor Gollancz, London, 1997, p. 198.

7. Serial Killers

1. Publicity brochure for *A Place for Gold*, the Worshipful Company of Goldsmiths.

2. Anthony Hinds in conversation with the author.

3. Respectively as Carter, in *Crescendo*

(Alan Gibson, Warner/Hammer [Michael Carreras], 1970), the Countess, in *Lust for a Vampire*, and Alan Bax, in *The Witches* (Cyril Frankel, Warner/Hammer [Anthony Nelson-Keys], 1966).

4. George Rose later became a very successful actor, both in London and on Broadway in New York. According to John Gielgud, who told the tale to Bernard, Rose was eventually found dead (suspected murder) in the Dominican Republic. Bernard felt that this macabre event prefigured the murder of Ken McGregor in Jamaica.

5. Lady Huntingdon was the writer Margaret Lane. She and Dehn had become friends when broadcasting frequently together on the radio program *The Critics*. The Huntingdons' daughter, Selena Hastings, like her mother, became a successful writer.

6. Rascher taught saxophone at the Royal Danish Conservatory in Malmö, Sweden, and made his American debut in 1939. Paul Hindemith, Darius Milhaud and Jacques Ibert have also composed works for him.

7. Colin Graham, the director of *Twelfth Night*.

8. Lennox Berkeley had already collaborated with Paul Dehn on the opera *A Dinner Engagement* (first performed in 1954 at Aldeburgh). They would collaborate again on *Castaway* (first performed in 1967, also at Aldeburgh). Speaking on BBC Radio 3's program *Private Passions*, Bernard recalled to Michael Berkeley how he first met Lennox Berkeley: "It was I really, who brought Paul and Lennox and your very dear mother, Frieda, together. I was still, I think, a student at the Royal College of Music, and somebody I met at a party—and I just cannot remember who—said he knew Lennox Berkeley and would I like an introduction. I said, of course, I'd love one. So I had this introduction and I rang them up and was immediately invited along for a cup of tea. From that we became great friends and they soon invited me and Paul, and the cups of tea turned into the most wonderful gourmetic dinners, which we used to exchange in each other's houses [...] One of my most vivid memories of Lennox would be at the beginning of a dinner party when he'd be mixing the drinks, and he loved mixing dry Martini cocktails—and his Martinis were the real thing: a great deal of gin or vodka with just the merest hint of Vermouth; and I can see him mixing them now with a kind of sparkle about him and a boyish zest and happiness."

8. Virtue and Danger

1. James Bernard, *Virtue in Danger*, Mermaid Theater program, April 10, 1963.

2. Intriguingly, *Quake, Quake, Quake* was illustrated by the American artist Edward Gorey, who would later design the drop-curtain for the Nantucket Stage Company's 1973 production of John Balderston and Hamilton Deane's play of *Dracula*. In 1979, Gorey went on to design the Broadway revival of this play, starring Frank Langella in the title role.

3. Marcus Hearn and Alan Barnes, *The Hammer Story*, London, Titan Books, 1997, p. 67.

4. Charles Rosen, *The Romantic Generation*, London, HarperCollins, 1996, pp. 468–71.

5. Gamley went on to compose the music for several films made by Amicus, Hammer's principle British rival.

6. A Wagnerian precedent for this is the metamorphosis of the Rhine daughter's cry of "Rheingold!" in the opera of that name. It too consists of a descending tone, which, later in the cycle, is transformed into a semitone fall to symbolize the corruption of their once pure gold.

7. John Huntley, *British Film Music*, London, Skelton Robinson, 1947, p. 54.

8. Mike Murphy (ed.), *Dark Terrors*, Issue 14, St. Ives, 1997, p. 13.

9. Mike Murphy (ed.), *Dark Terrors*, Issue 14 (Note 7), pp. 15–16 : "Under John Hollingsworth's guidance, Barry Warren quickly learn't [sic] the intricate fingering required to 'play' the piano. "He's a natural," was Hollingsworth's verdict. "He should study the piano seriously."

10. The idea of a vampire hypnotizing his victim by means of music had been filmed before in *House of Dracula* (Erle C. Kenton, Universal [Paul Malvern], 1945). In that film, it is not John Carradine's Count Dracula who plays the piano but rather his victim, who is innocently amusing herself with the first movement of Beethoven's "Moonlight" Sonata. It then fell to film composer Edgar Fairchild to inject progressively Debussian and Scriabinesque harmonies into the piece as Dracula's will makes itself felt in the mind of the hapless pianist. *Torture Garden* features a more extreme variation on this theme in which the piano itself becomes the attacker. Jealous of the pianist to whom it belongs, the piano forces its female rival out of an upper story window from which she falls to her death, accompanying the proceedings with Chopin's *Marche funèbre*.

11. *The Kiss of the Vampire* also has certain things in common with Arthur Schnitzler's 1926 *Traumnovelle* (*Dream Novel*), in which the hero, Fridolin, similarly attends a sinister and erotically charged masque ball.

12. Faubion Bowers, *The New Scriabin—Enigmas and Answers,* Newton Abbot, David and Charles, 1974, p. 189.

13. The Lisztian connotations of the "Vampire Rhapsody" are more than merely a reflection of Bernard's personal musical taste. Although Bram Stoker's Dracula is never shown at the piano, Stoker may well have been influenced by the appearance and reputation of the world's most famous pianist, when planning the world's most famous vampire novel. It is well-known that the personality of Stoker's egocentric and highly demanding employer, the actor-manager Sir Henry Irving, provided the author with a model for Count Dracula. Less well-known is the influence of Liszt, who attended one of Irving's celebrated Beefsteak Room banquets at the Lyceum Theater on April 14, 1886. At that time an old man of 75, Liszt none the less fascinated Stoker by his astonishing similarity to Irving:

"Liszt sat on the right hand of Ellen Terry who faced Irving. From where I sat at the end of the table I could not but notice the quite extraordinary resemblance in the profiles of the two men. After supper Irving went round and sat next him and the likeness became a theme of comment from all present. Irving was then forty-eight years of age; but he looked still a young man, with raven black hair and face without a line. His neck was then without a line or mark of age. Liszt, on the other hand, looked older than his age. His stooping shoulders and long white hair made him seem of patriarchal age. Nevertheless the likeness of the two men was remarkable." (Bram Stoker, *Personal Reminiscences of Henry Irving,* 2 vols., Heinemann, London, 1906, II, 146–7.)

The contrast of age between Irving and Liszt may well have given Stoker the idea of making Dracula grow younger throughout the course of his own novel, as he responds to the rejuvenating qualities of fresh English blood. In *The Roman Journals 1852–1874* (trans. G. W. Hamilton [London 1911], p. 230), Ferdinand Gregorovius described Liszt as "Mephistopheles disguised as an Abbé," and Liszt's attire as an Abbé certainly resembles that of Dracula as "a tall, old man [...] clad in black from head to foot." Liszt's persona also seems to have contributed to Dracula's character. For further information on this subject see David Huckvale, "Wagner and Vampires" in *Wagner,* the Journal of the Wagner Society (ed. Stewart Spencer), vol. 18, no. 3, Sept. 1997, pp. 127–41.

9. Femmes Fatales

1. H. Rider Haggard, *She,* 1974, Collins, London, chapter 12, p. 151.

2. The wife of Olivier Messiaen, and a virtuoso on the Ondes Martenot.

3. The soprano who sang the siren call was Patricia Clark, a folk opera singer whom Bernard described as having "a high pure voice from which she could remove expression and warmth, so as to give a sense of the inhuman." She had previously recorded the soprano solos in *The Phantom of the Opera* (Terence Fisher, Universal/Hammer [Anthony Hinds], 1962.)

4. Marcus Hearn & Alan Barnes, *The Hammer Story,* Titan, London, 1997, p. 90.

5. H. Rider Haggard, *Ayesha,* Ward Lock, London, 1911, p. 7.

6. Carl Gustav Jung (ed.), *Man and His Symbols,* Aldus Books/Jupiter Books, London, 1964, p. 177.

7. op. cit., p. 186.

8. op. cit., pp. 178–79.

9. Richard Klemensen (ed.), *Little Shoppe of Horrors,* vol. 10/11, Elmer Valo Appreciation Society, Iowa, U.S.A., p. 96. Philip Martell quoted.

10. Eero Tarasti, *Myth and Music,* Suomen Musiikkitieteellinen Seura, Helsinki, 1978, p. 77.

11. For a detailed analysis of the effect of consecutive triads see the section on *The Devil Rides Out* in chapter 11 of this study.

12. H. Rider Haggard, *She,* Collins, London, 1974, p. 297.

10. Back from the Dead

1. Sir Jack Westrup and F. Lt. Harrison, *Collins Encyclopedia of Music,* Chancellor Press, 1984, p. 340.

2. Hollander had been a familiar figure in London musical life at the turn of the century, often mentioned by Bernard Shaw in his celebrated musical criticism. On December 20, 1893, for example, Shaw reported that "Miss Beatrice Langley played Spohr's ninth concerto. [...] In the rondo the snapping of a string compelled her to borrow Mr. Hollander's fiddle to

finish with. I have seen that happen before; but I cannot recollect any other violinist whose first proceeding on borrowing a violin from the band was to hastily alter its tuning. Mr. Hollander's chanterelle no doubt sounded flat to Miss Langley's sharp ear, though his and mine were satisfied; but it seemed ungrateful to criticize the tuning of the leader's fiddle before the audience" (Bernard Shaw, *Music in London*, Vol. 3, Vienna House, New York, 1973, p. 121).

It was Martell's long-standing ambition to mount a performance of one of Hollander's many ambitious orchestral compositions, the *Roland* Symphony, at the Royal Festival Hall. Sadly, this never came to pass and over the years the painstaking manuscripts of his former teacher literally rotted in the cellar of his Highgate home.

3. Philip Martell in conversation with the author in 1988.

4. Richard Klemensen (ed.), *Little Shoppe of Horrors*, Elmer Valo Appreciation Society, Iowa, No. 10/11, p. 96.

5. Bernard was a great fan of lavish West End pantomimes and used to collect original scene designs when he could. One afternoon, he showed the author of this book one of a snow scene called "The Kingdom of Cool Whiteness." "I think I was more into hot blackness at the time," he explained, with a charming smile.

6. Bernard in fact once actually met Elizabeth Taylor at a party, and recalled enjoying a "very interesting and pleasant chat by the fire with her."

7. Christopher Lee, *Tall, Dark and Gruesome*, Victor Gollancz, London, 1997, p. 231.

8. Susana Walton, *Behind the Façade*, Oxford University Press, Oxford, 1989, p. 175.

9. *op. cit.*, p. 194.

10. *op. cit.*, p. 200.

11. Black and White Music

1. Dennis Wheatley, *The Devil Rides Out*, Hutchinson and Co., London/ Edito-Service, S.A., Geneva, 1972, Chapter XVI, p. 15.

2. *The Times*, London, September 15, 1967.

3. Walter Hussey, *Patron of Art*, Weidenfeld and Nicolson, London, 1985, p. 133.

4. *To the Devil a Daughter* (Peter Sykes, EMI/Hammer-Terra Filmkunst [Roy Skeggs], 1976), also based on a Wheatley novel of the same name, was produced at the end of Hammer's existence as a filmmaking concern.

5. Marcus Hearn & Alan Barnes, *The Hammer Story*, Titan Books, London, 1997, p. 121.

12. Assorted Aristocrats

1. Cecil Beaton, *Self-Portrait With Friends, The Selected Diaries of Cecil Beaton* (ed. Richard Buckle), Pimlico, London, 1991, p. 298.

2. Laurence Schifano, *Luchino Visconti—the flames of passion* (trans. William S. Byron), Collins, London, 1990, p. 118.

3. Fulco Santostefano della Cerda, *The Happy Summer Days*, Weidenfeld & Nicolson, London, 1998, p. 39.

4. *op. cit.*, pp. 52–53.

5. Tim Stout (ed.), *Supernatural Horror Filming*, No. 1, Dorset Publishing Co., 1969, p. 17.

6. Eero Tarasti, *Myth and Music*, Suomen Musiikkitieteellinen Seura, Helsinki, 1978, pp. 93–94.

7. Marcus Hearn & Alan Barnes, *The Hammer Story*, Titan Books, London, 1997, p. 127.

8. Veronica Carlson recalls the difficulties which this scene caused:

"They were trying to work out how to tear my nightgown off without exposing me because there was no nudity in my contract. I didn't want to be exposed. And every alternative was more vulgar than the last, and it was just the most horrendous thing. Peter and I discussed it at length very quietly together. Just him and me. We tried to argue about it but it wasn't any good. But I can remember Terry [Terence Fisher] cut it short. He said, 'Cut! That's enough.' And he just turned away. And we stopped and Peter and I just stayed there and held onto each other. We felt very bad about it" (Tim Greeves, *Veronica Carlson, An Illustrated Memento*, 1-Shot Publications, Eastleigh, p. 12).

9. James Bernard, *The Horror of Dracula*, Silva Screen FILMCD 708, CD Booklet.

13. Kapellmeister to Count Dracula

1. Christopher Lee, *Tall, Dark and Gruesome*, Victor Gollancz, London, 1997, p. 306.

14. Sunset in the East

1. From the soundtrack album of *The Leg-*

end of the Seven Golden Vampires, Warner Brothers, K56085, 1974.

2. Bogarde had previously played two musical characters. In 1960 he appeared as Liszt in *Song Without End* (George Cuckor/Columbia [William Goetz]) and before that, in 1948, as a much less successful would-be pianist in an adaptation of W. Somerset Maugham's short story "The Alien Corn" in *Quartet* (Harold French/GFD/Gainsborough [Anthony Darnborough]). Bernard had been introduced to Maugham many years before and had been presented with a signed copy of one of Maugham's books inscribed "To Jimmy ... from a very old party."

3. Marcus Hearn & Alan Barnes, *The Hammer Story*, Titan, London, 1997, p. 160.

4. Marcus Hearn & Alan Barnes, *The Hammer Story*, *op. cit.*, p. 161.

5. Franz Liszt, Preface to *Les Préludes*, translated from the original French by Humphrey Searle, Ernst Eulenburg, London, 1977.

6. Philip Martell in conversation with the author.

15. Danger in Paradise

1. *The Legend of the Seven Golden Vampires*, original soundtrack album, Warner Brothers K56085, 1974.

2. Dennis van Thal's brother, Herbert van Thal, edited Pan Books' very successful series of paperback horror story anthologies. In a more musical vein, he edited a tribute to the music critic Ernest Newman (*Fanfare for Ernest Newman*, Arthur Barker, London, 1955).

3. *The Daily Gleaner*, "Brutal Murder in Mobay" by Margaret Morris, August 18, 1992.

16. Resurrection

1. Paul Patterson and John McCabe scored two episodes of the *Hammer House of Horror* television series ("Rude Awakening" and "Guardian of the Abyss" respectively).

2. "Since it's quite obvious to science-fiction fans that Prince of Darkness is an homage to Nigel Kneale's *Quatermass* films, it would be appropriate to state that one of my favorite and primary influences is James Bernard. Although his best known score is probably *Horror of Dracula* I have loved all his Hammer work throught [sic] the fifties and sixties."—John Carpenter, the soundtrack album of *Prince of Darkness*, Varese Saraband STV 81340, 1987, Universal City Studios.

3. Bram Stoker, *Dracula*, Constable, London, 1904, pp. 221–222.

4. *Edna, the Inebriate Woman*, BBC TV Play for Today, written by Jeremy Sandford and starring Patricia Hayes in the title role. First broadcast October 21, 1971.

Select Bibliography

Berlioz, Hector. *Treatise on Modern Instrumentation and Orchestration.* Trans. Mary Cowden Clarke. London: Novello, 1855.
Bowers, Faubion. *The New Scriabin— Enigmas and Answers.* London: David and Charles, Newton Abbot, 1974.
Buckle, Richard, ed. *Self-Portrait with Friends— The Selected Diaries of Cecil Beaton.* Pimlico, London, 1991.
Buscombe, Edward. *Making "Legend of the Werewolf."* British Film Institute, London, 1976.
Carpenter, Humphrey. *Benjamin Britten— A Biography.* London: Faber and Faber, 1992.
Cerda, Fulco Santostefano della. *The Happy Summer Days.* London: Weidenfeld & Nicolson, 1998.
Conan Doyle, Sir Arthur. *A Treasury of Sherlock Holmes* (selected and edited by Adrian Conan Doyle). New York: International Collectors Library, 1955.
Cooke, Deryck. *Introduction to "Der Ring des Nibelungen."* London: Decca Records, 1968.
Cushing, Peter. *Peter Cushing: An Autobiography.* London: Wiedenfeld and Nicolson, 1987.
Eyles, Allen, Robert Adkinson, and Nicholas Fry. *The House of Horror.* London: Lorrimer Publishing, 1981.
Greeves, Tim. *Veronica Carlson: An Illustrated Memento.* Eastleigh: 1-Shot Publications, 1993.
Gregorovius, Ferdinand. *The Roman Journals 1852–1874.* trans. G. W. Hamilton. London, 1911.
Haggard, H. Rider. *Ayesha.* Ward Lock, London, 1911.
_____. *She* (1887). London: Collins, 1974.
Hearn, Marcus, and Alan Barnes. *The Hammer Story.* London: Titan Books, 1997.
Huckvale, David. "Wagner and Vampires" in *Wagner,* ed. Stewart Spencer. Wagner Society, London, Vol. 18, No 3, September 1997.
Hussey, Walter. *Patron of Art.* London: Weidenfeld and Nicolson, 1985.
Jung, Carl Gustav, ed. *Man and His Symbols.* London: Aldus Books/Jupiter Books, 1964.
Lee, Christopher. *Tall, Dark and Gruesome.* London: Victor Gollancz, 1997.
Liszt, Franz. Preface to *Les Préludes.* Trans. Humphrey Searle. London: Ernst Eulenburg, 1977.
Lockspeiser, Edward. *Debussy: His Life and Mind.* 2 vols. London: Cassell, 1965.
Lutyens, Elizabeth. *A Goldfish Bowl.* London: Cassell, 1972.
Mann, Thomas. *Thomas Mann, Pro and Contra Wagner.* Trans. Allan Blunden. London: Faber and Faber, 1985.
Manvell, Roger, and John Huntley. *Technique of Film Music.* London: Focal Press, 1975.
Marsden, Simon. *The Haunted Realm— Echoes from Beyond the Tomb.* London: Little, Brown, 1998.
Millington, Barry, ed. *Selected Letters of Richard Wagner.* Trans. Stewart Spencer. London: Dent, 1987.
Prendergast, Roy M. *Film Music— A Neglected Art.* New York: W. W. Norton, 1992.
Rosen, Charles. *The Romantic Generation.* London: HarperCollins, 1996.
Schifano, Laurence. *Luchino Visconti— The Flames of Passion.* Trans. William S. Byron. London: Collins, 1990.

Schnitzler, Arthur. *Dream Story.* Trans. J. M. Q. Davis, Harmondsworth: Penguin, 1999.
Shaw, George Bernard. *Music in London.* 4 vols., New York: Vienna House, 1973.
Shelley, Mary. *Frankenstein.* London: Dent, 1941.
Simpson, Robert. *The Essence of Bruckner.* London: Victor Gollancz, 1992.
Smith, Michael. *Station X.* London: Channel 4 Books, 1998.
Stoker, Bram. *Dracula.* Constable, London, 1904.
_____. *Personal Reminiscences of Henry Irving.* 2 vols. London: Heinemann, 1906.
Tambling, Jeremy, ed. *A Night in at the Opera.* John Libbey/Arts Council, London, 1994.
Tarasti, Eero. *Myth and Music.* Helsinki: Suomen Musiikkitieteellinen Seura, 1978.
Walton, Susana. *Behind the Façade.* Oxford: Oxford University Press, 1989.
Wells, H.G. *Selected Tales.* Harmondsworth: Penguin, 1958.
Westrup, Sir Jack, and F. Lt. Harrison. *Collins Encyclopaedia of Music.* London: Chancellor Press, 1984.
Wheatley, Dennis. *The Devil Rides Out.* London: Hutchinson and Co., and Geneva: Edito-Service, S. A., 1972.

Discography

LP Vinyl Discs

Hammer Presents Dracula *with Christopher Lee,* EMI, TWOA 5001, 1974
The Legend of the Seven Golden Vampires, Warner Brothers, K56085, 1974.
Prince of Darkness, Varese Saraband, STV 81340, 1989.
Virtue in Danger, Decca, SKL 4536, 1963

CDs

The Devil Rides Out, GDI Records, GDICD013, 2000.
The Devil Rides Out: Horror, Adventure and Romance. Music for Hammer Films Composed by James Bernard, Silva Screen FILMCD 174, 1996.
The Hammer Film Music Collection — Vols. 1 & 2, GDI Records, GDICD002, 1998.
The Hammer Frankenstein Film Music Collection, GDI Records GDICD011, 2000.
Hammer — The Studio That Dripped Blood!, Silva Screen, FILMXCD 357, 2002.
The Hammer Vampire Music Collection, GCI Records, GDICD017, 2001.
A History of Horror, Silva Screen, FILMXCD 331, 2000.
Horror, Silva Screen, FILMCD 175, 1996.
The Horror of Dracula, Silva Screen, FILMCD 708, 1992.
Music from the Hammer Films, Silva Screen FILMCD 066, 1989.
Nosferatu — A Symphony of Terror, Silva Screen, FILMCD 192, 1997.
Scars of Dracula, GDI records, GDICD014, 2000.
She/The Vengeance of She, GDI Records, CDICD018, 2001.
Taste the Blood of Dracula—Original Motion Picture Soundtrack, GDI Records GDICD010, 2000.

Index

Page numbers in ***bold italics*** indicate illustrations.